# FRANCE

## *A Culinary Journey*

# FRANCE

## *A Culinary Journey*

CollinsPublishersSanFrancisco
*A Division of* HarperCollins*Publishers*

First published in USA 1992
by Collins Publishers San Francisco

Produced by Weldon Owen Pty Limited
43 Victoria Street, McMahons Point, NSW 2060, Australia
Telex AA23038; Fax (02) 929 8352
Weldon Owen Inc.
90 Gold Street, San Francisco, CA 94133, USA
Fax (415) 291 8841
Member of the Weldon International Group of Companies
Sydney•San Francisco•Chicago•London•Paris

President: John Owen
General Manager: Stuart Laurence
Publisher: Wendely Harvey
Foreign Editions Director: Derek Barton
Editor: Gillian Hewitt
Assistant Editor: Lu Sierra
Editorial Assistant: Tristan Phillips
Picture Editor: Jenny Mills
Wine Consultant: James Halliday
Indexer: Dianne Regtop
Design Concept: John Bull, The Book Design Company
Designer: Stan Lamond, Lamond Art & Design
Maps and Illustrations: Stan Lamond, Lamond Art & Design
Jacket Artwork Concept: John Bull, The Book Design Company
Production Director: Mick Bagnato
Food Styling: Janice Baker
Food Photography: Peter Johnson



Library of Congress
Cataloging-in-Publication data:

France: a culinary journey.
p. cm.
Includes index
ISBN 0-00-255031-8
1. Cookery, French. 2. France--Description and travel
I. Collins Publishers San Francisco
TX719.F774 1992
641.5944--dc20
92-4926



Typeset by Letter Perfect, Sydney, Australia
Produced by Mandarin Offset, Hong Kong
Printed in Hong Kong

A Weldon Owen Production

*Poppies blooming in the valley of the Auvézère in the Dordogne.*
JEAN-PAUL FERRERO/AUSCAPE INTERNATIONAL

*Page 1: Duck Terrine with Calvados, Foie Gras Soup with Lentils, Oysters in Pommeau, Omelette de la Mère Poulard (recipes pages 227-8)*
PETER JOHNSON

*Pages 2-3: Daybreak on the Dordogne river at Sainte-Foy-la-Grande.*
MICHAEL BUSSELLE/TONY STONE WORLDWIDE/THE PHOTO LIBRARY

*Pages 4-5: Corsican Cheesecake with Caramel, Lemon and Almond Tart, Lavender and Toasted Almond Ice-Cream (recipes pages 109-10)*

STAURANT

# CONTRIBUTORS

**Maria Donovan**
Paris-based author of several books on cooking and travel, including *The Far Eastern Epicure*

**Peter Graham**
French resident for thirty years, author of a number of books on travel and food, and writes regularly on food and wine for the *Sunday Times Magazine*, the *Times*, the *Guardian*, and *The Good Food Guide*

**Diane Holuigue**
Director of The French Kitchen Cookery School in Melbourne, author of *The French Kitchen*, and Food Editor for the *Australian* newspaper

**Philip and Mary Hyman**
French residents for twenty years, translators of cookbooks written by some of today's top French chefs, and co-authors of *Webster's Wine Tours: France*

**Alexandra Michell**
Studied cooking in Paris, has owned a restaurant and cooking school in Melbourne, writes regularly on food for a number of newspapers and magazines, and is author of six cookbooks

**Robert Noah**
President of Paris en Cuisine, a gastronomic tour company that uses France's top restaurants as classrooms, regular contributor to international magazines, and publisher of a bimonthly French food newsletter

**Martha Rose Shulman**
Caterer and cookery writer resident in Paris, and author of twelve cookery books, including *The Vegetarian Feast* and *Mediterranean Light*

**Gregory Usher and Isabelle Bachelard**
Gregory Usher is the Director of the Ecole de Gastronomie Francaise Ritz-Escoffier in Paris and in 1989 was made a Chevalier du Mérite Agricole by the French government. Isabelle Bachelard writes widely on food and wine and is a regular member of French wine-tasting juries

**Joanne Weir**
International cooking instuctor at Tante Marie's Cooking School, San Francisco and teaches in Canada, Australia, and New Zealand. Currently writing a book on Mediterranean cookery

*Menton on the Côte d'Azur, the Baroque church of Saint-Michel looking out over the rooftops.*
AUSTRALIAN PICTURE LIBRARY

# CONTENTS

# C O N T E N T S

United Kingdom
London
La Manche
Les Iles Anglo-Normandes
Belgique
Lille
Flandres
Luxembourg
Deutschland
Amiens
Picardie
Rouen
Caen
Eure
Calvados
Normandie
Orne
Paris
Reims
Champagne
Lorraine
Metz
Strasbourg
Alsace
Troyes
Brest
Finistère
Côtes-du-Nord
Rennes
Bretagne
Morbihan
La Manche
Maine
Le Mans
Orléanais
Orléans
Nantes
Anjou
Angers
Tours
Pays Nantais
Touraine
Nivernais
Dijon
Besançon
Franche-Comté
Bourgogne
Bourges
Berry
Poitiers
Poitou
Vendée
Océan Atlantique
France
Bourbonnais
Limousin
Auvergne
Clermont Ferrand
Lyon
Bresse
Lyonnais
Savoie
Jura
Charentes
Limoges
Massif Central
Saint-Etienne
Dauphiné
Grenoble
Périgord
Cantal
Bordeaux
Les Landes
Quercy
Armagnac
Nimes
Avignon
Provence
Biarritz
Gascogne
Toulouse
Languedoc
Camargue
Montpellier
Marseille
Toulon
Pays Basque
Pyrénées
Roussillon
Golfe du Lion
Andorra
Perpignan
España
Mer Méditerrané
0 20 40 60 80 100 120 M
0 50 100 150 200 Km

# INTRODUCTION

A trip through France is a delightful journey of discovery, both scenically and gastronomically. The provinces each have their own distinctive style, a style that is particularly evident in their cuisines. Food is one of life's principal pleasures for the French, and everywhere it commands great interest and respect.

Throughout the country the terrain and climate vary a good deal, so produce differs considerably from region to region. In addition, mountain ranges and the myriad of rivers which criss-cross the country often act as natural barriers between provinces. It was not until the coming of the railways in the nineteenth century that communications and trade became widespread, and even today, mountainous areas still remain relatively cut off, especially in winter when upland areas are covered with snow.

Language barriers also prevailed in much of the country until the beginning of this century, with many French people not actually speaking the national language. In the south their native tongue might have been Basque, or Occitan; in Brittany people spoke Breton; in the Alps many spoke Italian; and in the northeast Alsatian and Flemish were widely used.

While these barriers have helped to keep the country's regional cuisine virtually intact, international fast-food outlets and supermarket chains are now posing a threat to traditional ways. This is causing many French people concern, and there is a growing appreciation of the skills and long hours worked by people like the cheesemakers, the bakers, the winemakers, and those who cure the olives. In provincial centers it can be rewarding to seek out books on regional culture and cuisine, many of which will never reach the stores in Paris.

The two areas where the cuisine could be described as generally French rather than regional are the Ile de France, around Paris, and the Loire valley, which is within easy reach of the nation's capital. Over the centuries the eating habits of the bourgeoisie in these regions were considerably influenced by those of the nobility. Paris has always been the center of the French food trade, importing produce from overseas as well as from throughout the country. In any reputable Parisian grocery store in the eighteenth century you could buy such items as Gruyère from Switzerland, Parma ham from Italy, and salt cod from Canada. The capital's many migrants also influenced its cuisine. Parisians were quick to adopt any regional dish that appealed to them, such as *quiche lorraine*, *choucroute garnie*, *madeleines*, *rum babas*, and *tarte Tatin*. In the rest of the country, however, the cuisine has always been an integral part of regional culture, people using the products that they grow and make themselves.

One of the great differences between the north and the south of the country is that olive oil is the cooking medium in the south, while butter is used in the north. In the southwest, walnuts provide oil for salad dressings and flavorful goose fat is used for cooking.

In Provence and Languedoc the marvellous Mediterranean climate provides a basis for a simple, fully flavored cuisine. Colorful cooked vegetable dishes abound, such as *ratatouille*, *tomates à la provençale*, and *artichauts à la barigoule,* and food is redolent with onions, garlic, and fresh herbs.

In the Dauphiné, Savoie, and Franche-Comté, the mountainous regions in the east, centuries-old culinary methods are still followed, and food is preserved for the long winter months. During the summer, cheeses such as Comté and Saint-Marcellin are made; then in autumn smoked pork sausages, and smoked, salted and dried beef are prepared, and cherries are preserved in liqueur. Wild mushrooms, chestnuts, and walnuts are also used in many recipes.

To the west, the sophisticated cuisine of Burgundy and the Lyonnais makes them particulary appealing regions to visit. Not only is Burgundy known for its excellent wine, but also for its beef, pork, and chickens, and the mustard from Dijon. In this part of the country, pork fat is used as the basis for cooking. The city of Lyon, at the heart of the Lyonnais, draws on all the best products from rich neighboring provinces, and is acknowledged as France's gastronomic center. In addition, the city has the good fortune to be surrounded by some of the best wine-producing areas in the country.

Further north, Alsace and Lorraine, over the centuries alternately claimed by France and Germany, have dishes which are distinctly their own. Alsace is famous for *choucroute garnie*, sauerkraut with pork meats, *foie gras* from Strasbourg, fine white wines, and *eaux-de-vie*. Butter and cream are used widely, notably in the beautiful pastries that are part of any good cook's repertoire. Lorraine is perhaps best known for its *quiche lorraine*. The potato was grown in this part of the country, as well as in Savoie and the Dauphiné, long before it was introduced into Parisian cooking, and is used in all sorts of dishes.

In the west, cream, butter, and apples are the ingredients *par excellence* of Norman cuisine, but the region is also known for its excellent sausages, *rillettes*, pâtés, and terrines. A bountiful supply of fish and shellfish is provided by the fishing fleets that operate all along the coastline, and delicate *pré-salé* lamb is raised on the salt marshes near Le Mont-Saint-Michel. Brittany, too, shares in the wealth of the sea, providing French markets with seafood such as oysters, scallops, mussels, and lobsters, and nowhere in France are there finer *crêpes*.

In the southwest the rolling vineyards of Bordeaux produce some of the word's best wines, and a cuisine that is robust and simple, and further inland lies *foie gras* and truffle territory. Southwards, in the Basque country, there are specialties such as *jambon de Bayonne*, and the bell pepper reigns supreme in a flavorful, straightforward cuisine.

From the vineyards of Champagne to the olive groves of Provence, from the oyster beds of Brittany to the alpine meadows of Savoie, France is a glorious land of contrasts, and nowhere in the world could one make a more rewarding culinary journey. *Bon appetit!*

ALEXANDRA MICHELL

*A group of farm workers in the Pyrenees, sitting down to a hearty lunch in the open air.*

FRANCOIS PERRI/COSMOS

La Manche
Calais
Dunkerque
Bruxelles
Flandres
Tourcoing
Roubaix
Lille
Belgique
Boulogne-sur-Mer
Meuse
Douai
Arras
Arleux
Cambrai
Abbeville
Amiens
Somme
Charleville Mézières
Picardie
Ardennes
Aisne
Beauvais
Meuse
Oise
Compiégne
Soissons
Reims
Verdu
Seine
Sainte-Menehould
Marne
Epernay
Châlons-sur-Marne
Paris
Champagne
Versailles
Ile de France
Saint-Dizie
Chartres
Fontainbleau
Seine
Troyes
0 10 20 30 40 50 M
0 20 40 60 80 Km
Chaumont
Yonne
Orléans
Loire
Auxerre
Chablis

# PARIS, CHAMPAGNE, AND THE NORTH

*Philip and Mary Hyman*

Northeastern France offers unexpected culinary contrasts. The finest Brie is made only thirty minutes from Paris; there are roads in French Flanders lined with garlic fields; and eels are grilled at picnics in the valley of the Somme. The region boasts the strongest cheeses in the country, the finest beer, and one of the world's most sought-after wines. Nevertheless, the average French person finds it hard to name a single dish from Champagne, the north, or even Paris. Perhaps it is because this densely populated part of France (Paris and Lille are the country's two largest cities) attracts few French vacationers and is generally associated with hard work rather than revelry. But those who explore the northeast will be surprised by the wealth of specialties they find.

Paris is commonly thought of as a gourmet's paradise, but even here a certain amount of exploration is needed in order to find local specialties. "Paris," the French like to say, "is not France." It is a cosmopolitan city, an elegant crossroads where ideas are exchanged, fashions started and fortunes spent. Creativity is applauded and ambitious chefs, who feel obliged to astonish diners with personal creations, rarely, if ever, serve the kind of fare that might be called traditional Parisian cuisine. Such dishes survive only in bistros, modest establishments with limited menus and, despite a revival in recent years, they are becoming harder and harder to find. Nonetheless, Parisians still trade addresses for places serving such favorites as *filets de hareng pommes à l'huile*, lightly smoked herring fillets with warm potato salad, *andouillettes*, tripe sausages, *boeuf miroton*, boiled beef and onions, *petit salé aux lentilles*, salt pork with lentils, and *tête de veau sauce gribiche*, calf's head with gribiche sauce.

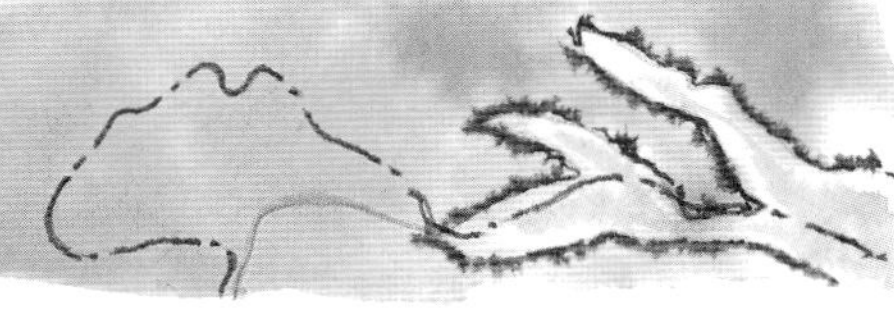

LEO MEIER

*A glistening array of the most elegant fish dishes in aspic displayed in the window of a* traiteur *in Paris.*

## "The Belly of France"

In addition to bistros, Parisians have another source for these and various other typically Parisian dishes — *charcuteries*. These shops, which specialize in selling a wide range of pork products, such as pâtés, sausages, and salt pork, also prepare hot take-out food of all kinds. They will always provide a counter full of freshly made *crudités*, vegetable salads, and advertise such Parisian favorites as *hachis parmentier*, a French version of shepherd's pie, and *côtes de porc charcutière*, pork chops with a tangy tomato sauce. On Fridays they might well serve *raie au beurre noir*, skate with nut-brown sauce. Indeed, ordering lunch at a modest *charcuterie* counter is often the best way to sample the kind of cooking that the people of Paris tend to take for granted.

On the whole, Parisians live a privileged existence insofar as food is concerned. Indeed, to paraphrase Zola, Paris might be called "the belly of France." The central market, Les Halles, until recently in the center of the city, is now located at Rungis, near Orly airport. Alleyways are piled high with crates of fruit and vegetables, and throngs of market strongmen move sides of beef or crates of fish from sellers' stalls to purchasers' trucks. A national network of suppliers has made this sprawling new market the largest in Europe and specialties from every province (and from around the world) flow towards Paris both day and night.

Paradoxically, the availability of such a wide range of produce, the spread of the city, and increasingly fast means of transportation have led to the disappearance of certain specialties that were once identifed with the Ile de France. Gone, for instance, are the fat white asparagus from the Paris suburb of Argenteuil, the chickens from nearby Houdan, cherries from Montmorency, and the peas from Clamart. Though these products come from elsewhere now, the traditions associated with each remain: Parisians still love asparagus, and peas (from the south) are still prepared *à la parisienne*.

Paris is a haven for lovers of cheese, whatever style they prefer. Nowhere in the country are there as many cheeses on display. Parisians, however, have a weakness for *fromage blanc*, fresh cream cheese, which is eaten with or without cream and sugar at the end of the meal. The most famous *fromage blanc* sold in Paris comes from Fontainebleau, and is known by that name.

## Simple Food from the Flatlands

If Parisian cooking can be hard to track down, the cuisine of Champagne is positively elusive. Indeed, there is no tradition of bistros in Champagne, and some cooks go as far as to say that no regional specialties even exist. (Others claim that anything doused with the region's famous sparkling wine is "typically" champenois.) In fact, Champagne boasts a list of specialties, but some chefs find them too embarrassing to serve.

Let us be more explicit. This area, whose name evokes the most glamorous wine in the world, has long been one of the poorest regions in France. The vineyards of Champagne have never exercised the romantic appeal of nearby Burgundy, and the local dishes are hardly what one would expect to serve with the "local wine," that is, Champagne. "Who's going to order bacon and dandelion salad, or boiled salt pork and cabbage, to eat with a vintage *brut*?" some chefs complain. Since the local cooking is not of the kind people associate with

Champagne (the wine), it simply is not served. That is, it is not served in restaurants, but in the homes far from the palatial establishments of Reims and Epernay, local traditions are preserved.

In this region, whose name evokes festivities and elegance, one expects wealth and finds it in the large towns where the famous wine is made; but there is another Champagne, a glamorless land of farmers, and it is their cuisine that is of interest — the only true *cuisine champenoise*. Keep in mind that vineyards cover no more than 5 per cent of Champagne, and that the famous wine is produced mainly by big houses, not small growers. Most people here live in simple homes, and grow wheat or sugar beets, not grapes.

The oft-repeated truism that regional dishes are best with the wines of the region from which they come simply does not apply in Champagne. In this vast area of flat land which extends from the Belgian border to Chablis, hearty, simple dishes abound. Towns like Troyes boast *andouillettes*, and in Sainte-Menehould, pigs' feet have been simmered, breaded, and grilled in the same way for centuries. Cabbage is a staple, and root vegetables are used in many dishes, such as *hochepot*, *pot-au-feu*, and *potée champenoise*, the traditional boiled dinner. If you are lucky, you might be offered a *matelote* stew made with fresh-water fish, or a venison pâté made from the deer that abounds in the forest of the Ardennes but, on the whole, the traditional cooking of Champagne is strikingly plain.

*The Ile Saint-Louis in the heart of Paris, surrounded by the river Seine. In the middle distance stands Notre Dame, with its twin towers and flying buttresses, and away to the left is the outline of the Eiffel Tower.*

TRIPELON-JARRY CEDRI

DANIEL THIERRY/DIAF/IFA-BILDERTEAM

*A prospective customer reads through the menu of a Paris restaurant. Throughout France the restaurants, bistros and cafés display their menus outside, or in the window.*

## FLANDERS AND PICARDY

If you venture north to French Flanders, however, everything changes. Cooks swell with pride when the cooking of their province is mentioned, and regional specialties are in evidence everywhere you go. The food, the people and, particularly, the landscape, have little in common with Champagne. As you travel toward Lille, grapevines disappear and farms give way to small brick houses where coalminers used to live. Belgium is a few miles to the east, and the English Channel an hour's drive further north. You pass factory towns where beer flows instead of wine, and *genièvre,* gin, is the local *eau-de-vie*. This is not a picturebook vision of France, but many colorful traditions have survived, and culinary surprises are in store for those who look behind the brick façades, study the region's history, or simply observe the customs which set the north apart.

Some regional tastes seem inexplicable at first. For instance, people here have, for France, an unusually sweet tooth. Hard candies are extremely popular, with the mint-flavored *bêtise* from Cambrai being perhaps the most famous hard candy in the country. Sugar is used in cooking both vegetables and meat (red cabbage and beef stews) and the most famous dessert is simply a sugar tart. But look at the fields. One leafy plant seems to dominate — the sugar beet. Its large, white roots have replaced the oleaginous rapeseed that once grew here, ever since Napoleon was angered by an English embargo in the early nineteenth century that deprived France of imported cane sugar. The Emperor sponsored experiments for extracting sugar from native plants, resulting in French sugar "independence" in 1812. Now most French sugar comes from these northern fields, and the local people have an almost inordinate fondness for it.

Other typically Flemish penchants are rooted in history as well. The tenacity of a man from neighboring Picardy changed the local diet, and to some extent, that of the world. In the late eighteenth century, after a series of disastrous wheat harvests, Antoine-Auguste Parmentier led a campaign to turn the humble potato into a staple food that, he hoped, could replace bread as the mainstay of the French peasants' diet. Today the potato is the most popular vegetable in France, and it is most popular of all in the north.

The north is also an area of "pockets" where unexpected local specialties can be encountered. Take garlic from Arleux, for example. The south has no monopoly on this condiment, and this little town, 20 miles (30 kilometers) from Lille, holds a garlic festival every year. This region is in fact the eighth largest garlic-producing area in France, but the garlic here is quite different from that found elsewhere. It is smoked like ham or bacon, until it has become a dark caramel color. Local people say that smoking keeps the garlic from sprouting, which means that it can be easily kept for a year or more. Vendors' stands line the highway, festooned with skeins of the dark brown bulbs, and the tourists can hardly believe their eyes. In the winter months along some of these same roads there will be stands selling *endives*, another northern specialty.

Confusingly known as Belgian endive in the US and chicory in Britain, what the French call *endive* is appropriately known as *witloof*, white leaf, in Flanders. Indeed, this hand-length vegetable is a compact collection of snow-white leaves with pale yellow borders. The plant is a relative newcomer to French tables, appearing first in Brussels markets in the early nineteenth century and moving to France at the end of the century. In fact, it is only in the last forty years or so that

*Few cafés in Paris are more famous than Les Deux Magots on the Left Bank in Saint-Germain-des-Prés. It was a favorite haunt of American writers such as Hemingway during the 1920s.*

NIK WHEELER

*endives* have become commonplace in the markets of Paris. Neatly wrapped in blue or purple tissue paper, they announce the arrival of winter just as surely as the first flakes of snow.

Today France, and more specifically the north, is the world's largest producer of *endives*. Highway 17 is called *la route de l'endive*, though travelers will never glimpse this versatile plant as it is cultivated in total darkness, either in cavernous vaults or beneath the ground in deep trenches that cross the fields.

From a culinary standpoint, both Flanders and Picardy are much richer, and easier to explore, than either Champagne or the Ile de France. Specialties are omnipresent and proudly displayed. Indeed the Picard town of Amiens "merited a detour" for many years before the *Guide Michelin* created its stars. (Rabelais praised the cuisine of "Guillot en Amiens," and the duck pâté from that city was for many years considered to be the finest in France.) Visit a market and you will find slices of

CATHERINE KARNOW

## NORTHERN CHEESES

Found throughout France, Brie's home is in the northeast. The best Bries are yellow-gold, whole milk farmhouse cheeses, soft but not runny, and have an almost nutty taste. Wedges of Brie are typically cut from a whole wheel of the cheese.

Chaource from Champagne is a small, round cheese with a snowy white crust and a mild, milky taste. It is best from the fall to early spring, and smells faintly of mushrooms and cream.

Maroilles from Flanders is considered too strong by some, though its defenders call it "the most delicate of strong cheeses, and the strongest of delicate cheeses." It is used in cooking, whereas Brie and Chaource are not, and is just as likely to be used in tarts and waffles as it is to be served on a cheese platter.

One specialist has counted up to forty cheeses in the north alone, most of which are notably pungent. Some have revealing names, like the Puant de Lille ("the stinker of Lille"), while others are flavored with herbs and spices.

Few cheeses are made in Champagne, but in addition to Chaource there are *cendrés*, small cheeses ripened in wood ashes, and Langres from the south, which resembles the famous Burgundian Epoisses.

LEO MEIER/WELDON TRANNIES

*flamiche*, home-baked leek pie, or of the cheese-rich *goyère au Maroilles* for sale. Near Amiens a table might be covered with tall, buttery cakes, the famous *gâteaux battus*, while in Arras and Cambrai the merits of the local *andouillettes* will be vaunted.

Nowhere are *gaufres*, waffles, more popular than in northeastern France, and throughout the region outdoor stands selling crisp, freshly made waffles are a common sight, particularly at festival time. Talk to the locals, however, and you will be given a bewildering variety of recipes. The batter invariably contains yeast, but may be made with beer, milk, or cream. Sometimes, in Picardy, purèed pumpkin is mixed with the milk. Waffles are generally served with sugar or jam, and topped with whipped cream, but some cooks make savory versions.

Everywhere a wide variety of beer is served, delicious beers, both dark and light, to drink with mussels from Boulogne or Dunkerque, or beef, and to cook with as well. Dark beer is used like wine, and everything from chicken to eel can be simmered in it to make memorable stews. Both the northern *carbonnade,* beef and onions stewed in dark brown beer, and *coq à la bière,* rooster stewed in dark brown beer, rival their famous wine-based counterparts from Burgundy — *boeuf bourguignon* and *coq au vin*. A meal orchestrated around several beers is a gastronomic treat, darker and darker beers being served until the blackest brew of all is served with a slice of local cheese to round off the meal.

Those who know only the cooking of creative chefs in Paris are missing a glorious tradition of simple food in the capital's cafés and bistros, and those who disdain the homely pleasures of a *poteé champenoise* will never understand Champagne. To consider this northeastern corner of France a drab flatland is to sorely underestimate it. Take the time to explore the region and you will find a wealth of good food as varied as the natural resources that have sustained its economy and shaped its cuisine for centuries.

*Hunters out in the fields with their guns, trying their luck for some rabbit or pigeon for the pot.*

*Opposite: A basketful of freshly baked* baguettes *hangs over the arm of a baker in a street in Montmartre.*

*Following pages: Champagne vineyards spread over the plains south of Epernay, the grapes almost ready for havesting.*

R. TRUMAN/LANDSCAPE ONLY

# CHAMPAGNE!

According to Webster's Dictionary, Champagne is "a white sparkling wine made in the old province of Champagne, France; also a similar wine made elsewhere." A connoisseur would disagree. The method used to make Champagne *does* produce sparkling wines throughout the world, but true Champagne comes only from France and *must* be made in one of five departments: the Marne, the Aube, the Aisne, the Seine-et-Marne and the Haute-Marne. Similar wines are "sparkling," but nothing more.

Webster's overlooks the fact that although most Champagne is white and sparkling, it can also be pink and sparkling, or red, rosé, or white and *not* sparkling.

In fact, none of the wines originally produced in Champagne was sparkling. The earliest references to Champagne describe a non-sparkling red wine and, indeed, the red wine from Champagne was long a rival to the best wines of Burgundy. To this day, the red wines of Champagne (known as Côteaux Champenois) are still made with the same Pinot Noir grape as the famous reds further south.

White Champagne, originally a novelty, had a natural tendency to be slightly fizzy, but it was not until a seventeenth-century monk, Dom Pérignon, tightly tied corks onto the newly bottled wine that a truly sparkling wine was born. Interestingly enough, this famous white wine continues to be made mainly from the same dark-skinned Pinot Noir grape as the once-famous red. When Champagne is made from the white-skinned Chardonnay grape it is called Blanc de Blancs, white from whites. Non-sparkling whites, like the reds mentioned earlier, continue to be made in Champagne, and are also labeled Côteaux Champenois. Lastly, in addition to pink sparkling Champagne, a non-sparkling rosé with its own *appellation*, Rosé des Riceys, is produced in small quantities, and is well worth tasting.

Webster's does not mention that sparkling Champagne can be vintage and non-vintage, *brut intégral*, very dry, *brut*, dry, *sec*, not so dry, *demi-sec*, sweet, and *doux*, very sweet. Vintage Champagne is the wine of one particular year, while non-vintage Champagne is made by mixing wines made in different years. Vintage wines are rarer, more expensive and generally preferable, although non-vintage Champagnes can be quite good. These days,

J.-N. REICHEL/AGENCE TOP

*Remuage is the process of giving each Champagne bottle a daily turn, so that the sediment slips into the neck of the bottle and adheres to the base of the crown cork.*

ost Champagne, vintage or not, is *brut*. White or red, sparkling or not, wines om Champagne are always served chilled d they can be drunk with meat or fish. n "all Champagne" dinner can either be ie in which the same Champagne enerally *brut*) is served from beginning end, or one in which a variety of nampagnes is served throughout the eal. In the latter case you might, for ample, start with a very dry Champagne an apéritif, drink a non-sparkling white ôteaux Champenois with the first course, red Côteaux Champenois or a Rosé des ceys with the main dish and the cheese, d a sweet Champagne with the dessert, fore finishing with coffee and a Marc Champagne.

After investigating the variety of wines oduced in this region and experiencing eir distinctive tastes, one looks sadly at 'ebster's inadequate definition, and can ly pity those people who, disregarding e wine list, presumptuously shout, Vaiter, Champagne!"

SCOOPIX

*Dom Pierre Pérignon, the cellarmaster of the Benedictine Abbey of Hautvilliers, was a most gifted winemaker and is considered to be the "father of Champagne."*

## CHAMPAGNE

### CHAMPAGNE

*The best known of the Grandes Marques, great name, Champagnes:*

*Ayala (2)*
*Billecart-Salmon (2)*
*Bollinger (2)*
*Deutz and Geldermann (2)*
*Alfred Gratien (3)*
*Charles Heidsieck (1)*
*Heidsieck and Co (1)*
*Henriot (1)*
*Krug (1)*
*Lanson (1)*
*Laurent-Perrier (2)*
*Moët et Chandon (3)*
*Mumm (1)*
*Joseph Perrier (5)*
*Perrier-Jouët (3)*
*Piper Heidsieck (1)*
*Pol Roger (3)*
*Pommery (1)*
*Louis Roederer (1)*
*Dom Ruinart (1)*
*Salon (4)*
*Taittinger (1)*
*Veuve Clicquot (1)*

### STILL WINES OF CHAMPAGNE

*Côteaux Champenois (2)*
*Rosé des Riceys (6)*

All French wine is subject to *Appellation Contrôlée*. The system is based upon precisely defined geographical boundaries, but also prescribes approved grape varieties, cultivation methods, yields, and alcohol levels. There are three main types of *Vin d'Appellation*:

- d'Appellation d'Origine Contrôlée (AOC)
- Vin Delimité de Qualité Superieure (VDQS)
- Vin de Pays

Almost all the best French wines, and most of those exported, are in the top category of AOC. The wines listed in this book are of this classification, unless otherwise stated.

PETER JOHNSON

# RECIPES OF PARIS, CHAMPAGNE AND THE NORTH

*Philip and Mary Hyman*

## Salade au Lard

*Salad Greens with Bacon*

Versions of this simple farmer's salad can be found all over France, but nowhere is it as popular as in Champagne. Most people agree that "bitter" greens, such as dandelion greens or chicory, should be preferred, but debates rage as to whether shallots, onions, and/or potatoes should be included.

*2 lb (1 kg) dandelion greens or chicory (curly endive)*
*6 thick bacon slices, finely sliced crosswise*
*6 potatoes, boiled in their skins and peeled (optional)*
*3 large shallots or 1 onion, chopped*
*3 tablespoons red or white wine vinegar*
*salt and freshly ground pepper*

Cut off the base of the dandelion greens, remove damaged leaves, but keep any buds. If using curly endive or escarole, separate the leaves and break them into two or three pieces. Pour boiling water into a large salad bowl to heat it while the bacon is cooking.

In a large skillet, allow the bacon to render its fat over low heat for 5 to 10 minutes. The pieces should brown but not harden. Thickly slice the cooked potatoes, if using, add to the pan and sauté to reheat.

Pour the hot water from the salad bowl, dry rapidly and place the greens in the bowl. Sprinkle the bacon pieces and potatoes over the greens, along with any fat the bacon has rendered. Add the shallots to the skillet, pour in the vinegar and boil just long enough to soften them. Pour the vinegar and shallots over the salad, salt lightly, pepper generously and toss. Taste for seasoning and serve immediately.

SERVES: 6

*Salad Greens with Bacon,*
*Eels with Cream,*
*Leek Pie,*
*Arleusian Garlic Soup*

## *Anguilles à la Crème*

*Eels with Cream*

In both Picardy and Flanders eel recipes abound. This one was provided by Madame Seminet who runs a small restaurant in Cappy near Amiens.

If eels are unavailable, scallops are equally delicious prepared in this way. Scallops should be poached for no more than 5 minutes.

*2 lb (1 kg) small, young eels, skinned and cut into 2-in (5-cm) lengths*
*8 cups (2 qt/2 l) water*
*1 tablespoon coarse salt*
*6 peppercorns*
*1 carrot, thinly sliced*
*2 shallots, thinly sliced*
*bouquet garni: 1 bay leaf, 2 thyme sprigs, 2 parsley sprigs*
*3 large shallots, finely chopped*
*1 teaspoon butter*
*3 tablespoons chopped chives*
*1 cup (8 fl oz/250 ml)* crème fraîche *or heavy (double) cream*
*salt and freshly ground pepper*

Make a *court-bouillon* by heating the water, salt, peppercorns, carrot, shallots, and bouquet garni in a large saucepan. Bring to a boil then lower the heat and simmer for 20 minutes. Add the eels and poach gently for 10 minutes. Drain the eels and keep warm in a serving dish.

Melt the butter in a high-sided skillet, add shallots and cook gently until transparent. Add the cream and chives and heat just enough to warm. (If the cream is very thick, add a little of the *court-bouillon*.) Season to taste, pour over the eels and serve.

Serves: 6

## *Flamiche aux Poireaux*

*Leek Pie*

A *flamiche* can also be made with vegetables such as pumpkin, onions, and potatoes. This recipe is from the Somme valley.

*Pastry:*
*$2^1/_2$ cups (10 oz/315 g) all purpose (plain) flour*
*5 tablespoons ($2^1/_2$ oz/75 g) .butter, in pieces*
*5 tablespoons ($2^1/_2$ oz/75 g) lard, in pieces*
*1 egg*
*1 teaspoon salt*
*2 tablespoons water*

*Filling:*
*1 egg for glazing*
*1 tablespoon butter*
*2 lb (1 kg) leeks, white parts only, sliced not too thinly*
*1 cup (8 fl oz/250 ml) milk*
*$^2/_3$ cup (5 fl oz/150 ml)* crème fraîche *or heavy (double) cream*
*1 egg, plus 1 egg yolk*
*salt, freshly ground pepper, and freshly grated nutmeg*

For the pastry: Place the flour on a work surface and dot it with the pieces of butter and lard. With a rapid pinching motion, coarsely combine the flour and fat. Beat the egg, salt, and water lightly with a fork and gradually incorporate into the flour-fat mixture until the dough can be packed into a ball. Roll out two-thirds of the dough and line a 9-in (23-cm) pie pan, leaving a border of about $^1/_2$ in (1 cm) all around the edge. Place the lined pan and the remaining dough in the refrigerator to chill while preparing the leeks.

For the filling: In a skillet, melt the butter, add the leeks and cook gently for a few minutes to soften, then add the milk and cook until it has entirely evaporated. When the leeks are done, remove from the heat and allow to cool a little. Preheat the oven to 425°F (220°C). In a mixing bowl, whisk together the *crème fraîche*, eggs, salt, pepper, and nutmeg, then stir into the leeks.

Roll out the remaining dough into a circle large enough to cover the pie. Beat the remaining egg with a little salt in a small bowl. Pour the filling into the pie pan, smooth with a fork, then set the top crust in place. Trim the edge of the crust, brush with the egg glaze and fold the border of the bottom crust over the top, pressing with the tines of a fork to seal. Brush the surface of the pie with egg, cut a hole in the middle and make a few slits in the top of the pie with the tip of a knife. Bake for 40 minutes to 1 hour, or until golden brown. Serve warm.

Serves: 6

## *Soupe à l'Ail Arleusienne*

*Arleusian Garlic Soup*

Arleux, a town midway between Douai and Cambrai, is the "garlic capital of the North." Some recipes for this local soup call for up to a head of garlic per person.

*2 tablespoons butter*
*$^3/_4$ cup ($3^1/_2$ oz/100 g) whole garlic cloves, peeled*
*$1^1/_4$ lb (600 g) potatoes, quartered*
*2 carrots, quartered*
*8 cups (2 qt/2 l) water*
*2 teaspoons coarse salt*
*freshly ground pepper*
*butter and/or cream to taste*

In a large saucepan, melt the butter and gently cook the garlic, stirring often, until it barely begins to brown. Add all the other ingredients except butter and/or cream, bring to a boil, cover partially, and cook gently for 1 hour. The vegetables should be very soft. Purée the soup using a food mill or a food processor. Reheat, taste for seasoning, add butter and/or cream and serve.

Serves: 6

## *Goyère de Maroilles*

*Maroilles Cheese Tart*

Unlike other soft, fully ripened cheeses, Maroilles is frequently used in cooking.

*$^1/_3$ oz (10 g) fresh (compressed) yeast or $^1/_2$ teaspoon ($^1/_6$ oz/5 g) dry yeast*
*2 tablespoons lukewarm water*
*$1^3/_4$ cups (7 oz/200 g) all purpose (plain) flour*
*$^1/_2$ teaspoon salt*
*2 eggs*
*1 tablespoon sugar*
*$3^1/_2$ tablespoons butter, softened*
*1 Maroilles cheese*
*3 tablespoons* crème fraîche *or heavy (double) cream*
*freshly ground pepper*
*butter for serving*

*Maroilles Cheese Tart*

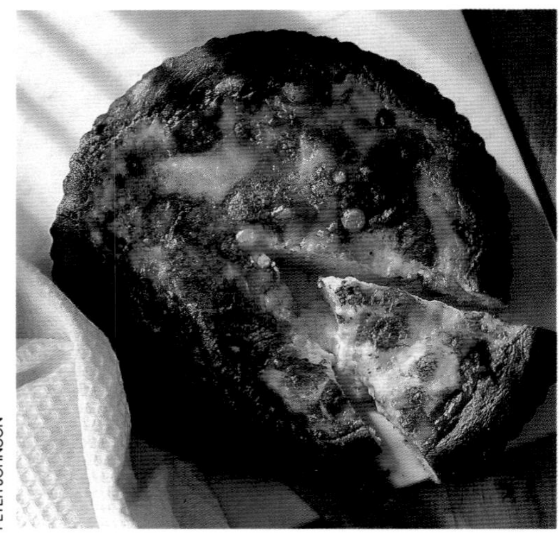

PETER JOHNSON

*Duck Pâté from Amiens*

Dissolve the yeast in the water. Place the flour in a large mixing bowl, sprinkle with salt and make a well in the center. Place the eggs, sugar, and yeast mixture in the well and mix together, then gradually begin incorporating the flour. When all the flour has been added, incorporate the butter and beat the dough, either by hand or using an electric dough hook, until the dough detaches from the sides of the bowl (and no longer sticks to the fingers, if mixing by hand). The finished dough should be very soft.

Lightly butter and flour a 10-in (25-cm) tart pan. With your hands, spread the dough out and place it in the pan, pulling it up the sides with your fingers. Cover the pan with a damp cloth and leave in a warm place to rise for 1 hour.

Preheat the oven to 400°F (200°C). Scrape the crust off the Maroilles (the edges may be cut off, if preferred), then slice the cheese thinly. Cover the risen dough entirely with the slices of cheese, except for a border around the edge. Spread the cream over the top, season with pepper, and bake for about 30 minutes, or until the edge of the crust is brown. Serve warm, dotted with butter, or provide butter at the table for people to serve themselves.

SERVES: 6 to 8

## *Pâté de Canard d'Amiens*

### *Duck Pâté from Amiens*

Virtually no one makes traditional *pâté de canard d'Amiens* using an unboned duck any more. It's easier for restaurants and take-out specialists to serve slices of rich duck "pie" (which sometimes includes such atypical ingredients as *foie gras de canard*). The following recipe is based on old accounts of the pâté found in early French cookbooks.

*lard-butter short pastry made with double the recipe given for* flamiche aux poireaux, *page 30*
*1 duck, about $2^1/_2$ to $3^1/_4$ lb (1.2 to 1.5 kg)*
*5 oz (150 g) lean veal*
*10 oz (300 g) lean pork*
*8 oz (250 g) pork fatback*
*2 shallots, finely chopped*
*4 oz (125 g) mushrooms, finely chopped*
*2 teaspoons butter*
*1 cup (2 oz/60 g) fresh breadcrumbs, broken very small or grated*
*2 apples, peeled, cored, and grated*
*1 egg*
*2 to 3 tablespoons* eau-de-vie de genièvre, *gin, or Cognac*
*20 g truffle shavings (optional)*
*2 teaspoons salt*
*$1^1/_2$ teaspoons freshly ground pepper*
*1 teaspoon* quatre-épices *(see glossary)*
*1 bay leaf, broken into pieces*
*7 tablespoons ($3^1/_2$ oz/105 g) soft butter*
*about 8 oz (250 g) barding fat*
*1 egg for glazing*

Make the short pastry. Clean the duck. Cut off the neck and wings and reserve for making aspic. Reserve the heart, liver, and gizzard for the stuffing.

Grind the veal, pork fatback, duck heart, liver, and gizzard in a food processor, or through a meat grinder equipped with a fine grill. In a skillet, cook the shallots and mushrooms rapidly in the butter until they soften.

Stir the shallots and mushrooms into the chopped meat then add breadcrumbs, grated apple, egg, *eau-de-vie de genièvre*, and truffles, if using. Season with salt, pepper, and *quatre-épices*. Stir vigorously to perfectly combine, then fill the duck with this stuffing. Make sure there is a little stuffing left over.

Preheat the oven to 400°F (200°C). Divide the dough in half. Roll out one half into an oval considerably larger than the duck and slightly thicker in the middle than around the edges. Place the duck in the center. Spread the entire surface of the duck with the reserved stuffing, then place pieces of bay leaf here and there on top, dot generously with the butter, and lay a sheet of barding fat over the breast and legs. (Trim off any excess.)

Roll out the rest of the dough into an oval slightly larger than the first and of even thickness. With a fork, lightly beat the egg for glazing with a little salt and water. Brush the edge of the first sheet of dough with a little egg, lay the second sheet over the duck and press the sheets of dough together. Trim the edges (keep the trimmings), then roll them in toward the duck and crimp with your fingers or the prongs of a fork.

Roll out the trimmings and cut into leaf shapes to decorate. Glaze the surface of

*French Boiled Dinner*

PETER JOHNSON

the pâté with egg then, using an apple corer or knife, cut a hole in the center of the crust and insert a nonstick paper or aluminum foil "chimney" into the hole. Decorate the surface with the pastry leaves and glaze again. Bake for 30 minutes, then lower the heat to 325°F (160°C) and bake for 2 hours more.

When the pâté is done, remove from the oven, discard the chimney and allow to cool to room temperature. Place the pâté in the refrigerator and chill for at least 24 hours before serving. To serve, remove the top crust, slice the breast and leg meat and place a little of each on serving plates. Garnish with the stuffing.

SERVES: 8

## Pot-au-Feu

*French Boiled Dinner*

Boiled beef dinners are served in homes throughout the country, but Parisians are particularly fond of *pot-au-feu*.

The goodness of a *pot-au-feu* depends on the cuts of meat, the quantity of water and, especially, the proper salting of the water in which the beef is cooked. Only a few rules apply to the vegetables: cabbage is never cooked in the broth, and potatoes (if served) are best boiled separately. Only a few simple root vegetables are cooked with the meat, the amounts being left to the discretion of the cook.

A *pot-au-feu* should be served with a wide range of condiments — *cornichons* and other vinegar-based pickles, French mustards of all kinds, and freshly grated horseradish — and a little coarse sea salt should be sprinkled over the meat and vegetables on each plate.

Leftover meat and vegetables can be served cold with a mustardy vinaigrette, and the meat can also be made into another Parisian favorite, *boeuf miroton*.

*4½ to 6 lb (2.25 to 3 kg) boiling beef, such as thick, lean short ribs, brisket, or chuck*
*1 teaspoon of coarse salt for every quart (liter) of water used*
*pinch of peppercorns*
*bouquet garni: 1 bay leaf, 2 thyme sprigs, 2 parsley sprigs*
*1 garlic bulb (optional)*
*1 onion stuck with 3 cloves*
*1 lb (500 g) carrots, quartered*
*1 lb (500 g) young turnips, quartered*
*2 lb (1 kg) leeks, white part only with just a little of the green, tied into 2 bunches*
*6 celery stalks, strings removed, halved and tied into 2 bunches*
*1 lb (500 g) potatoes (optional)*
*six 1-in (2.5-cm) sections of marrow bones or three 2-in (5-cm) sections, tied inside a cloth*
*various pickles, a selection of mustards, and coarse salt for serving*

Place the meat in the bottom of a large pot and add enough water to cover by a few inches — use approximately 1½ qt (1½ l) for every 2 lb (1 kg) meat. Bring to a boil, skim off any foam that rises, then add the salt. Skim again, then add the peppercorns and all the vegetables except the potatoes. Bring to a gentle boil, cover and cook over very low heat for 3½ to 4 hours. About 30 minutes before the cooking time is up, add the marrow bones and cook the potatoes (if using) in boiling salted water.

Lift the meat, the vegetables, and the bag of marrow bones out of the stock and keep warm. Discard the bouquet garni, the garlic and the onion, and strain the stock. Leave the stock to rest for about 15 minutes, then skim off as much fat as possible. (Do not discard the fat. It can be used to make *boeuf miroton*.)

Reheat the stock and serve as a first course. Place the meat on a large platter, top with the marrow from the marrow bones, surround with vegetables and serve with an assortment of *cornichons*, vinegar pickles, mustards such as Dijon or Meaux, coarse salt, and a little extra stock for those who want to moisten the meat and vegetables.

SERVES: 6

## Carbonnade à la Flamande

*Beef Braised in Beer*

The most famous *carbonnade* is made in northern France, and contains beef, onions, and dark beer. Some people add bread and mustard, or *pain d'épices*, gingerbread. It should be served with the same dark beer as is used to cook the meat.

*6 tablespoons (3 oz/90 g) lard*
*2 lbs (1 kg) onions, thinly sliced*
*4 tablespoons dark brown sugar*
*4 lb (2 kg) lean braising beef, such as chuck or brisket*
*salt and freshly ground pepper*
*4 tablespoons cider vinegar*
*1 bottle (3 cups/24 fl oz/750 ml) dark beer, preferably from the north of France or Belgium*
*bouquet garni: 1 bay leaf, 2 thyme sprigs, 2 parsley sprigs*
*2 large slices country-style bread*
*Dijon-style mustard*

Melt about 4 tablespoons of the lard in a large pot, add the onions and cook over moderate heat until they begin to brown. Add brown sugar and simmer gently while preparing the meat.

Cut the meat into slices about ¾ in (2 cm) thick and then into 2-in (5-cm) rectangles; season with salt and pepper. In a large skillet, melt about a tablespoon of the lard and brown a few pieces of beef. Avoid overcrowding the pan. Remove the meat and brown the remaining beef in small batches. Pour off the fat and deglaze the skillet with the vinegar, scraping the bottom to dissolve the caramelized meat juices. Stir this liquid into the onions.

Remove most of the onions from the pot, leaving just enough to cover the bottom. Add a layer of meat, cover with a layer of onions, and continue layering until all the meat is in the pot, ending with a layer of onions. Add the beer, bouquet garni, salt and pepper, then cover the pot. Bring to a boil, then immediately lower the heat and simmer slowly for 2½ hours.

Spread the slices of bread with the mustard, then cut each one into three pieces. Lay these in the pot, mustard side down, and gently press them into the liquid. Cover and simmer for an additional 30 minutes. Serve the *carbonnade* inthe cooking pot.

SERVES: 6

## Boeuf Miroton

*Beef Miroton*

A perfect *miroton* must be simmered slowly, it should have just the right proportion of onion to meat, and have a slightly acid tang.

It can be served "as is," the braised onions being both sauce and garnish, with boiled potatoes, or spooned over toasted slices of country-style bread that have been "buttered" with *pot-au-feu* fat before serving.

PETER JOHNSON

*Beef Braised in Beer, Beef Miroton*

*3 tablespoons* pot-au-feu *fat*
*6 onions, thinly sliced*
*1 tablespoon all purpose (plain) flour*
*$2^1/_2$ cups (20 fl oz/600 ml) beef stock*
*4 tablespoons red wine vinegar*
*salt and freshly ground pepper*
*$1^3/_4$ lb (800 g) boiled beef*
*white wine (optional)*
*lemon juice or vinegar for serving (optional)*

In a high-sided skillet, melt the fat and add the onions. Cook over moderate heat, stirring occasionally, until the onions are golden brown. Sprinkle in the flour and cook over low heat, stirring frequently, for 5 minutes, then add the stock, vinegar, salt and pepper. Cover and simmer for 15 minutes.

Remove any excess fat from the beef, then slice thinly. When the cooking time for the onions is up, stir in the beef: if the sauce seems too thick, add a little more stock or a little white wine. Cover and simmer over very low heat for 25 to 30 minutes. Taste for seasoning. If desired, a little lemon juice or extra vinegar may be added before serving.

SERVES: 6

## *Caqhuse*

*Cold Pork and Onions*

A *caqhuse* is always made with "fresh ham" — a slice cut from the thick end of a leg of pork. It is generally eaten cold as a main course, with a green salad, and a glass of beer.

*5 tablespoons ($2^1/_2$ oz/75 g) butter*
*$2^1/_2$ lb (1.25 kg) pork from the thick end of a leg, sliced across bone*
*2 lb (1 kg) onions, quartered or thickly sliced*
*salt and freshly ground pepper*
*$^1/_4$ cup (2 fl oz/60 ml) red wine or cider vinegar*
*$^3/_4$ cup (6 fl oz/180 ml) water*
*$^2/_3$ cup (5 fl oz/150 ml) white wine*

Preheat the oven to 400°F (200°C). Melt a lump of the butter in a large baking dish, place the pork in the center and surround it with onions. Dot with the remaining butter, season generously with salt and pepper and bake for about 45 minutes to 1 hour, or until the pork and onions have begun to brown. Baste from time to time.

Turn the pork over, add vinegar, water, and white wine, and continue baking for about 1 hour more. Test to see if the pork is done by piercing the thickest part of the meat with a needle: if the juices run clear, it is cooked.

Remove from the oven and allow to cool. Serve cold in the baking dish.

SERVES: 6

*Cold Pork and Onions*

PETER JOHNSON

## Potée Champenoise

*Boiled Dinner from Champagne*

*Potées* are made throughout France and their contents vary. This one, from Champagne, is sometimes called the *potée des vendangeurs*, the grape-pickers' dinner, since it is traditionally served during the grape harvest.

The contents of a *potée* vary with the budget and the season. White beans are optional and, in the spring, fresh green peas can be added about 30 minutes before serving.

Lightly salted pork need be soaked for only a couple of hours, but heavily salted pork should be soaked for 48 hours in cold water, and the water should be changed every 6 hours.

*8 oz (250 g) dried white beans*
*1 lb (500 g) salt (pickled) pork belly, desalted as described above*
*1¾ lb (800 g) salted ham hocks or shoulder, desalted as described above*
*bouquet garni: 1 bay leaf, 2 thyme sprigs, 2 parsley sprigs*
*1 boiling hen (optional)*
*6 large carrots, quartered*
*4 small to medium turnips, quartered*
*1 large rutabaga, quartered (optional)*
*salt and freshly ground pepper*
*1 large cabbage, quartered*
*6 potatoes, peeled*
*1 large boiling sausage*
*8 oz (250 g) smoked ham (optional)*
*bread*

Soak the white beans overnight, then drain. Place the salt pork and ham hocks in a large pot with the beans and fill with enough cold water to cover by several inches. Bring to a boil, skimming any foam that surfaces. Add the bouquet garni, the boiling hen (if using) and all the vegetables except the cabbage and potatoes. Return to a boil, then lower the heat and simmer very slowly for 2 hours. After the time is up, taste, add a little salt, if necessary, and season with pepper. Add the cabbage, cook 1 hour longer, then add the potatoes, boiling sausage and ham, if using, and cook 45 minutes more.

Ladle the liquid into a tureen and serve with slices of stale bread or bread dried in a moderate oven. Place the meat and vegetables on a large platter and serve as a second course with Dijon mustard.

SERVES: 6 to 8

PETER JOHNSON

*Boiled Dinner from Champagne, Green Peas and Lettuce French Style*

## Petits Pois à la Française

*Green Peas and Lettuce*

The best green peas in France were once grown in what is now a drab suburb of Paris — Clamart.

*3 lb (1.5 kg) green peas, shelled*
*7 tablespoons (3½ oz/105 g) butter*
*30 pearl onions, or small pickling onions*
*1 head Bibb lettuce, tender leaves only, cut into strips*
*a few parsley sprigs and 1 green onion (scallion or spring onion) tied together*
*salt and freshly ground pepper*
*1 teaspoon sugar*
*2 egg yolks*
*5 tablespoons* crème fraîche *or heavy (double) cream*

In a heavy-bottomed pot, place all the ingredients except the egg yolks and cream, and toss together. Cover and leave for 1 to 2 hours. (The vegetables will give out moisture during this time.)

Place the pot over low heat and stir about every 5 minutes, pushing the vegetables that are on top down to the bottom until the liquid comes about half way up. Bring to a boil, then lower the heat. Cover and cook gently for about 15 minutes or until the peas are tender.

In a bowl, whisk the eggs and cream; season with salt and pepper. When the peas are done, pour this mixture into the pot, stirring. Stir for a few minutes, allowing the sauce to thicken slightly, but do not boil. Transfer to a dish and serve.

SERVES: 6

## *Gâteau Battu*

*Beaten Cake*

This rich yeast cake is traditionally baked in a special fluted mold that is approximately 5½ in (14 cm) tall and 6 in (15 cm) wide, but a can of about the same height with a 2 qt (2 l) capacity will do.

The cake is normally served with jam at breakfast, or with stewed fruit at the end of a meal.

*¾ oz (20 g) fresh (compressed) yeast or 1 teaspoon (⅓ oz/10 g) dry yeast*
*3 tablespoons lukewarm milk*
*½ cup plus 2 tablespoons (2½ oz/75 g) all purpose (plain) flour*
*pinch of salt*
*3 small egg yolks*
*5 tablespoons (2½ oz/75 g) softened butter*
*1½ tablespoons sugar*
*1 tablespoon rum*

Dissolve the yeast in the lukewarm milk. Place the flour in a large mixing bowl, sprinkle with salt, and then make a well in the center. Place the egg yolks, softened butter, sugar, rum, and yeast mixture in the well.

With the fingers, mix the ingredients in the well together, then gradually begin incorporating the flour. When all the flour has been added, beat the dough, lifting and stretching it to incorporate as much air as possible. The dough should be beaten for 15 to 20 minutes, or until it detaches from the sides of the bowl and no longer sticks to the fingers. (An electric mixer with a dough hook can be used.)

Place the dough in a lightly buttered *gâteau battu* or *brioche* mold. (It should be no more than one-third full.) Cover the mold with a moist, thick cloth and leave in a warm place away from draughts to rise for about 2 hours.

Preheat the oven to 350°F (180°C). When the dough almost reaches the edge of the mold, place in the oven and bake for about 30 to 45 minutes, or until a skewer inserted into the center of the cake comes out clean. Remove from the oven and wait 5 minutes before turning out onto a cake rack. Allow the cake to cool completely before serving.

Serve with stewed fruit (rhubarb is especially recommended) or homemade jam.

SERVES: 6 to 8

## *Tarte au Sucre*

*Sugar Tart*

This is one of the most famous desserts in Flanders. The "filling" varies from family to family. Some simply dot the sugar with butter before baking, others pour cream over the sugar, and still others use the mixture below.

*Pastry:*
*$1/3$ oz (10 g) fresh (compressed) yeast or $1/2$ teaspoon ($1/6$ oz/5 g) dry yeast*
*2 tablespoons lukewarm water*
*2 cups (8 oz/250 g) all purpose (plain) flour*
*$3/4$ teaspoon salt*
*1 tablespoon white sugar*
*1 egg*
*$1/2$ cup (4 oz/125 g) softened butter*
*Filling:*
*1 egg*
*2 tablespoons milk*
*approximately 1 cup (6 to 8 oz/185 to 250 g) white, light brown, or dark brown sugar*
*3 tablespoons butter, in small pieces*

Dissolve the yeast in the water. Place the flour in a mixing bowl, sprinkle with salt, and make a well in the center. Place the sugar, egg, butter, and yeast mixture in the well. Mix all of these ingredients together then incorporate the flour, working very quickly with the tips of the fingers until a smooth, homogeneous dough is produced. Pack the dough into a ball, cover with a damp cloth and place in the refrigerator for 1 hour.

Roll out the dough and line a 10-in (25-cm) pie pan or flan ring, then roll the edge of the dough toward the inside to form a sort of rope around the edge. Prick the dough base all over with a fork. Preheat the oven to 400°F (200°C).

For the filling: Mix the milk and egg together. Spread the sugar in an even layer over the bottom of the tart — it should be about $1/8$ in (3 mm) thick. Sprinkle the milk and egg mixture over the sugar using a pastry brush or fork, as if sprinkling laundry to be ironed. Place dabs of butter all over the top and bake for about 30 minutes, or until the pastry has browned lightly. Serve warm or cold.

SERVES: 6 to 8

*Beaten Cake, Sugar Tart, Snow Eggs*

PETER JOHNSON

## *Oeufs à la Neige*

*Snow Eggs*

Early recipes suggest serving *oeufs à la neige* either hot or cold and flavoring the cream with orangeflower water and lemon peel. By the 1830s, vanilla was the recommended flavoring when serving cold, and only this version has survived.

*4 cups (1 qt/1 l) milk*
*1 vanilla bean, halved lengthwise*
*8 eggs, separated*
*1 cup (7 oz/210 g) sugar*

Place the milk in a high-sided skillet. Scrape the inside of the vanilla bean into the milk, whisk, then drop the vanilla bean in as well. Bring just to a boil, then remove from the heat, cover the pan and allow to infuse for 10 minutes.

Beat the egg whites until thick and foamy. Sprinkle in one-third of the sugar and continue beating until very firm but not "dry." Whisk in half the remaining sugar.

Place the milk back over low heat and remove the vanilla bean. When the milk is simmering, take a rounded tablespoon of egg white and shape the top with a second tablespoon or a knife, forming a large "egg." Slide it into the milk, then form two or three more eggs in the same way and add them to the skillet. Do not crowd the skillet. When the milk begins to foam up around the base of an egg, turn it over and cook for 10 to 20 seconds more, then remove from the pan with a slotted spoon and drain on a cloth. Place the drained snow eggs on a large platter and chill until ready to serve.

PETER JOHNSON

*Waffles*

When all the snow eggs have been made, strain the milk and measure: about 3 cups (24 fl oz/750 ml) are needed for the custard. If there is not enough, add a little extra milk. In a mixing bowl, beat the egg yolks with the remaining sugar until they lighten and form a ribbon. Heat the milk in a saucepan until almost boiling, then whisk a little into the egg yolks. Pour the egg yolks into the saucepan and stir, over low heat, until the bubbles disappear and the custard coats a spoon. Do not allow the milk to boil, or the custard will curdle. When done, strain the custard into a bowl and allow to cool, then chill until ready to serve.

To serve, pour the custard into a deep, wide dish. Pour off any liquid in the bottom of the snow egg platter, slide the snow eggs on top and serve.

SERVES: 6

## Gaufres

*Waffles*

In northern France, waffles such as these have been made since Medieval times. Heart-shaped irons are often used, and the waffles are usually served with sugar or jam.

*1/3 oz (10 g) fresh (compressed) yeast or 1/2 teaspoon ((1/6 oz/5 g) dry yeast*
*2 tablespoons lukewarm water or milk*
*2 cups (8 oz/250 g) all purpose (plain) flour*
*3 eggs*
*pinch of salt*
*2 tablespoons sugar*
*1 cup (8 fl oz/250 ml) light (blond) beer, lukewarm or at room temperature*
*about 1/2 cup (4 fl oz/125 ml) warm water or milk*
*2 tablespoons melted butter*
*piece of pork fatback*

Dissolve the yeast in the 2 tablespoons of water. Place the flour in a mixing bowl, make a well in the center and add the eggs, salt, sugar and yeast mixture. Stir the flour gradually into these ingredients then, little by little, stir in the beer, followed by the warm water. Finally stir in the butter. The batter should be runny but thick enough to coat a spoon. Cover with a cloth and leave in a warm place for 2 hours to rise.

Heat the waffle iron over moderate heat (or use an electric one) and rub both halves with pork fatback. Stir the batter and ladle it into the bottom half of the waffle iron until the surface is covered. Close the iron and cook for about 4 to 5 minutes, or until the waffle is golden brown and it separates easily from the iron when pried with a fork.

SERVES: 6 to 8

Belgique
Luxembourg
Luxembourg
Deutschland
Thionville
Saarbrücken
Boulay
Verdun
Metz
Montigny-les-Metz
Moselle
Haguenau
Meuse
Lorraine
Nancy
Toul
Lunéville
Strasbourg
Marlenheim
Alsace
Obernai
Mittelbergheim
Itterswiller
Charmes
Moselle
Saint-Dié
Dambach-la-Ville
Marne
Riquewihr
Ribeauvillé
Vittel
Epinal
Kaysersbourg
Niedermorschwihr
Colmar
Contrexéville
Chaumont
Munster
Vosges
Rhein
Thann
Mulhouse
Belfort
Basel
0 10 20 30 40 50 M
0 10 20 30 40 50 60 70 80 Km

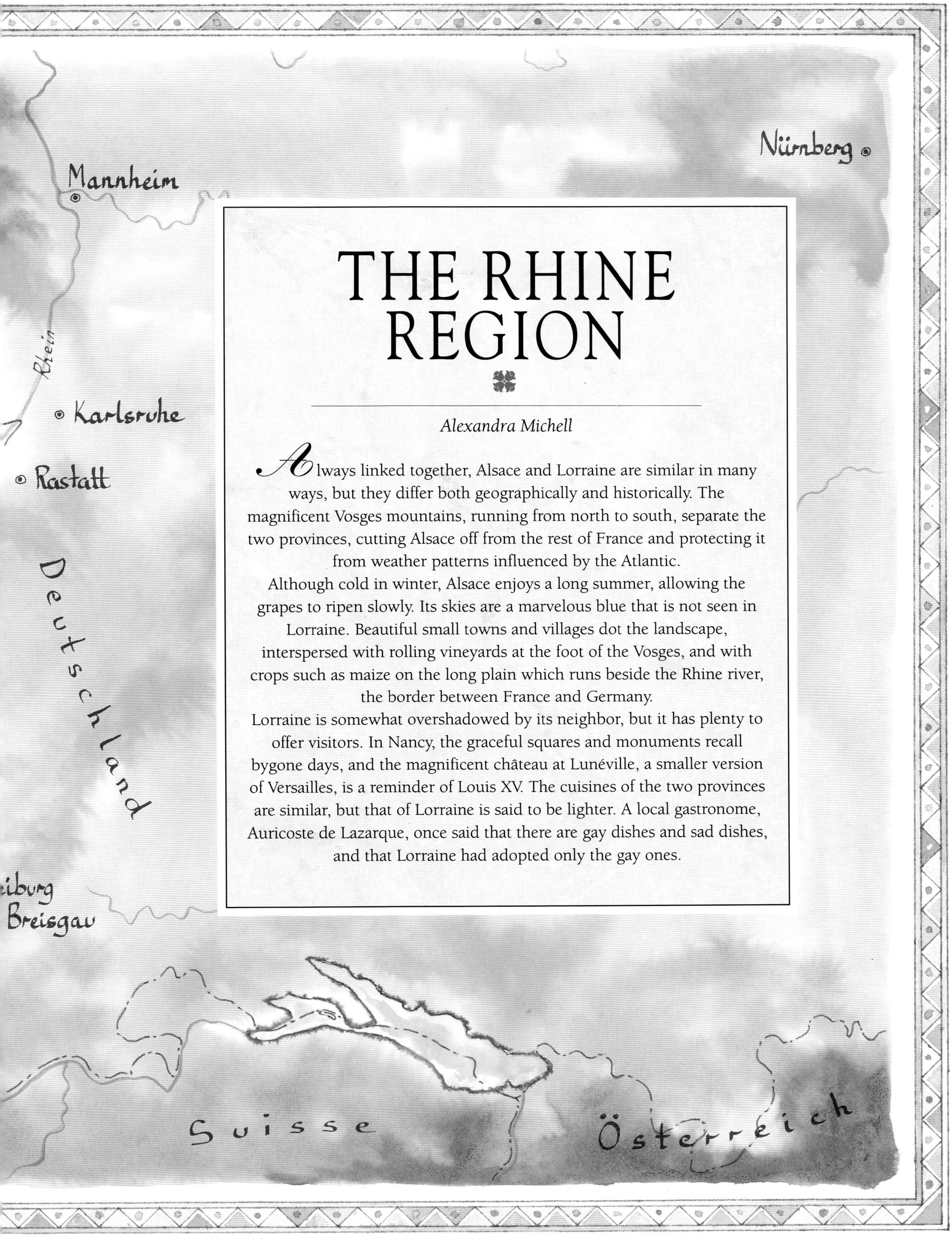

# THE RHINE REGION

*Alexandra Michell*

Always linked together, Alsace and Lorraine are similar in many ways, but they differ both geographically and historically. The magnificent Vosges mountains, running from north to south, separate the two provinces, cutting Alsace off from the rest of France and protecting it from weather patterns influenced by the Atlantic.

Although cold in winter, Alsace enjoys a long summer, allowing the grapes to ripen slowly. Its skies are a marvelous blue that is not seen in Lorraine. Beautiful small towns and villages dot the landscape, interspersed with rolling vineyards at the foot of the Vosges, and with crops such as maize on the long plain which runs beside the Rhine river, the border between France and Germany.

Lorraine is somewhat overshadowed by its neighbor, but it has plenty to offer visitors. In Nancy, the graceful squares and monuments recall bygone days, and the magnificent château at Lunéville, a smaller version of Versailles, is a reminder of Louis XV. The cuisines of the two provinces are similar, but that of Lorraine is said to be lighter. A local gastronome, Auricoste de Lazarque, once said that there are gay dishes and sad dishes, and that Lorraine had adopted only the gay ones.

Mannheim
Nürnberg
Rhein
Karlsruhe
Rastatt
Deutschland
Breisgau
Suisse
Österreich

CHRISTIAN SAPPA/CEDRI

*In Dambach-la-Ville, oak barrels labeled with the names of grape varieties serve as a sign for one of the local winemakers.*

## ALSACE

Alsace consists principally of a plain no more than 20 miles (32 kilometers) wide which runs north-south between the Vosges and the Rhine river. The land is rich in alluvial deposits, which favor agriculture, and the sheltered lower slopes of the Vosges produce the wines for which Alsace is so well known.

For seven centuries Alsace was a Germanic state. In 1648 the Treaty of Munster gave France rights to most of Alsace, but even today, with its half-timbered Bavarian architecture, the region looks more like part of Bavaria or Austria than France. The Alsatians still speak a German dialect, and it is often easier to converse with the older people in German rather than French.

## STRASBOURG, THE CROSSROADS OF EUROPE

Strasbourg, the capital of Alsace, was in the past on major military and trade routes, and it now plays host to the Council of Europe and the European Parliament. Despite outside influences, it remains staunchly Alsatian — neither French nor German. In the old part of the city, quaint houses that are centuries old seem to lean against one another, offering support.

The city's cuisine features the abundant produce of the province. In the eighteenth century Savary des Bruslons wrote in his *Dictionnaire Universel de Commerce* that Strasbourg traded principally in *eaux-de-vie,* saffron, and large cabbages. Saffron has now disappeared, but *eaux-de-vie* and cabbages are as important as ever. *Choucroute*, sauerkraut (pickled cabbage) with ham and sausages, appears on menus everywhere, from workers' cafés to elegant restaurants. Like many Alsatian specialties, most of the dish's ingredients are salted and preserved, a legacy of the days when people relied on provisions stored away at harvest time. The new season's sauerkraut is still celebrated with festivals in various towns and villages in the early fall.

F. JALAIN/EXPLORER

*An array of sausages from Charcuterie Bruxer in Kaysersberg, one of the many wine-producing towns in the Vosges foothills.*

DALLAS AND JOHN HEATON/SCOOPIX

*With its old Alsatian houses, canals, and restaurants, La Petite France is one of Strasbourg's most picturesque districts.*

Another Alsatian favorite is the *flammekueche* or *tarte flambée*. In the village of Pfulgriesheim, not far from the capital, this tart is prominent among the many regional specialties that are served. Bread dough is rolled out until it is paper-thin, spread with thick cream, onions, and bacon, and cooked in an extremely hot, open bread oven. The tart must be served piping hot, so usually everyone at the table shares one, before the next is served.

The other great specialties of the Strasbourg area are, of course, *foie gras*, and *pâté de foie gras*. Very much part of the cuisine of the well-known restaurants, this delicacy can be found in such dishes as terrine of truffled *foie gras*, a warm salad of pork cheeks and *foie gras* with green lentils from Puy, *foie gras en brioche*, fresh asparagus with fried *foie gras* and crayfish, and terrine of *foie gras* with Riesling.

# PÂTÉ DE FOIE GRAS

The *pâté de foie gras* of which Strasbourg is so proud is said to have been the invention of a cook from Lorraine by the name of Jean-Pierre Clause. According to the *Dictionnaire de l'Académie des Gastronomes* (1962), the Marquis of Contades was named military governor of Alsace in 1768, and when he went to Strasbourg to take up the post, he was accompanied by his extremely able cook. Clause discovered the merits of *foie gras,* and is said to have improved it by surrounding it with finely chopped veal and a pastry case. This new pâté was baptized *pâté à la Contades*. In 1788, when Contades was replaced, Clause remained in Strasbourg, married the widow of a *pâtissier* named Mathieu, and for the rest of his life carried on a successful business making and selling the pâté that he supposedly invented.

The claim that Clause was the first to make this pâté is, however, disputable, since some decades earlier the author of *Le Cuisinier Gascon* (1740) gave a recipe for *petits pâtés de foyes gras aux truffes*, small pâtés of *foie gras* with truffles. Pastry cases were lined with a *farce* of *foie gras*, then a piece of *foie gras* studded with truffles was added, everything was covered with more *farce*, and the pastry was glazed with egg before baking. Admittedly, the *farce* is of *foie gras* rather than veal, but otherwise the two recipes sound as if they are almost identical.

*Foie gras* with the greatest reputation comes from geese raised in Alsace and in the southwest of France. However, it is estimated that about one-third of the livers processed in these areas is now imported from Hungary, Bulgaria, Poland, and Israel. The ancestral tradition of force-feeding has been maintained in these countries, as in Alsace, by Jewish farmers. The quality of *foie gras* from Hungary has always been recognized, and one of the best-known French companies has imported *foie gras* from there since before the Second World War.

*Foie gras* from ducks is also a great delicacy, and over 3000 tons are produced annually in France, in sharp contrast with only 600 tons of goose livers, making it much more readily available.

Great care must be taken with the preparation of *foie gras* because it is extremely delicate. Seasoning should be slight, and it should always be cooked slowly, or it will melt. At its best, *foie gras* is pink inside. Canned *foie gras* can therefore never be of the highest quality because sterilization requires it to be cooked at too high a heat.

*Foie gras* is the most highly regarded of all Alsatian dishes, and it is always served on special occasions. Production of *foie gras* peaks in early December, and it is an integral part of the *réveillon* dinner on Christmas Eve and at New Year.

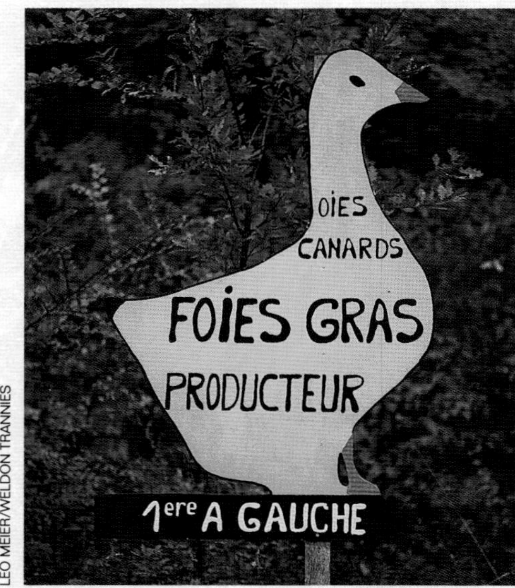


LEO MEIER/WELDON TRANNIES

*Geese on an Alsatian farm, destined for the foie gras market.*

LEO MEIER

KLAUS BOSSEMEYER/BILDERBERG

*A serving of Munster cheese, freshly baked bread, and a bottle of local red wine are cause enough for a smile.*

## The Route du Vin

On leaving Strasbourg the Route du Vin beckons, especially at vintage time, when the vineyards are buzzing with activity. Tractors pull wooden carts loaded with empty wooden barrels along the roads, which are then piled high with grapes and taken slowly and carefully back to the wineries. At dusk, the tractors' lights can be seen moving home all along the valley. Visitors are welcome at the vineyards, and the winemaker will happily pour a tasting of his produce and tell you about his vines, while keeping an eagle eye on the grape crushing. All the wines are made using traditional methods — not a stainless steel tank can be seen.

Alsatian wines are mainly white, and are primarily labeled by grape type. The main varieties are Sylvaner, Riesling, Muscat, Tokay Pinot Gris, Gewürztraminer, and Pinot Blanc. Red and rosé wines are made from Pinot Noir. Edelzwicker, a blend of various grape types, is the everyday wine of the region. At vintage time, restaurants proudly indicate that they are serving *vin nouveau,* milky fermenting grape juice which may only be a few weeks old. *Eau-de-vie,* the equivalent of schnapps or clear brandy, is made from almost every type of local fruit, from raspberries to plums, and each vineyard appears to produce its own.

The Route du Vin, which runs from Marlenheim in the north to Thann in the south, winds through one of the prettiest areas in Europe. Strasbourg is a romantic city, yet it cannot compare with the enchanting towns and villages with their Medieval half-timbered houses through which this road passes. The villages of Ribeauvillé and Riquewihr are home to some of the best known vineyards. Their houses are crowded together, window boxes filled with flowers hanging over the

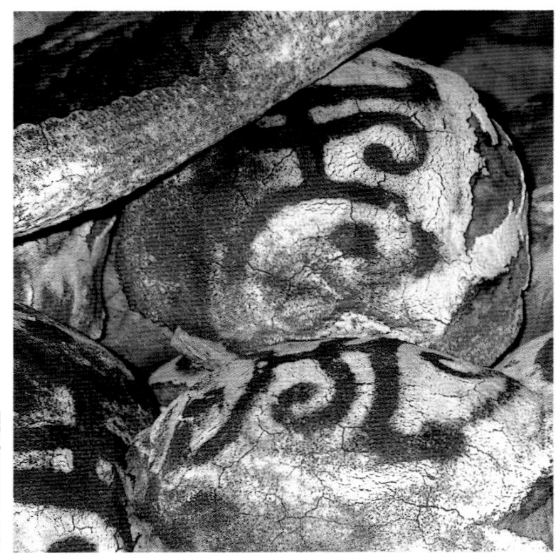
ALEXANDRA MICHELL

*In addition to its splendid pastries, Alsace is noted for its bread, which comes in a great array of shapes, sizes, patterns and flavors. Bread here is still often baked at home.*

narrow streets. Elaborate signs hang outside the many excellent food shops, restaurants and *winstubs*, wine bars, that serve local produce and traditional dishes. And there are so many more places to visit: Obernai, Itterswiller, Dambach-la-ville, Zellenberg, Kaysersberg, Munster, and, of course, Colmar, at the region's center. If you make a detour to the château of Haut-Koenigsbourg, from the ramparts you can look out over the plain of Alsace and across the Rhine towards Germany.

Some of the regional dishes which should be tried are *zewelwaï*, onion tart, *tourte aux viandes de la vallée de Munster*, meat pie from the Munster valley, *eierkuchas*, thick pancakes served with salad, and *foie gras en brioche*. An Alsatian feast is incomplete without *charcuterie*, and there is a tremendous selection to choose from, including bierwurst; *zungenwurst*, an enormous tongue sausage; *saucisses type Montbéliard*, sausages that are eaten hot with horseradish sauce; stuffed pork fillets; kassler; galantines and ballottines made with game and poultry; and *galerei*, pork brawn. Pork chops are served hot or cold with horseradish, and suckling pig is stuffed and roasted, or boned and treated as a galantine. Pies of all sorts are filled with pork, chicken, young wild boar, or venison.

Much of the game supplied to three-star restaurants elsewhere in France comes from Alsace, particularly from around Ribeauvillé and Riquewihr. While hares and rabbits are now practically non-existent, and it is difficult to find wild pheasant, there is no shortage of large game, such as deer and wild boar, which are traditional Christmas fare in the province.

The river Ill provides trout, pike, roach, perch, and eel. Carp comes from the ponds of Sundgau in the south, and is cooked in beer, stuffed, fried, or baked. The principal fish dish is *matelote alsacienne*, a fresh-water fish stew. Now in short supply, crayfish, frogs, and snails are often imported, but they continue to be very much part of the regional cuisine. Frogs' legs are served in soup with eggs, or in Riesling with cream and *fines herbes*. Snails are served with snail butter or in bouillon, and crayfish are often poached in Sylvaner.

In the realm of vegetables, the cabbage is definitely king. *Choucroute garnie à l'alsacienne* appears on all regional menus, and indeed on many bistro menus elsewhere in France. Red cabbage cooked in goose fat with onions and vinegar, or cooked with bacon, chestnuts, or apples, is also popular. Potatoes form a substantial part of the diet, and are served, steamed, with *choucroute*, and as potato cakes, known as *grumbeerekiechle*. They are also often used in salads.

## Fruit Tarts and Alsatian Breads

The province's desserts show Rhenish and Austrian influences, and many have pastry bases. Fruit in abundance provides fillings for all sorts of tarts, such as plum, apple, bilberry, and grape. Fruit sorbets also appear on most menus and, although they look quite innocent, a good slug of the appropriate *eau-de-vie* has invariably been poured over them prior to serving. Yeast-based cakes include the kugelhopf, and *birewecke*, pear bread, a Christmas specialty made almost entirely of dried fruit and heavily spiced with cinnamon. A bakery in Colmar, which has been handed from father to son since 1776, is renowned for this bread, and also specializes in other beautiful Alsatian breads, such as bretzels, salted bread sticks, and *christstolle*, sugary brioches with bitter almonds and crystallized fruit, sold during the month before Christmas.

*Warfare, both in the last century and this, brought devastation to Alsace. Following the Second World War the vineyards were replanted with high quality vines, and business now prospers.*

F. JALAIN/EXPLORER

*Opposite: With its many fine examples of Baroque architecture, Nancy is one of the loveliest cities in France. The Bastille Day festivities held here, in Place Stanislas, are rivaled only by those in Paris.*

## MUNSTER AND GÉROMÉ

Cheesemaking in Alsace and Lorraine began in the seventh century, when Irish monks came to the Munster valley to spread the gospel. They settled on both sides of the Vosges, raising dairy cattle and making cheese, and as a result the cheeses, Munster in Alsace, and Gérome in Lorraine, are much the same. More than 8000 tonnes of Munster, a beautiful orange-crusted cheese, is produced annually and exported throughout the world.

The cheesemaking traditions of the monks have been continued by over four hundred farms. Each year in late May the herds are taken to the high pastures, where they remain until late September. The cheese is made and stored in simple two-room stone structures, many of which are now *fermes-auberges*, offering regional dishes to travelers. These include *baeckeoffe*, beef, lamb, pork, potatoes, and onions, stewed in wine; ham in Riesling; *tarte flambée;* Munster tart; and cheesecake made with *fromage blanc* and farm eggs. On the other side of the Vosges, Géromé is sold as *fromage frais* on Saturdays at the Epinal market, and the cheeses that remain unsold are later ripened in the traditional way.

*For centuries cabbages have been grown in great quantities in Alsace, and sauerkraut can be found on practically every restaurant menu.*

KLAUS BOSSEMEYER/BILDERBERG

CHRISTIAN SAPPA/CEDRI

## LORRAINE

On the western side of the mountains the slopes are more gentle, and the landscape of Lorraine is less dramatic than that of Alsace. The greater part of the region consists of a rolling plateau of pasture and farmland, with industry concentrated mainly in the north near iron ore deposits, or exiled to small areas where it is relatively unobtrusive.

Lorraine was created in 843 by the division of Charlemagne's empire, the central part becoming Lotharingia, later known as Lorraine. In the last two centuries it has been, like Alsace, both French and German, but unlike its eastern neighbor, it is without Germanic characteristics. The province's sombre architecture is similar to that in other parts of France, but the graceful Place Stanislas in Nancy, with its ornate gilded grills, pavilions, balconies, and fountains, is an appealing sixteenth-century legacy from Stanislas Leszczynski, father-in-law to Louis XV, who once ruled Lorraine.

At that time, Savary des Bruslons wrote that the the area's trade was based principally on salt, honey, and *eaux-de-vie*. Metz, Toul, and Verdun were known for their wines, jams, and sugared almonds. The best jams from Metz were those made from Mirabelle plums and white raspberries, and Verdun produced a great quantity of *dragées*, known as *anis de Verdun*. The pastures of the Vosges mountains provided the three towns with beef, butter, and cheese.

Until recently, salting food was the only way it could be preserved, and salt was therefore an extremely valuable commodity. Lorraine's trade in salt was a major source of revenue from the Middle Ages onwards, and it came to be known as "the province of salt." Today the province still has more than twenty salines. In the town of Marsal there is an interesting little museum, the Maison du Sel, which is devoted solely to the history of salt.

## THE MACAROONS OF NANCY

Macaroons are a specialty of Boulay, Toul, and Nancy in Lorraine, but those of Nancy have a long history. In the seventeenth century they were already famous, and were known as *benoitons* because they were made by the Benedictine nuns in the rue de la Hache. When the convent was shut down by the revolutionaries in 1793, two nuns were given refuge by the family Gormand in the same street. Sister Suzanne and Sister Elisabeth, in order to pay for their keep, helped in the kitchen, where they made the convent's macaroons. These were put on sale, and soon their fame spread throughout the city.

When Sister Suzanne died, Sister Elisabeth called on her niece to come from Savigny to help her. The niece and her husband successfully carried on the business with Sister Elisabeth, eventually buying the house in rue de la Hache.

The secret recipe was passed from one to another, with the result that these macaroons are still baked in the same house in the same street, after nearly two hundred years. In honor of the two sisters, the town of Nancy changed the name of the rue de la Hache to rue des Soeurs-Macarons in 1952.

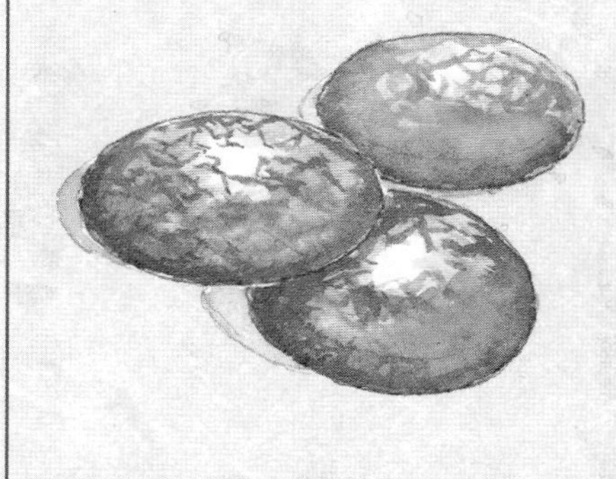

CHRISTIAN SAPPA/CEDRI

*One of the many beautiful lakes in the Vosges ranges. In summer the mountain pastures provide grazing for cattle, and in winter they become skiing territory for cross-country enthusiasts.*

## Food from the Wild

The food and cuisine of Lorraine continue to depend almost totally on regional produce. Game and wild foods are important, and there are many recipes in local cookbooks for quail, partridge, wild duck, wood grouse, and pheasant. Among the fruits that grow so well are all sorts of berries, such as bilberries, cranberries, mulberries, and wild strawberries, and there are sloe plums, wild apples, sorb apples, medlars, and rosehips. Wild vegetables include lamb's lettuce, wood asparagus, borage, thyme, watercress, sorrel, and samphire, and there are many varieties of wild mushrooms. The region is also known for its mineral springs, especially in Contrexéville and Vittel in the south.

The people of Lorraine are great soup eaters, and the *potée lorraine,* originally a peasant soup, is made with smoked sausages, onions, carrots, different sorts of beans (fresh in summer, dried in winter), anything from the kitchen garden, and above all cabbage, which must dominate the other vegetables. It is served with slices of toast, the vegetables piled on top of slices of ham.

Freshwater fish found in the district include trout, pike, gudgeon, carp, tench, bream, and eel. Trout is served *au bleu*, *meunière*, or as a pâté; pike is cooked as *quenelles*, or with cabbage and potatoes; gudgeon is deep fried and served with lemon wedges; carp is cooked in beer or *à la juive*; tench is cooked in local wine, and eel is presented in a tart, with champignons. As in Alsace, frogs and crayfish are rare, and are now mainly imported.

Perhaps the province's most famous dish is *quiche lorraine,* which, according to the experts, should never contain cheese. Apparently the cheese was a Parisian addition. Originally *quiche lorraine* was made with a bread dough base; nowadays it is cooked in a pastry shell. The eggs and cream mixture, known as *migaine*, is also used in desserts such as *pommes à la migaine* and rhubarb tart.

Lorraine is truly the province of tarts. Fillings include cherries, plums, apples with raisins and cinnamon, poppyseeds, and cream cheese. It is also renowned for its *pâtisserie*, especially its *babas*. Stanislas Leszczynski is said to have particularly enjoyed kugelhopf dipped in wine, and gave it the name of Ali-Baba, his favorite story. Since then, rum syrup has replaced the wine. Another famous local cake is the small, shell-shaped *madeleine*. Madeleine, a Commercy girl, replaced Stanislas' pastrycook at short notice one day and made the only cake she knew. The king and his guests much enjoyed it, and Stanislas decided to call it after the girl. Other cakes and candies include the chocolate cakes from Nancy and Metz; a cheesecake known as *gâteau lorrain au fromage blanc*; *tarte au maugin,* a cream cheese tart; macaroons from Boulay, Toul, and Nancy; *bergamotes,* honey sweets, from Nancy; the *dragées* of Verdun; and the barley sugar from Charmes. The province is also famous for its fruit conserves and jellies.

Despite the horrors and devastation of two world wars, Alsace and Lorraine have managed to retain their old ways and their individuality. Tradition is important in the day-to-day life of the towns and villages, and the centuries-old methods of food and wine production, along with the wonderful old recipes that continue to be used, make these regions a delight for the visitor.

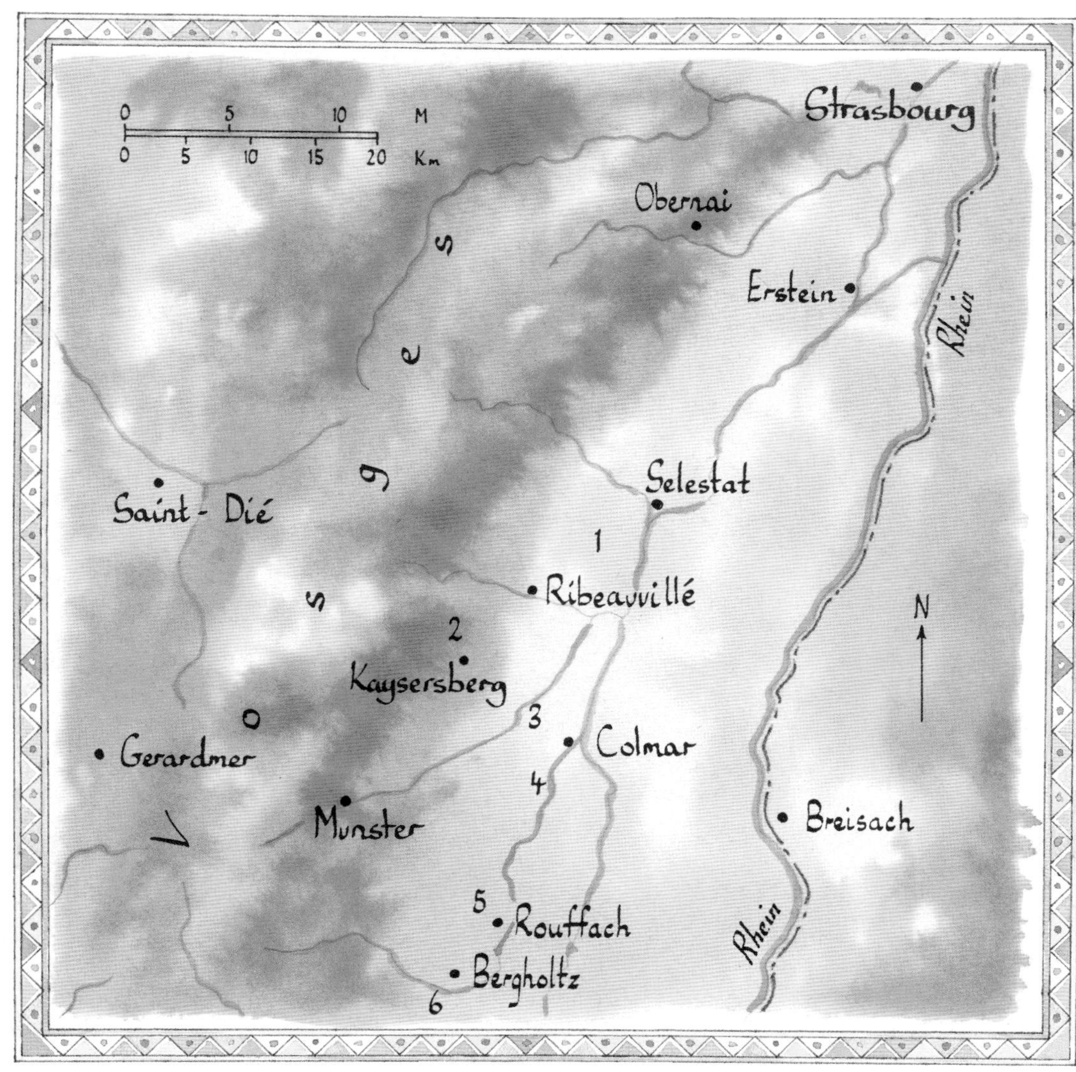


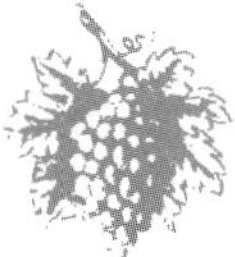

## ALSACE

*Riesling, Gewürztraminer, Tokay-Pinot Gris, Muscat, Sylvaner, Pinot Blanc and Pinot Noir are the noble grape varieties. Edelzwicker is a blend from two or more varieties. The entire Alsace region is of AOC status.*

*Leading wine producers:*

*Léon Beyer (4)*
*Blanck (2)*
*Dopff "Au Moulin" (2)*
*Dopff and Irion (2)*
*Hugel (2)*
*Kuentz-Bas (3)*
*Jos Meyer (3)*
*Muré (5)*
*Rolly Gassmann (1)*
*Schlumberger (6)*
*Louis Sipp (2)*
*Pierre Sparr (3)*
*F. E. Trimbach (2)*
*Domaine Weinbach (2)*
*Domaine Zind Humbrecht (4)*

# RECIPES OF THE RHINE REGION

*Alexandra Michell*

PETER JOHNSON

## *Matelote de Poissons au Riesling*

*Fish Stew with Riesling*

Alsace is blessed with two rivers, the Rhine and the Ill, which are well stocked with fish, so fresh-water fish are prominent in the Alsatian diet. A *matelote* is usually a stew of different fresh-water fish and other local ingredients, and is found in various provinces. In Alsace Riesling is used to moisten and flavor it whereas in Normandy cider is added.

*4 lb (2 kg) freshwater fish, such as pike, eel, tench, carp, perch and trout, cut into large chunks (retain heads and bones)*
*4 cups (1 qt/1 l) water*
*2 leeks, white parts only, sliced*
*2 carrots, chopped*
*2 garlic cloves, peeled*
*2 parsley sprigs*
*6 tablespoons (3 oz/90 g) butter*
*4 shallots, finely chopped*
*1¼ cups (10 fl oz/310 ml) Riesling*
*10 oz (300 g) champignons (button mushrooms), sliced*
*juice of 1 lemon*
*2½ tablespoons all purpose (plain) flour*
*1 egg yolk*
*⅔ cup (5 fl oz/150 ml), heavy (double) cream or* crème fraîche

At the fishmarket, arrange for the fish to be scaled and cleaned. The head and bones are needed for the stock.

Place the head and bones in a saucepan with the water, leeks, carrots, garlic, and parsley, and bring to a boil. Reduce the heat, simmer for 20 minutes, then strain the stock into a bowl.

Melt one-third of the butter in a saucepan, add the shallots and cook over low heat until they are soft and translucent. Then add the fish and lightly brown them. Eel and tench require longer cooking than the other types of fish so, when browned, remove the pieces of pike, carp, perch, and trout to a plate. Continue cooking the eel and tench a little longer. Pour the Riesling and 1¼ cups (10 fl oz/310 ml) fish stock into the saucepan, season with a little salt and pepper and simmer for about 7 minutes. Then add the reserved fish and simmer a further 10 minutes, or until cooked.

Meanwhile, slice the champignons and place them in a saucepan with one-third of the butter and the lemon juice. Cook over a low heat for about 5 minutes. Blend together the remaining butter and the flour to make a *beurre manié*. When the fish is just cooked, remove from the saucepan with a slotted spoon and keep warm. Add the champignons to the saucepan and thicken the liquid with the *beurre manié*. Blend the egg yolk with the cream and stir in. Season to taste. Place the fish on a warmed serving dish, pour the sauce over the fish and serve immediately.

SERVES: 6

## *Potage aux Lentilles à l'Alsacienne*

*Alsatian Lentil Soup*

This is a very hearty soup which, with a crusty loaf of bread and a green salad, could be a meal in itself.

*8 oz (250 g) lentils*
*8 cups (2 qt/2 l) water*
*14 oz (440 g) carrots, chopped*
*14 oz (440 g) potatoes, chopped*
*1 leek, sliced*
*1 onion, sliced*
*2 garlic cloves, peeled*
*½ cup chopped parsley*
*1 bay leaf*
*2 cloves*
*7 oz (220 g) bacon, sliced crosswise*
*8 peppercorns*
*salt*
*6 to 8 Strasbourg sausages or other smoked pork sausages, cut into rounds or pieces (some sausages may need to be precooked)*
*¾ cup (6 fl oz/180 ml) cream (optional)*

Soak the lentils for several hours, preferably overnight, then drain. Place them in a large saucepan with the water, and add the vegetables, parsley, bay leaf, cloves, bacon, and peppercorns. Bring everything to a boil, reduce heat and simmer for 2 hours.

Pass the soup through a food mill, using the coarse blade, and return to the saucepan. If the soup is too thick, add more water. Taste for seasoning. Just before serving, add the sausages and reheat. Add the cream, if desired, and serve.

SERVES: 6 TO 8

*Left: Fish Stew with Riesling, Alsatian Lentil Soup, Flaming Tart*

## *Tarte Flambée*

*Flaming Tart*

*Tarte flambée* is traditionally cooked in an open bread oven where the flames literally lick at its sides.

This recipe yields 2 lb (1 kg) of dough. Only 1 lb (500 g) is needed for the *tarte flambée*, but the dough is also suitable for making *baguettes*, other white breads, and *birewecke*, see page 59. Bread flour is richer in gluten than ordinary flour, giving it elasticity, and is available from health food stores.

*Bread Dough:*
*1²/₃ cups (13 fl oz/400 ml) water*
*¹/₃ oz (10 g) fresh (compressed) yeast or ¹/₆ oz (5 g) dry yeast*
*4³/₄ cups (1 lb 3¹/₂ oz/600 g) bread flour*
*2 teaspoons salt*
*Tart:*
*3 tablespoons butter*
*1 small onion, finely chopped*
*2³/₄ oz (80 g) rindless bacon, finely sliced crosswise*
*1³/₄ cups (14 fl oz/430 ml) heavy (double) cream*
*salt*
*freshly grated nutmeg*
*1 lb (500 g) bread dough*
*1 tablespoon rapeseed oil*

For the dough: Place the water in the bowl of a mixer, add the yeast and whisk until dissolved. Add the flour and, using a dough hook, knead with the machine for 15 minutes, adding the salt after 5 minutes. The dough can be made by hand, but must be kneaded for longer to give it the necessary elasticity.

Place the dough in a bowl in a warm spot to rise for an hour, or until it has doubled in size. Knock it down and place in the refrigerator until needed. It can be prepared up to about 12 hours ahead.

For the tart: Melt the butter in a small saucepan. Add the onion and cook over low heat until it is soft but not browned. Turn it into a bowl to cool. Add the bacon to the saucepan and cook over low heat until cooked but not crisp. Stir the cream into the cooled onion mixture and season to taste with salt and grated nutmeg.

Preheat the oven to its maximum temperature, preferably more than 480°F (250°C). Weigh out two 8 oz (250 g) portions of bread dough, and roll each into a rectangle 12 x 16 in (30 x 40 cm). At first this will seem an impossible task with the small amount of dough, but it must be rolled out paper-thin for the tart to be a success. Place on baking trays. Spread the onion and cream mixture over the top, sprinkle with the bacon then the rapeseed oil and bake for 10 to 12 minutes.

The tarts must be served immediately, so cook each one as needed.

SERVES: 6

PETER JOHNSON

*Alsatian Onion Tart*

## *Tarte à l'Oignon*

*Alsatian Onion Tart*

Onion tart is to Alsace what the *quiche* is to Lorraine, and is found on most café and *winstub* menus. The filling can be made with a simple mixture of eggs, milk, and cream, or with a béchamel sauce, as in the following recipe.

*Pastry:*
*2 cups (8 oz/250 g) all purpose (plain) flour*
*6 tablespoons (3 oz/90 g) unsalted butter, diced*
*1 teaspoon salt*
*3 egg yolks*
*about 3 tablespoons cold water*
*Filling:*
*1 lb (500 g) onions, finely sliced*
*5 tablespoons (2¹/₂ oz/75 g) butter*
*3 oz (90 g) lean rindless bacon, finely sliced crosswise*
*4 tablespoons (2 oz/60 g) butter*
*¹/₂ cup (2 oz/60 g) all purpose (plain) flour*
*2 cups (16 fl oz/500 ml) milk*
*salt and freshly ground pepper*
*ground nutmeg*
*2 egg yolks*

For the pastry: Place the flour, butter, and salt in a bowl and with a rapid pinching motion combine until the mixture resembles fine breadcrumbs. Then add the egg yolks and enough water for the pastry to form a ball. This can also be done with a food processor. Cover the dough with plastic wrap and chill.

For the tart: Preheat the oven to 425°F (220°C). Melt the butter, add the onions and cook over a low heat until soft and lightly browned. Blanch the bacon in boiling water for 1 minute. Melt 4 tablespoons butter, add the flour, then stir in the milk and cook over low heat until it thickens. Remove from heat and season with salt, pepper, and nutmeg. Stir in the egg yolks and onions, and taste for seasoning again.

Roll out the pastry and line an 11-in (27-cm) tart pan. Fill with the onion mixture and sprinkle the top with bacon. Bake at 425° (220°C) for about 20 to 25 minutes. Serve hot.

SERVES: 6

## Baeckeoffe

*Alsatian Hotpot*

*Baeckeoffe* means "cooked in the baker's oven." In earlier days Alsatian housewives would take this hotpot to to be cooked in the baker's oven after the bread had been baked. As this dish is mainly prepared the evening before, it was generally cooked on Mondays — washing day.

*1 lb (500 g) loin of pork, cut into 2-in (5-cm) cubes*
*1 lb (500 g) boned shoulder of lamb, cut into 2-in (5-cm) cubes*
*1 lb (500 g) topside or rump steak, cut into 2-in (5-cm) cubes*
*2 onions, finely sliced*
*3 garlic cloves, coarsely chopped*
*2 leeks, white parts only, finely sliced*
*2 cups (16 fl oz/500 ml) Riesling*
*bouquet garni: 2 bay leaves, 2 thyme sprigs, 3 parsley sprigs*
*2 lb (1 kg) potatoes, sliced*
*salt and freshly ground pepper*

Place the meat, onions, garlic, and leeks in a large bowl, pour over the Riesling, and add the bouquet garni. Cover and place in the refrigerator overnight.

Preheat the oven to 375°F (190°C). Place a quarter of the potatoes in a layer in the bottom of a large casserole dish, then add a layer of meat and vegetables and season with salt and pepper. Continue layering, using up all the meat and vegetables, topping the dish with a layer of potatoes.

Cover and bake for 3 hours. This dish can be taken straight to the table. Serve with a green salad.

SERVES: 6

## Poulet au Riesling

*Chicken in Riesling*

Because of the amount of corn and barley grown in Alsace, poultry raised in the province is known for its delicate flesh, and chicken recipes are numerous.

*6 tablespoons (3 oz/90 g) butter*
*1 chicken, about 3 lb (1.5 kg), trussed*
*2 onions, sliced*
*1 carrot, sliced*
*2 garlic cloves, chopped*
*bouquet garni: 1 bay leaf, 1 thyme sprig, 3 parsley sprigs*
*2 cups (16 fl oz/500 ml) Riesling*
*8 oz (250 g) champignons (button mushrooms)*
*2 egg yolks*
*3/4 cup (6 fl oz/180 ml) cream*
*salt and freshly ground white pepper*

Melt two-thirds of the butter in a large saucepan that has a cover. Add the chicken and lightly brown all over. Then add the onions, carrot, garlic, and bouquet garni, and cook for several minutes. Pour in the Riesling, bring to a boil, then reduce the heat, cover, and simmer for about 50 minutes, or until chicken is cooked.

Meanwhile, cut the champignon stalks level with their caps, and cook the champignons over low heat in the remaining butter for 3 to 4 minutes.

When the chicken is cooked, remove it to a serving platter and keep warm. Strain the cooking juices into another saucepan and reduce to half over high heat.

Mix the egg yolks with the cream, and whisk in a little of the hot liquid. Pour the egg yolk mixture and the reduced cooking juices into the saucepan, add the champignons, and stir over a very low heat until the sauce begins to thicken. Season to taste. Spoon a little of the sauce over the chicken and surround it with the champignons. Serve the remaining sauce separately.

The chicken can also be cut into serving pieces and cooked as above. However, the cooking time will be about 35 minutes, and only half the amount of wine should be used.

SERVES: 4

*Alsatian Hotpot, Chicken in Riesling*

PETER JOHNSON

PETER JOHNSON

Beet Salad with Walnuts

## *Salade de Betteraves aux Noix*

*Beet Salad with Walnuts*

Walnut trees grow along the edges of many of the vineyards, providing welcome shade in the summer. The nuts are used in salads and ice-creams, and are made into salad oil.

*$1^1/_2$ lb (750 g) beets (beetroot)*
*4 shallots, finely sliced*
*6 tablespoons chopped parsley*
*$^3/_4$ cup ($2^1/_2$ oz/75 g) coarsely chopped walnuts*
*$^1/_4$ cup (2 fl oz/60 ml) white wine vinegar*
*$^1/_3$ cup (3 fl oz/90 ml) walnut oil*
*$^1/_4$ cup (2 fl oz/60 ml) grapeseed oil*
*salt and freshly ground pepper*

Place the beets in lightly salted water, bring them to a boil, reduce the heat and simmer for about 1 hour, or until tender when pierced with a small skewer. Cool, then slip off their skins and cut them into large chunks.

Place the beets in a salad bowl with the shallots, parsley and walnuts. Pour over the vinegar and oils, season with salt and pepper, and serve.

SERVES: 6

## *Grumbeerekiechle*

*Potato Galettes*

In this recipe potatoes are cooked as small round flat cakes — *galettes*. The word *galette* covers an infinity of cakes and savory or sweet tarts, and in Brittany it is a pancake, usually made with buckwheat flour. The essential thing is that it is flat.

*2 lb (1 kg) potatoes, grated coarsely*
*1 onion, grated coarsely*
*1 garlic clove, crushed*
*1 tablespoon chopped parsley*
*1 tablespoon chopped chives*
*2 eggs*
*1 tablespoon all purpose (plain) flour*
*salt and freshly ground black pepper*
*$^1/_2$ cup (4 fl oz/125 ml) grapeseed oil*

Place the potatoes and onion in a bowl and add the garlic, parsley, chives, eggs, and flour. Season to taste with salt and pepper. Heat several tablespoons of oil in a large skillet, add spoonfuls of the mixture and flatten each to a *galette*. Cook over a low heat until golden on one side, then turn to brown the other. Drain on paper towels and serve immediately.

SERVES: 6

## *Chou Rouge aux Pommes et aux Marrons*

*Red Cabbage with Apples and Chestnuts*

The cabbage has always provided food for the people of Alsace, and continues to be a significant source of income for the province's farmers.

*Choucroute* festivals are held in September in Colmar and several other towns in the area. This is the time of year when the new sauerkraut first appears on the market.

*$^1/_2$ red cabbage*
*1 small onion, finely chopped*
*2 tablespoons grapeseed oil*
*2 Granny Smith apples*
*$^1/_2$ cup (4 fl oz/125 ml) dry white wine*
*2 to 3 tablespoons white wine vinegar*
*1 14-oz (440-g) can chestnuts*
*salt and freshly ground pepper*

Remove the thick central stalk from the cabbage. Cut the cabbage into thick chunks and then slice it finely. This is most easily done by using the slicing blade of the food processor.

Heat the grapeseed oil in a medium saucepan, add the onion and cook over a low heat until soft and translucent.

Meanwhile, peel, core, and slice the apples. Add the cabbage, apples, white wine, and vinegar to the saucepan. Cover and cook for about 45 minutes. Season to taste with salt and pepper, and if necessary add a little sugar or a dash more vinegar. Stir in the chestnuts, and serve either hot or cold.

This dish is traditionally served with pork or ham.

SERVES: 4 to 6

Red Cabbage with Apples and Chestnuts, Potatoes with Onions and Bacon, Potato Galettes

PETER JOHNSON

PETER JOHNSON

*Madeleines*

## *Pommes de Terre aux Oignons et au Lard*

*Potatoes with Onions and Bacon*

The potato was grown as a vegetable in Alsace, Lorraine, the Dauphiné, and the Lyonnais long before Parmentier managed to persuade the Parisians that it made a cheap alternative to bread.

*2 lb (1 kg) potatoes, sliced thinly*
*8 oz (250 g) bacon, finely sliced crosswise*
*2 large onions, sliced*
*$^1/_2$ cup (4 oz/125 g) butter*
*salt and freshly ground black pepper*

Preheat the oven to 400°F (250°C). Sprinkle the bottom of a cast-iron casserole with bacon, then cover it with a layer of potatoes, a layer of onions, season with salt and pepper, and dot with butter. Continue layering the ingredients, topping the dish with a layer of potatoes generously dotted with butter. Cover the casserole and bake for about 1 hour, until the potatoes are golden brown.

This dish is often served with smoked neck of pork and a green salad.

SERVES: 6

## *Madeleines*

Today, more than two hundred years after they were first made, the town of Commercy is still famous for its madeleines. These small cakes, baked in molds resembling scallop shells, are now sold widely throughout France.

*8 tablespoons (4 oz/125 g) unsalted butter, plus butter for the molds*
*4 eggs, separated*
*$^1/_3$ cup (3 oz/90 g) superfine (caster) sugar*
*1 cup (4 oz/125 g) all purpose (plain) flour*
*1 teaspoon orangeflower water*

Preheat the oven to 350°F (180°C). Liberally butter about 24 madeleine molds. Soften the butter in the microwave oven or a double boiler.

Mix the egg yolks with half the sugar, then add the butter and stir well. Whisk the egg whites until stiff, adding the remaining sugar as needed. Then, alternating with spoonfuls of flour, fold the whites into the egg yolk mixture and add the orangeflower water.

Spoon the mixture into the molds, filling them two-thirds full. Bake at 350°F (180°C) for 13 to 15 minutes, until they are risen and lightly browned.

MAKES: 20 to 24 madeleines

## *Birewecke*

*Alsatian Pear Bread*

Also known as *berawecka*, this rich bread is made almost entirely of dried fruits and nuts. It is a treat that is served on special occasions and at Christmas time.

*1½ cups (7 oz/220 g) dried pear pieces*
*1 cup (3 oz/90 g) dried apple pieces*
*½ cup (3 oz/90 g) stoned prunes*
*½ cup (3 oz/90 g) dried figs*
*1⅓ cups (7 oz/220 g) chopped candied peel*
*1 tablespoon golden raisins (sultanas)*
*⅓ cup (3 fl oz/90 ml) Kirsch*
*2 cups (8 oz/250 g) coarsely chopped walnuts*
*5 oz (150 g) bread dough (see* tarte flambée, *page 54)*
*1¼ cups (5 oz/150 g) all purpose (plain) flour*
*¾ cup (6 oz/185 g) superfine (caster) sugar*
*2 tablespoons ground cinnamon*
*walnut kernels, for decoration*

Place the dried pears, apples, and prunes in a saucepan. Cover with water, bring to a boil and simmer for 7 to 10 minutes, or until the fruit is soft.

Drain the fruit and let it cool, then chop coarsely, along with the figs. Place the chopped fruits in a bowl with the candied peel and golden raisins, pour over the Kirsch, and let stand overnight. Add the walnuts to the mixture.

Place the bread dough in the bowl of an electric mixer and, using a dough hook, gradually add the fruit mixture. This will take time at first. Preheat the oven to 375°F (190°C). Mix the flour, sugar, and cinnamon together, and work this into the mixture when everything else is well combined.

Divide the mixture into thirds and, with wet hands, form three small loaves on a nonstick baking tray. They should all be of the same thickness so that they cook evenly. Decorate the tops of the loaves with walnut kernels and bake for about 40 minutes, then cool.

Wrap the loaves and keep for a week before serving. The bread should be sliced thinly and is best served with a small glass of Kirsch.

MAKES: 3 small loaves

*Alsatian Pear Bread*

PETER JOHNSON

## *Visitandines*

The recipe for these delicate teacakes is thought to have been created by the nuns of the Order of the Visitation.

*¾ cup (3 oz/90 g) ground almonds*
*½ cup (3 oz/90 g) powdered (icing) sugar, sifted*
*½ teaspoon vanilla extract (essence)*
*1 egg, separated*
*7 tablespoons (3½ oz/105 g) unsalted butter, plus butter for the molds*
*½ cup (2 oz/60 g) all purpose (plain) flour*
*1 egg white*

Preheat the oven to 410°F (210°C). Butter and flour about 15 small molds — preferably rectangular ones that have low sides.

Place the ground almonds, powdered sugar, vanilla extract, and the egg white in the food processor and work to blend. Soften the butter until it is nearly liquid. Add this to the mixture in the processor with the egg yolk and flour, and blend once again. Turn the mixture into a bowl. In another bowl, whisk the remaining egg white until stiff. Work half into the mixture, then carefully fold in the remainder. Spoon the mixture into the molds, filling them to the brim, and bake for 12 to 15 minutes, until they are risen and lightly browned.

MAKES: about 15 small visitandines

## *Babas au Rhum*

*Rum Babas*

Instead of baba molds, *dariole* molds can be used. The resulting cork-shaped babas are known in Paris as *bouchons*. These are usually served without cream.

*1/2 oz (15 g) fresh (compressed) yeast, or 1/4 oz (7 g) dry yeast*
*1/3 cup (3 fl oz/90 ml) lukewarm water*
*2 cups (8 oz/250 g) bread flour*
*1 1/2 tablespoons superfine (caster) sugar*
*1 teaspoon salt*
*3 eggs*
*grated peel of 1/2 lemon*
*6 tablespoons (3 oz/90 g) unsalted butter, softened, plus butter for the molds*
*1/4 to 1/3 cup (3 to 4 oz/90 to 125 g) smooth apricot jam*
*Rum Syrup:*
*1 cup (8 oz/250 g) sugar*
*2 cups (16 fl oz/500 ml) water*
*grated peel and juice of 1 orange*
*grated peel and juice of 1/2 lemon*
*3 tablespoons rum*
*Chantilly Cream:*
*1 1/4 cups (10 fl oz/310 ml) cream*
*1 tablespoon superfine (caster) sugar*
*1/2 teaspoon vanilla extract (essence)*

Liberally butter 8 to 10 baba molds. Place the yeast in the water and whisk until it dissolves. Then add the flour, sugar, salt, eggs, and lemon peel. Stir the mixture using your hand, gradually drawing in the flour to form a smooth dough. Knead the dough, raising it and letting it fall back into the bowl until it is very elastic. This will take about 5 minutes. Alternatively, it can be mixed in a mixer with planetary action. When elastic, dot the surface with the butter, cover the bowl with a cloth and leave the dough to rise in a warm spot for about an hour. Then mix in the butter.

Place the dough in a piping bag with a large plain nozzle, and pipe into the prepared molds until two-thirds full. Alternatively, it can be spooned in. Cover and let the babas rise for a further 30 minutes, or until they have doubled in size.

Preheat the oven to 400°F (200°C), and place a baking tray in it to heat.

Make the rum syrup: Place the sugar, water, peel, and juices in a saucepan and simmer for 5 minutes. Remove from the heat and add the rum.

When the babas are risen, place them on the hot tray and bake for about 10 to 12 minutes, or until brown. Turn them out immediately, soak both sides in hot rum syrup and place on a cake rack.

Melt the apricot jam with a little water or Kirsch, stirring until smooth. If necessary, pass it through a fine sieve to remove any lumps. Brush the babas with it.

Make the Chantilly cream by whipping the cream with the sugar and vanilla extract until stiff. Pipe a large swirl of Chantilly cream in the center of each baba, using a piping bag with a large star nozzle.

MAKES: 8 to 10 babas

## *Gâteau au Chocolat de Nancy*

*Chocolate Cake from Nancy*

This rich chocolate cake should be served on its own or, at the most, with whipped cream or a vanilla custard.

*6 1/2 oz (200 g) unsweetened (bitter cooking) chocolate*
*1/2 cup (4 oz/125 g) unsalted butter, plus butter for the cake pan*
*5 eggs, separated*
*1/2 cup (4 oz/125 g) superfine (caster) sugar*
*1/2 cup (2 oz/60 g) ground almonds*

Preheat the oven to 320°F (160°C). Liberally butter an 8-in (20-cm) spring-form cake pan. Cut the chocolate into chunks, then work it into fine crumbs in a food processor. Place it in a bowl with the butter and melt in the microwave oven or a double boiler. The chocolate must only become lukewarm, not hot. Stir in the egg yolks and half the sugar.

Whisk the egg whites until stiff, adding half the remaining sugar at the beginning and the rest by degrees. Stir the ground almonds into the chocolate mixture, and add a third of the egg whites to lighten it. Scrape the chocolate mixture into the bowl with the remaining egg whites and fold everything together carefully.

Turn the mixture into the pan and bake at 320°F (160°C) for approximately 45 minutes, or until a skewer inserted in the center comes out clean. Let the cake cool in the pan before turning it out.

SERVES: 6 to 8

*Rum Babas, Chocolate Cake from Nancy, Visitandines*

PETER JOHNSON

0 10 20 30 40 50 M
0 10 20 30 40 50 60 70 80 Km
Ronchamp
Mulhouse
Belfort
Montbéliard
Saône
Dijon
Doubs
Besançon
Ornans
Dole
Neuchatel
Autun
Berne
Pontarlier
Chalon-sur-Saône
Suisse
Franche-Comté
Jura
Lausanne
L. Léman
Saône
Mâcon
Genève
Bourg-en-Bresse
Rhône
Villefranche-sur-Saône
Chamonix
Annecy
Loire
L. d'Annecy
Mont Blanc
Savoie
Lyon
Villeurbanne
L. du Bourget
Vénissieux
Aix-les-Bains
Isère
Chambéry
Massif de la Chartreuse
Vienne
Saint-Etienne
Beaurepaire
Voiron
Belledonne
Dauphiné
Rhône
Grenoble
Tain-l'Hermitage
Isère
Valence
Vercours
Drac

# FRANCHE-COMTE AND THE ALPS

*Maria Donovan*

Between the river Saône and the highest regions of the Jura mountains, bordering Switzerland, lies Franche-Comté, Burgundy's country cousin. To the south lie Savoie and Dauphiné — the French Alps. Savoie is snow country, dominated by Mont Blanc, Europe's highest peak. Dauphiné, one of the country's largest regions, has one face turned towards the Alps, the other turned towards Provence and the warmth of the Mediterranean. This picture-postcard world of rich, undulating pastures grazed by cows with tinkling bells around their necks, alpine villages, and towering peaks, in many ways resembles Switzerland, but it could not be more French.

Franche-Comté is a delight to explore. Countless clear mountain streams tumble down to its two main rivers, the Saône and the Doubs, and the densely wooded mountains are criss-crossed by many hundreds of miles of tracks, providing access for hikers, cyclists, and horseback riders. There is beauty underground, too, in the fairytale landscapes of numerous caves and grottoes. In the winter months the land is blanketed with snow, and the area becomes a paradise for cross-country skiers. In January the Trans-Jurassienne race is held here, which is for skiers what the Tour de France is for cyclists.

At one time belonging to the Duchy of Burgundy, Franche-Comté was part of the Holy Roman Empire in the sixteenth and seventeenth centuries, a period of great wealth and artistic achievement. The Spanish influence can still be seen in the flamboyant, late Gothic architecture of many of its towns. Louis XIV defeated the Spanish in 1678 and Franche-Comté then became part of France, with Besançon as its capital.

*A forested hillside is reflected in the still, blue waters of the river Doubs, not far from Villers-le-Lac in Franche-Comté.*

Built on the banks of the river Doubs, Besancon was an important town in Roman times, and from the Middle Ages to the seventeenth century was a richly endowed bishopric. Its massive great fortress, rising from sheer rock, dominates the town, and houses several museums. Once France's watch-making capital, Besançon boasts a fascinating astrological clock, with mechanical puppets that perform when it strikes.

South, not far from Bescançon, Ornans looks down at her reflection in the waters of the river Loue. This is Courbet country, painted many times by the great romantic master. His home is now a museum, housing many of his works. Near Ornans is the Gouffre de Poudrey, a most spectacular cave.

Further south, close to the Swiss border, lies the town of Pontarlier, high in the Jura mountains, offering easy access to the surrounding forests. This region provides one of Europe's last refuges for wildlife. Here you will see peregrine falcons, eagles, owls, woodpeckers, and the great featherfooted grouse. Male grouse can be heard at mating time in the spring, singing falsetto and shrieking. In the rocky mountains around Pontarlier there are chamois, agile antelope resembling goats, and deer are hunted in the forests of Belfort, to the north.

Not far from Belfort lies the town of Ronchamp. In 1955 Le Corbusier built Notre-Dame-du-Haut on one of the nearby hills, the site of an old bombed-out chapel. Some liken this extraordinary open-air cathedral to a bird in flight, while others think it looks more like a *cèpe* mushroom. It is well worth a visit, the views alone from the hilltop being remarkable.

Wines from the Jura are not widely known, but a number of fine ones are produced in the region, notably Vin Jaune, a sweet aged wine that is similar in flavor to sherry. The Route du Vin meanders through villages, past abbeys and châteaux from Salins-les-Bains southwards to Saint-Amour, giving the traveler opportunities to visit vineyards and sample the produce. Wine tastings are offered by growers everywhere. Arbois, not far from Salins-les-Bains, was the boyhood home of Louis Pasteur who, among his numerous scientific achievements, did much pioneering work on the aging and fermentation of wine, using produce from his family's vineyard. This pretty mountain town, with its tiny backstreets, has an interesting wine museum and holds its Fête du Vin on the third Sunday in July.

A glass of Vin Jaune with a slice of Comté cheese and a loaf of bread still warm from the oven will give you an unforgettable taste of the Jura.

CHRISTIAN SAPPA/CEDRI

*Morbier cheese being made in a dairy in Franche-Comté. The dark grey streak that runs horizontally through the middle of the cheese was traditionally soot or wood ash, but a vegetable product of some sort is now generally used instead.*

## Cheeses and Smoked Goods

Comté is dairy country, and the cattle which graze in the meadows of the alpine foothills are the much coveted Montbéliard breed. Sturdy, white and russet-patched animals, the finest are said to produce as much as 2200 gallons (10 000 liters) of high quality milk a year. Prize-winning cows can be seen at the annual agricultural fair in Besançon in spring.

Milk from Montbéliard cows is used to make traditional Gruyère de Comté, known simply as Comté, and vast quantities of this fine cheese are produced — 40 000 tons annually. Cheeses are the glory of this part of France. Here you will also find Emmental, Morbier, and Vacherin Mont-d'Or. At the Cooperative Laitière et Fromagère in Arbois, as in many other places in the Jura, you can watch Comté being made. A fine table cheese, Comté is used in sauces, meat dishes, omelettes, and fondues, and makes a delicious topping on vegetable soup.

LEO MEIER/WELDON TRANNIES

*Gruyère de Comté cheese, commonly known simply as Comté, among a tempting display in a Jura store.*

*Opposite: Glorious alpine scenery at the foot of Mont Blanc, Europe's highest peak. Tourists flock here in the summer for the hiking and rock climbing, and in the winter for the skiing.*

COMNET/WELDON TRANNIES

Smoked goods are also the pride of the Jura. Twice a year, on 11 November, Saint Martin's Day, and in the week that precedes Ash Wednesday, farmers slaughter their pigs and prepare the meat according to methods that have been handed down from generation to generation. The huge chimneys on the stone houses in the Doubs area, some of them many hundreds of years old, are still used as smoking chambers for hams, bacon, and sausages. Best known of all is the *saucisse de Morteau*, a type of smoked pork sausage, but fine hams come from Luxeuil, and wurst-like sausages are made in Montbéliard. *Saucisse aux choux*, cabbage sausage, is traditionally eaten on Saint Sylvester's Day, the last day of the year. Smoked and salted beef, served in paper-thin slices with bread and butter, is called *brési* here; across the border in Switzerland it is commonly known as *viande séchée des Grisons.*

In the forest clearings fragrant morels can still be found, available for only a short season in the spring. These brown, pitted fungi are the most highly regarded of all the wild mushrooms, and are delicious with meat or chicken. One of Franche-Comté's finest dishes is *poulet au Vin Jaune et aux morilles*, chicken cooked in Vin Jaune with morels. Fish, particularly trout, are in plentiful supply from the region's many rivers and lakes. Trout is usually fried in butter and served with a cream sauce, or sometimes with hazelnuts. Eating in Franche-Comté is a delight for lovers of genuine traditional French cooking. Dishes are robust, to suit the climate, but delicately flavored.

*Hams and dried sausages on sale in Val d'Isère. The crisp, dry mountain air of Savoie is ideal for maturing hams and sausages.*

JEAN-PAUL FERRERO/AUSCAPE/INTERNATIONAL

TRIPELON-JARRY CEDRI

*Brown-capped, succulent* cèpe *mushrooms can be found from the end of August, through to November, growing in the leaf litter from oak and chestnut trees.*

## SAVOIE

Savoie offers breathtaking alpine scenery and is the home of rich, creamy food and a range of exceptional cheeses. Game is abundant, and it is said that cooks from Savoie invented the *civet*, a dish in which game is cooked in red wine and its own blood. Civets of hare, venison, and deer are specialties of the region.

Though most people consider Savoie essentially snow country (a billboard on the way to the Mont Blanc tunnel proclaims Chamonix "the world capital of skiing"), since Roman times, from Chambéry to Aix-les-Bains, grapes have been grown on the sunny slopes of the Alps. Subtle, fruity, and often sparkling wines, such as Roussette de Savoie, Crépy, Seyssel, and Apremont (of the Vin de Savoie appellation), go well with the rich, creamy food and local cheeses like Tomme, Reblochon, Beaufort, and Emmental.

Snow-capped Mont Blanc, on the border with Italy, dominates the region, its slopes often shrouded in cloud, and there are glaciers, tumbling waterfalls, and sparkling, clear rivers. Lakes dot the landscape, like Lake Annecy, Lake de Bourget near Aix-les-Bains, and huge Lake Léman which lies on the border between France and Switzerland. In the summer the alpine meadows resemble oriental carpets, brilliant with gentians, anemones, asters, tiny bluebells, and pansies. Burning red mountain rhododendrons grow profusely above the tree line. In the cool forests below, strawberries, raspberries, and cranberries can be found, along with an abundance of mushrooms — *cèpes,* morels, *girolles*, and *mousserons*. Fruit is also grown commercially in the valleys, Savoie being particularly known for its raspberries.

From the eleventh century until the plebiscite in 1868, when it became part of France, Savoie belonged to the House of Savoie, one of Europe's oldest royal houses, whose lands stretched from the Rhône to the Po. Chambéry, the ancient capital, shows its long history in stone and brick, dominated by the austere château from which the dukes of Savoie once ruled. There is a fascinating fountain, the Fontaine des Eléphants, built in the early nineteenth century, and in the old town there are many stone houses that date from earlier times. A little out of town lies the Musée des Charmettes, once the home of Jean-Jacques Rousseau, which contains exhibits relating to the philosopher's life.

The lakeside town of Annecy is filled with tourists during the summer months. The old town is a delight, with its canals, cobbled streets, and Medieval houses, their window-boxes brimming with geraniums, petunias, and pansies and the market on rue Sainte-Claire is well worth a visit. Throughout the town there are small, cosy restaurants, pubs, and cafés where, in fine weather, one can eat out and admire the panorama of darkly etched mountains. Lake Annecy is the area's biggest summer attraction, and old-fashioned passenger boats depart frequently from the wharf on pleasure trips. The scenery is enchanting, with a succession of old villages, hilltop castles, vineyards, and inns along the shore. Thanks to pressure from environmentalists, the lake has now been restocked with fish — pike, carp, perch, trout, and the delicious pink-fleshed *omble chevalier*, which is similar to salmon trout. Local restaurants make a specialty of fish dishes.

In winter the action shifts to the resorts in the mountains. Val d'Isère, once a sleepy mountain village, is filled with skiers in the winter months. In this part of the country the Italian influence is evident in such pasta dishes as *ravioles au chèvre*, ravioli filled with goat's milk cheese.

*Opposite: A farmer in the Hautes Alpes spreads potatoes out to dry in the sun. Following pages: Patrons of the Café des Arts in Annecy, enjoying their lunch.*

ANTHONY STONE/THE PHOTO LIBRARY

Chamonix, nestling at the foot of Mont Blanc, has more fine cake shops, cafés, restaurants, and hotels along its main street than any other ski resort in the world. Here you can sample such regional specialties as *fondue savoyarde*, made with Gruyère and white wine, and *jambon fumé de montagne*, the delicious local ham. Chamonix is a year-round favorite with the French, offering hiking and rock climbing in the summer and excellent skiing once the snow falls. A prime attraction is the cablecar that rises at a breathtaking angle to the Aiguille du Midi in France and then descends into Italy. Nowhere in the world can you travel higher in a cablecar, and the views are unsurpassable.

JEAN-PAUL FERRERO/AUSCAPE/INTERNATIONAL

## EAUX-DE-VIE AND LIQUEURS

With recipes often dating back to the Middle Ages, *eaux-de-vie* are obtained by distilling fruit and herbs, and are usually colorless. Originally they were sold as elixirs ensuring long life. Liqueurs are made from sugar and alcohol, flavored with plants, fruits, or herbs, and are generally brightly colored and sweet.

In Franche-Comté, Fougerolles is the home of Kirsch, distilled from wild cherries, and from the Pontarlier region comes Liqueur de Sapin, made from herbs and pine buds. Anise de Pontarlier is made from plants such as hyssop and balm, to which green aniseed is added. Gentiane, a popular digestif, is one of a number that are made from the distilled roots of the gentian plant that grows in the mountains.

No liqueur boasts more secrets than Chartreuse, first made by Carthusian monks in the Alps above Grenoble. Legend has it that the secret formula for the liqueur was originally given to the monks by Henri IV's General d'Estrées. Though the monastery was destroyed and the monks dispersed, they managed to guard the recipe down through the centuries. Today Chartreuse, both yellow and green, is made in Voiron.

CAFE des ARTS
4
CAFE DES ARTS
MENU 50F NET
TERRINE DE CAMPAGNE
OU
SaLade Composée
STEAK au grill
OU
Truite Meunière
Frites et Haricots

MENU 50F

# THE WALNUTS OF GRENOBLE

All along the Isère valley in Dauphiné there are plantations of shady walnut trees. Eaten fresh with wine and cheese, walnuts are also found in many traditional recipes, are baked in breads, and are used increasingly for oil, served on salads. They are also made into liqueur, and pickled whole.

Walnut trees are said to have originated in the Caspian and in northern India. They were known to the Romans and figure in the recipes of Acipius, the first known cookery writer of antiquity. According to legend, the trees made their first appearance on French soil around the fourth century, when the lord of Vinay, a castle not far from Saint-Marcellin, planted them on his territory.

In the Middle Ages, farmers used to pay their rent with walnuts. In the record book of Saint-Hugues, dating from the eleventh century, a number of such payments are noted.

Most famous are the walnuts of Grenoble, which have their own *appellation controllée*. A decree issued in 1938 regarding the *noix de Grenoble* limits the varieties that can be grown and the area in which they can be cultivated. Packets of these nuts carry a red label that guarantees their provenance, and they are exported all over the world.

LEO MEIER

## DAUPHINÉ

Dauphiné, facing both the Alps and the Mediterranean, is one of the largest regions in France. Grenoble, the capital, built at the junction of the Isère and Drac rivers, is surrounded by formidable mountains — the Massif de la Chartreuse, the Vercors, and the Belledonne chains. It is a cosmopolitan, spreading city, with some fine old buildings, and its university is one of the country's largest. Famous for winter sports, visitors also come here in large numbers in the summer for walking and rock climbing.

The Vercors, a vast limestone bastion, is a mysterious, thickly forested mountain chain with thousands of caves and grottoes, where many members of the French Resistance took refuge during the Second World War. This is a region of torrents and gorges, and remote cliff-hanging villages where old ways survive.

The sunny face of Dauphiné looks west. From Vienne, just south of Lyon, the department of Drôme's western border follows the Rhône southwards through Tain-l'Hermitage and Valence. Vienne was once a major Roman town, and a number of important Roman monuments remain, but perhaps it is best known for La Pyramide, the restaurant of the late Fernand Point, one of the finest French restaurateurs of this century and mentor and model to many of today's great chefs. At Tain-l'Hermitage, on the banks of the Rhône, are the prestigious Hermitage vineyards, the vines growing on steep granite slopes. The wines produced here are equal to the best from Burgundy and Bordeaux. At the Cave Coopérative in Tain wines from throughout the northern Rhône can be tasted and bought.

Dauphiné's cheeses are exceptional. From the Vercors comes the incomparable Saint-Marcellin, once a goat's milk cheese although now made mostly from cow's milk, and near Beaurepaire a rare Tomme made from goat's milk can still be found. As in Franche-Comté and Savoie, cheese and milk are used widely for cooking, particularly in vegetable *gratins*, but the classic version of *gratin dauphinois*, potato gratin with cream, is not made with cheese.

In spring, the Rhône valley is decked with cherry blossoms. It was the Roman legionaries of Lucullus who introduced cherry trees to the region from Asia. A cherry liqueur is made in the area around Côte Saint-André, and liqueur cherries in chocolate are a notable specialty of Grenoble.

Franche-Comté, Savoie, and Dauphiné provide an inexhaustible treasure trove that is best visited off-season: in early June when the cherries are starting to ripen; in October when the forested hillsides are painted a russet-gold; and in late spring, when the skiing is at its best.

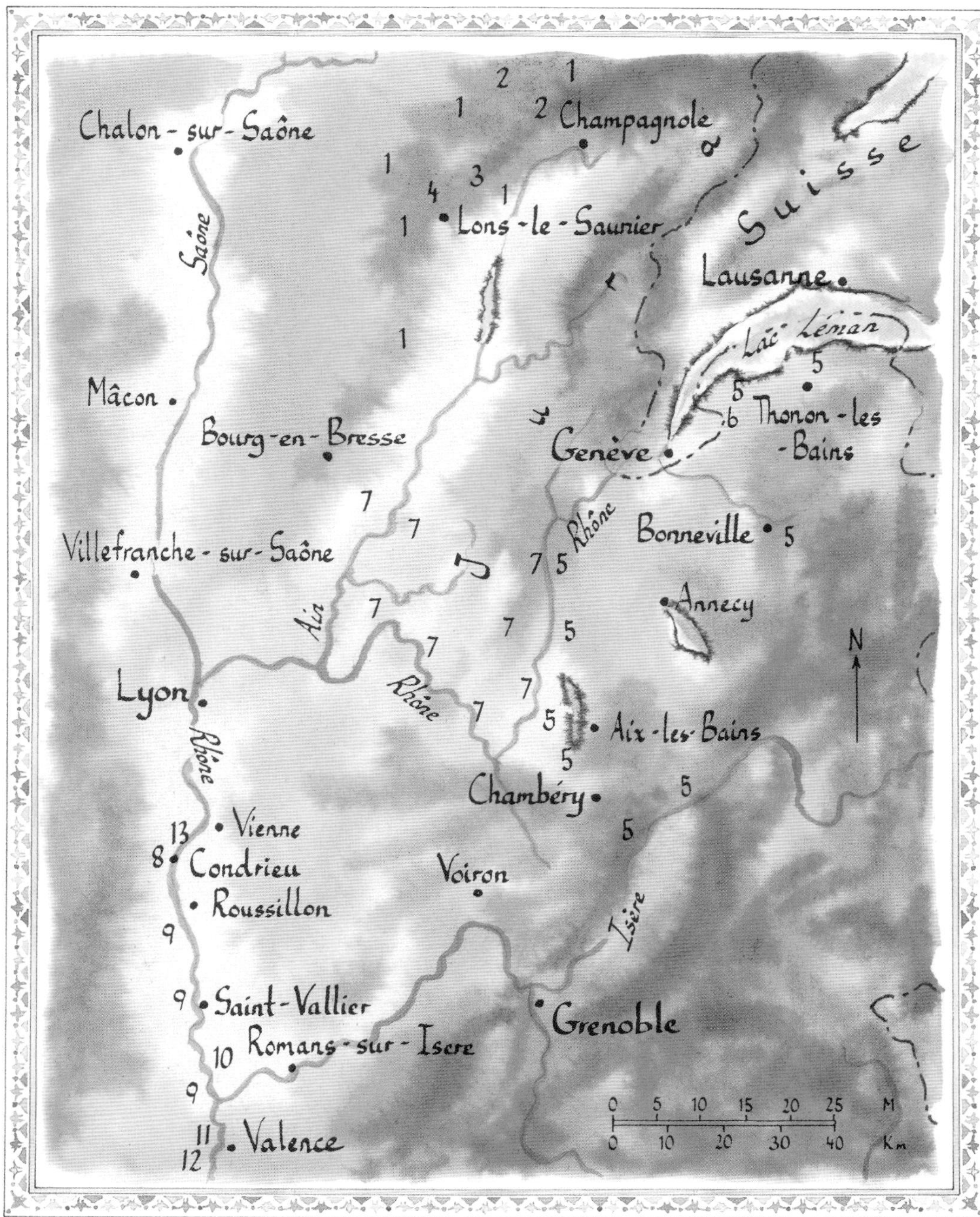


*Opposite: Rows of vegetables growing in Saint-Pierre-de-Chartreuse, near Grenoble.*

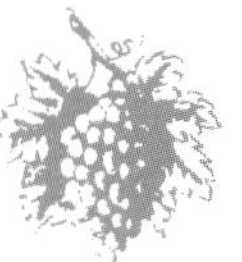

## JURA

*Principal wines:*

*Arbois (2)*
*Château-Chalon (3)*
*Côtes de Jura (1)*
*L'Etoile (4)*

*The AOC-recognized styles within the above regional appellations include:*

*Mousseux (sparkling)*
*Vin de Paille (sweet white wines made from dried grapes)*
*Vin Jaune (aged, potent, sherry-like white wine)*

*The grape varieties are generally obscure.*

## SAVOIE

*Principal wines:*

*Crépy (6)*
*Rousette de Savoie (5)*
*Seyssel (7)*
*Vin de Savoie (5)*
*Vin de Bugey VDQS (7)*

*The AOC-recognized styles within the above regional appellations include:*

*Petillant and Mousseux (both sparkling) dry white and red table wines*

*The grape varieties range from noble, such as Chardonnay, to obscure.*

## DAUPHINE (NORTHERN RHONE)

*Principal wines:*

*Condrieu (and Château Grillet) (8)*
*Cornas (11)*
*Côte-Rôtie (13)*
*Crozes-Hermitage (10)*
*Hermitage (10)*
*Saint-Joseph (9)*
*Saint-Péray (12)*

# RECIPES OF FRANCHE-COMTE AND THE ALPS

Maria Donovan

PETER JOHNSON

## *Aubergines Farcies*

*Stuffed Eggplants*

Typical of Provence and the warm southern regions, eggplants are available year-round throughout France, even in the mountains. This recipe is from the Jura.

*8 small eggplants (aubergines), halved*
*vegetable oil for the baking dish*
*salt and freshly ground black pepper*
*6 oz (185 g) freshly grated Comté or Gruyère cheese*
*6 oz (185 g) smoked raw ham, finely chopped*
*1 cup (3 oz/90 g) cooked long-grain rice*
*1¼ cups (10 fl oz/310 ml) cream*

Preheat the oven to 400°F (200°C). Place the eggplants in an oiled baking dish and bake for 25 minutes.

With a spoon, carefully scoop out the insides of the eggplants. Transfer the pulp to a mixing bowl and season with salt and pepper. Mash with a fork and mix well with the cheese, ham, and rice.

Fill the eggplant skins with this mixture and lay them side by side in a buttered ovenproof serving dish. Moisten each eggplant with cream. Reduce oven setting to 300°F (150°C) and bake for a further 20 minutes. Serve hot.

SERVES: 4

## *Asperges et Morilles*

*Asparagus and Morels*

In March and early April, when morels are in season, and the first bunches of asparagus appear in the market, this unusual combination is possible. Cultivated mushrooms may be used instead of morels.

*2 lb (1 kg) asparagus, stalks scraped, if necessary*
*2 tablespoons white wine vinegar*
*½ cup (4 oz/125 g) butter*
*salt and freshly ground black pepper*
*1 lb (500 g) morels or cultivated mushrooms, cleaned and sliced*
*2 tablespoons chopped parsley*
*2 tablespoons lemon juice*

Tie the asparagus in bunches and place upright in a tall, narrow saucepan filled with boiling salted water, to which the vinegar has been added. Cook until crisp-tender. Undo the bunches and drain the asparagus completely on a cloth. If long-stemmed asparagus has been used, the spears can be cut in half.

In a large, heavy skillet melt half the butter and stir-fry the asparagus for 3 minutes. Season with salt and pepper and transfer to a serving plate. Keep warm.

Place the remainder of the butter in the skillet and stir-fry the morels for 3 to 4 minutes over high heat. Sprinkle with salt and pepper and the parsley.

Add the morels to the asparagus. Sprinkle with lemon juice, pour the pan juices over them, and serve.

SERVES: 4

## *Oeufs Brouillés au Fromage*

*Scrambled Eggs with Cheese*

This recipe is ideal for using up a mixture of leftover pieces of cheese. Almost any kind is suitable. It was supplied by a cheese merchant in Paris, who came originally from the Jura.

*6 eggs*
*salt and freshly ground black pepper*
*1½ tablespoons cold water*
*2 tablespoons butter*
*1 lb (500 g) assorted cheese, such as Comté, Emmental, Gruyère, blue, or Brie*
*2 tablespoons cream*
*French bread, cut into croûton-sized cubes*

Break the eggs into a bowl. Add salt, pepper, and water. Beat with a wire whisk for 2 minutes.

In a nonstick saucepan, over low heat, melt the butter. Add the cheese and carefully melt it, stirring continuously with a wooden spatula.

Stir in the beaten eggs, gently moving the mixture around with a fork for 4 minutes until the eggs thicken. Add cream and mix well. Serve immediately with the bread cubes.

SERVES: 6

*Left: Stuffed Eggplants, Asparagus and Morels, Scrambled Eggs with Cheese*

PETER JOHNSON

Ingredients for Trout in Cream Sauce

## Brochet à l'Ail

*Baked Pike*

Pike is a flavorful fresh-water fish with firm, white flesh, and it is used widely in French cooking. In this recipe perch, mullet, or bass can be substituted.

*1 pike, 3 to 4 lb (1.5 to 2 kg), washed, scaled and gutted, but with the head and tail left on*
*vegetable oil for coating the baking dish and the fish*
*6 garlic cloves, peeled*
*salt and freshly ground pepper*
*2 cups (12 oz/375 g) finely chopped parsley*
*$1^1/_2$ cups (12 fl oz/375 ml) cream*

Baked Pike

PETER JOHNSON

## Truites à la Crème

*Trout in Cream Sauce*

The rivers, streams, and lakes of Franche-Comté are well stocked with trout.

*6 trout, about 12 oz (375 g) each, filleted*
*milk for dipping*
*all purpose (plain) flour for dusting*
*salt and freshly ground black pepper*
*6 tablespoons (3oz/90 g) butter*
*$^3/_4$ cup (6 fl oz/180 ml) dry white wine*
*3 oz (90 g) champignons (button mushrooms), chopped*
*$1^1/_2$ tablespoons finely chopped chives and parsley*
*5 tablespoons cream*
*juice of $^1/_2$ lemon*

Dip each trout fillet first in milk, then in flour seasoned with salt and pepper.

Heat butter in a skillet and cook fillets for about 4 minutes on each side, until golden. Transfer to a heated serving dish and keep warm.

Pour the wine into the skillet, stirring to scrape up any brown bits clinging to the bottom, then add the champignons and the chives and parsley. Stir-fry over high heat for 2 minutes before stirring in the cream and lemon juice. Do not reboil as the mixture will curdle. Pour the sauce over the fish and serve with boiled parsleyed potatoes.

SERVES: 6

Preheat the oven to 350°F (180°C). Place the fish in an oiled baking dish. Stud the fish with the garlic cloves, season with salt and pepper, and coat with oil. Bake for 45 minutes.

While the fish is cooking, prepare the sauce. Put two-thirds of the parsley in a saucepan with the cream and cook over low heat for 20 minutes. Remove from heat and add the remaining parsley. Rub sauce through a strainer and keep warm.

Once the fish is cooked, remove the garlic and place the fish on a warmed serving dish. Pour the parsley sauce over it and serve with boiled potatoes.

SERVES: 4 to 6

PETER JOHNSON

*Ravioli Filled with Goat's Milk Cheese*

## *Ravioles au Chèvre*

*Ravioli Filled with Goat's Milk Cheese*

These tasty, cheese-filled ravioli are a specialty of the Val d'Isère. They are usually cooked in a strong chicken stock, and are either served in the cooking liquid, or are drained and served separately, with grated Gruyère.

*Dough:*
*4 cups (1 lb/500 g) all purpose (plain) flour*
*salt*
*3 eggs*
*2 tablespoons olive oil*
*Filling:*
*1 chèvre, goat's milk cheese, weighing about 8 oz (250 g)*
*1 egg*
*1 tablespoon melted butter*
*12 oz (375 g) Gruyère cheese, finely and freshly grated*
*2 teaspoons finely chopped parsley*
*salt and freshly ground pepper*
*3 oz (90 g) Gruyère cheese, finely and freshly grated, for serving*

For the dough: Sift the flour and salt onto a work surface. Make a well in the center and add the eggs and oil. Combine ingredients. When dough is mixed, knead until elastic. Roll into a ball, cover with a cloth and let it rest in a cool place for 30 minutes.

For the filling: In a bowl mash the *chèvre* with a fork. Blend in the egg, butter, Gruyère, parsley, and salt and pepper, and work into a smooth paste.

To make the ravioli: Divide the dough in two and roll each half out thinly, into a rectangular shape. Place heaped teaspoons of the filling over one half of the dough, leaving 1/2 in (1 cm) between mounds. Place the second sheet of dough on top, pressing down firmly with your fingers around each mound. Cut out the ravioli with a ravioli cutter or a crimp-edged pastry wheel.

Drop the ravioli one by one in plenty of boiling stock or water and cook for 4 minutes or until *al dente*. Drain and serve, passing the cheese separately.

SERVES: 4 to 6

PETER JOHNSON

*Meat Loaf with Walnuts*

## Terrine aux Noix

*Meat Loaf with Walnuts*

This meat loaf can either be served cold, as a terrine, or hot, as a main course.

*1½ lb (750 g) lean pork or veal, or half and half, finely ground (minced)*
*8 oz (250 g) walnuts, coarsely chopped*
*salt and freshly ground black pepper*
*3 tablespoons walnut oil or vegetable oil*
*2 egg yolks*
*2 tablespoons chopped chives*
*¾ cup (4 oz/125 g) raisins, soaked overnight and drained*
*2 tablespoons yellow Chartreuse*

Place meat and walnuts in a mixing bowl. Season with salt and pepper, and add the oil, egg yolks, chives, raisins, and Chartreuse. Mix all ingredients until they are well combined.

Lightly oil a round or rectangular terrine mold and fill with the mixture. Bake in a bain-marie in a 350°F (180°C) oven for 1½ hours.

SERVES: 6 to 8

## Côtes de Veau aux Morilles

*Veal Chops with Morels*

In this dish from Franche-Comté, dried morels or other fresh mushrooms can be used when fresh morels are unavailable.

*9 oz (280 g) morels or any other fresh mushrooms, or 5 oz (155 g) dried morels*
*6 veal chops (cutlets), 1½ in (4 cm) thick*
*salt and freshly ground pepper*
*3 tablespoons butter*
*2 tablespoons vegetable oil*
*1 cup (8 fl oz/250 ml) heavy (double) cream*

If using fresh morels, they should be rinsed several times in water and left whole, with only a small part of the stem cut off. Dried morels must be soaked for several hours, and then rinsed several times in water. Other fresh mushrooms should be sliced.

Season chops with salt and pepper. Heat butter and oil in a large heavy skillet and fry chops on both sides until golden. Reduce heat and cook chops slowly for 10 minutes. Remove and keep warm.

Add the morels to the skillet and stir-fry for 2 minutes. Add the cream, stir, and cook for a further 2 minutes. Pour the cream sauce over the chops and serve with fried potatoes.

SERVES: 6

*Veal Chops with Morels*

PETER JOHNSON

## Cuissot de Chevreuil Sauce à la Crème

*Leg of Venison in Cream Sauce*

In the more mountainous parts of Savoie and the Jura there are still many deer.

Fillet of beef can be substituted for venison in this recipe, and does not need as much marinating.

*4 cups (1 qt/1 l) red wine*
*2 tablespoons Cognac*
*1 onion, sliced*
*3 garlic cloves, peeled*
*2 carrots, sliced*
*2 tablespoons juniper berries*
*bouquet garni: 1 bay leaf, 1 thyme sprig, 5 parsley sprigs*
*salt and freshly ground black pepper*
*1 cut from a leg of venison, or a piece of fillet of beef, about 3 lb (1.5 kg)*
*3 oz (90 g) fat bacon, for larding*
*2 or 3 tablespoons softened butter*
*1/2 cup (4 fl oz/125 ml) cream*

In a large earthenware or glass bowl mix together the wine, Cognac, onion, garlic, carrots, juniper berries, and bouquet garni. Salt and pepper the meat and place in the marinade. Let stand in the refrigerator for 4 days (2 days for beef), turning twice a day.

Preheat the oven to 450°F (230°C). Remove meat from marinade, dry thoroughly. Cut the bacon into small strips. With a larding needle, insert the bacon into the meat, parallel to the grain. Rub the meat all over with softened butter, and transfer to a baking dish. Roast for 15 minutes, turning to seal on all sides.

Strain marinade (having discarded the bay leaf and garlic) and pour over the meat. Reduce the oven to 350°F (180°C) and continue roasting for 30 minutes, basting the meat from time to time with the marinade. Both venison and beef should be underdone inside and browned on the outside.

Remove the meat from the oven, pour over the cream and let stand for a few minutes in a warm place. Remove the meat from the gravy, carve into 1/4-in (5-mm) slices and arrange on a warmed serving dish. Pour gravy over the meat and serve.

SERVES: 8

## Gratin Dauphinois

*Potato Gratin with Cream*

There are many versions of this popular dish, but the classic gratin is certainly never made with cheese.

*5 garlic cloves, peeled*
*4 cups (1 qt/1 l) milk*
*3 lb (1.5 kg) potatoes, thinly sliced, and dried thoroughly*
*salt and freshly ground pepper*
*grated nutmeg (optional)*
*1 1/2 cups (12 fl oz/375 ml) cream*
*1/2 cup (4 oz/125 g) butter*

*Leg of Venison in Cream Sauce, Potato Gratin with Cream*

PETER JOHNSON

Preheat the oven to 350°F (180°C). Put the garlic in a saucepan with the milk and bring rapidly to a boil. Add the sliced potatoes, season with salt and pepper, and nutmeg, if desired. Cook for 12 minutes, taking care that the milk does not boil over. Discard the garlic.

Transfer the potatoes to a well-buttered ovenproof dish. Pour the cream over the top and dot with small pieces of butter.

Bake in the oven for 45 minutes, or until the top is golden brown and all the milk has been absorbed.

SERVES: 6 to 8

## *Soufflé à la Chartreuse*

*Chartreuse Soufflé*

Soufflés are to French cooking what *haute couture* is to the world of fashion — the quintessence of elegance.

*4 tablespoons (2 oz/60 g) butter*
*2 tablespoons all purpose (plain) flour*
*1 teaspoon cornstarch (cornflour)*
*1 cup (8 fl oz/250 ml) milk*
*3 oz (90 g) superfine (caster) sugar*
*2 tablespoons green Chartreuse*
*2 tablespoons yellow Chartreuse*
*4 eggs*
*1 egg white*
*pinch of salt*
*powdered (icing) sugar for dusting*

Preheat the oven to 400°F (200°C). With one-third of the butter, grease a 6-in (15-cm) soufflé dish. Sprinkle it with 1 tablespoon of the superfine sugar and turn the dish so that the sugar coats the entire inside surface.

Melt the remaining butter in a saucepan and when frothing blend in the flour and cornstarch. Stir and cook for a minute as if for a béchamel sauce. Add the cold milk all at once and remove the pan immediately from the heat. Stir well. Whisk in the sugar and add the liqueurs, stirring continuously.

Separate the eggs and beat the whites with a pinch of salt until stiff. Stir the yolks into the milk mixture one by one. Lastly fold in the egg whites, very carefully, little by little.

Pour the mixture into the soufflé dish, filling it only three-quarters full. Bake for 30 minutes, or until puffed and golden. Dust the top generously with powdered sugar and serve immediately.

SERVES: 4

## *Bûche aux Marrons*

*Chestnut Log*

The Yule log is a must at every French table at Christmas time.

*4 lb (2 kg) fresh chestnuts*
*4 cups (1 qt/1 l) milk*
*1 piece of vanilla bean (pod) about 1 in (2 cm) long, opened lengthwise*
*1 cup (7 oz/220g) superfine (caster) sugar*
*pinch of salt*
*10 oz (315 g) unsweetened (bitter cooking) chocolate*
*10 tablespoons (5 oz/150 g) softened butter*
*2 oz (60 g) unsweetened cocoa powder*
*whipped cream and walnut halves, or crystallized violets, for decoration*

With a sharp knife make an incision in each chestnut. Bring a large saucepan of water to a boil and drop in the chestnuts, cooking them for 5 minutes. Drain and peel off both the outer skin and the furry inner skin.

Put the milk, vanilla pod, sugar, and salt in a saucepan, together with the chestnuts. Bring to a boil and simmer for 30 minutes. Break the chocolate into small pieces and soften in a double boiler.

Drain chestnuts and transfer to a food processor, together with the butter and melted chocolate. Blend into a smooth paste, adding, if necessary, a little of the cooking milk.

On a glass or marble slab, shape the paste to resemble a log. Dust with the cocoa and refrigerate for several hours before serving. Decorate with whipped cream and walnut halves or crystallized violets.

SERVES: 8 to 10

## *Mont Blanc*

*Chestnut Purée*

Originally from Savoie, this dessert stars in pastry shops from France to Austria and Hungary. This version, using canned chestnut purée, can be made year round.

*1/2 cup (4 oz/125 g) butter*
*3/4 cup (6 oz/185 g) superfine (caster) sugar*
*1 piece of vanilla bean (pod) about 1 in (2 cm) long*
*2 tablespoons rum*
*1 lb (500 g) canned unsweetened chestnut purée*
*2 cups stiffly whipped cream*
*meringues (optional)*

Cream the butter and sugar in a blender or by hand. Transfer this mixture to a mixing bowl and add the rum, the seeds scraped from the vanilla pod, and the chestnut purée. Mix well with a wooden spatula.

Let the mixture stand in the refrigerator for 2 hours then press through the holes of a food mill, or through a wire strainer with large holes. Garnish with stiffly whipped cream. The dessert can also be served with meringues placed under the purée.

SERVES: 4 to 6

## *Crêpes au Kirsch*

*Kirsch Pancakes*

*Crêperies*, cafés serving only pancakes, are to be found in every mountain resort and are popular with the skiers.

*1 1/2 cups (6 oz/150 g) all purpose (plain) flour*
*2 eggs*
*pinch of salt*
*2 teaspoons olive oil*
*1 teaspoon brandy*
*2 cups (16 fl oz/500 ml) milk*
*butter for frying*
*powdered (icing) sugar for dusting*
*Kirsch, or any liqueur or brandy*

Place the flour in a bowl. Break in the eggs, and add salt, oil, and brandy. Beating with a wire whisk, add the milk gradually until the batter becomes the consistency of smooth thick cream. (A food processor can be used instead.)

Melt a walnut-sized piece of butter in an 8-in (20-cm) cast-iron skillet over high heat. When hot, pour in half a small ladleful of batter, tilting the skillet so that the batter fully covers the base. After about 40 seconds, when it is golden on the bottom, turn the pancake over and cook for a further 30 seconds or so, then transfer to a warmed plate. The skillet must be kept hot.

Dust pancakes with powdered sugar and sprinkle generously with Kirsch. Serve hot, folded in quarters.

SERVES: 4 to 6

*Following pages: Chestnut Log, Chartreuse Soufflé, Chestnut Purée, Kirsch Pancakes*
PETER JOHNSON

Isère
Valence
Durance
Gap
Montélimar
Haute Provence
Rhône
Valréas
Alpes-Marit
Alès
Orange
Digne
Carpentras
Alpes de Provence
Avignon
Vaucluse
Durance
Nîmes
Arles
Grasse
Nice
Monac
Ment
Provence
Antibes
Cannes
Côte d'Azur
Camargue
Salon-de-Provence
Aix-en-Provence
Fréjus
Marseille
Saint-Tropez
Cassis
Golfe du Lion
La Ciotat
Toulon
Mer Méditerranée
0 10 20 30 40 50 60 M
0 20 40 60 80 100 Km

# PROVENCE AND CORSICA

*Joanne Weir*

Blessed by the strong southern sun, Provence is in many ways closer to other Mediterranean countries than to the rest of France, and the neighboring island of Corsica, though French, has much in common with Italy. Here in the south the people are exuberant and outspoken, and their cooking is strongly flavored, redolent of herbs, garlic, olives, anchovies, and spices. Fruit grows in abundance, vines flourish, fields of lavender perfume the air. This is a land that will enchant any visitor: not without good reason do so many people flock to the Côte d'Azur each summer.

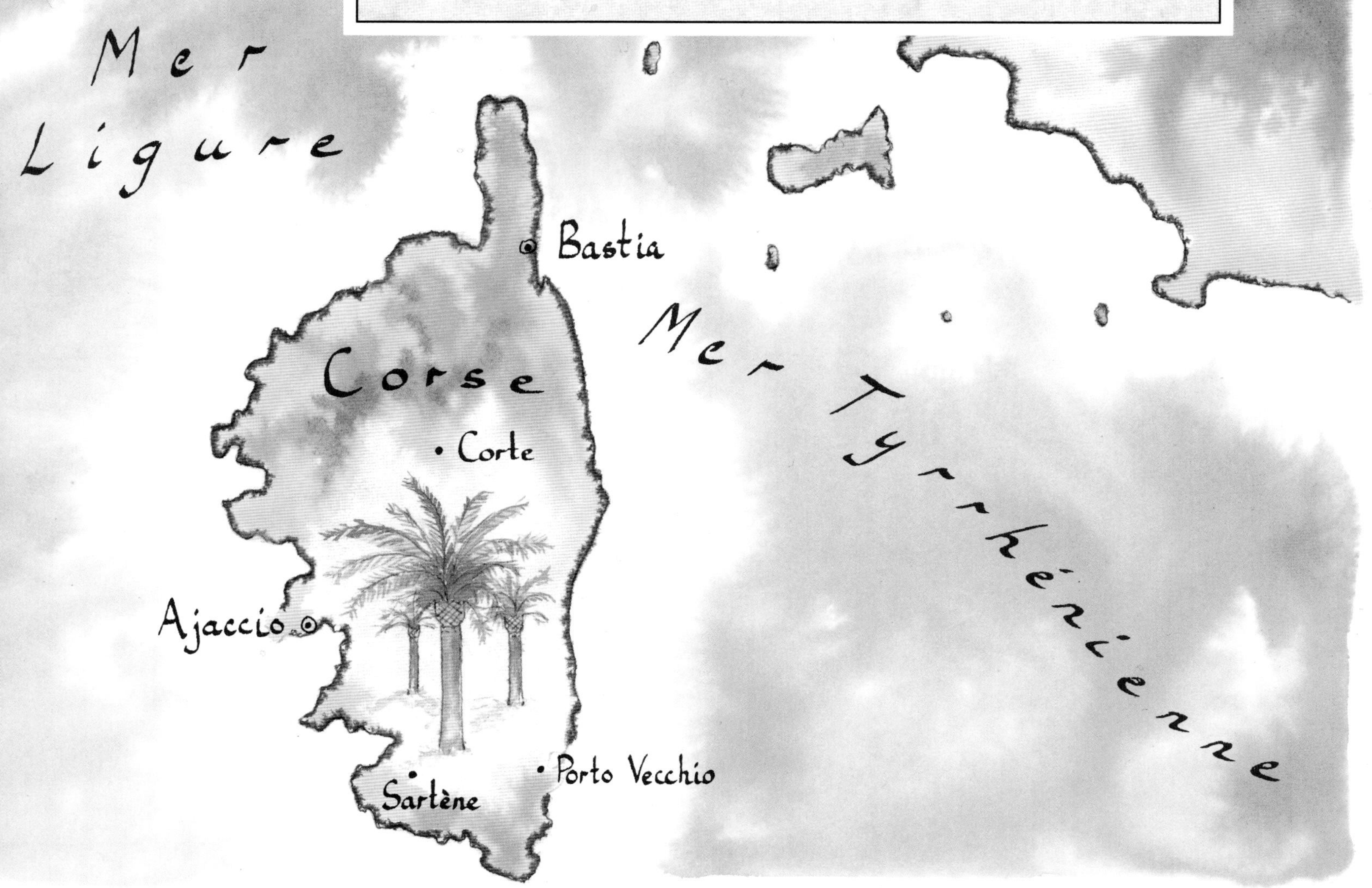

DALLAS AND JOHN HEATON/SCOOPIX

## Provincia Romana

Provence was born Greek but it grew up Roman. The Greeks set up a trading settlement in Marseille in the sixth century BC and in time established trading posts along the coast and inland as far as Nîmes and Avignon. In 125 BC the Greeks asked the Romans for help in defending "their" land, and the Romans not only came, but they stayed. They called the region Provincia Romana, and many impressive reminders of Roman times remain in the form of roads, triumphal arches, baths, temples, amphitheaters, bridges, and aqueducts. The climate here made the Romans feel at home, as did the vines and the olive trees.

In the early fourteenth century the pope settled in Avignon, which remained the first city in Christendom until 1377, when the papacy returned to Rome. A legacy of these times remains in the massive Palace of the Popes, which dominates the city, and the extensive ramparts which surround the city. In 1481 Provence became a province of France.

Provence is bounded on the south by the Mediterranean, on the east by the Alpes de Provence, and on the west by the Rhône river. It is an area of great diversity. In the north, the Haute-Provence, the soil is rich in some areas, arid and barren in others. The Côte d'Azur, in the south, stretches from the wild and sometimes desolate Camargue, the Rhône delta, to the resorts of Nice and Menton. Sun-drenched Provence has a gentle feel to it, except when the mistral is blowing, a bitter cold wind that sweeps down the Rhône valley. Rows of solemn cypress trees stand tall and act as windbreaks. Groves of citrus and olives grow alongside vineyards on rolling, herb-scented hillsides which are dotted with terracotta-roofed farmhouses. Out of the haze, villages can be seen high on the rocky hills, perched like eagles' nests. It is no great wonder that this enchanting land provided such inspiration for painters such as Van Gogh and Cézanne.

LEO MEIER

*Boxes of baby tomatoes on display at the Cours Saleya market in Nice.*

## The People of Provence

The people of Provence are a passionate, jovial, and fiery lot. They have great respect for their land, and in return the land provides them with an abundance of produce. Virtually self-sufficient, they enjoy a simple life, but they revel in interminable discussions about anything from the best way to travel to the market to how to make *bouillabaisse*, *salade niçoise*, or *brandade*. To hear some full-blooded arguing, go and watch the men play *pétanque*, a form of bowls. You will find them gathered under shady plane trees wherever there is a flat patch of earth. But don't take the arguing too seriously.

Steeped in tradition, the people of Provence have the greatest respect for their heritage. Festivals and celebrations of all sorts are held throughout the year in every little hamlet. A particularly tasty festival, which thanks the land for her bounty, takes place in a small village near Toulon called Solliès-Toucas. At noon, summer's last day is celebrated with large platters of green beans, hard-boiled eggs, artichokes, carrots, beets, potatoes, flaky salt cod, and of course the beloved *aïoli*, golden mayonnaise spiked with plenty of garlic. There are loaves of crusty bread, and the meal is washed down with rosé. It is a simple meal, but a perfect one, in which all the villagers partake.

A most colorful festival, the Festival of Autumn, takes place in the town of Courthézon on the first weekend in September. There is a street market with

*Opposite: In amongst the yachts in Cannes harbor a fisherman sits in his boat, sorting nets. The fish markets of the Riviera sell a wide variety of fish and seafood from the waters of the Mediterranean.*

## OLIVE OIL

The olive was first planted in Provence by the Greeks, along with fruit trees and vines, and has flourished here ever since.

To make olive oil, the olives are first washed and then crushed with large rotating wheels into a paste. The paste is then pressed and the oil extracted. It takes 11 pounds (5 kilograms) of olives to produce 1 quart (1 liter) of the top quality, cold pressed olive oil, known as *extra vierge*. Heated pressings of the paste then yield progressively lower grades of oil.

In Provence olive oil flows in the cooking as a fundamental element, contributing both flavor and nutrition. It is an excellent frying medium as it has a hotter smoking point than most other oils. It is the only oil that comes from a fresh fruit and should be stored away from light and heat. It should be a clear, amber color, have a sweet, fruity nose, and a clean taste, without acidity or bite.

Moulin à Huile Autrand, founded in 1847, is a working mill open to the public, where you can see the extraction process take place and taste the excellent oil and cured olives. It is located in Nyons, the premier olive-growing area of Provence.

*Cold pressed, extra virgin olive oil*

vendors selling pottery, honey, wines, and family specialties like pâtés, *tians, boeuf en daube*, and pastries. Everyone walks the streets in costumes taken from the attic — everything from grandmother's dresses, veils, and lace, to grandfather's top hat and tails. On Sunday there is a great procession of local identities, such as the hunter, the whittler, and the shepherd with his sheep — no one from the past is missing. Changes are now taking place, but people are keen to maintain traditional ways. As an old friend from the region says: *"Vive la cheminée, et le vrai feu de bois!"* "Long live the fireplace and the real log fire!"

## TOMATO, OLIVE, AND GARLIC

The tomato, the olive, and garlic are synonymous with Provence. Garlic and onions are pulled from the earth with their long stems intact, dried in the sun and woven into braids which are hung on kitchen walls and from the rafters. Artichokes are omnipresent, a traditional dish being *artichauts à la barigoule*, in which they are stuffed with onion, garlic, parsley, thyme, and diced ham, then braised. Also important are asparagus, eggplant, squash, cardoons, onions, green beans, and fennel, which grows wild.

Fish and shellfish are a mainstay along the coast. There are three great Provençal fish soups, but the one to receive top billing is the *bouillabaisse*, a robust, crimson masterpiece. Ingredients such as onions, tomatoes, and saffron are essential, but also added are garlic, fennel, parsley, thyme, bay leaves, orange peel, and, of course, the fish. Controversy abounds, but all agree that the fish must be very fresh and caught locally. *Bouillabaisse* is served as two courses; the broth first, then the fish garnished with *rouille*, a spicy hot *aïoli*. *Bourride,* another sumptuous dish, is a white fish soup that has been tempered with *aïoli* and egg yolks. Finally there is the *soupe de poissons*, a puréed soup made with small rock fish. This is a flavorful broth, served with croûtons and cheese.

Marseille is certainly the place to taste the widest variety of seafood. One of the restaurants along the Vieux Port that features *coquillages*, shellfish, will set you up with a plateful, supplied by the man in the blue smock out front, one of the many independent fishmongers who maintain their own boats and sell their catches to the restaurants. It will be a feast for both your eyes and your stomach: mussels and oysters from Bouzigues, and *oursins*, sea-urchins, delicacies resembling spiny golf balls that contain a sweet coral. There are clams of all kinds: small *clovisses,* large *praires*, and the thumb-nail sized *tellines* from the Camargue. Sardines are grilled, stuffed, or served raw doused with olive oil.

## SIMPLE AROMATIC FOOD

Provençal cooking is straightforward home cooking, not restaurant cuisine. The cook does not use an overabundance of ingredients in any one dish, or complicated techniques. Ingredients are used in their purest, freshest state, and cooked simply. The less that is done to adulterate the food, the better it tastes. This is a cuisine where the maximum amount of flavor is derived from the minimum amount of work. Spit-roasting and grilling are favored cooking methods, and most kitchens are equipped with a fireplace and grill for just that purpose. What could be better than a freshly caught fish dressed with olive oil and cooked over an open fire with thyme and fennel burning with the embers?

LEO MEIER

On his farm near Castallane, in Haute-Provence, a farmer casts an eye over his sheep. Lamb raised in this alpine country feed on wild herbs and yield the most delectable meat.

There is an aromatic fortitude to the food, ranging from sour, to bitter, to pungent and salt, accomplished through the use of herbs, garlic, anchovies, lemon, and olive oil. Take, for example, the *aïoli*. This sauce is made from garlic pounded to a paste, added to a mayonnaise base. It gives its name to a dish where it is served in a large bowl surrounded by such accompaniments as small potatoes boiled in their skins, sweet carrots, Jerusalem artichokes, tender green beans, artichokes, beets, hard-boiled eggs, freshened salt cod, snails, and olives. *Aïoli* turns up in many other dishes as well, such as grilled lamb chops, *bourride*, octopus *daube,* and, of course, *bouillabaisse*. The simple *salade niçoise* is made with radishes, hard-boiled eggs, potatoes, green beans, tomatoes, bell peppers, anchovies, and tuna. Pizza from this area, the *pissaladière*, is made with sweet caramelized onions, which contrast with the salty anchovy and olive garnish.

Slow cooking is popular in Provence, a result of people spending long hours working in the fields. Ingredients are thrown into a pot and left to gently stew, to be eaten later. The *ratatouille* is such a dish. Squash, onions, garlic, bell peppers, eggplant, tomatoes, and herbs are cooked together for hours. A shortage of pasture means little meat, and the meat that there is has much more muscle than fat, so tends to be tough. Long, slow cooking, in combination with marinating, does the trick. In the winter months *estouffades* and *daubes* of all sorts are served. Initially the meat, mainly beef or lamb, is marinated for several days in red wine and herbs, then slowly cooked with an assortment of aromatics — garlic, olives, mushrooms, leeks, tomatoes, onions, and invariably a piece of dried orange peel. Sisteron lamb from the Alpes de Provence is an exception. These animals graze in herb-rich alpine pastures and yield a delectable cut of meat.

*Following pages: Lavender flourishes in Provence, particularly on the Vaucluse Plateau and north of Nîmes. Lavender essence is used in perfumes and cleaning products, and pretty lavenderbags are sold in the markets.*

COMNET/WELDON TRANNIES

*Opposite: The game of* pétanque, *or* boules, *is an institution in Provence. Every town has an open stretch of ground somewhere central where the men play for hours and hours.*

*Tian* is a popular vegetable casserole which uses up leftovers. Its name derives from the heavy earthenware terrine in which it is cooked, and originally it was made at home and then taken to the village bakery to be cooked. Versatility is its strength, as it can be made with nearly any vegetable, it can be expanded with rice, beans or macaroni, and can also be enriched with eggs and cheese. *Aigo boulido* is a garlic broth in which are floated crusts of bread that have been doused in olive oil. This soup is widely regarded as a cure-all.

The mortar and pestle are essential in the Provençal kitchen, *pistou* being the local word for pestle. *Pistou* is also a sauce made from basil, garlic, olive oil, and cheese, pounded into a paste and swirled into a minestrone-style soup. The sauce is the same as Italian *pesto*, minus the pine nuts. Mortar and pestle are also used to make *tapenade*, an aromatic paste of olives, capers, garlic, anchovies, and lemon, which can be served with hard-boiled eggs, mixed with vegetables, spread on bread, or used as a dip. *Anchoïade* is a similarly pungent spread, focussing more strongly on anchovies. *Brandade de morue* is salt cod and potato, ground into a creamy concoction. This is made mainly in Haute-Provence where fresh fish is not always readily available.

In Provence there is a passion for stuffed food, such as eggplant, tomatoes, squash and zucchini blossoms, small game birds, artichokes, sardines, and leg of lamb. *Pieds et paquets,* a notable specialty from Marseilles, consists of lamb's feet and tripe which are stuffed with salt pork, garlic, onions, and parsley, then cooked slowly in white wine and tomatoes.

## HERBES DE PROVENCE

Wild herbs grow in profusion in the region, from the fertile fields to the craggy limestone cliffs which wall the Mediterranean. The assortment ranges from mint to chervil, basil, marjoram, oregano, rosemary, thyme, and savory. During the heat of the day the vapors are intoxicating as they rise from the ground, and at night the aroma is carried on the breeze. In the cooking, a specific combination of these herbs, called *herbes de Provence*, is used sparingly to enhance natural flavors. *Tisanes* are teas made with all sorts of herbs such as mint, linden blossom, verbena, lime, sage, wild thyme, or camomile. A cup before you retire will calm the nerves, cure indigestion, and promote sound sleep.

The traditional bread of the region is *fougasse*, a flat loaf into which slits are cut before baking. When the dough rises, the slits expand, opening out into a large laced pattern. A *fougasse* can be flavored with olives, herbs, small pieces of ham, anchovies, orangeflower water, or garlic. When you are in Nyons tasting olive oil, pick up a loaf of olive bread at the *boulangerie* in the square.

Rice is a relatively new crop in the region, having only been grown in the Camargue since the Second World War. Initially it was planted as an interim crop while the area was drained and irrigation systems were set up for cultivating vines, but it proved so popular that substantial quantities continue to be grown. Two-thirds of France's rice requirements are met from here. The Camargue is the vast area of the Rhône delta between Arles and the Mediterranean. The northern part of the delta is extensively cultivated, but further south it is wild country, half ranch-land, half quagmire, which is the domain of *gardians*, Provençal cowboys, with their herds of sheep and bulls, and wild white horses. Much of this area is a nature reserve, and a paradise for birdwatchers.

*Banon cheeses on sale at the market in Digne, Haute-Provence. These little parcels are aged and full of flavor.*

LEO MEIER

NIK WHEELER

## NOUGAT

Nougat has become synonymous with the little town of Montélimar in the northwest corner of Provence. It was first made here in the seventeenth century by artisans and their families, and even though thousands of pounds now leave the factories each day, producers strive to retain traditional production methods, and use only the highest quality natural ingredients.

First grade honey from Provence and sugar are mixed together in a large copper pan and cooked, stirring constantly, until the mixture reaches 300°F (130°C). Then stiffly beaten egg whites are added, giving the mixture its white, airy quality, followed by grilled Aix-en-Provence almonds, pistachios, and vanilla. The mixture is then poured into a mold lined with wafer paper, the top covered with paper, and the mold weighted. In due course the nougat is cut, dried, and wrapped ready for selling.

There are two kinds of nougat made in Montélimar; the soft one, described above, called *nougat tendre*, and *nougat noir*, which is a brittle caramel version.

If you would like to see this delightful confection being made you can visit Chabert et Guillot on 1 rue André-Ducatez, 26200 Montélimar. The factory is open daily and tours can be arranged by appointment.

Most of the cheeses in Provence are made from goat's milk, but there are some that are made from sheep and cow's milk. The goat's milk cheeses are sold either fresh, when they are sweet and moist, or aged, when they are more strongly flavored. Banon, a small fortified town in Haute-Provence, gives its name to the region's most prized cheese. These small, flat, rounded cheeses are traditionally made from goat's milk, and are wrapped in chestnut leaves that have been soaked in *eau-de-vie* or wine, and then tied with raffia. A number of commercial varieties are made with cow's milk.

Picodon, a goat's milk cheese from the mountainous region of northern Provence, has a strong, somewhat nutty flavor and a soft center. It is one of the latest French cheeses to obtain its *appellation d'origine contrôlée*. *Brousse* is a creamy, mild curd cheese made from goat or sheep's milk which is frequently served as a dessert, with sugar and cream.

## FRUIT IN PROFUSION

For dessert fruit is favored, particularly figs. It is hard to beat the flavor of tree-ripened figs, simply cut in half and the pulp scooped from the cracked, purple skin. A real must is a slice of Cavaillon melon — tiny, juicy melons which are available in the markets from July to September.

There are a multitude of orchards along the Rhône, where pomegranates, persimmons, peaches, apricots, plums, quinces, and cherries grow. Around Menton groves of lemons, blood oranges, and tangerines flourish. And there are all sorts of irresistible ice-creams to be sampled, like rose geranium, lavender, and nougat. *Fruits glacés, fruits confits*, nougat, and *calissons*, little oval-shaped sweetmeats of almond paste from Aix-en-Provence, are a delight for the sweet-toothed. *Fruits confits* are brightly colored candied fruit — clementines, cherries, melons, apricots, even whole pineapples — which burst with fruity sweetness when you bite into them.

LEO MEIER

LEO MEIER/WELDON TRANNIES

*One of the many corner stores in the streets of Nice that sells fruit and vegetables.*

## At the Markets

To find the markets in Provence you simply follow the inviting smells and the women bustling along the alleys with their empty shopping baskets. It is at the markets that you will really appreciate the cornucopia of produce Provence has to offer. Take the enticing market of Avignon, its stalls nestled against the city's ramparts. It seems to extend for miles, offering everything from spices and olives to creamy *brandade de morue*.

Every market has its own flavor and rhythm. The Carpentras market rambles through the town's streets and alleys like a maze, the Friday winter market famous for its tables piled with black truffles. In the small town of Richerenches, just outside Valréas, there is also an excellent truffle market held every Saturday from late November to mid-March.

The Arles market, which is held on Wednesday and Saturday, is well worth visiting. Here you can sample the *saucisson d'Arles*, a dried sausage made with pork, beef, and plenty of garlic, as well as the Tomme de Camargue and the Tomme Arlésienne, creamy white rounds of cheese made with a blend of goat's milk and cow's milk, sprinkled with summer herbs. *Saucisson d'Arles*, Tomme, warm *fougasse*, and a bottle of local red wine make a sumptuous picnic.

Probably the most appealing market of all is the sunny one held on Cours Saleya in Nice, where the produce market and the flower market are side-by-side. Here you will find mountains of baby lettuces, known as *mescluns*, lavender honey, baby artichokes, braids of garlic, and tubs of salted anchovies and

*Opposite: A selection of the fish and seafood that can be found at the markets all along the coast of Provence. Fishmongers often own their own fishing boats, and can guarantee the freshness of their produce.*

*Perched on a rocky point high above the sea, the village of Eze offers a magnificent view of Cap Ferrat in the distance, and on a clear day it is possible to see as far as Corsica.*

COMNET/WELDON TRANNIES

*cornichons*, small gherkins. In the winter there are dark, scented wild mushrooms from the woods. If all this makes you hungry you can buy a *socca*, a thin chickpea pancake that has been cooked over a wood fire on a little vending cart. *Soccas* are served with olive oil and coarse black pepper. Another irresistible Niçoise snack is the *pan bagna*, a roll or piece of *baguette* doused in olive oil and *aïoli,* filled with tuna, tomatoes, bell peppers, hard-boiled eggs, onions, radishes, olives, and capers. On the shadier side of Cours Saleya are the fish stalls, many of which double as restaurants. On Fridays, throughout Provence, there are markets selling fish, their eyes bulging and clear, their scales bright.

## Southern Wines

Provence can be divided into two areas when it comes to wines: the southern Rhône valley and southern Provence. The southern Rhône produces many fine wines, plus great quantities of straightforward Côtes du Rhône. Avignon is the best center from which to tour the vineyards. Perhaps the finest of the southern Rhône wines is the long-lived Châteauneuf-du-Pape, which dates from the time the papacy was in Avignon. The *appellation* applies to red and white wines from vineyards that surround the ruined summer house of the popes. The prized full-bodied yet subtle red is made from a skillful blend of up to thirteen grape varieties. Distinctive of the vineyards in the southern Rhône are the large, white, smooth stones which blanket the hillsides under the vines. They retain the heat from the scorching sun, and assist drainage.

The town of Tavel is said to produce the best rosé in all France, its high alcohol content masked by its velvety smoothness. Muscat de Beaumes-de-Venise is a sweet, fortified wine which is widely drunk as an aperitif and is delicious served with fruit desserts.

The southern Provence wine area borders the Mediterranean. Bandol, a picturesque seaside village, produces some outstanding full-bodied red wines which age well. Of this appellation, Domaine Tempier produces red wines of distinction, plus a high quality rosé and a white. In neighboring Cassis, a spicy white wine is produced, which pairs well with *bouillabaisse* and other fish dishes, but supplies are limited as the vineyard area is very small. To the east is Bellet, a minute *appellation* nestled in the hills behind Nice. Steeped in history, these wines are so good, and their production so limited, they rarely find their way out of the region. To experience this Niçoise secret, order a bottle of the white from Chateau de Crémat to accompany your *bourride* at one of the restaurants along the *quai* in old Nice. Côtes de Provence is the largest viticultural area and probably the best known, and the appellation covers some excellent red wines and rosés. Domain Ott heads the list of producers.

*Following page: In the back streets of Ajaccio, in Corsica, washing hangs out to dry, and a jovial cut-out waiter encourages passers-by to step into one of the little restaurants.*

## The Island of Corsica

Corsica lies 100 miles (160 kilometers) south of Provence, and just north of Sardinia — a mountainous island that seems to jump out of the Mediterranean. Corsica has lovely gentle beaches which are popular with the tourists and, in the interior, rugged mountain peaks that are an attraction for both the hunter and climber. The capital, Ajaccio, birthplace of Napoleon, is a palmy, balmy city of pastel shades. Its small outdoor market is rustic and colorful, with tables of clementines, crisp watercress, and tiny purple artichokes.

Corsicans are good-natured people, whose lives are rustic and robust. Ruled over the years by numerous invaders — the Greeks, Romans, Phoenicians, Moors, and Genoese — the island continues to reflect much of Italian culture, although it has been part of France since the middle of the eighteenth century. The language of the islanders is distinctive — a combination of French and Italian.

Traveling through inland Corsica it is easy to think you have gone back in time, to what Provence would have been like two hundred years ago. The pace of life is slow, but conditions are not as harsh as they once were. Until recent times the population had to rely on produce from the hill country — notably game and flour made from chestnuts. Now a greater range of food is available. Strong and intriguing combinations of flavors are used to create simple country fare. Pasta, *minestrone*, *risotto* and *polenta* show the Italian influence, whereas *bouillabaisse, daubes, anchoïade*, stuffed vegetables, and garlic sauce are closely related to the cooking of Provence. From Spain comes pimento and salt cod, and the Arab influence is reflected in the country-style grills, *galettes* of maize or chestnut flour, and the use of spices.

*The French are keen drinkers of tisanes, herbal teas. This selection ranges from hawthorn to camomile and dandelion, and there is a mixture specifically to aid the circulation of the blood.*

LEO MEIER

SPECTRUM COLOUR LIBRARY/SCOOPIX

Corsicans are known for their delicious pork products. *Lonzo* is boned pork fillet that has been pickled in brine with herbs and then hung to dry, *prizzutu* is similar to *prosciutto,* and *figatelli* are smoked sausages made from pork liver. The island's blackbirds, which feed on arbutus, juniper, and myrtle, are grilled and roasted to make pâté and *ragoût*. In the interior, chestnut flour and maize meal are used to make *polenta*, fritters and pastries. *Brocciu*, made from fresh sheep's milk, is very similar to the *brousse* of Provence. It is served with fruit, or is cooked in tarts, cakes, *ravioli*, and *cannelloni*.

Corsican wines are, for the most part, gutsy reds. Fruity, high in alcohol and somewhat harsh on the palate, they go well with the island's strongly flavored food. The best wines are from south of Ajaccio, Sartène, Porto Vecchio, and Patrimonio. Sweet liqueurs like Cédratine, made with sweet lemons, and Pastis, are extremely popular. Myrte is a potent *eau-de-vie*, often drunk as a digestif.

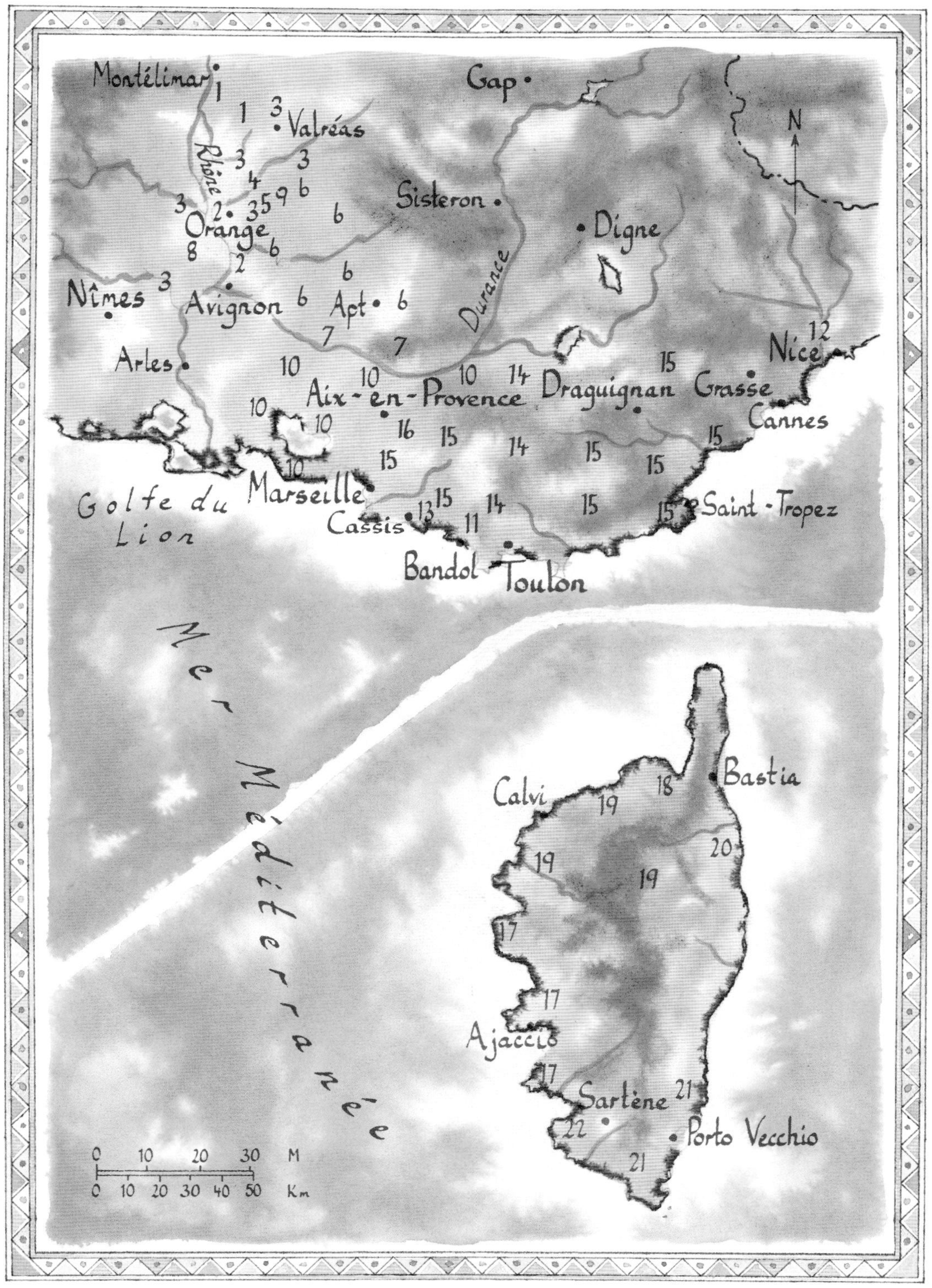

*The following three regions mainly produce red wine, with Cinsault, Carignan, Grenache, Mourvèdre, and Syrah the principal grape varieties used.*

## SOUTHERN RHONE

*Principal wines:*

*Châteauneuf-du-Pape (2)*
*Coteaux du Tricastin (1)*
*Côtes du Lubéron VDQS (7)*
*Côtes-du-Rhône (3)*
*Côtes-du-Rhône Cairanne (4)*
*Côtes-du-Rhône Vacqueyras (5)*
*Côtes du Ventoux (6)*
*Gigondas (9)*
*Lirac (8)*
*Muscat de Beaumes-de-Venise (5)*
*Tavel (8)*

## PROVENCE

*Principal wines:*

*Bandol (11)*
*Bellet (12)*
*Cassis (13)*
*Coteaux D'Aix-en-Provence (10)*
*Coteaux Varois VDQS (14)*
*Côtes de Provence (15)*
*Palette (16)*

## CORSICA

*Principal wines:*

*Ajaccio (17)*
*Patrimonio (18)*
*Vin de Corse Calvi (19)*
*Vin de Corse Coteaux du Cap Corse (20)*
*Vin de Corse Porto Vecchio (21)*
*Vin de Corse Sartène (22)*

PETER JOHNSON

# Recipes of Provence and Corsica

Joanne Weir

## Pissaladière

*Onion and Anchovy Pizza*

A *pissaladière* is best baked either on a pizza brick or on unglazed quarry tiles, covering an area 12 x 15 in (30 x 38 cm). If there is an electric element, place the brick or tiles on the bottom shelf, otherwise place them on the oven floor.

*Dough:*
*1/4 cup (2 fl oz/60 ml) lukewarm water*
*2 teaspoons (2/3 oz/20 g) dry yeast*
*1/4 cup (4 oz/125 g) whole wheat (wholemeal) flour*
*1/2 cup (4 fl oz/125 ml) lukewarm water*
*3 tablespoons extra virgin olive oil*
*1/2 teaspoon salt*
*1 3/4 cups (7 oz/220 g) all purpose (plain) flour*
*Topping:*
*4 tablespoons extra virgin olive oil*
*5 white onions, thinly sliced*
*2 garlic cloves, chopped*
*1 teaspoon fresh thyme, chopped*
*1/2 teaspoon fresh rosemary, chopped*
*salt and freshly ground pepper*
*2 oz (60 g) flat anchovy fillets in olive oil, drained*
*1/2 cup (3 oz/90 g) pitted Niçoise olives*

For the dough: Combine the lukewarm water, yeast, and flour in a bowl. Let it stand for 20 minutes. Add the rest of the ingredients and mix thoroughly. Knead on a floured board for about 10 minutes until the dough is soft yet still a bit moist. This moistness is what will give a crispy crust. Place in an oiled bowl, turning once. Cover the bowl with a cloth and put in a warm place, about 75°F (25°C). Let the dough rise for 2 hours, or until it has doubled in size.

Set the oven to its hottest temperature, and place the pizza brick or tiles inside at least 30 minutes before cooking the pizza, so they will be well heated.

For the topping: Heat 3 tablespoons oil in a skillet and add the onions, garlic, and herbs. Cook over low heat for 25 to 30 minutes, stirring frequently, until the onions are very soft and golden. Season with salt and pepper and allow to cool.

Soak the anchovy fillets in cold water for 5 minutes. Drain and pat dry with paper towels, then halve lengthwise.

*Salade Niçoise,*
*Onion and Anchovy Pizza,*
*Chickpea Pancake,*
*Anchovy Spread*

To assemble: Roll the dough out to form a large rectangle $1/4$ in (5 mm) thick. Place the dough on a well floured pizza peel, the wooden implement used for placing pizzas in a hot oven. Cover the dough to within 1 in (2.5 cm) of the edge with the onions and herbs. Arrange the anchovy fillets in a lattice on top of the onions and place a pitted olive in each section. Drizzle with the remaining oil. Place the *pissaladière* on the brick in the oven and bake for 10 to 12 minutes, or until the crust is golden brown and the bottom is crisp and has some color.

SERVES: 6 to 8

## *Salade Niçoise*

This colorful salad can be served as a first course or as a light lunch.

*Vinaigrette:*
*3 garlic cloves, finely minced*
*$1/4$ cup (2 fl oz/60 ml) red wine vinegar*
*salt and freshly ground pepper*
*$1/2$ cup (4 fl oz/125 ml) extra virgin olive oil*
*Salad:*
*1 lb (500 g) fresh tuna, or canned water-packed albacore tuna*
*2 tablespoons olive oil*
*salt and freshly ground pepper*
*12 oz (375 g) small, new red potatoes*
*12 oz (375 g) green beans, trimmed*
*2 oz (60 g) flat anchovy fillets in olive oil, drained*
*1 head salad greens, such as romaine (cos) lettuce, or chicory (curly endive)*
*1 very small red onion, thinly sliced*
*$1/2$ red bell pepper (capsicum), seeded and thinly sliced*
*4 small ripe tomatoes, cut into wedges*
*$1/2$ cup (3 oz/90 g) Niçoise olives*
*2 hard-boiled eggs, thinly sliced*
*handful of mixed fresh herbs such as thyme, parsley, rosemary, chervil, tarragon, and chives*

For the vinaigrette: Whisk the garlic, vinegar, salt, and pepper together in a bowl. Stir the oil in slowly and whisk well. Reserve.

For the salad: Marinate the tuna in olive oil, salt, and pepper for 1 hour. Either grill the tuna on a barbecue or sauté it in olive oil in a skillet. It should be lightly cooked so that it is still pink inside. Remove and cool. (If using canned tuna, omit this step.)

LEO MEIER

*Olives for sale in Nice.*

Boil the potatoes in salted water until just soft. Drain and cool. Blanch the green beans and rinse under cold water. Drain and cool. Soak the anchovies in cold water for 5 minutes. Drain and pat dry with paper towels.

Thinly slice the potatoes and cut the green beans into bite-sized pieces. Break the tuna into large bite-sized pieces and toss with one-quarter of the vinaigrette. Taste for seasoning.

Layer the salad in a large glass bowl in the following order; the greens, potatoes, beans, onion, pepper, tomatoes, tuna, olives, eggs, anchovies, and herbs. At the table, season the salad with salt and pepper and pour over the remaining vinaigrette. Toss lightly and serve immediately.

SERVES: 6

## *Socca*

*Chickpea Pancake*

These little pancakes are usually served as a snack. They do not look very interesting and the first bite is unremarkable, but after a further bite or two most people are addicted. Chickpea flour is available at health food stores.

*1 cup (4 oz/125 g) chickpea flour*
*$3/4$ teaspoon salt*
*scant $1/2$ teaspoon cumin*
*1 cup plus 1 tablespoon ($8^1/2$ fl oz/ 270 ml) water*
*2 tablespoons extra virgin olive oil*
*$1/4$ cup (2 fl oz/60 ml) olive oil*

Combine the dry ingredients. Place the water and the extra virgin olive oil in a bowl and sift the dry ingredients into it little by little, whisking constantly. Let the batter stand at room temperature for at least 2 hours.

Preheat the oven to 450°F (230°C). Oil the insides of two 10-in (25-cm) round shallow pans and divide the batter between them. It should coat the bottom to a depth of about $1/4$ in (5 mm). Bake in the top of the oven for 25 to 35 minutes, or until golden brown and crisp.

Remove from the pan and cut into wedges. Serve with freshly cracked black pepper and drizzled with extra virgin olive oil.

SERVES: 6

## *Anchoïade*

*Anchovy Spread*

This simple, strongly flavored snack is for those who love anchovies. The anchovies are tempered by the pungency of the garlic and the red wine vinegar, and a certain sweetness comes from the large amount of parsley that is used.

*20 slices of* baguette *(French bread), cut diagonally into $1/4$-in (5-mm) slices*
*3 oz (90 g) flat anchovy fillets in olive oil, drained*
*2 to 3 tablespoons extra virgin olive oil*
*1 tablespoon red wine vinegar*
*4 garlic cloves, finely chopped*
*freshly ground black pepper*
*$1/3$ cup chopped parsley*

Toast the bread slices until golden brown on both sides. Soak the anchovies in cold water for 5 minutes. Drain and pat dry with paper towels. Finely chop the anchovies with the extra virgin olive oil. Add the vinegar, garlic, black pepper, and parsley and mix together.

Thinly spread the *anchoïade* on the toast and broil (grill) for about 1 minute until just warm. Serve immediately.

SERVES: 6 to 8

*Provençal Fish Stew with Garlic Toast and Red Pepper Mayonnaise*
PETER JOHNSON

## *Bouillabaisse et Rouille*

*Provençal Fish Stew with Garlic Toast and Red Pepper Mayonnaise*

Every cook on the Provençal coast has his or her own version of this dish, and most claim that it cannot be made elsewhere. Originally the fishermen cooked the soup on the beach in a huge pot over a driftwood fire, using the fish which they could not sell.

*3 lb (1.5 kg) assorted white fish such as sea bass, flounder, red snapper, grouper, perch, sole, pike, haddock, and cod*
*1/3 cup (3 fl oz/90 ml) olive oil*
*5 garlic cloves, chopped*
*a few saffron threads*
*pinch of thyme*
*2 large onions, coarsely chopped*
*3 lb (1.5 kg) clean fish bones (remove fins, skin, etc. and all traces of blood)*
*5 large tomatoes, peeled, cored, seeded, and chopped*
*bouquet garni: 1 bay leaf, 1 thyme sprig, 6 parsley sprigs*
*pinch each of grated orange peel, ground fennel seeds, basil, and oregano*
*2 carrots, coarsely chopped*
*2 leeks, coarsely chopped*
*salt and freshly ground pepper*
*6 cups (1 1/2 qt/1.5 l) water*
*1 1/4 cups (10 fl oz/310 ml) dry white wine such as Sauvignon Blanc*
*2 lb (1 kg) clams, washed*
*1 teaspoon saffron threads*
*2 teaspoons Pernod*
2 baguettes *(French bread) cut diagonally into thin slices*
*2 large garlic cloves, peeled*
rouille *(see following recipe)*

Fillet the fish or have your fishmonger do it for you. Save the bones. Cut the fish into 1-in (2.5-cm) chunks. Marinate with 2 tablespoons olive oil, 1 clove chopped garlic, a few saffron threads, and a pinch of thyme for at least 1 hour.

Sauté the onions and remaining chopped garlic in 4 tablespoons olive oil for 4 minutes. Add the fish bones, tomatoes, bouquet garni, orange peel, fennel seeds, basil, oregano, carrots, leeks, salt and pepper, and cook covered for 10 minutes. Add the water and 1 cup of the wine and bring to a boil. Simmer uncovered for 30 minutes, using a wooden spoon from time to time to crush the bones. Remove from the heat. Blend the mixture in a blender for a few seconds and then strain it into a soup pot through a fine strainer lined with cheesecloth. Discard the residue in the strainer. Taste the stock for seasoning. If it tastes a little thin, reduce over high heat for a few minutes until the flavor is more fully developed.

Add the clams and simmer until they just begin to open. Add the fish and the remaining wine and cook at a rolling boil for 10 minutes. Add the saffron threads and continue to cook for another 5 minutes. Taste and season with Pernod, salt and pepper. Pour into warmed individual bowls.

Meanwhile dry the *baguette* slices in the oven for a few minutes and then rub them with the whole cloves of garlic. Top the slices of bread with plenty of *rouille* and float them in the bowls of soup. Serve immediately.

SERVES: 6

PETER JOHNSON

*Braised Stuffed Artichokes*

## Rouille

*Red Pepper Mayonnaise*

This fiery red sauce, the name of which means "rust," is almost always served with *bouillabaisse*. It also goes well with *soupe de poissons* and broiled fish.

*1/2 red bell pepper (capsicum)*
*1 small slice white bread, crust removed*
*2 tablespoons clam juice*
*a few saffron threads*
*cayenne pepper to taste*
*2 garlic cloves, mashed finely*
*2 teaspoons Dijon mustard*
*2 egg yolks*
*3/4 cup (6 fl oz/180 ml) olive oil*
*3/4 cup (6 fl oz/180 ml) peanut oil*
*juice of 1/2 lemon*
*salt and freshly ground pepper*
*2 tablespoons chopped parsley*
*2 teaspoons tomato paste*

Roast the bell pepper under the broiler (grill) until the skin turns black. Remove from the heat and place in a plastic bag for 5 minutes, or until the pepper is soft. When it is cool, peel it and discard the skin and seeds. Mash to a fine paste.

Soak the bread in the clam juice with the saffron and cayenne until it is saturated. Add the mashed garlic to the bread. Combine the mustard with the egg yolks and mix well. Add the yolks to the bread with 1 tablespoon olive oil. Mix until an emulsion is formed. Combine the olive oil and peanut oil. Drop by drop, add all the oil to the emulsion, whisking constantly. Do not add the oil too quickly and be sure that the emulsion is homogeneous before adding more oil. Season with lemon juice, salt, pepper, parsley, and tomato paste. Then add the mashed pepper.

Season with cayenne, lemon juice, salt and pepper as needed.

MAKES: about 2½ cups (2 fl oz/625 ml)

## *Artichauts à la Barigoule*

*Braised Stuffed Artichokes*

Use a ham which is only slightly smoked, otherwise it will overwhelm the artichokes.

*4 tablespoons olive oil*
*¼ cup (1 oz/30 g) chopped onion*
*4 garlic cloves, finely chopped*
*3 tablespoons chopped parsley*
*½ teaspoon chopped thyme*
*5 basil leaves, chopped*
*6 oz (185 g) country ham, finely diced*
*salt and freshly ground pepper*
*6 artichokes*
*1 lemon, halved*
*3 onions, thinly sliced*
*2 small carrots, thinly sliced*
*bouquet garni: 1 bay leaf, 1 thyme sprig, 6 parsley sprigs*
*1¼ cups (10 fl oz/310 ml) dry white wine*

For the stuffing: Heat half the olive oil in a skillet over medium heat, add the onion and sauté until it softens. Add the garlic, parsley, thyme, and basil, along with the ham. Mix well. Taste for seasoning.

Cut the stems off the artichokes, remove the outer leaves, and cut off the leaf tips. Rub the cut surfaces with the lemon. Blanch the artichokes in boiling salted water for 8 minutes. Drain and cool. Force the inner leaves open and scoop out the chokes with a spoon. Fill the centers of the artichokes and between the leaves with the stuffing.

In a flameproof casserole just large enough to hold the artichokes, heat the remaining olive oil over medium heat. Add the onions and carrots. Place the artichokes on top and season with salt, pepper and bouquet garni. Sauté for 6 to 8 minutes, or until the vegetables start to brown. Add the wine and deglaze for a minute. Reduce heat, cover and cook gently for 45 minutes. Check from time to time to see that the vegetables are not drying out. Remove the lid, raise the heat and boil down the sauce until syrupy.

Place the vegetables on a serving plate, topped with the artichokes. Spoon the sauce over the top. Serve warm.

SERVES: 6

## *Croûtons avec Tapenade*

*Toasted Bread with Olive Paste*

*Tapenade* takes its name from the Provençal word for caper, *tapéno.*

*1 large garlic clove*
*1 cup (6 oz/185 g) pitted Niçoise olives*
*1 tablespoon chopped capers*
*2 flat anchovy fillets in olive oil, drained, patted dry, and mashed*
*1½ tablespoons lemon juice*
*2 tablespoons olive oil*
*freshly ground pepper*
*20 slices of* baguette *(French bread), cut diagonally into ¼-in (5-mm) slices*

Place the garlic in a food processor and blend until finely chopped. Add three-quarters of the olives and process to a rough paste. Add the capers and anchovies and pulse a few times. Add the rest of the olives and pulse a few more times. Remove the mixture from the processor and place in a mixing bowl. Add the lemon juice and olive oil, seasoning to taste with freshly ground pepper. Toast the bread and spread with the *tapenade.*

SERVES: 6 to 8

*Toasted Bread with Olive Paste, Vegetable Soup with Basil*

PETER JOHNSON

## Soupe au Pistou

*Vegetable Soup with Basil*

*Pistou* is made around Nice, and is similar to the Italian *pesto*.

*4 oz (125 g) dried white beans*
*16 cups (4 qt/4 l) water*
*2 small carrots, diced*
*2 small potatoes, diced*
*1 lb (500 g) tomatoes, peeled, cored, seeded, and chopped*
*1 onion, chopped*
*1 leek, tender parts only, diced*
*bouquet garni: 1 bay leaf, 1 thyme sprig, 12 parsley sprigs*
*salt and freshly ground pepper*
*4 oz (125 g) green beans, trimmed, cut into $\frac{1}{2}$-in (1-cm) lengths*
*2 small zucchini (courgettes), diced*
*$\frac{2}{3}$ cup (3 oz/90 g) elbow macaroni*
*Pistou:*
*4 garlic cloves, peeled*
*1 packed handful of fresh basil leaves*
*freshly ground pepper and a pinch of salt*
*1 cup (4 oz/125 g) freshly grated Parmesan cheese*
*$\frac{1}{2}$ cup (4 fl oz/120 ml) olive oil*

Soak the white beans overnight in cold water, then drain. Put them in a pot with 6 cups ($1\frac{1}{2}$ qt/1.5 l) of water. Bring to a boil and simmer for 1 hour, then drain.

Put the beans, carrots, potatoes, tomatoes, onion, leek, and bouquet garni in the pot and add 10 cups ($2\frac{1}{2}$ qt/1.5 l) of water. Add salt and pepper, bring to a boil and simmer for 30 minutes.

Add the green beans, zucchini, and macaroni and cook for 15 minutes, or until the macaroni is just cooked. Discard the bouquet garni. Taste for seasoning.

For the *pistou*: (This should be made while the soup is cooking.) Pound the garlic, basil, pepper and salt in a large mortar. Work in some of the Parmesan until the mixture is a stiff paste, then add the oil little by little, adding more Parmesan until the mixture is barely fluid. Do not add the olive oil too quickly or the mixture will separate. Alternatively, you can use a food processor or blender.

Ladle the hot soup into bowls and pass the *pistou* separately.

SERVES: 6

*Provençal Summer Vegetable Stew, Gratin of Eggplant, Tomatoes, and Chickpeas, Stuffed Tomatoes Magaly*

PETER JOHNSON

## Tian de Legumes

*Gratin of Eggplant, Tomatoes, and Chickpeas*

This *tian* is delicious served as a light vegetarian main course, or as a side dish with grilled lamb chops.

*1 cup (6 oz/185 g) dry chickpeas (garbanzos)*
*bouquet garni: 1 bay leaf, 1 thyme sprig, 6 parsley sprigs*
*1 large eggplant (aubergine), about $1\frac{1}{2}$ lb (750 g), cut into 1-in (2.5-cm) cubes*
*2 tablespoons kosher (sea) salt*
*$\frac{1}{2}$ cup (4 fl oz/125 ml) olive oil*
*1 onion, finely chopped*
*6 tomatoes, peeled, cored, seeded, and chopped*
*$\frac{1}{2}$ teaspoon ground allspice*
*$\frac{1}{2}$ teaspoon dried crushed hot red chili pepper*
*12 to 15 shredded basil leaves*
*salt and freshly ground pepper*
*$\frac{1}{2}$ cup (2 oz/60 g) freshly grated Parmesan cheese*

Soak the chickpeas overnight in cold water. Drain and place in a saucepan, covering them with water by 2 in (5 cm). Add the bouquet garni. Bring to a boil and simmer for 45 minutes, then drain. Place the eggplant in a colander and sprinkle with the kosher salt. Leave for 30 minutes. Rinse and pat dry with paper towels.

Heat half the oil in a large skillet and sauté the eggplant over moderately high heat until lightly browned, adding more oil if necessary. Remove the eggplant and set aside in a bowl. Add half the remaining oil and sauté the onion until translucent. Add the tomatoes and cook until the liquid has evaporated. Preheat the oven to 375°F (190°C).

Combine the eggplant, onion and tomato mixture, allspice, red chili pepper, basil, and chickpeas. Taste for seasoning. Spoon into an oiled baking dish. Sprinkle with the Parmesan and the remaining olive oil. Bake in the oven for 40 minutes. Serve hot or at room temperature.

SERVES: 6 to 8 as a side dish

*A Provençal baker at his oven, carved in wood.*

PETER JOHNSON

## Ratatouille

*Provençal Summer Vegetable Stew*

In this variation of *ratatouille* the vegetables are sautéed separately and only stewed together at the end, thus maintaining their brilliant color.

*1 large eggplant (aubergine), about 1½ lb (750 g) cut into 1-in (2.5-cm) cubes*
*2 tablespoons kosher (sea) salt*
*5 tablespoons olive oil or more, as needed*
*3 yellow or red bell peppers (capsicums), cored, seeded, and cut into 1-in (2.5-cm) strips, and the strips halved*
*4 small zucchini (courgettes), cut into 1-in (2.5-cm) slices*
*2 onions, chopped*
*4 garlic cloves, finely chopped*
*5 tomatoes, peeled, cored, seeded, and cut into 1-in (2.5-cm) slices*
*2 bay leaves*
*3 tablespoons chopped parsley*
*½ teaspoon fresh thyme leaves, chopped*
*freshly ground pepper*
*1 to 2 tablespoons red wine vinegar*
*20 basil leaves*

Place the eggplant in a colander and sprinkle with the kosher salt. Leave to drain for 30 minutes. Rinse and pat dry with paper towels.

Heat 2 tablespoons of olive oil in a large heavy casserole. Add the eggplant and brown on all sides. Remove and reserve. Add a tablespoon more oil to the pan and sauté the bell peppers until they begin to wilt. Remove and reserve. Add the zucchini and sauté until lightly browned. Remove and reserve. Add a few more tablespoons of olive oil and sauté the onions and garlic over medium heat until translucent. Add the tomatoes, bay leaves, parsley, thyme, and black pepper and cook for 20 minutes. Return the reserved vegetables to the casserole and cook for 10 minutes. Taste and season with salt, pepper, and vinegar.

Serve at room temperature, sprinkled with basil leaves.

Serves: 6

## Tomates Farcies Magaly

*Stuffed Tomatoes Magaly*

Magaly Fabre, along with her husband Raymond, are the proprietors of Domaine du Mont Redon, which produces some of the finest Châteauneuf du Pape wines. This is one of her excellent recipes.

*6 large, ripe red tomatoes, cored*
*2 tablespoons olive oil*
*½ cup (2 oz/60 g) finely chopped onion*
*12 oz (375 g) fresh pork sausage, crumbled*
*½ cup (4 fl oz/125 ml) milk, scalded*
*1 cup (2 oz/60 g) fresh breadcrumbs*
*1 egg, whisked*
*salt and freshly ground pepper*
*4 tablespoons chopped parsley*
*¼ teaspoon fresh thyme*
*½ teaspoon fresh savory*
*2 garlic cloves, finely chopped*
*1 tablespoon butter*
*thyme, parsley, and savory for garnish*

Halve the tomatoes and squeeze slightly to remove excess moisture. Sprinkle the insides with salt and place tomatoes cut side down on paper towels for at least 1 hour to drain.

Heat half the oil in a skillet over medium heat and cook the tomato halves, cut side down, for 5 minutes. Season with salt and pepper, then carefully turn them over and cook for a further 3 minutes. Remove and place in an oiled gratin dish. Add the onion to the juices and oil in the skillet and sauté until translucent. Add the sausage and cook over medium heat until it colors. Transfer to a mixing bowl and add the milk and breadcrumbs. Cool slightly. Add the egg, salt and pepper, half the parsley, thyme, and savory. Taste for seasoning.

Stuff the tomatoes with this mixture. Combine remaining parsley and the garlic and sprinkle on top. Dot with butter and broil (grill) until golden.

Let the tomatoes cool before serving. Garnish with thyme, parsley, and savory.

Serves: 6

## Nougat Montélimar

This nougat is very similar to the melt-in-the-mouth *nougat tendre* from Montélimar.

*½ cup (5 oz/150 g) honey*
*2 tablespoons light corn syrup*
*1 cup (8 oz/250 g) sugar*
*¼ cup (2 fl oz/60 ml) water*
*pinch of cream of tartar*
*2 egg whites*
*pinch of salt*
*2 teaspoons vanilla extract (essence)*
*⅓ cup (2 oz/60 g) candied cherries, chopped*
*2½ cups (13 oz/400 g) blanched almonds, coarsely chopped*

In a heavy saucepan, combine the honey and corn syrup over moderately high heat and cook until a candy thermometer registers 260°F (125°C). In another heavy saucepan, heat the sugar, water, and cream of tartar to 285°F (140°C). The sugar should be dissolved before the syrup boils. Wash any sugar crystals that accumulate on the sides of the pan with a brush dipped in cold water.

In the bowl of an electric mixer, beat the egg whites until they form stiff peaks. With the mixer set at moderate speed, add the sugar syrup in a slow stream. The mixture will become thick. Add the honey mixture and continue beating until the mixture is

very stiff. With a wooden spoon, fold in the salt, vanilla, cherries, and almonds.

Pour the nougat into an oiled 8-in (20-cm) square pan or a nougat frame lined with rice paper. Leave overnight. Cut the nougat into 2 x 1-in (5 x 2.5-cm) pieces and wrap in waxed paper.

MAKES: about 30 pieces

## *Fiadone*

*Corsican Cheesecake with Caramel*

This Easter specialty is usually made with *brocciu*, which is similar to the *brousse* of Provence and Italian ricotta.

*2/3 cup (5 oz/155 g) sugar*
*2 tablespoons water*
*1/2 cup (4 oz/125 g) sugar*
*1/3 cup (3 fl oz/90 ml) milk*
*2 teaspoons vanilla extract (essence)*
*12 oz (375 g) ricotta*
*grated peel of 1/2 lemon and 1/2 orange*
*6 eggs*

Combine 2/3 cup of sugar and water in a heavy saucepan over medium heat and stir with a metal spoon until combined. Bring to a boil and simmer, swirling the pan occasionally. As soon as the syrup turns golden brown, remove from the heat and pour into a 9-in (23-cm) tart pan. Swirl the dish to coat the sides.

Preheat oven to 325°F (160°C). Scald 1/2 cup of sugar and the milk. Cool and add the vanilla. Place the ricotta in a bowl and slowly stir in the milk, mixing well. Add lemon and orange peel. Add the eggs one at a time, beating well. Pour this mixture into the prepared pan. Place the pan in a bain-marie and bake for about 1 hour in the oven until set. Remove the pan from the bain-marie and run a knife around the inside. Let the cheesecake cool for 20 minutes and then turn out. Serve warm.

SERVES: 6

*Nougat Montélimar*

PETER JOHNSON

## Tarte au Citron et Amandes

*Lemon and Almond Tart*

Around Menton, close to the Italian border, Meyer lemons flourish. The Meyer is a sweet lemon with a thick shiny skin, and is ideal for this tart, but Eureka or Lisbon lemons can be substituted.

*Pastry:*
*1 cup (4 oz/125 g) all purpose (plain) flour*
*1 tablespoon sugar*
*pinch of salt*
*¾ teaspoon grated lemon peel*
*10 tablespoons (5 oz/150 g) butter, not too cold*
*1 to 2 teaspoons water*
*½ teaspoon vanilla extract (essence)*
*Filling:*
*2 eggs*
*⅓ cup (3 oz/90 g) sugar*
*juice of 2 lemons*
*3 tablespoons grated lemon peel*
*8 tablespoons (4 oz/125 g) butter, melted*
*⅓ cup (2 oz/60 g) blanched almonds, toasted and ground*
*¾ cup (6 fl oz/180 ml) heavy (double) cream for serving*

For the pastry: Mix the flour, sugar, salt, and lemon peel directly on the work surface. Cut the butter into thin slices and work it into the flour mixture with your fingertips until the mixture resembles cornmeal.

Combine the water and vanilla and add only as much as is needed to blend the pastry together. Gather the pastry into a ball, flatten into a 6-in (15-cm) cake then cover in plastic wrap. Let rest in the refrigerator for 1 hour.

With the palm of your hand and your fingertips, press the pastry into a 9-in (23-cm) tart pan, making sure that it is of an even thickness. Set the shell in the freezer for 30 minutes.

Bake the shell in a 375°F (190°C) oven for 20 to 25 minutes, or until light golden in color and baked through.

For the filling: (This should be made while the shell is baking.) Beat the eggs and sugar until a stiff ribbon is formed which leaves a trail when the whisk is lifted. Stir in the lemon juice and grated peel, then the butter and ground almonds.

Pour the filling into the shell and bake for 25 to 30 minutes, or until the filling is set and golden. Serve warm with lightly whipped cream.

SERVES: 6 to 8

## Glace à la Lavande et Amandes

*Lavender and Toasted Almond Ice-cream*

Dried lavender flowers are available in health food stores or you can buy fresh lavender and dry it yourself. Lavender ice-cream is fairly common in Provence, but this combination with toasted almonds is particularly delightful.

*⅓ cup (2½ oz/75 g) sugar*
*2 tablespoons dried lavender flowers*
*¾ cup (4 oz/125 g) almonds*
*2 cups (16 fl oz/500 ml) milk*
*2 cups (16 fl oz/500 ml) heavy (double) cream*
*⅓ cup (3 oz/90 g) lavender honey*
*9 egg yolks*

In a small heavy saucepan, combine the sugar, lavender, and 1 tablespoon water. Cook over moderately high heat for 2 to 3 minutes, until the mixture caramelizes. Pour onto an oiled baking sheet and cool. Grind to a fine powder in a spice grinder. Remove any larger pieces. Reserve. This can be made in advance and stored in an airtight container for up to a month.

Toast the almonds in a 350°F (175°C) oven for 5 minutes or until they are aromatic and just too hot to hold. Cool and chop into ¼-in (5-mm) pieces.

Combine the milk, cream, and lavender honey in a saucepan and scald. In another saucepan, place the egg yolks and break them up with a whisk. Add the scalded mixture to the yolks, drop by drop at first, and tablespoon by tablespoon after a minute. This tempering should be done slowly so that you do not scramble the yolks. When all the milk mixture has been added to the yolks, add the lavender powder. Stir well with a wooden spoon. Place the pan over low heat and stir constantly until the mixture lightly coats the back of the spoon. Do not let the mixture boil. Remove from the heat immediately and strain into a bowl. Whisk to cool, then chill for several hours in the refrigerator.

Churn in an ice-cream maker until frozen, adding the almonds during the last 2 minutes and mixing well. Scoop into ice-cream dishes or parfait glasses.

SERVES: 8 to 10

*Lavender and Toasted Almond Ice-cream, Lemon and Almond Tart, Corsican Cheesecake with Caramel*

PETER JOHNSON

Massif Central
Aurillac
Le Puy
Dordogne
Lot
Cahors
Rodez
Caussade
Quercy
Cévennes
Millau
Alès
Roquefort-sur-Soulzon
Montauban
Tarn
Albi
Nîmes
Languedoc
Montpellier
Toulouse
Castres
Bouzigues
Garonne
Pézenas
Sète
Bassin de Thau
Castelnaudary
Béziers
Agde
Carcassonne
Narbonne
Limoux
Golfe du Lion
Foix
Salses
Pyrénées
Perpignan
Andorra
Roussillon
(Pays Catalan)
Collioure
Port-Vendres
Céret
Banyuls-sur-Mer
España

# LANGUEDOC

*Martha Rose Shulman*

The Languedoc is part of the ancient land of Occitania, which includes all southwestern France, and whose language was the *langue d'Oc,* the language of the troubadours. Today this part of France, which stretches along the Mediterranean from west of Arles down to the Spanish border, west into the Pyrenees and north into the Massif Central and the country around Toulouse, is also referred to as the Languedoc-Roussillon. A country of mountains, sea, and brush-covered high plains, it comprises three distinct gastronomic regions: the Languedoc Méditerranéen, whose cuisine is redolent of olive oil and garlic, and fragrant with herbs; the Roussillon, or Pays Catalan, whose cuisine marries olive oil and garlic with the rustic flavors of sausage, ham, and lard; and the Languedoc Toulousain, the mountainous country around Albi and Toulouse, where olive oil gives way to goose fat, and dishes, like *cassoulet*, are hearty, meaty, and earthy.

NIK WHEELER

*Bouzigues' renowned oysters and mussels are grown on wooden frames throughout the calm waters of the Bassin de Thau.*

## The Languedoc Méditerranéen

The Languedoc Méditerranéen, from the eastern border of the region in the Camargue — that flat, hot, marshy country of the Rhône delta south of Nîmes and Arles — down to just north of Perpignan, has a cuisine that is very similar to that of its Provençal neighbors. It is a cuisine of the sun and the sea, with its versions of Provençal dishes like *brandade de morue*, purée of salt cod, and the rich *aïoli*-thickened fish soup called *bourride*. Salt cod is much loved, and the region has a *bouillabaisse* which contains ham as well as fish. Its heady lobster stew, called *civet de langoustine*, can be found from Sète to Banyuls, but changes in character once you reach Catalan country, Cognac being replaced by the fortified Banyuls wine.

Bouzigues is famous for its mussels and oysters from the Bassin de Thau, a large salt-water lagoon near Sète, where one-third of France's mussels are cultivated. Traditionally these shellfish are served *à la marinière,* but they can also be eaten raw, and are sometimes stuffed with sausage and simmered in tomato sauce. Roadside mussel and oyster stands dot the highway which runs along the coast. Other specialties from Thau and the towns nearby are delicate grilled *cigales de mer*, sea-crickets, like tiny crayfish; little clams called *tellines*, which are cooked with olive oil and garlic; and briny shellfish called *violets*, which are eaten raw from the shell, and cooked in omelettes.

But the Camargue is also cowboy country, and one of its most popular dishes is *gardiane*, a rich bull meat stew containing black olives — southern France's answer to *boeuf bourguignon*. This dish is most often served with delicious nutty, chewy Camargue rice, and may be followed by the Languedoc's firm and slightly piquant Pélardon goat cheese.

This is fruit country, too. From roadside fruitstands during the summer you can buy small, round, fragrant Cavaillon melons that are so ripe they are splitting. At these stands you will also find juicy ripe peaches, both white and yellow, and nectarines, sold by the crate.

## Pays Catalan

Officially Catalonia is an administrative region in the northeastern corner of Spain, but culturally and gastronomically the *paios catalans* extends into France as far as Salses, about 10 miles (16 kilometers) north of Perpignan, and as far south in Spain as Alicante. Perpignan is the proud capital of the French Pays Catalan (which is administratively the Roussillon), and the second city of Catalonia. In the thirteenth century, before this part of the world became Catalonia, it was the capital of the kingdom of Mallorca, which stretched from the Balearic Islands (where old Languedoc recipes can still be found) to Montpellier.

Catalan cooking reflects a rich history. The Romans occupied the region from the third century BC to the fifth century AD, and it was they who planted olives and grapes, introduced bread, chickpeas, lentils, and broad beans, and taught the people to cure ham. The Moors also left their mark on Catalan cuisine. They popularized rice, eggplant, almonds, hazelnuts, spinach, oranges, cane sugar, and saffron. They also brought with them the most wonderful pastries and a taste for sweet and sour combinations.

Catalans love to eat, and they eat heartily. Theirs is a unique cuisine, which often uses olive oil, lard, and ham or salt pork in the same dishes, like *poulet à la*

*Opposite: A pair of fishing boats moored in the inlet at Agde, a small town lying southwest of the Bassin de Thau.*

NIK WHEELER

*catalane*, in which chicken is sautéed in olive oil with red peppers, tomatoes, onions, salt pork, and lots of garlic. The olive oil and pork combination even occurs in seafood dishes, such as *civet de langoustine*. Tomatoes and eggplant are much loved, while garlic and onions are ubiquitous.

There are four fundamental sauces used in Catalan cooking: *allioli*, a garlic mayonnaise (which is the same as Provençal *aïoli*) served with meats, fish, snails, vegetables, soups, stews, and rice dishes; *sofregit*, a sauce base which is made by slowly melting down onions and tomatoes together; *picada*, a paste of garlic, almonds, bread, and olive oil, used as a thickening agent; and a *ratatouille*-like vegetable mixture called *samfaina*, often served with meats, as a sauce or as a side dish. When sauces are made, the base is frequently *sofregit*, and *picada* is used at the end, to add body.

## Cargols and the Cargolada

*Petits gris* and *escargots de vigne*, small, grey land snails, are popular throughout the Languedoc. Those that come from the inland scrublands are called *escargots de garrigue*.

Snail recipes abound. They are cooked in their shells in lard with lots of garlic, then sprinkled with parsley and breadcrumbs, or cooked with pork liver and salt pork. Some recipes include tomatoes, and in one they are cooked with potatoes and eaten with *aillade*. There are snail fricassees and there is even a snail *bouillabaisse*.

But the *cargolada* is nothing less than a snail feast. *Cargol* is Catalan for snail, and a *cargolada* is a big snail barbecue, where snails are cooked over vine cuttings. It is a major family event in the Pays Catalan, often held on religious holidays.

Everyone participates. Some clean the snails, some prepare the grill, and others make the sauce. In Spain the sauce is often made with raw tomato and garlic, whereas in France *allioli* is the usual accompaniment.

It is common for people to eat up to a hundred snails each, followed by sausages and lamb chops, all washed down with red wine from the Roussillon. Bread and salads are served on the side.

## Collioure Anchovies

Along this coast, anchovies and sardines are not only important gastronomically, but also big business (or small, depending on the luck of the catch). Collioure is a charming fishing village close to the Spanish border, famous for its anchovies. In nearby Port-Vendres the anchovies are cured in salt, packed, aged then shipped all over France. Those that remain, and plenty do, go into *salade catalane,* the Roussillon's version of *salade niçoise*, and into tomato and anchovy salads. Anchovies are pounded and mixed with olive oil or butter for spreading on toast or filling puff pastry. The *anchoïade*-filled puff pastry is a typical hors d'oeuvre, called *pâté aux anchois de Collioure*. Anchovies often accompany *pain catalan*, lightly toasted bread rubbed with tomato and garlic, and are delicious served fresh in a marinade of vinegar, lemon juice, and olive oil.

The Perpignan area is also an important fruit and vegetable center. Farmers in the region bring their melons, peaches, apricots, cherries, and strawberries to the market daily in summer. Fresh fruit is made into granita-like ices, which you can enjoy in the cafés while, if you are lucky, dancers in the square perform the Catalan folkdance called La Sardane.

*Opposite: A Camargue farmer hand-feeds a tame member of her flock.*
*Below: Sausages, prepared meats, and pâtés in a* charcuterie *in Caussade, with stuffed animals set out on the counter.*

LEO MEIER

CHRISTIAN SAPPA/CEDRI

## Into the Pyrenees

As you head inland you quickly find yourself in the Pyrenees. In the foothills, peach orchards give way to apples and pears. The charming town of Céret is famous for its cherries. In 1922 farmers from here sent a crate of the first-of-the-season crop to the president of the republic, and the gesture became an annual tradition. Céret's Saturday morning market, set out in the shade of sycamore trees, is one of the most colorful in the Roussillon.

In the mountains pork is a mainstay, and there are many types of hams and sausages. Some of the sausages are highly spiced, while others, like the white *botifarra,* are simply seasoned with salt and pepper. Country pâtés are varied, hearty, and complex. Other mountain specialties are game, snails, and rich stew-like soups which combine pork, vegetables, herbs, and beans. One of these, called an *ouillade*, is considered by some to be Catalonia's national dish. It is made in two cooking vessels called *ouilles* — one for beans, the other for pork and vegetables.

The Catalans use garlic abundantly in dishes like *mouton, agneau,* or *perdreau en pistache*, mutton, lamb, or patridge cooked with raw ham or salt pork, onions, carrots, wine, stock, and fifty whole cloves of garlic. The dish stews slowly and the garlic sweetens as it cooks. Almost as much garlic is combined with lemon and simmered with chicken in stock and Banyuls wine in one of the most marvelous of Catalan dishes, *poulet au citron à la catalane*. Another popular dish is *boles de Picolat*, highly seasoned beef meatballs cooked with green olives and often served with white beans. Beef is a rarity in Spanish Catalonia, but it is eaten widely in the Roussillon.

The Catalans inherited from the Moors a great love of sweets. A local snack in Céret is a made-to-order fried donut filled with cream and rolled in sugar, called a *chichi*. The dessert found everywhere is *crème catalane*, a rich, creamy flan, pure and simple, often served with a caramel topping like *crème brulée*, sometimes flavored with fennel or cinnamon, or containing chestnuts.

## Le Rose d'Albi

It is said that the most prized garlic in France is the pink-skinned garlic from the Languedoc, *le rose d'Albi*. There is an element of sweetness in its pungency that is enhanced by long simmering in soups and stews. This same sweetness accounts for the lack of acrid flavor in the many variations of garlic mayonnaise found throughout the Languedoc-Roussillon.

These sauces are essential for some of the region's best known dishes. *Bourride nîmoise* would not be a *bourride* were it not for the rich *aillade* that is stirred into each serving of this luscious fish soup. In the Pays Catalan, that same garlic mayonnaise is as ubiquitous as ketchup in an American diner.

*Aillade* can also refer to a garlic soup in the Languedoc, of which there are many versions, or it can be a dish in which garlic or garlic mayonnaise plays a central role, such as *aillade d'escargots*, in which snails and potatoes are cooked together and spread with the sauce.

At one time garlic was even instrumental in bringing wedding ceremonies to a close. It was the custom in many villages for members of the wedding party to bring the bride and groom, once they had gone to bed, bowls of garlic soup, black with pepper.

KLAUS BOSSEMEYER/BILDERBERG

*Roquefort cheese is prized the world over, but nowhere more than in the Languedoc, where it is made.*

## The Languedoc Toulousain

Traveling north from Montpellier, or west towards Albi and Toulouse, you soon find yourself in rugged mountainous country with deep, dramatic gorges and winding mountain roads. In the small villages, signs advertise goose and duck *foie gras* and *confits*. These specialties are associated with the southwest — Périgord, Quercy, and Gascony — but the gastronomic borders here are somewhat fluid.

*Confits*, from the word *confire*, meaning "to preserve," are the backbone of southwestern cuisine. They are preserved meats — duck, goose, and pork — which have been salted to draw out moisture, slowly cooked in rendered fat, then stored in the fat. They are traditionally preserved in heavy earthenware jars in cool, dry storage rooms, or they are refrigerated. *Confit* occurs everywhere on menus in this part of the Languedoc: on its own as a main dish, as an ingredient in various salads and stews, and in *cassoulet*.

*Cassoulet* is probably the best known dish of the Languedoc Toulousain. All over the southwest people are passionate about their *cassoulets*, insisting they can only be made this way or that, with or without mutton, partridge or sausage, *confit* or breadcrumbs. The dish is similar to the *ouillade* of the Pays Catalan — a rich combination of meats and beans cooked slowly in an earthenware pot.

## The Home of Roquefort

One of the most famous of French cheeses, Roquefort, is produced in the Languedoc. It is made from ewe's milk, and all of it — about 17 000 tons a year — is aged in the cool limestone caves of Roquefort-sur-Soulzon, a mountain village north of Montpellier. Originally it could only be made from the milk of local sheep, but now it can legally be made with sheep's milk from the Pyrenees and Corsica. About 80 per cent of all Roquefort is made by machine, the penicillin spores which give the cheese its blue-green veins being produced in a laboratory and introduced into the cheese at the curd stage. A small number of artisans still produce the cheese by hand, using natural penicillin obtained from rye bread. Their cheese is ivory-white, with the veins spreading evenly to the edges of the cheese. Industrial Roquefort is yellower and drier, and the veins tend to be clustered in the middle. The handmade cheeses are also less salty than their commercial counterparts.

Chestnuts have been important for centuries in the Languedoc. They were at one time the main source of food for the peasants of the Cévennes, who referred to chestnut trees as *arbres à pain,* bread trees, because they made bread from chestnut flour. Roasted chestnuts with milk still comprise the evening meal in some areas, and they are made into wonderful chestnut cakes.

A polenta-like porridge, called *millas*, dating from ancient times, is still eaten in rural areas. Cornmeal, wheat, buckwheat, barley, millet, or chestnut flour is boiled in milk or water, which is then seasoned with lard or salt pork, and sometimes mixed with vegetables like squash and onions. Sliced, fried, and sprinkled with sugar, *millas* is also served as a dessert.

Another favored dessert is a covered fruit pie made with strudel-like pastry, called a *croustade*. One of the most common and delicious *croustades* is filled with preserved quinces and prunes. Its flavor is deep and intense, like so much of the food of the Languedoc.

# A Sea of Vines

No matter where you go in the Languedoc Méditerranéen and the Roussillon, you are never far from vineyards. From the autoroute that hugs the coast from Montpellier to the Spanish border, a sea of vines can be seen from the car window, stretching away to the west. Here is where the notorious European wine lake is produced, thousands of industrial wines that fill the supermarket shelves. Forty per cent of France's wine is made here, and a good deal of it is poor quality. Not all of it is mass produced, though, and it is worth seeking out the good ones.

As well as extending along the coast, there are vineyards in the high mountains of the Massif Central north of Montpellier, and in the foothills of the Pyrenees, in the hilly scrublands, and on the alluvial plain which slopes down from the highlands. Vines and olive trees are the only viable crops in parts of the province, where year-round temperatures are the highest in France, and rainfall is scant.

Some of the best wines from the region are sweet, fortified wines, like Muscat de Rivesaltes, Rivesaltes, and Banyuls from the Roussillon. Muscat de Frontignan, from just east of Sète in the Languedoc, is another fine wine of this type.

Excellent reds can also be found. The Pays Catalan produces velvety, fruity Collioure, and Côtes du Roussillon and Côtes du Roussillon Villages, which should be drunk young. The best red wines from the Languedoc come from Corbières and l'Hérault. Little white wine is made in this part of the country, but a number of good rosés are available.

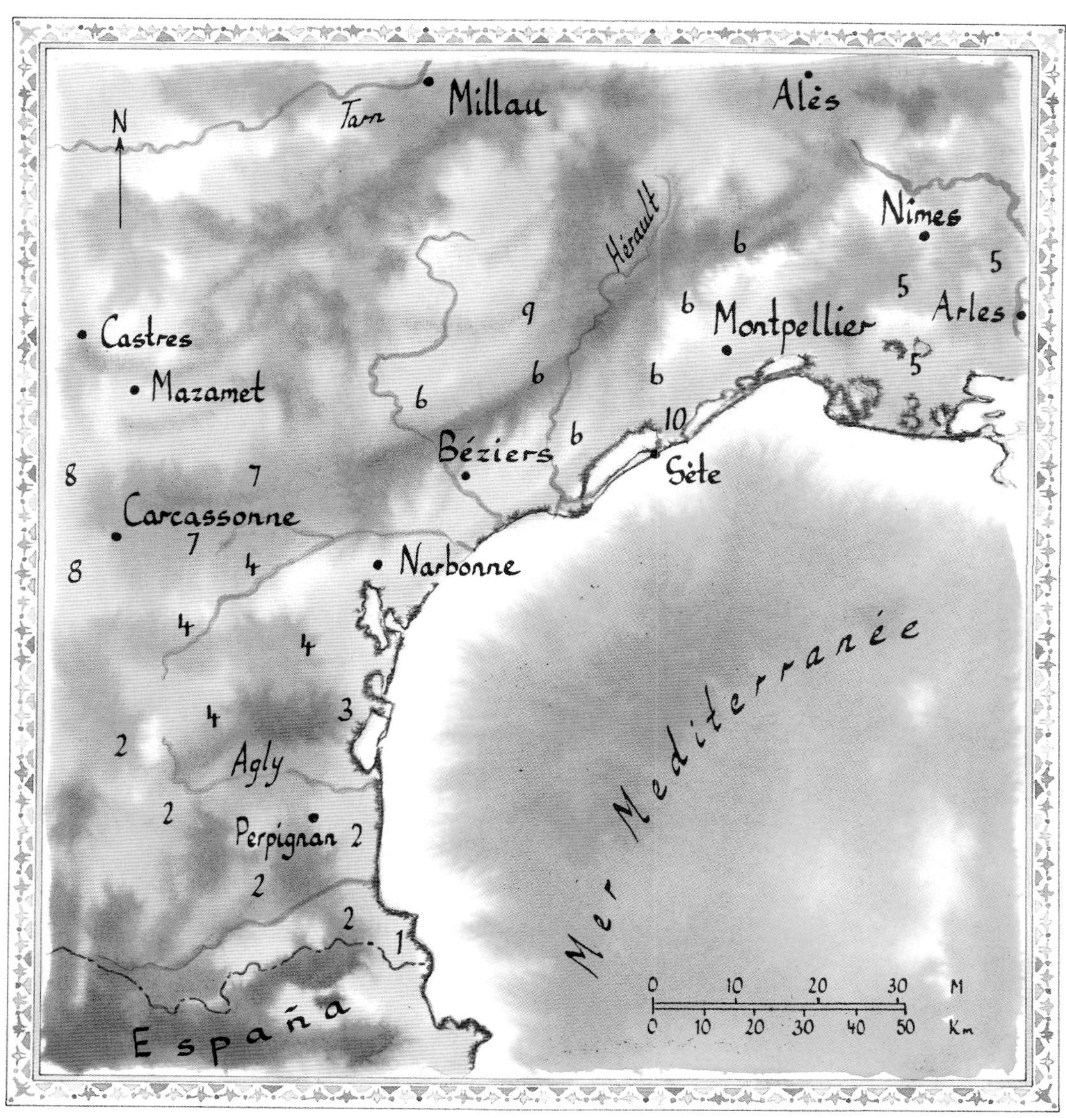

## LANGUEDOC

*Principal sweet and fortified wines:*

*Banyuls (1)*
*Clairette du Languedoc (9)*
*Muscat de Frontignan (10)*
*Muscat de Rivesaltes (2)*
*Rivesaltes (2)*

*The following districts produce mainly red wines, but rosé and white wines are also made:*

*Collioure (1)*
*Corbières (4)*
*Costières du Gard VDQS (5)*
*Coteaux du Languedoc (often with a village name added) (6)*
*Côtes de la Malepère VDQS (8)*
*Côtes du Cabardès et de l'Orbiel VDQS (8)*
*Côtes du Roussillon (2)*
*Faugères (6)*
*Fitou (3)*
*Grand Roussillon (2)*
*Minervois (7)*
*Saint-Chinian (6)*
*Vin de Pays de l'Hérault (6)*

# RECIPES OF LANGUEDOC

Martha Rose Shulman

PETER JOHNSON

## Salade Catalane

Wherever you go in the Roussillon, you will find this salad on the menu. It is the Catalan version of *salade niçoise*, but differs significantly, as it rarely contains tuna or potatoes. In its simplest form it consists only of tomatoes, which are preferred slightly green, and young red or green onions, dressed with a simple vinaigrette and a *persillade* of chopped parsley and garlic. Other ingredients that can be found in the salad include young purple artichoke hearts, thinly sliced; minced cucumber; sliced celery; radishes; young raw broad beans; roasted red bell pepper; raw ham; and beets.

*Vinaigrette and* persillade:
*$2^1/_2$ tablespoons good quality red wine or sherry vinegar*
*salt and freshly ground pepper*
*$^1/_2$ cup (4 fl oz/125 ml) olive oil*
*1 to 3 garlic cloves, finely chopped (optional)*
*4 or 5 parsley sprigs, finely chopped*
*Salad:*
*6 to 12 flat anchovy fillets in oil, drained*
*1 small head salad greens, such as romaine (cos) lettuce, leaf lettuce, or chicory (curly endive)*
*3 large tomatoes, slightly green, quartered*
*1 red onion, or 5 green onions (scallions or spring onions), finely chopped*
*1 green bell pepper (capsicum), seeds and membranes removed, thinly sliced*
*handful of black or green olives (Spanish or French)*
*2 or 3 hard-boiled eggs, quartered*

For the vinaigrette and *persillade*: Mix together the vinegar, salt and pepper, and olive oil. Combine well and add the garlic, if desired, and the parsley. Set aside.

For the salad: Soak the anchovies in cold water for 1 hour. Drain and pat dry with paper towels. Line a large serving bowl or platter with the salad greens. Place tomato wedges here and there, sprinkle with the onions and pepper slices. Top with the anchovy fillets and distribute the olives and quartered eggs evenly among the tomatoes. Just before serving, pour the dressing over the salad. Bring the salad to the table, toss, and serve.

SERVES: 6

*Salade Catalane, Catalan Tomato Bread*

## Pain Catalan

*Catalan Tomato Bread*

This simple snack, known as *pa amb oli* in Catalan, is eaten at any time of the day, and is a particular favorite with children when they arrive home after school.

*6 to12 thick slices country-style bread*
*6 ripe tomatoes, halved crosswise*
*olive oil*
*salt*

Grill the bread lightly over a wood-burning fire or coals, or toast lightly in a toaster or oven. It should be crisp on the outside and slightly soft in the middle.

Rub the toasted bread on one or both sides with the cut side of a tomato, gently squeezing the tomato as you do so. The bread should have little bits of tomato on the surface. Drizzle on a thin film of olive oil, and sprinkle with salt to taste.

Variations: Rub the toasted bread with a cut clove of garlic; drizzle on a little good quality red wine vinegar; top with a few anchovy fillets that have been soaked in water and milk for 10 minutes to an hour and then dried; or top with a thin slice of Bayonne ham or *prosciutto*.

SERVES: 6

## Sauce Catalane

*Tomato, Garlic, and Orange Sauce*

This garlicky tomato sauce is from the Perpignan area. What makes it Catalan is the addition of bitter orange. It goes well with all meats, especially partridge and pork, as well as with fried eggs and fish.

*2 tablespoons olive oil*
*4 to 6 garlic cloves, coarsely chopped*
*$1^1/_2$ lb (750 g) tomatoes, skinned, seeded, and chopped*
*salt and freshly ground pepper*
*$^1/_4$ teaspoon sugar, or a little more to taste*
*1 Seville or bitter orange, unpeeled, sliced, seeds removed*

Heat the oil over medium heat in a heavy-bottomed skillet. Add the garlic and sauté over medium heat until it begins to color. Add the tomatoes, salt and pepper to taste, and sugar, and simmer uncovered for 10 minutes. Add the orange and continue to simmer for 20 minutes. Do not cook for much longer than this as the sauce will become bitter. Remove from the heat and taste for seasoning. Remove the orange slices if you wish. Serve hot or cold.

SERVES: 6

*Tomato, Garlic, and Orange Sauce; Fried Eggs with Eggplant and Tomato*

PETER JOHNSON

## *Oeufs à la Catalane*

*Fried Eggs with Eggplant and Tomato*

This dish can be served as a main dish or as a starter. Serve one egg per person as a starter, two for a main dish.

*2 medium-sized eggplants (aubergines), cut in thin lengthwise slices*
*salt*
*1/3 cup (3 fl oz/80 ml) olive oil*
*6 large garlic cloves, finely chopped*
*4 to 6 parsley sprigs, finely chopped*
*3 fairly large, firm, ripe tomatoes (depending on the number of eggs), halved crosswise*
*salt and freshly ground pepper*
*6 large eggs*

An hour or so before cooking, place the eggplant slices in a colander and sprinkle liberally with salt. Let stand 1 hour. Rinse well and pat dry with paper towels.

Heat 4 tablespoons olive oil over medium-high heat in a well-seasoned or nonstick skillet and brown the eggplant slices on both sides. Drain on paper towels, set aside and keep warm. Sprinkle with half the garlic and parsley.

Reduce the heat, add another tablespoon of oil to the skillet and place the tomatoes in it, cut side down. Cook over very low heat until they begin to "melt" but remove from the pan before they fall apart. Set aside, cut sides up, and keep warm. Sprinkle with salt and the remaining garlic and parsley.

Turn the heat up to medium-high. Fry the eggs in the remaining tablespoon of oil until the whites are set. Carefully remove from the pan with a spatula and place beside the tomato halves. Serve at once, with a slice or two of eggplant.

SERVES: 6

## *Omelette au Roquefort*

*Roquefort Omelette*

This rich, flat omelette is cooked in lard, which gives it a characteristic southwestern flavor. The ingredients here are based on those in a recipe in André Bonnaure's *La Cuisine en Languedoc.*

*12 large eggs*
*7 oz (220 g) good quality Roquefort*
*1 tablespoon Armagnac*
*salt and freshly ground pepper*
*1 tablespoon lard*
*1 to 2 tablespoons butter or olive oil*

Beat the eggs in a large bowl. Crumble in the Roquefort. Stir in the Armagnac and add salt and pepper. (Little salt will be needed as the cheese is quite salty.)

Heat the lard and 1 tablespoon of the butter or oil together in a 10 or 12-in (25 or 30-cm) well seasoned or nonstick skillet over medium-high heat. When the fat is sizzling, pour in the mixture. Shake the skillet gently and turn the heat down to medium-low. Cook the omelette, shaking the skillet and lifting the sides of the omelette every once in a while to let the mixture run under, for about 10 minutes, or until just about set.

Light the broiler (grill). Dot the top of the omelette with the additional tablespoon of butter, or drizzle on the remaining olive oil, if desired. Brown the omelette under the broiler for 1 or 2 minutes. Alternatively, you can slide the omelette out of the skillet onto a large plate when it has just about set, put it back into the skillet the other way up and cook another 2 minutes. Serve hot.

SERVES: 6

*Roquefort Omelette*

PETER JOHNSON

PETER JOHNSON

*Braised Chicken Legs with Lemon and Banyuls Wine*

## *Poulet au Citron à la Catalane*

*Braised Chicken Legs with Lemon and Banyuls Wine*

The fortified wine from Banyuls is what makes this a Catalan dish. In other parts of the Languedoc it is made with white wine. This is based on a recipe by Richard Olney.

*30 large, firm garlic cloves, unpeeled*
*4 cups (1 qt/1 l) chicken stock*
*6 chicken legs*
*salt and freshly ground pepper*
*3 tablespoons olive oil*
*1 tablespoon butter (or use all olive oil)*
*1½ large lemons, peeled, pith and seeds removed, sliced in thin rounds*
*2½ tablespoons all purpose (plain) flour*
*¾ cup (6 fl oz/180 ml) Banyuls wine*

Bring a large pot of water to a boil and blanch the garlic cloves for 30 seconds. Transfer to cold water, drain and remove the skins without crushing the cloves. Place the garlic and chicken stock in a saucepan and bring to a boil. Cover and simmer gently for 40 minutes.

Lightly season the chicken legs with salt and pepper. Heat the olive oil and butter together in a skillet. Add the chicken legs and brown them for 15 to 20 minutes, turning regularly so that they are evenly colored. Transfer to a large, heavy-bottomed casserole.

Strain the chicken stock and set aside. Scatter the garlic cloves over the chicken pieces, along with the lemon slices. Cover the casserole and set aside. Preheat the oven to 375°F (190°C).

Strain off most of the fat from the skillet, leaving about 2 or 3 tablespoons. Sprinkle in the flour and cook for 1 or 2 minutes over medium heat, stirring all the while with a wooden spoon, until the roux begins to brown. Add the Banyuls wine and deglaze, stirring constantly with a wooden spoon over high heat until the bottom of the pan is relatively clean. Whisk in the chicken stock and transfer to a small saucepan. Bring to a boil and simmer, skimming the fat off the top of the sauce, for 15 minutes. Taste for seasoning.

Pour the sauce over the chicken in the casserole and cover. Place in the oven and bake for 40 to 45 minutes. Taste for seasoning. Serve with rice, pasta, or potatoes.

SERVES: 6

## Boles de Picolat

*Catalan Meat Balls with Green Olive Sauce*

This tasty dish is a particular specialty of the Roussillon.

*8 oz (250 g) lean ground (minced) beef*
*1 lb (500 g)* botifarra *sausage or mild Italian sausage, casings removed, crumbled*
*4 to 6 garlic cloves, finely chopped or put through a press*
*1 to 2 tablespoons chopped parsley*
*pinch of thyme*
*salt and freshly ground pepper*
*2 eggs, beaten*
*4 tablespoons all purpose (plain) flour*
*2 tablespoons olive oil*
*4 oz (125 g) salt pork, diced*
*1 onion, chopped*
*1 large ripe tomato, peeled, seeded, and chopped, or 2 tablespoons tomato paste*
*2 oz (60 g) Bayonne ham or* prosciutto *(optional)*
*1 small dried red pepper, hot or sweet, crumbled*
*1 to 2 teaspoons cinnamon*
*½ teaspoon paprika*
*1½ cups (12 fl oz/310 ml) water*
*1¼ cups (6 oz/185 g) French green olives, rinsed and pitted*

Combine the ground beef, sausage, garlic, parsley, thyme, salt and pepper in a bowl. Stir in the beaten eggs and form golfball-sized meatballs, about 1½ in (4 cm) in diameter. Roll lightly in flour.

Heat the olive oil over medium heat in a large, heavy-bottomed casserole and add the salt pork. Cook until it has released a good amount of fat then remove from the casserole and discard. Brown the meatballs in the oil and fat then drain on paper towels.

Reduce heat to low and add the onion to the casserole. Cook, stirring, until tender, and sprinkle with the remaining flour. Mix thoroughly, cook for about 30 seconds, stirring, then add the tomato, optional ham, red pepper, cinnamon, paprika, and water. Mix well and bring to a simmer. Add the meatballs and olives. If the sauce does not just cover the meatballs, add a little more water. Cover and cook for 30 to 45 minutes over low heat. The sauce should become thick. Taste for seasoning. Serve, with cooked white beans on the side.

SERVES: 6

## Agneau en Pistache

*Rolled Shoulder of Lamb with Garlic*

There are many versions of this Catalan dish, one of which is similar to *cassoulet* (see page 126), with the lamb cubed and cooked with sausage and beans. "*En pistache*" means cooked with garlic, and it certainly is, but the garlic becomes mild and sweet with the long cooking.

*1 shoulder of lamb, boned, rolled, and trimmed of fat*
*2 tablespoons olive oil, goose fat, or lard*
*2 slices Bayonne ham or* prosciutto*, diced*
*1 large onion, chopped*
*1 large carrot, sliced*
*3 garlic bulbs (about 50 cloves), unpeeled*
*1 cup (8 fl oz/250 ml) dry white wine*
*1 cup (8 fl oz/250 ml) chicken or meat stock*
*bouquet garni: 1 bay leaf, 1 thyme sprig, 3 parsley sprigs, 1 sprig rosemary or celery leaves, 1 strip dried orange peel*
*salt and freshly ground pepper*

Peel the garlic by lightly pounding the cloves with the flat side of a jar or knife. The skins will pop off and the garlic will remain relatively intact. Preheat the oven to 350°F (180°C).

Over medium heat, heat the olive oil or fat in a casserole that will accommodate the lamb. Brown the lamb on all sides and remove from the casserole. Add the ham, onion, carrot, and garlic and cook, stirring, over medium-low heat for about 5 minutes, until the onion is tender. Pour in the wine and stir the mixture to deglaze the pan. Bring to a boil and reduce by a quarter. Add the stock, bouquet garni, and a little salt and pepper. Push the vegetables to one side and return the lamb to the casserole.

Cover the casserole tightly and bake in the oven for 1 to 1½ hours, until the meat is tender.

Transfer the meat to a warm serving platter and carve. Remove the bouquet garni from the sauce. Mash the garlic to thicken the sauce or purée the sauce in a blender. Taste for seasoning, heat through, and serve with the lamb.

SERVES: 6 to 8

*Cassoulet, Catalan Meat Balls with Green Olive Sauce, Rolled Shoulder of Lamb with Garlic*

PETER JOHNSON

## Cassoulet

Everyone in the Languedoc who makes this dish feels passionately that theirs is the authentic version, and every recipe is different. The amount given here serves a crowd, but leftovers are good.

*Beans:*
*1½ lb (750 g) dried white beans*
*8 oz (250 g) fresh pork rind with fat, cut into strips*
*8 oz (250 g) salt pork, diced*
*1 large onion stuck with 6 cloves*
*4 large garlic cloves, finely chopped*
*2 carrots, sliced*
*bouquet garni: 2 bay leaves, 1 stick of celery, 3 thyme sprigs, 3 parsley sprigs*
*salt and freshly ground pepper*
Cassoulet:
*2 legs duck or goose* confit *(optional)*
*4 tablespoons drippings from the* confit, *or lard or bacon drippings*
*1 lb (500 g) boned shoulder of lamb, cut into 2-in (5-cm) cubes*
*8 oz (250 g) lean pork, cut into 2-in (5-cm) cubes*
*6 garlic cloves, finely chopped*
*2 medium to large onions, chopped*
*1 lb (500 g) garlic sausage, halved lengthwise and cut into 3-in (8-cm) lengths*
*2 large tomatoes, chopped, or an 8-oz (250-g) can of tomatoes*
*8 oz (250 g) dried spicy garlic sausage, halved lengthwise and sliced (optional)*
*salt and freshly ground pepper*
*3 tablespoons fresh breadcrumbs*

For the beans: Soak the beans overnight, or for at least 6 hours in cold water. Drain.

Place the pork rind in a saucepan, cover with water and bring to a simmer. Simmer for 10 minutes and remove from the heat. Take the rind from the water, run under cold water until cool enough to handle, then roll up and secure with string.

Combine the beans with the pork rind and the rest of the ingredients for the beans in a large heavy-bottomed saucepan. Cover by 2 in (5 cm) with water and bring to a boil. Skim off any scum which rises. Reduce heat, cover and cook for 1 hour, until the beans are just cooked but not mushy. Remove from the heat and discard the onion and bouquet garni. Remove the pork rind and allow to cool. Untie and cut into large pieces. Strain off the liquid from the beans and retain.

For the *cassoulet*: Put the *confit* in a pot of warm water to melt the fat. Take out the legs and remove the meat from the bones.

Heat 4 tablespoons of the fat and brown the lamb. Remove with a slotted spoon and set aside. Add the pork and half the garlic, and brown. Remove with a slotted spoon and set aside. Fry the onions with the remaining garlic until golden. Remove from the heat and pour off the remaining fat into a bowl.

Brown the fresh sausage on the cut side in a little fat. Remove from heat. Preheat the oven to 275°F (140°C).

Lay the pork rind in a large, heavy-bottomed, preferably earthenware casserole, fat side down (the skin side will stick). Place one-third of the beans in a layer over the pork rind. Layer half the meats, with half the onions, garlic, and tomatoes, and top with half the fresh and dried sausage. Layer another third of the beans over the meat, and layer the remaining meats, vegetables, then sausage, over the beans. The top layer should be the final third of the beans. Taste the cooking liquid from the beans and add salt if necessary, and some pepper. Pour over the mixture so that it barely covers the beans. Sprinkle with breadcrumbs and drizzle 2 tablespoons of the fat poured off from the meat over the top.

Place in the oven and bake 1½ to 2 hours. If the *cassoulet* dries out during cooking, add a small amount of boiling water or stock. By the end of the cooking it should have a good crust.

Remove from the oven and serve from the casserole with a green salad.

SERVES: 10

## Biscotins

*Crisp Orange Cookies*

These delicately flavored cookies are much like Italian *biscotti.*

*3 eggs*
*½ cup (4 oz/125 g) sugar*
*2 tablespoons orangeflower water*
*grated peel of 1 large orange*
*2½ cups (10 oz/300 g) sifted all purpose (plain) flour*
*½ teaspoon baking powder*
*¼ teaspoon salt*
*1 egg white, lightly beaten*

Preheat the oven to 375°F (190°C). Lightly butter a baking sheet, and dust with flour. Beat together the eggs and sugar. Add the orangeflower water and orange peel. Sift together 2¼ cups of the flour, the baking powder, and salt, and gradually add the egg and sugar mixture.

Using the remaining flour to dust the board and your hands, scrape the dough, which will be sticky, from the bowl and knead for a few minutes, adding flour as necessary. Divide the dough in half and shape into two logs, about 2 in (5 cm) in diameter. Place on the baking sheet and brush with the beaten egg white.

Bake the logs in the oven for 20 minutes and then remove. Turn the heat down to 275°F (140°C). Slice the logs on the diagonal into ¼-in (5-mm) thick rounds. Place on the baking sheet. Return to the oven and bake for another 40 minutes, until the cookies are lightly browned. Remove from the oven and cool on racks.

MAKES: 45 to 50 cookies

## Flan Catalan

*Catalan Custard*

A traditional *flan catalan* has burnt sugar on top, but there are now versions without topping, like this one. It comes from Collioure via Patricia Wells, with alterations.

*1⅓ cups (11 fl oz/340 ml) milk*
*1 cup (8 fl oz/250 ml) half-and-half, or an additional ½ cup (4 fl oz/125 ml) milk plus ½ cup (4 fl oz/125 ml) cream*
*1 tablespoon fennel seeds, crushed*
*1 vanilla bean, split in half*
*⅓ cup (3 oz/90 g) sugar*
*3 large egg yolks*
*grated peel of 1 lemon and ½ orange*

Combine the milk, half-and-half and fennel seeds in a saucepan and bring to a simmer. Remove from the heat at once and let stand for at least 30 minutes. Preheat the oven to 350°F (180°C).

Scrape the seeds out of the vanilla bean and combine with the sugar. (Keep the pod for other uses.) Beat the eggs and sugar with a whisk until thick. Stir in the peel. Strain in the milk mixture (discard the fennel seeds), beating all the while.

Pour the mixture into six cup-sized ramekins, cover with aluminium foil and bake in a bain-marie in the oven for 30 minutes, or until just set. Remove from the heat, uncover and allow to cool completely, then chill in the refrigerator.

SERVES: 6

*Catalan Custard, Crisp Orange Cookies*

PETER JOHNSON

Périgueux
Brive-la-Gaillarde
Rouffignac
Lascaux
Périgord
Les Eyzies-de-Tayac
Dordogne
Saint-Cyprien
Souillac
Aurillac
Lalinde
Sarlat
Bergerac
La Roque Gageac
Domme
Rocamadour
Beaumont de Périgord
Eymet
Monpazier
Lot
Cahors
Saint-Cirq-Lapopie
Lalbenque
Quercy
Rodez
Agen
Tarn
Montauban
Condom
Albi
Armagnac
Auch
Toulouse
Castres
Gascogne
Béziers
Garonne
Carcassonne
Narbonne
Foix
Pyrénées
Perpignan

# THE CENTRAL SOUTHWEST

Diane Holuigue

A neat geographical unit bordered by Spain and the waters of the Atlantic and the Mediterranean, the southwest corner of France is the home of the Basques, the Gascons, and the Provençals. While the traditional dishes of these people have little in common, a line drawn north-south down the center of the region links the ancient provinces of Périgord, Quercy, and Gascony (roughly equivalent to the departments of the Dordogne, the Lot, and the Gers) which together form one of the country's most definable gastronomic entities. For this is goose territory — France's *foie gras* country. It is here that most of the geese and ducks force-fed for *foie gras* are raised.

Goose fat as a cooking medium defines the region's cuisine as a whole, while local products dictate the dishes and the detail. And there is a rich array of produce to be found here. Périgord and Quercy together yield all but a tiny percentage of France's truffles. The town of Agen is known internationally for its superlative prunes, although it is also widely associated in France with all manner of fruit trees — pears, apples, and cherries — and spring vegetables, known as *primeurs*. Strawberries are now grown widely, and walnuts have long been a staple. In the south Quercy ranks second only to the Pyrenees in lamb breeding, and small farms across all three provinces raise pigs. Game such as venison and hare can still be found, particularly in the forested areas of Gascony and the neighboring province of Landes, and wild mushrooms are plentiful, particularly *cèpes* and morels.

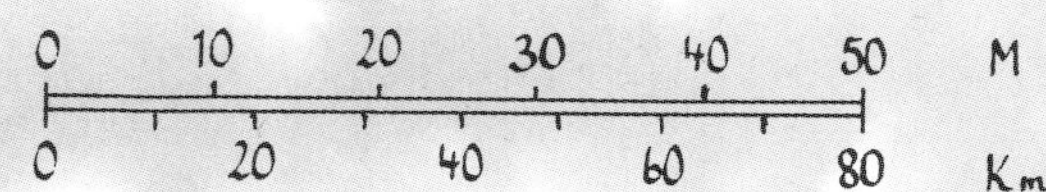

BRUNO BARBEY/MAGNUM

*A couple busy harvesting grapes near Cadillac in the Dordogne, on the right bank of the Garonne river. Sweet wines are made from grapes such as these.*

To accompany the produce, the region boasts high quality wines from the vineyards of Cahors, in the Lot valley, and Bergerac, on the Dordogne. The red wines of Cahors are dark and powerful, as are those of Madiran, in the Gers. The communes of the Bergerac region produce a variety of wines, among them the great sweet white wine of Monbazillac. The undulating hills to the west of the Gascon capital of Auch produce Armagnac, one of the great brandies of the world. The local aperitif, Floc de Gascogne, is a light liqueured wine made from unfermented grape juice fortified with young Armagnac, and aged in oak for two to three years. *Eau-de-vie de prunes*, distilled from freshly picked plums, is a staple of the farms of the area, and many a farmer makes their own *eau-de-vie de noix* from green walnuts. There is also a rough, bitter aperitif called Quinquina made from the leaves of the walnut tree macerated in white wine.

## Mountains and Gorges

The three provinces boast some of the most beautiful and varied countryside in all France. Here the Massif Central descends to the soft, undulating hillsides of Gascony, which in turn lead to the mountainous Pyrenees and the border with Spain. Rivers tumbling down from the central plateau over the ages have carved a landscape of spectacular gorges, above which perch castles and towns. Prior to the Hundred Years War there were said to be as many as one thousand castles standing on Périgord's rocky heights.

The Dordogne is one of the country's longest rivers, and from its source high in the Massif Central it dashes wildly between cliffs and wooded limestone gorges, becoming calmer by the time it reaches the beautiful Medieval town of Souillac. Here it is sufficiently tame and wide to be navigable, and over the centuries the people of Souillac established a flourishing trade network based on the river. Heavily laden barges used to trade downstream in timber, and on their return from the Atlantic they would bring coffee, sugar, rum, and salt. When the railways were built, such river traffic ceased. Nowadays you can rent a canoe in Cénac-et-Saint-Julien and paddle with the swiftly flowing current past towering cliffs and enchanting villages like La Roque Gageac and Beynac, and return the canoe several breathtaking miles further downstream at Saint-Cyprien.

## Traces of the Stone Age

The limestone rock of Périgord and Quercy is so porous that underground torrents are nearly as numerous as the rivers above, and the region is studded with a vast network of caves and subterranean springs. The giant Gouffre de Padirac with its vaulted grotto and magnificent stalagmites and stalagtites is one of Quercy's major attractions. In part a visit has to be made by boat, and torch-bearing guides help visitors negotiate the pathways that wind over several levels beside the high rock walls, tracing with their lights such forms as a bison's back or a mammal's tusk, etched into the rock by people of the stone age.

There are more than two hundred prehistoric sites in the Périgord region, of which more than half are in the valley of the Vézère near the village of Les Eyzies-de-Tayac. The walls of caves and rock shelters are covered with numerous paintings of animals, such as mammoths, horses, and charging bison, sometimes pierced by spears and arrows, and in places there are outlines of human hands.

*Opposite: High on a cliff above the Dordogne river stands the castle of Beynac, an outstanding example of thirteenth-century military architecture.*

LEO MEIER/WELDON TRANNIES

LEO MEIER

Fascinating examples can be seen at Rouffignac, Font-de-Gaume, and Pech-Merle, but the best known cave paintings of all are those at Lascaux, which were painted with consummate skill. This cave, discovered in 1940 by some boys chasing a dog, has been closed for twenty years because of damage caused by lighting and air-conditioning, but a facsimile, known as Lascaux 2, has recently been constructed nearby.

In 1868, when the railway was being built from Sarlat to Les Eyzies-de-Tayac, workmen unearthed a number of skeletons in a rock shelter at Cro-Magnon. These were found to be at least 40 000 years old. Scientists consider Cro-Magnon man to be the first evidence of *Homo sapiens* — today's humans. This discovery, along with numerous other subsequent finds of skeletons, tools, and jewelry, and the many cave paintings in the region, has led to the area being known as the capital of prehistory. The National Museum of Prehistory, which is in a thirteenth-century castle overlooking Les Eyzies, contains a wide variety of exhibits discovered locally over the last eighty or so years.

The Medieval fortified town of Rocamadour, perched high on a cliff above the Alzou river, was once one of the principal places of pilgrimage in Christendom, and is another great attraction for visitors. Its fortified gate, the only entrance to the town, is followed by a single narrow street now lined with tourist shops. On the highest level, up a great many steps which pilgrims once ascended on their knees, stands the fort and the Chapel of Notre-Dame, which houses the famous statue of the Black Madonna. From the ramparts of the fort, which are situated above a vertical drop, there is a remarkable view of the tiered buildings of the town lying below and the vast, rocky panorama beyond.

East of Cahors lies the equally enchanting town of Saint-Cirq-Lapopie, perched high on a rocky escarpment above the river Lot. This tiny town has scarcely changed since Medieval days. Its stone houses, with their brown rooftops and high-walled gardens, cluster together along the narrow, sloping streets. A path leads to the ruins of the castle on the cliff top above the town, from which there is a breathtaking view.

Among the more remarkable features of Gascony and Périgord are the *bastides*, feudal villages built in the thirteenth century to identical grid plans by both the French and the English. They were established for economic and political reasons on uncultivated land that was suitable for farming, and prospective inhabitants were encouraged to come and build the towns with the offer of various privileges, grants of land, and protection. During the Hundred Years War many of the *bastides* were fortified, but even so many of them changed hands as fighting ranged over the region. Domme, Lalinde, Monpazier, and Eymet are the most interesting *bastides* to visit, being the ones that are best preserved, and Beaumont du Périgord, built in the shape of an "H" in memory of Henry III of England, Duke of Aquitaine, also merits a detour.

Sarlat, a jewel in the crown of French Medieval towns, attracts tourists in their thousands during the summer and is a major commercial center for the farmers of the Dordogne. Its Saturday market is a lively affair. Centered around a sixteenth-century cathedral, the city, with its steep roads and alleys, is still largely contained within its Medieval walls. Many beautiful Renaissance houses built of honey-colored stone remain — homes of the city's wealthy merchants. It has featured in many films, including the Hollywood version of Dumas' *The Three Musketeers*. The celebrated d'Artagnan in fact came from neighboring Gascony.

*Opposite: Most farms in the region grow a little tobacco. Here a crop of tobacco leaves hangs in a drying shed.*

*Ducks, geese and* foie gras *feature prominently at the Sarlat market, and the customers are most discerning.*

JEAN-PAUL FERRERO/AUSCAPE INTERNATIONAL

## Small Family Farms

Although conditions in this part of the country are favorable for farming, and over 70 per cent of the region's production is agricultural, the rural sector is poorly developed. In the sixteenth century a system of *métayage*, share cropping, was set up, which has only recently died out. Farmers would work the landowner's land in return for a proportion of the harvest, and to ensure that they each had an equal share both of fertile and less productive soil, the land was divided into small parcels. This has resulted in small plots of land being passed from generation to generation, and in holdings of multiple separate parcels of land stemming from several inheritances. Small farms do not warrant mechanization or capital investment, and therefore rarely prove profitable. In recent years the government has been encouraging landowners to exchange their small plots of land with one another, to consolidate their holdings, and has also promoted the planting of cash crops, particularly tobacco.

Most farms breed a few pigs and chickens, and grow a little corn and tobacco, leaving a corner for some walnut trees and a few oaks from which they hope to gather truffles. The walnut harvest is in September, and most of the crop is made into oil. Sarlat is the largest walnut growing center in France, and it is here that much of the pressing and canning of the oil is done.

Some of the most intensively cultivated fields in the area are where the grape vines for Armagnac grow, although here too holdings are relatively small, as they are in the Gascon wine areas. Most of the winemaking is done by cooperatives in order to make the best use of expensive equipment.

*Sprinklers send up clouds of spray around a farm laborer walking through a field of poppies in the Dordogne.*

JOE MCNALLY/COLORIFIC!

# BLACK DIAMONDS

Known as the black diamond of gastronomy, the black truffle is a ball-like subterranean fungus, roughly the size of a walnut, and those gathered in the Périgord and Quercy are the most highly esteemed in France. Although research is being done into possible cultivation, the world market still depends almost entirely upon farmers harvesting truffles that grow wild on their own lands.

Truffles grow on the roots of oak trees, and are found between November and March. Their presence is said to be indicated by a drying off of the grass around the base of the tree or the presence of a certain sort of fly. At the foot of likely trees, the hunter sets to work with a dog or pig trained to scent out mature truffles. Once the animal starts to dig it is given a tasty morsel to divert it, and the truffle is unearthed with a minimum of digging to avoid disturbing any future growths.

Regular markets in townships such as Cahors and Lalbenque, and annual fairs account for about 70 per cent of French truffle supplies. Nowadays, truffle markets in the smaller villages are fast disappearing, for despite the tuber's ability to command high prices, supplies are on the decline.

At these markets, bargaining is highly skilled. The sellers are often astute peasant grandmothers dressed in their black Sunday best, complete with hat and large handbag. One by one the truffles are taken from the handbag and closely examined. Scarcely a word is exchanged. Prices penciled on pieces of paper are passed back and forth between seller and purchaser until agreement is reached, and then the truffles change hands.

Most of the world's truffle production ends up in small, expensive cans, after brushing and sterilizing (cooking). Buyers should check labeling for both quality and grading. Styles of canning are as follows: *truffes brossées*, whole and cleaned; *truffes pelées*, whole and peeled; *truffes en*

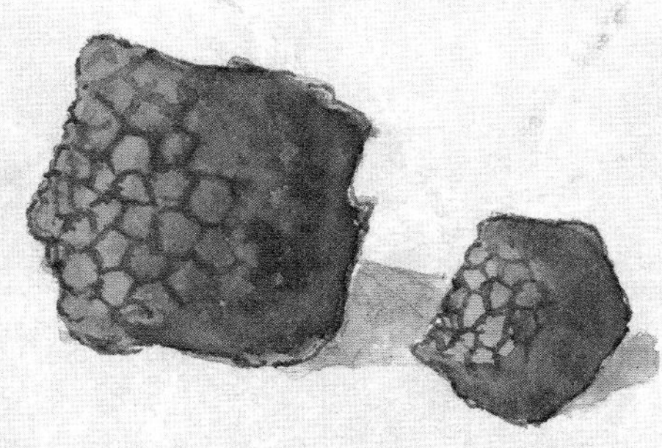

*morceaux*, pieces; *truffes en pellures*, peelings, bits; *truffes préparées*, *eau-de-vie*, brandy, or wine added; *truffes au naturel*, only water and salt added. The best distributors sterilize their truffles only once, and this should be credited on the can.

Good distributors also supply fresh truffles. Only mature ones, with good color and aroma, are sold fresh. They are brushed, packed in tiny plaited straw boxes, and air-freighted direct to the buyers, usually top ranking restaurants, like little treasures. Great chefs recommend that they be cooked simply, in recipes designed to bring out their natural perfume and texture. Preferred are methods in which the truffle is encased in puff pastry, bread dough, clay, or even rock salt compacted with egg white, and then baked in the oven or *sous les cendres*, under the coals. The cooked package is then taken to the table and broken open before the diner, so that the truffle's heady aroma can be appreciated to the full.

Modern chefs use the truffles in a myriad of ways from spooning a purée into a soft-boiled egg, through soups and salads. They have even been known to make truffle ice-creams. The people of the truffle region, however, will generally offer you their beloved tubers with scrambled eggs, and will insist that the truffles are left to rest in the egg basket for a few days beforehand, so that their aroma can permeate the eggshells for added effect.

*A truffle hunter sets out with his pig. Hardly a farm in Périgord or Quercy is without a stand of oak trees, as it is on their roots that the elusive truffle grows.*

BRUNO BARBEY/MAGNUM

LEO MEIER

*Ducks taking to the water. Because geese can be difficult to handle, a growing number of farmers are using ducks for* foie gras.

## GEESE, DUCKS, AND FOIE GRAS

The breeding of geese and ducks for the *foie gras* industry is also in the hands of small, family farms. Throughout the summer the birds wander around in the open, feeding on grass and weeds, but come the autumn they are put in pens and force-fed on corn so that their livers become plump. The traditional method by which they are fattened, known as *le gavage,* is to take each bird firmly between the knees, insert a funnel into its beak, and with one hand massaging its neck, while murmuring encouraging sounds, entice it to swallow the corn. The famous, large Toulouse geese of the region consume around 2 pounds (1 kilogram) of corn a day, but they can be quite hard to handle, and in many cases have been replaced by ducks.

Nowadays, most farms have upgraded their *gavage* with a simple mechanized system into which the geese or ducks are harnessed. Above the perches hang a series of funnels connected to a feed belt which allows a certain amount of food per minute to run through them. The farmers still insert the funnels individually, but the process is more efficient than hand feeding.

Many farmers preserve the *foie gras*, using either a simple canning system, or spring-lidded preserving jars. Sometimes truffles and Armagnac or Port are added to enhance the flavor of the rich, satin-textured flesh. Much of this home produce is then sold direct from the farms, or at the local markets, while some is sent to the larger cities. Professional companies, based largely in Sarlat, Périgueux, and Cahors, can a range of pâtés, *foies gras*, truffles, soups, oils, and local mushrooms for international sales. Only a relatively small number of people are employed in the canning industry, but they account for a good deal of the region's export earnings.

## BY-PRODUCTS OF THE FOIE GRAS INDUSTRY

A by-product of the *foie gras* industry, and over-fatty from the way it was bred, the goose itself is not very good for roasting and cannot be sold outside the area. The fat, however, is used to fry almost anything from fish to desserts, and every other part of the bird is also put to good use. The rind, crisped in its own fat, goes into many a soup pot for flavor. It is also chopped into little crisp offerings called *grelots*. These are generally mixed with chopped shallots, and served as a crunchy accompaniment to an aperitif.

The breast of goose, known as the *magret* for its contrasting leanness, and the even more flavorful breast of duck, is either roasted or sautéed, and is eaten rare like beef. Recent developments in vacuum packing have enabled local fattened duck breasts to find markets elsewhere in France, and overseas as well. This has created a penchant for rare, fanned-out slices of duck breast on the tables of many esteemed restaurants worldwide.

The limbs, along with the gizzards, are generally preserved by cooking for several hours, very slowly, in the rendered fat. This is the famous *confit* — *confit d'oie*, *confit de canard,* or *gésiers confits* — one of the principal local dishes. The *confit* is traditionally placed in large earthenware crocks, covered with the clarified fat, and then stored in the cool under the house. Even if it is not to be stored, *confit* tastes considerably better if it has been kept for at least a week before being eaten.

*Opposite: Following an age-old recipe, this elderly woman is preparing goose* confit. *The meat is simmered for several hours in goose fat then stored, in the fat, in earthenware pots.*

FRANCOIS PERRI/COSMOS

## Armagnac

Among brandies, second only in age to Calvados, and many years older than Cognac, it is surprising that pungent, flavorful Armagnac has been so little recognized beyond its region of production.

Armagnac is made from grapes grown in the Gers, the Landes and the Lot-et-Garonne, principally from Ugni Blanc, Folle Blanche, and Colombard grapes. The *appellation contrôlée* divides the production area into three districts: the Haut Armagnac, Ténarèze, and Bas Armagnac. The principal centers are Auch for the Haut Armagnac, Condom for Ténarèze, and Eauze for Bas Armagnac, and all boast markets at which local brandies are tasted and sold.

In contrast with the great Cognac merchants, Armagnac distillation is still in the hands of small companies, with much of it produced and sold by the growers themselves. Quality and styles vary considerably, and it has a somewhat less refined, more earthy taste than its younger brother.

After distillation, the brandy is aged in oak casks, which give it its characteristic color and flavor. It is then sold in flat, round, long-necked bottles known as Basque bottles, or in green wine bottles, the label generally stating the region of origin, the maker's name, and the year of distillation. Many distillers also sell fruit bottled in Armagnac.

ADAM WOOLFITT/SUSAN GRIGGS AGENCY

## Taking Soup Seriously

The staple of the region is soup. In the hearty, rustic, peasant diet of the Gascon, soup is taken very seriously. *Bougras* is a soup made in the pig-slaughtering season, just before Lent. The water in which blood pudding has been cooked forms its base, and root vegetables, cabbage, and potatoes are added to give it thickness. Bean soups, cabbage soups, and broths of all sorts are common, and a particular regional touch is often provided by the addition of what is known as *fricassée*. This is made from a mixture of vegetables, removed from the broth after cooking. They are chopped, tossed in flour, and then sautéed in goose fat before being returned to the pot. Broths are often poured over slices of stale white bread placed in the plate or the soup tureen. This is typical of *soupe aux abats,* turkey or goose giblet soup, and of *tourin périgordin*, an onion and tomato soup thickened with egg yolks. The *tourin gascon* is a puréed onion soup made with a good deal of garlic, and is generally served with stuffed goose neck.

The *garbure*, a dish of Gascony and the Béarne, is both a soup and a whole meal, for the broth is made using a piece of salt pork, a chicken and some *confit*, and as many whole vegetables as are in season. The broth is served first, followed by the meat and vegetables as a main course, and the ritual finish, known locally as the *chabrot,* is to leave a little of the broth in the plate and swill it out with red wine. The *mique* was once the traditional accompaniment, but it is now going out of style. This yeast dumpling was boiled in the broth like a pudding, then drained and served separately like bread.

*"A la périgordine"* denotes a dish of a certain sophistication that has been built on the foundations of a peasant recipe. The added allure is provided by the addition of a truffle or the combination of *foie gras* and truffles. *Oeufs à la périgordine* is a dish of eggs stuffed with *foie gras*, and *cou d'oie farci à la périgordine* is goose neck with the skin filled with minced pork and goose flesh, *foie gras*, and chopped truffle. *Poulet périgordine* is chicken stuffed with *foie gras* and truffles flavored with Cognac, and the famous *sauce périgueux* is a rich brown sauce enriched with truffles, truffle juice, and Madeira.

The people of the southwest make great use of the game of the area, such as small birds, venison, rabbit, and hare, and the fish of the local rivers and ponds, most often carp and trout. This supplements the annual killing of the pig, the meat of which is also stored in its own fat as a *confit*, with some pieces salted and the fattier portions used for pâtés and sausages. Lamb that is raised in the area is usually regarded as a saleable commodity and thus too great a luxury to be used for domestic consumption.

Local fruits feature in tarts and flans, particularly apples, pears, and stone fruit. There is a version of the Limousin-style *clafoutis*, made with both cherries and prunes, and the name Jacques in this part of the country often refers to a type of apple pancake. The *flagnarde aux pruneaux* is a melting blend of dried fruits embedded in a creamy baked custard, and the *millou* or *millassou* is a thick baked custard flan, often cooked with apples.

The best known apple dessert is the *pastis*. Its extremely fine pastry is reminiscent of the pastry of Moroccan *pastilla,* a pigeon pie flavored with cinnamon and sugar, suggesting that it originated with the Moorish invasion of southern France. The *pastis* is flavored with orangeflower water and Armagnac or rum, with no hint of the anise-based liqueur called Pastis. In the Landes, however, to the west, there is a high, domed cake resembling a kugelhopf that is flavored with Pastis, which carries the same name. Gastronomic terminology is not easily settled in this part of France. If you ask the older people in various villages the difference between a *tourtière*, a *croustade,* and a *pastis* you will stimulate heated debate and considerable confusion.

As for cheeses, the best known in the region are Bleu des Causses, a cow's milk cheese similar to Bleu d'Auvergne, and the tiny goat's milk cheese from Quercy, known as Cabécou. Cabécou can be eaten fresh, or at various stages of ripening, and occasionally mature ones macerated in *eau-de-vie de prunes* can be found, which provide a rare and most delicious treat.

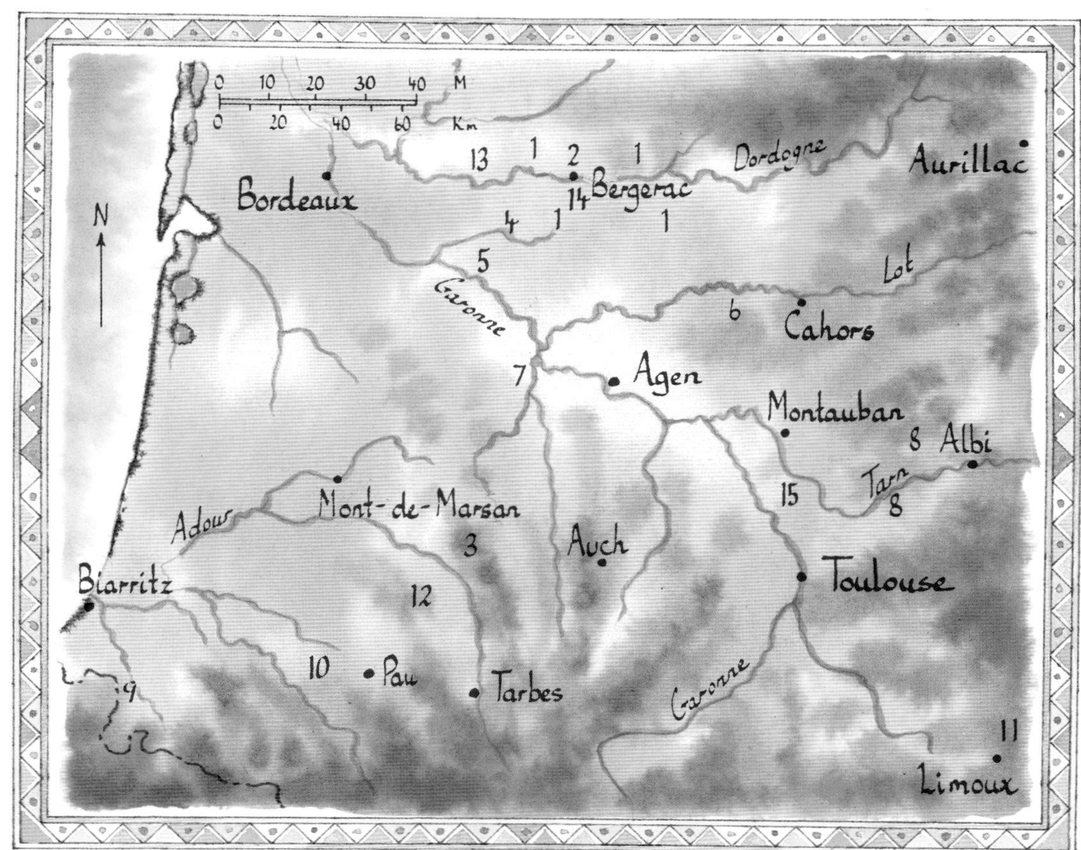


*Opposite: A hearty lunch and a bottle of local wine is provided for these grape pickers during harvest-time.*

## THE CENTRAL SOUTHWEST

*A kaleidoscopic array of wine styles permeate this region. In the north, the grapes of Bordeaux dominate; in the south, obscure local varieties are used.*

*The following districts produce mainly red and dry white wines:*

*Bergerac (1)*
*Cahors (6)*
*Côtes de Bergerac (1)*
*Côtes de Buzet (7)*
*Côtes de Duras (4)*
*Côtes de Saint-Mont (3)*
*Côtes du Frontonnais (15)*
*Côtes du Marmandais VDQS (5)*
*Gaillac (8)*
*Irouléguy (9)*
*Limoux (11)*
*Madiran (12)*
*Pécharmant (2)*

*Principal sweet white wines:*

*Côtes de Bergerac Moelleux (1)*
*Côtes de Montravel (13)*
*Gaillac Doux (8)*
*Jurançon (10)*
*Monbazillac (14)*
*Pacherenc du Vic-Bilh (12)*

*Sparkling wines include:*

*Blanquette de Limoux (11)*
*Gaillac Mousseux (8)*

PETER JOHNSON

## *Omelette aux Cèpes*

*Cèpe Omelette*

Possibly the meatiest of all the wild mushrooms, the large flat *cèpe* is found in abundance in southwestern France. This omelette is a regional treasure. More than a recipe, it is a tradition.

*4 oz (125 g)* cèpes (porcini *mushrooms) or other large field mushrooms, washed, trimmed, and cut into chunks*
*2 tablespoons butter or goose fat*
*2 tablespoons chopped parsley*
*5 large eggs*
*salt and freshly ground pepper*
*1 tablespoon water*

Heat half the butter in a 10-in (25-cm) omelette pan and fry the mushrooms for 2 minutes, or until softened. Add parsley, stir, then set aside on a plate. Break the eggs into a bowl. Add salt and pepper to taste, and the water.

Heat the omelette pan well, particularly the curved edge opposite the handle, then add the remaining butter. Quickly stir the eggs with a fork, then pour into the pan. Continue forking the eggs through with a scrambling motion until they start to firm (about 20 seconds), then, with the fork, spread them out so that they fill the bottom of the pan.

Lay the mushrooms in a line along the center of the omelette. The eggs will now have cooked a little on the base and will hold their shape. Carefully lift one corner of the omelette and fold one-third of it towards the center, over the mushrooms. The skilled Gascon cook now leans the pan forward and taps her wrist so that the folded omelette is shaken over to the far side of the pan, directly opposite the handle. If it does not slip easily it can be pushed with the back of the fork. When the side of the omelette protrudes over the lip of the pan, fold this third back over the mushrooms.

Finish the cooking with the omelette nestling in the curve of the pan, where it will take on the characteristic omelette shape. Grasping the handle of the pan firmly, invert the omelette onto a warmed plate. Serve immediately. It should still be moist in the center.

SERVES: 2

*Broad Bean Soup,*
*Cèpe Omelette,*
*Salad of Mixed Greens with Foie Gras*

## Salade au Foie Gras

*Salad of Mixed Greens with Foie Gras*

The immense appeal of this modern presentation derives from the vinaigrette offsetting the richness of the *foie gras*. Enhanced with truffle, this simple combination enters the realm of the sublime.

This type of salad is served as a first course, never after the main course.

*about 6 cups mixed salad greens, such as butterhead (cabbage) lettuce, oakleaf, mignonette,* radicchio, *chicory (curly endive), lamb's lettuce, and coral lettuce*
*12 to 16 walnut halves*
*2 tablespoons olive oil for frying*
*8 oz (250 g) fresh* foie gras *(if using canned, it must be served cold, therefore ignore frying instructions)*
*1 small canned truffle, sliced (optional)*
*Vinaigrette:*
*1 cup (8 fl oz/250 ml) walnut oil*
*$^1/_4$ cup (2 fl oz/60 ml) red wine vinegar*
*salt and freshly ground pepper*

Place the salad greens in a bowl. Add the walnuts. Heat the olive oil in a small skillet and sauté the *foie gras* over high heat until lightly browned, but only just heated through. Remove and slice thinly.

Place the vinaigrette ingredients in a jar and shake well to combine. Scatter the warm *foie gras* through the greens, and the truffle slices (if using). Dress with the vinaigrette and toss. Divide amongst the six plates and serve immediately.

SERVES: 6

## Soupe aux Fèves

*Broad Bean Soup*

This simple soup is a great favorite in Gascony and Quercy in early spring. The larger beans tend to give the soup a grey-brown color and chefs suggest peeling the beans after hulling, but the country cook, keen on flavor and not fashion, rarely goes through this tiresome procedure.

*$^1/_4$ cup (2 fl oz/60 ml) goose fat or oil*
*7 oz (220 g) fresh pork rind, finely diced*
*4 garlic cloves, finely chopped*
*2 onions, chopped*
*8 lb (4 kg) broad beans, shelled (yielding about 1 lb/500 g beans)*
*1 small leek, washed and roughly sliced*
*water or chicken stock to cover the beans*
*salt and freshly ground pepper*

In a large pot, heat the fat and sauté the pork rind for about 30 seconds. Add the garlic and onion and continue to cook, turning, for a further 30 seconds. Add the beans and toss for a moment, then add the leek. Cover with water and season with salt and pepper. Bring to a boil, reduce heat and simmer gently for $1^1/_2$ to 2 hours.

Check seasoning and serve piping hot. A common variation places pieces of shredded omelette in each bowl, onto which the soup is ladled. The soup makes a light meal when served in this way.

SERVES: 6

## Garbure

*Gascon Vegetable Soup*

This is the southwestern version of the robust country meal-in-a-pot soups that are found throughout France. The use of salt pork as the meat base and the addition of pieces of *confit* of duck or goose are what gives the dish its regional character.

The ritual finish for old timers is to leave a spoonful or two of the broth in their plate and then to swill it out with a little red wine. This is known in the local *patois* as *le chabrot*, but the custom is now dying out.

*Gascon Vegetable Soup, Soup Dumpling Quercy Style*

PETER JOHNSON

*1 lb (500 g) salt (pickled) pork*
*1 ham bone*
*10 oz (300 g) ham pieces*
*8 cups (2 qt/2 l) water*
*1 cup (7 oz/220 g) dried white beans, soaked overnight*
*1 bouquet garni: 1 bay leaf, 1 thyme sprig, 6 parsley sprigs*
*1 oregano sprig*
*1 rosemary sprig*
*6 garlic cloves*
*2 lb (1 kg) potatoes*
*3 small onions*
*3 turnips*
*5 carrots*
*2 leeks, with a little of their green parts, halved lengthwise*
*1 small cabbage, cut into chunky strips*
*2 to 3 pieces* confit *of duck or goose*

In a large pot, place the pork, the ham bone and the ham pieces and cover with the water. Add the white beans. Bring to a boil, reduce to a simmer and skim. Add the bouquet garni, the additional herbs, and garlic, and cook for 30 minutes. Add all the vegetables except the cabbage, and cook for a further 45 minutes. Add the cabbage and the *confit*, and cook for another 20 minutes.

Serve in a large soup tureen so that everybody can help themselves to the soup and all the vegetables and meats. Thin slices of stale country-style bread are generally placed in everyone's bowl, and the soup is ladled over the top.

SERVES: 6

## La Mique Quercinoise

*Soup Dumpling Quercy Style*

Throughout the provinces of the southwest, until a generation ago, a simple broth, a cabbage soup, or even the hefty *garbure* was incomplete without its *mique*. Part dumpling, part bread, the *mique* is cooked in the stock, but served separately, sliced thickly at table while still warm. Fairly tiresome to make, because of the amount of kneading required to give the dough a light texture, and requiring considerable rising time, *mique* is now hard to find, but many a grandmother is delighted to roll up her sleeves and make one for those who are interested. Some recipes substitute cornmeal for half the flour, and insist on goose fat. This version is somewhat lighter.

*4 cups (1 lb/500 g) all purpose (plain) flour*
*7 large eggs*
*10 tablespoons (5 oz/150 g) softened butter or goose fat*
*1 oz (30 g) fresh (compressed) yeast or 2 envelopes (1/2 oz/15 g) dry yeast*
*1/3 cup (3 fl oz/90 ml) lukewarm water*
*salt*
*1 garlic clove, finely chopped (optional)*
*1/4 cup (2 oz/60 g) diced bacon (optional)*
*chicken, vegetable, or strained* garbure *stock to cover the* mique

Place the flour in a large bowl and make a well in the center. Add the eggs and the butter. Crumble the yeast into the water and stir to dissolve, then add to the well.

Using a wooden spoon, mix together the ingredients in the well, then bit by bit, blend in the flour, mashing the butter with the back of the spoon against the side of the bowl so that it is incorporated into the dough. Since salt kills yeast if it touches the yeast cells, only add the salt once the yeast has been fully incorporated. The optional bacon and garlic are also added at this stage.

The dough will initially be a little lumpy but as it is worked it will become homogeneous. When no lumps remain, add a little more water to make a thick dough, then turn out onto a floured board. Knead the dough, lifting it and banging it on the board, until it is elastic and lighter in texture. Great *mique* cooks claim success lies in the kneading, and say it should be kneaded for 30 minutes.

When the desired elasticity is obtained, return the ball of dough to the bowl, cover it with a cloth and leave it to rise at room temperature until it has doubled in size. This will take from 3 to 4 hours.

Poach the *mique* in a large pot of stock for 1 to 1¼ hours, until it is soft in the center. Traditionally it is cooked as a single dumpling, but it can be made into 3 smaller dumplings. Some say it cooks best when fitted tightly into the pot, while others claim it cooks more evenly when left free, since, like all dumplings, when the cooked section lightens the dumpling will roll upside down, allowing the less cooked side (which is weightier) to roll under. It will continue to turn itself until evenly cooked.

When the *mique* is cooked, drain and serve hot as an accompaniment to soup, carved in thick slices on a wooden board.

SERVES: 6

PETER JOHNSON

*Braised Frogs' Legs*

## Blanquette de Cuisses de Grenouilles

*Braised Frogs' Legs*

Frogs' legs are particularly popular in the Béarn. Here they are served with a traditional vinegar and egg binding.

*2 tablespoons goose fat or butter*
*2 lb (1 kg) frogs' legs*
*1 onion, chopped*
*1 tablespoon all purpose (plain) flour*
*4 garlic cloves, finely chopped*
*1 cup (8 fl oz/250 ml) chicken or fish stock*
*salt and freshly ground pepper*
*1 tablespoon white wine vinegar*
*2 eggs*
*1 tablespoon chopped parsley*

In a deep skillet, heat the goose fat and sauté the frogs' legs over moderate heat until golden, then sauté the onion. Set aside on a plate. Scatter the flour and the garlic over the base of the skillet. Stir until the mixture sticks a little, then add the stock and mix together. Return the frogs' legs to the skillet and simmer gently for 30 minutes. Season with salt and pepper.

Mix together the vinegar and eggs in a small bowl, then stir them quickly into the sauce. Do not allow the sauce to boil or the eggs will curdle. Finish with parsley and serve as a first course. (Cream is not commonly used in this area, but a more blanquette-style dish can be made by adding ¾ cup (6 fl oz/180 ml) cream to the sauce and bringing it to a boil before thickening it with the eggs, leaving out the vinegar.)

SERVES: 6

## *Confit d'Oie ou de Canard*

*Confit of Goose or Duck*

The *confit* is a method of preserving meat in its own fat, and is usually used for the limbs of duck and geese, whilst the large, force-fed breasts known as *magrets* are preferred roasted. It is quite possible however to "*confit*" the whole bird.

*Confit* is served in a number of ways. It is very flavorsome eaten cold, but in cooler weather it is generally heated. It is commonly warmed in a little of its own fat and served with potatoes (see following recipe for *pommes sarladais*), or with brown lentils, flavored with bacon and a generous amount of thyme. It is added to soups such as the *garbure* (see page 142) and also makes an appearance in *cassoulet* (see page 126).

*4 lb (2 kg) goose or duckling, cut into pieces*
*rock salt*
*1 thyme sprig*
*goose fat to cover (at least three 120-oz/375-g cans), which may be extended with rendered duck fat saved from a roast*
*1 large garlic clove*
*2 bay leaves*

If using a whole bird, divide into thick pieces, cutting the breast across the breastbone. A duck will give only two breast pieces, while a goose breast should give four or six pieces. Only the fleshy parts of the wings should be used.

Lay the pieces of meat on a platter and sprinkle with rock salt and a little thyme. Leave for 24 hours. The next day, rinse off the salt, and pat the pieces dry with paper towels.

Pack the meat into a large cast-iron casserole dish. Warm the goose fat and pour it over the top until the meat is just covered. Poke the garlic and thyme beneath the surface of the fat and lay the bay leaves between the layers of meat.

Bring very slowly to a simmer and then cook with a meat thermometer in the casserole to ensure that the temperature remains at 210°F (105°C). The purpose is to impregnate the meat with fat, which acts as a preservative, *not* to deep-fry it. Continue cooking for 2 to $2^1/_2$ hours until a metal skewer pierces the meat readily. The juices should run a clear yellow.

Remove the meat with tongs and pack it into a deep earthenware bowl or large wide-necked glass container. Raise the heat beneath the casserole slightly for 5 minutes to evaporate any moisture accumulated in the fat, then pour the fat through a sieve over the meat. The fat must cover the meat. Although in southwestern France the pots of *confit* are kept in the cool under the house, they are best stored in the refrigerator, where they will keep for 2 to 3 months.

Reheat the pieces of meat in some of the fat used to cover them.

SERVES: 8 to 10

*Confit of Duck, Potatoes Sarlat Style*

PETER JOHNSON

## *Pommes Sarladaise*

*Potatoes Sarlat Style*

This dish is served as a traditional accompaniment to *confit*.

*5 to 7 oz (150 to 220 g) goose fat*
*2 lb (1 kg) potatoes, thinly sliced*
*3 garlic cloves, finely chopped*
*salt and freshly ground pepper*
*2 tablespoons chopped parsley*

Heat half the goose fat in a large skillet. Add the potatoes and fry gently, regulating the heat so that they cook through as they brown, adding more fat as needed. Turn the potatoes from time to time, taking care not to break the slices. Add the garlic when the potatoes are partially cooked: it loses its flavor if it is browned too much. Season with salt and pepper and just before serving add the parsley and toss. The luxury of a sliced truffle or so is a common addition.

SERVES: 6

PETER JOHNSON

*Calfs' Kidneys Flamed in Armagnac*

## Rognons de Veau Flambés à l'Armagnac

*Calfs' Kidneys Flamed in Armagnac*

A treat in Gascony is the much-loved calf's kidney. Here it is served at its richest, with the addition of cream and Armagnac. Bear in mind that a kidney will only remain tender if it is lightly cooked.

*6 small or 4 large calfs' kidneys*
*4 tablespoons (2 oz/60 g) butter*
*2 tablespoons peanut oil*
*8 oz (250 g) champignons (button mushrooms), sliced*
*4 shallots, finely chopped*
*1/4 cup (2 fl oz/60 ml) Armagnac*
*1/4 cup (2 fl oz/60 ml) dry white wine*
*1 tablespoon French mustard*
*juice of 1 lemon*
*2 tablespoons heavy (double) cream*
*salt and freshly ground pepper*

Cut the kidneys into small chunky pieces, trimming off as much fat as possible. Heat half the butter and half the oil in a large skillet and sauté the champignons for about 30 seconds, until they are well greased. Set aside on a plate.

Return the skillet to the stove and add the pieces of kidney. Toss over the heat for a minute or so, then place a lid on the skillet and set it aside for 5 minutes for the kidneys to give up their water. Strain off the liquid and set the kidneys aside in a bowl.

Place the skillet over high heat and when it is hot, add the remaining butter and oil, and sauté the kidneys until brown. Add the shallots, and the Armagnac, and set alight. When the flames have died down add the wine, mustard, and lemon juice. Bring to a boil, then remove the kidneys with a slotted spoon. Add the cream, then reduce the sauce until it coats the back of a spoon. Correct the seasoning, return the kidneys to the skillet and then serve immediately with fried bread triangles.

SERVES: 6

*Breast of Duck Gascony Style, Green Peas with Ham and Goose Fat*

## Magret de Canard

*Breast of Duck Gascony Style*

The breast of duck is a ubiquitous by-product of the *foie gras* industry. Weighing up to 2 lb (1 kg), these succulent breasts lend themselves to broiling and roasting, and are typically eaten rare. However, as duck breasts of this size are uncommon outside France, this recipe is for conventional duck breasts, which are best fried.

*6 single duck breasts, skinned*
*duck or goose fat for frying*
*salt and freshly ground pepper*

In a heavy skillet over high heat, fry the breasts as you would a minute steak. Cook the first side for a little longer than the second, and only salt and pepper the breasts after they have been turned. Do not cook to more than rare, as the meat tendons will toughen and become grey.

To serve, carve each breast thinly and fan it out over the warmed plate. Serve with *pommes sarladaise* (see page 144), and green beans blanched and sautéed in duck fat with garlic and diced ham.

SERVES: 6

## Petits Pois au Jambon

*Green Peas with Ham and Goose Fat*

Cooking green peas using the moisture of lettuce is a classic method of French cookery. Here, additional flavor is provided by the addition of goose fat, bacon and herbs. Broad beans can also be cooked in this way.

*4 oz (125 g) bacon, chopped*
*3 to 4 tablespoons goose fat*
*4 lb (2 kg) green peas, shelled*
*8 to 10 pearl onions, or small pickling onions*
*1 small lettuce heart, leaves separated*
*salt and freshly ground pepper*
*1 bouquet garni: 1 bay leaf, 1 thyme sprig, 6 parsley sprigs*
*3 mint sprigs*

In a shallow saucepan with a lid, sauté the bacon over moderate heat until it renders its fat, then add the goose fat, and peas, and toss. Add the onions and the lettuce leaves. Season with salt and pepper and add the bouquet garni and mint.

Close the lid of the pan firmly to retain all moisture. Reduce heat and cook until the peas are tender. Do not open the lid to test for 12 minutes. The peas will take from 15 to 20 minutes to cook, depending on their size and tenderness. Check the seasoning, discard the bouquet garni, and serve.

SERVES: 6

## Salmis de Pintade

*Braised Guinea-Fowl*

Braising in red wine is ideal for wild birds, the flesh of which can be quite tough.

*3 tablespoons goose or duck fat*
*1 large carrot, chopped*
*1 leek, white and green parts, sliced*
*2 large shallots, chopped*
*1 bottle (3 cups/24 fl oz/750 ml) red wine*
*1 thyme sprig*
*2 bay leaves*
*2 guinea-fowl, each cut into 4 pieces*
*1/4 cup (2 fl oz/60 ml) Armagnac*
*1 to 2 tablespoons all purpose (plain) flour*
*1 cup (8 fl oz/250 ml) water*
*salt and freshly ground pepper*

Heat 1 tablespoon goose fat and fry the vegetables until greased, then add the wine, thyme, and bay leaves. Bring to a boil, reduce heat and simmer for 2 hours. In a second pan, heat 2 tablespoons of goose fat and brown the guinea-fowl pieces thoroughly. Pour in the Armagnac and set alight.

Remove the guinea-fowl. Strain the juices and return to the pan. Sprinkle the flour over the juices. Stir until the mixture starts to stick a little, then add the water and the reduced wine mixture. Simmer for 30 minutes, then add the guinea-fowl. Season with salt and pepper and simmer for a further 30 minutes.

Turn off the heat, cover and leave the meat to absorb the flavor of the sauce. Reheat and serve the next day with green beans, blanched and sautéed quickly with shallots in goose fat.

SERVES: 6

## Porc aux Pruneaux

*Pork with Prunes*

The famous prunes of Agen, in Gascony, feature widely in the local cuisine.

*1 pork neck, boned, about 3 lb (1.5 kg)*
*salt and freshly ground pepper*
*10 slices streaky bacon*
*2 tablespoons oil for the pan*
*20 to 24 prunes, stoned, soaked in red wine for 1 hour*
*3 tablespoons* eau-de-vie de prunes *or Armagnac*
*3 tablespoons finely chopped shallots*

Preheat the oven to 400°F (200°C). Salt and pepper the pork, then wrap the bacon pieces around it. Oil the base of a roasting pan and in it place the pork. Roast in the oven for 1 1/4 hours.

Meanwhile, in a saucepan bring the prunes and wine to a boil. Reduce heat and simmer for 15 minutes. Turn off the heat. About 15 minutes before the meat is fully roasted, pour the prunes and half the wine around the pork in the pan.

When the pork is cooked, remove from the oven to a board. Spoon off the fat without removing any meat sediment. Place the pan over high heat. Replace the meat. Add the shallots and sauté for a minute or two, then add the *eau-de-vie de prunes* and set alight. When the flames have died down return the meat to the board. Add the remaining wine to the roasting dish and stir while bringing the mixture to a boil, stirring up the meat sediment. Season with salt and pepper.

Transfer the meat to a warmed serving dish and arrange the prunes around the meat. Strain the meat juices and pour over the meat, or serve separately in a sauceboat. Carve the meat at the table.

SERVES: 6

*Braised Guinea-Fowl, Pork with Prunes*

## *Pastis*

*Gascon Apple Pastry*

The *pastis*, pride of the Gascon dessert cook, boasts extremely fine pastry similar to Greek filo pastry, and to eastern European pulled strudel pastries. The art of pulling the dough is disappearing, but the dish is still a great specialty of the region's *pâtisseries*.

If the pastry recipe looks a little daunting, commercial Greek filo pastry will make an acceptable substitute.

*Pastry:*
*2½ cups (10 oz/300 g) all purpose (plain) flour*
*1 large egg*
*pinch of salt*
*1 tablespoon vegetable oil*
*few drops of orangeflower water*
*1¼ cups (10 fl oz/300 ml) water*
*Filling:*
*6 apples*
*¼ cup (2 fl oz/60 ml) Armagnac*
*½ cup (4 oz/125 g) goose fat or butter, warmed to liquid*
*1 tablespoon sugar*
*Syrup:*
*1 cup (8 fl oz/250 ml) Armagnac or rum*
*4 tablespoons sugar*
*½ cup (4 fl oz/125 ml) water*

For the pastry: Place the flour in a large bowl and make a well in the center. Add the egg, salt, oil, and orangeflower water. Mix together the ingredients in the well and then, with the fingertips, blend in the flour until a homogeneous mixture is obtained. Work into a ball, adding the water in a stream, and continue kneading until the dough forms a ball that will detach readily from the bowl.

Place the dough in an oiled bowl, cover with a plate, and leave to rest overnight in a cool place (but not in the refrigerator).

The next day, spread a large cloth over the kitchen table and flour it lightly. Place the ball of dough in the middle, flatten it into a disc with the palm of the hand or a rolling pin. With the thumb and first two fingers of each hand pull the edges of the dough outwards bit by bit, as for strudel, until the dough forms a tissue-paper layer covering the area of a card table. Leave to dry for at least 1 hour.

To assemble: While the pastry is drying, peel, core and slice the apples, and place the slices in the Armagnac. When the pastry is dry, drizzle a little goose fat over it and then sprinkle it with sugar. Cut into squares about 2 in (5 cm) larger than the diameter of your chosen tart pan. A 10-in (25-cm) tart pan would be the most suitable size.

Preheat the oven to 400°F (200°C). Line the base of the greased tart pan with three layers of pastry. Center them on the pan but rotate each one to lie at an angle to the one beneath, so that their corners stick up or overhang the rim evenly all the way round. Prick with a fork, then scatter a layer of the apple slices over the pastry base. Sprinkle lightly with sugar and add two more layers of pastry, again with each one lying at an angle to the one beneath.

PETER JOHNSON

*Gascon Apple Pastry*

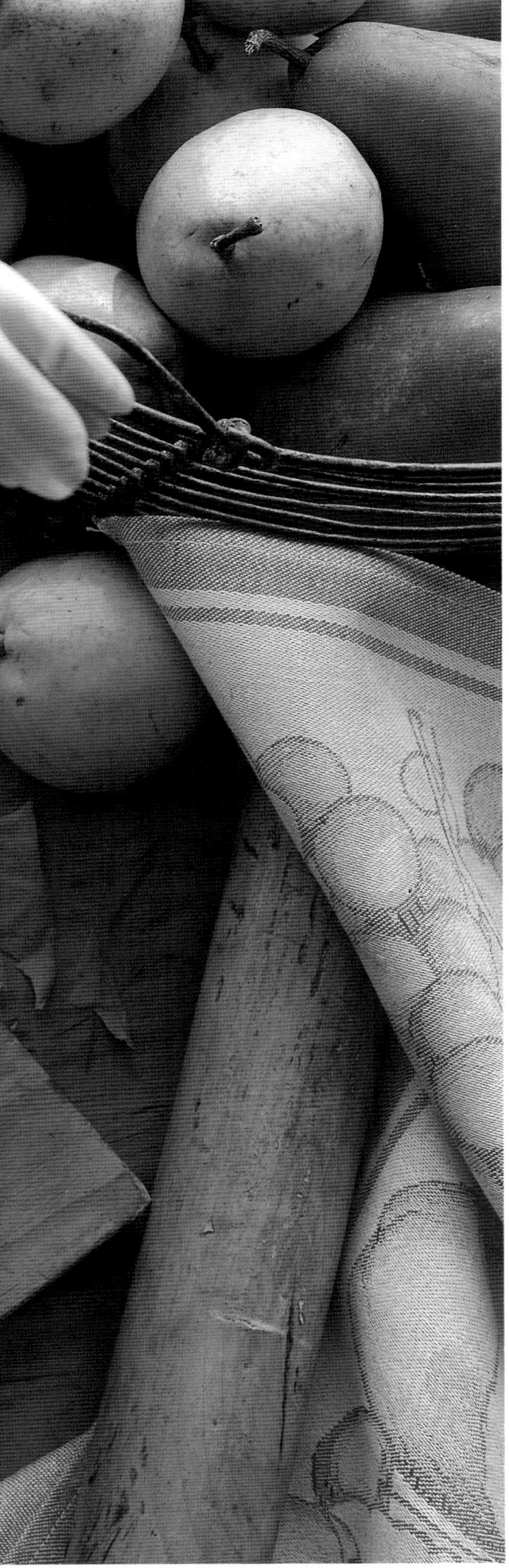

Add a further layer of apples and sugar, then two more layers of pastry. Use up the apples and the pastry, then fold the corners of the pastry inward. Drizzle the top with goose fat and sprinkle with sugar. Many cooks snip at the top layer of pastry with scissors to create jagged edges that brown during baking.

Bake the *pastis* in the oven for 30 minutes. Allow to cool then remove from the tart pan. Heat together the Armagnac, sugar, and water to make a light syrup and pour it over the *pastis*. Serve the *pastis* cut into wedges.

SERVES: 6

## Crème Brulée aux Noix

*Walnut Crème Brulée*

Walnut trees grow throughout the Dordogne, hence this regional version of an *haute cuisine* classic.

*1 vanilla bean, split lengthwise*
*3 cups (24 fl oz/750 ml) cream*
*8 egg yolks*
*1/2 cup (4 oz/125 g) superfine (caster) sugar*
*7 tablespoons walnut pieces*
*superfine (caster) sugar for the tops*

Preheat the oven to 350°F (180°C). Place the vanilla bean in a saucepan with the cream and bring to a boil. Set aside. Meanwhile, blend the egg yolks and sugar in a bowl, with a whisk. Mix a little of the hot cream in with the egg mixture, and then pour the mixture in with the cream. Whisk over moderate heat until the mixture thickens into a light custard. Do not allow the custard to boil, as it will curdle.

Pour the custard into ramekins, and share the walnuts between them. Stand the dishes in a bain-marie and bake in the oven for 8 minutes so that a light skin forms on top of the custard. Remove and leave to cool.

No more than 2 hours before serving, set the broiler (grill) on high. Dust the tops of the dishes with an 1/8-in (3-mm) layer of sugar, and place them under the broiler to "burn" the tops, or use a *brulée* iron or blow torch. Serve immediately, or chill and serve cold.

SERVES: 6

## Tartelettes aux Noix

*Walnut Tartlets*

Tartlets are classics of French cuisine, and walnuts and caramel make a delicious combination.

*Pastry:*
*1 3/4 cups (7 oz/220 g) all purpose (plain) flour*
*7 tablespoons (3 1/2 oz/105 g) butter, softened*
*4 tablespoons sugar*
*1 egg yolk*
*2 to 3 tablespoons water*
*Filling:*
*1 cup (8 oz/250 g) sugar*
*1/2 cup (4 fl oz/125 ml) milk*
*1/2 cup (4 fl oz/125 ml) cream*
*8 oz (250 g) walnuts, coarsely chopped*
*powdered (icing) sugar for dusting*

For the pastry: Place the flour on a marble or wooden surface and make a well in the center. Add the butter, sugar, egg yolk, and 2 tablespoons water. Mix together the ingredients in the well and then, with the fingertips, blend in the flour bit by bit until a homogeneous mixture is obtained. Drizzle in more water if needed. Knead the dough into a ball, cover with plastic wrap and chill for 20 minutes.

Preheat the oven to 425°F (220°C). Roll out the pastry and line six 4-in (10-cm) tartlet moulds. Prick the bases, line with aluminum foil, and bake blind in the oven for about 18 to 20 minutes, until cooked. Cool on a cake rack.

For the filling: Pour a little of the sugar into a small saucepan and place over high heat. Watch carefully until it starts to melt, then keep adding a little sugar at a time, shaking the pan to incorporate, and continue until all the sugar is dissolved. Without touching the sugar with a spoon, continue cooking until it turns a caramel color.

Meanwhile, pour the milk and cream into a saucepan and bring to a boil. When the sugar is a medium-brown caramel, add a little of the milk mixture to it. Wait for the bubbling to subside and then pour in the rest. Place a sugar thermometer in the mixture and continue to cook, stirring with the thermometer from time to time, until it registers 225°F (110°C). If the mixture is disturbed, or the sugar is coarse, the caramel may become grainy or separate. Stirring in 2 tablespoons of cream will enhance the texture.

Place the walnuts in a bowl, pour in the caramel and toss to coat the nuts. Dust the rims of the tartlets with powdered sugar and fill with the walnut mixture. Allow to cool before serving. For a more sophisticated appearance, a zig-zag pattern of chocolate can be piped across the top of each tartlet.

SERVES: 6

## *Glace à l'Armagnac et Pruneaux*

*Armagnac and Prune Ice-cream*

Ice-cream machines have turned what was once an arduous task, mainly undertaken only by chefs, into quite a simple procedure.

This creamy confection brings together two of the great products of the area in a stunning combination.

*10 prunes bottled in Armagnac or 10 plain prunes pricked with a skewer and soaked in the Armagnac overnight*
*1 cup (8 oz/250 g) sugar*
*4 cups (1 qt/1 l) milk*
*8 large or 10 small eggs*
*3/4 cup (6 fl oz/180 ml) Armagnac*

Drain the prunes, pit them, and chop them coarsely. Put them in a bowl. Place half the sugar with the milk in a saucepan and bring to a boil. Place the eggs and the remaining sugar in a bowl and beat until creamy.

Whisking all the time, pour half the milk onto the eggs, blend well, then return the mixture to the saucepan. Heat, whisking, until the mixture thickens to form a custard. Do not allow the custard to boil, as it will curdle. Remove from the heat and pour through a sieve onto the prunes. Stir in the Armagnac.

Cool the mixture, then churn in an ice-cream machine. Alternatively, freeze the mixture partially, then beat out any crystals, return to the freezer to firm, then beat again, before placing in the freezer to store. An ice-cream machine generally gives a better textured ice-cream.

Serve alone, scooped into parfait glasses, or with poached prunes, poached pears, or apple tartlets.

SERVES: 6

*Walnut Tartlets, Walnut Crème Brulée, Armagnac and Prune Ice-Cream*

PETER JOHNSON

Chaumont
Marne
Seine
Yonne
Joigny
Tonnerre
Auxerre
Chablis
Serein
Loire
Avallon
Epoisses
Vézelay
Saône
Sancerre
Pouilly
-sur-Loire
Sombernon
Dijon
Besaçon
Fixin
Yonne
Morvan
Doubs
Nuits-Saint-Georges
Dole
Nivernais
Beaune
Alloxe-Corton
Volnay
Meursault
Autun
Nevers
Chalon-sur-Saône
Monteeau-les-Mines
Louhans
Grosne
Moulins
Charolais
Cluny
Charolles
Saône
Mâcon
Allier
Loire
Nantua
Bourgogne
Bourg-en-Bresse
Vichy
Villefranche
-sur-Saône
Bresse
Clermond-Ferrand
Belley
Lyon
Rhône
Chambé
Lyonnais
Vienne
Saint-Etienne
Rhône

Grape pickers busy in one of the Beaujolais vineyards. Most of the vast amount of wine that comes from this region is best drunk while it is young.

MICHAEL BUSSELLE/TONY STONE WORLDWIDE/THE PHOTO LIBRARY

produced in the far north, on the hills south of Mâcon. But the best known Beaujolais, and by far the most widely drunk, is the Beaujolais *nouveau*, the young red wine for immediate drinking. This wine is shipped out from the region on a set date in November, by air, train, truck, and even balloon, to the four corners of the world, so that all those who wish to can join in the fun of drinking the new season's produce. Originally the race was in order to see who could get a case of the wine to Paris first.

After the grapepickers have finished and the new wine begins to ferment, feasts are held throughout the region to celebrate the completion of the harvest, featuring local produce such as *escargots*, *coq au vin*, *jambon persillé,* and many sorts of cheese. And of course everything is washed down with great quantities of fresh, grapy Beaujolais *nouveau*. The principal feast of the Beaujolais is held during the summer, and takes place at the end of June in Villefranche-sur-Saône, the main town of the region, which is almost at the gates of Lyon.

## The Nivernais

To the west of the wilds of the Morvan, and almost part of central France, lies the Nivernais, a region of rolling farmland, with Nevers, on the upper reaches of the river Loire as its capital. Ruled in Renaissance times by the Italian Gonzaga family, the city boasts a beautiful ducal palace dating from that period, perhaps the finest castle on the Loire. The highly civilized Gonzaga court fostered the arts and commissioned an Italian potter to set up a faience factory. The city continues to be known for its brilliant blue pottery.

The Nivernais is a rich agricultural region, and it has adopted the carrot as its symbol. If a meat dish is described as *"a la nivernaise"* it means that it has a garnish of glazed carrots and onions. *Soupe aux carottes nivernaises* is a local speciality, as are *le saupiquet*, a dish made with ham and juniper berries, *soufflé de chou-fleur*, cauliflower soufflé, *foie de veau sur compote de rhubarbe*, calf's liver with stewed rhubarb, and *panaché chaud de la Saint-Cochon*, an assortment of sliced hot sausages, ham, and bacon.

The most famous wine town of the Nivernais is Pouilly-sur-Loire — not to be confused with Pouilly and Fuissé, the twin villages near Mâcon. The wines produced in this area are the Pouilly-Fumé and the equally well-known Sancerre. The fortified hill town of Sancerre faces Pouilly across the Loire river. A major fair takes place in Pouilly-sur-Loire in the middle of August. Both Pouilly Fumé and Sancerre, though they come from Burgundy, are officially classified as Loire and not Burgundy wines.

*Chickens, ducks, and geese being fed in the yard of a Bresse farmhouse.*

JEAN-PAUL FERRERO/AUSCAPE INTERNATIONAL

## Burgundy's Cheeses

Burgundy is mainly cattle country, so cow's milk cheese predominates, the best known being Epoisses, which originally came from around the village of the same name near Auxerre. There are records of the Cistercian monks making it in the fifteenth century. It is soft and creamy, with a pink-gold crust formed by washing the cheese in Marc de Bourgogne, the local *eau-de-vie*.

Chaource, a less creamy and more rustic cheese than Epoisses, comes from the north-east, near the border with Champagne. Exclusively "hand-made," this soft, white cheese goes well with Chablis or with a Rosé d'Anjou.

Bresse has a reputation for fine cream cheese, *fromage blanc*, used widely in savories and desserts. It is often flavored with herbs or strawberries.

There are ninety kinds of *chèvre*, goat's milk cheese, registered around France. Burgundy's best known varieties are the Chavignol from around Sancerre, which includes the hard, dry, salty Crottin de Chavignol; the Chevreton de Mâcon, and the Pourly from near Tonnerre.

As a table cheese, *chèvre* is best served at below room temperature. It is also used in sauces, particularly with roasts, and is served in salads and mixed with walnuts and olives.

## Bresse's Famous Poultry

Bresse is a rural corner of France on the road to Switzerland, south of Dijon. The region has always been known for the excellence of its poultry, and in these days when a free-range chicken is no longer easy to find the *poularde de Bresse,* raised on farms in liberty, constitutes a gastronomic treat of the first order. (A *poularde* is a plump, mature bird with more flavor than a *poulet.*) Two ingredients go hand-in-hand with the *poularde*: truffles and morels. The morel is a rare mountain mushroom that wears a strange dunce's cap, and is available for barely a month in spring. The two great traditional dishes are *poularde en demi-deuil,* chicken with truffles inserted under the skin (sometimes morels are substituted for the truffles), and *poularde en vessie*, chicken stuffed in a pig's bladder.

Scarcely a gourmet would be unaware that it was in Belley, a sleepy country town in Bresse's Ain department, that the author of *Physiologie du Gôut,* Brillat-Savarin, was born in 1755. It is not widely known, however, that he was not a cook but a high court judge, who wrote his treatise on gastronomy in his chambers in his free time. Brillat-Savarin was a man of many talents. During the French Revolution he spent two years in exile in New York, giving French lessons and playing the violin in a theater orchestra.

Perhaps the loveliest town in Bresse is Louhans, with its old arcaded houses. Around Louhans there are still quite a few traditional Bresse farmhouses, timbered and shaded by overhanging eaves, where chickens, resembling patches of white fluff from a distance, roam freely in courtyards and are pampered and corn-fed by loving hands. In butcher's shops an authentic Bresse fowl is easy to recognize by the metal band, the *marque de contrôle*, attached to its leg.

The capital of Bresse is Bourg-en-Bresse, famous for its flamboyant Gothic church on the outskirts of town. The church and its monastery, which now houses the Musée de l'Ain, were built by Marguerite of Austria in memory of her adored husband, Phillip the Beautiful. In the museum's courtyard there is a reconstruction of an authentic Bresse farmhouse, while inside the cloisters a room is devoted to Bourg's most famous citizen: the Bresse rooster!

Bresse is a land of lakes, ponds, marshes, rivers, and brooks. These were once filled with plump *écrevisses*, crayfish, before the ravages of pollution. Today crayfish are imported from the rivers of Yugoslavia, to cater to local demand, and frogs' legs are flown in from as far away as Bangladesh.

## The Gastronomic Capital of France

Lyon, capital of the Lyonnais, is one of the country's principal cities. At first glance, usually cast from a car on the Autoroute du Midi, traveling through tunnels under the rivers and hills, the appeal of Lyon is not apparent. On the outskirts oil refineries light up the night sky, and the city is surrounded by industrial sprawl. But Lyon is a city of contrasts — a thriving business district of towering office blocks and a busy modern shopping center, with an old town of Renaissance buildings and narrow, dark cobbled streets. In Lyon one can eat as well as anywhere in the world. This is a city of both *haute cuisine* and traditional dishes served in inexpensive bistros.

The hills of Croix-Rousse and the Fourvière dominate the city, the latter topped by an extraordinary half-church, half-fortress — the richly decorated basilica of

Notre-Dame-de-Fourvière. From its tower (after walking up 3000 steps) there is a splendid view of the city straddling the Rhône and the Saône rivers. There's an old saying that Lyon is in fact washed not by two but by three rivers: the Rhône, the Saône, and the Beaujolais!

The surrounding countryside is extremely rich and offers up its finest produce on the altar of gastronomy: beef from the Charolais, cream from the Dauphiné, fish from the rivers, poultry from nearby Bresse, and lamb from the Auvergne. Then there is the wine. The people of Lyonnais have always claimed Beaujolais as their own, and they drink it all the time. They have also devised a particular snack they call *le mâchon,* served at any hour of the day, which is unknown in the rest of France. A little like Spanish *tapas, le mâchon* consists of an assortment of cooked pork meats with a *pot* of Beaujolais (a *pot* is what you ask for here, not a *bouteille).* Sometimes there is also tripe, which the Lyonnais love to eat pan-fried and crisp, calling the dish *"tablier de sapeur,"* "firemen's aprons."

A *charcuterie* is a cross between a butcher's shop and a delicatessen. Lyon is particularly famous for its *charcuteries*, but even the smallest village in the region has one. In these shops you will find all sorts of freshly prepared salads and a profusion of pork products (which is why they are sometimes known as *cochonailles).* Lyon produces some wonderful sausages, such as the long *rosette de Lyon,* and *sabodets*, made from pork, beef, pig's head and skin. Creations such as these, and hams, pig's trotters, *grattons*, crackling, and sows' ears are popular fare in the city's innumerable *bouchons,* bar/bistros.

*Lyon is known for its wonderful sausages, and practically every part of the pig is put to good culinary use, even the ears.*

PASCAL MAITRE/ODYSSEY

PIERRE BOULAT/COSMOS

*Lunchtime at the Brasserie Georges in Lyon. The city boasts an immense range of places to eat, from little back-alley bistros to three-star restaurants.*

Many years ago there were already many *rôtisseries* in Lyon, forerunners of today's restaurants. One of the earliest, in the eighteenth century, was called Mère Guy. Mère Guy was a housewife noted for her skill in making *matelotes,* a rich stew of eel, carp, perch, and other fresh-water fish cooked in wine. The most famous *mère* this century was La Mère Fillioux, and she laid down the principles of her cooking as follows: "It takes years of study and experience to serve a perfect dish. I have spent a lifetime perfecting five or six dishes. I will serve only these, but will do them perfectly." Regrettably, few *mères lyonnaises* remain. This is the era of great chefs, and Lyon's glory is Paul Bocuse, who continues the tradition of the *mères* at his restaurant at Collonges.

Some of the finest hand-made chocolates in all France are produced in Lyon by the Bernachon family, who view chocolate making as an art akin to making wine. Their shop on the fashionable Cours Franklin-Roosevelt is a delight to visit.

A fitting farewell to this city of gastronomic delights would be to ask a native to compose you a festive meal. Though *quenelles* are part of the cuisine of Burgundy, they are a Lyonnais invention, and the meal would probably begin with *quenelles de brochet*, pike dumplings. These would be followed by artichokes with *foie gras*, climaxing with *poularde de Bresse*, served either *demi-deuil*, or *en vessie*. For cheese you would álmost certainly be served a Saint-Marcellin from the Vercours in neighboring Dauphiné, or an Epoisses.

And what wines would a Lyonnais host select to accompany such a meal? A Montrachet perhaps with the *quenelles*, followed by a Gevrey-Chambertin with the main course. And with the cheese they would probably order a Moulin-à-Vent — for chauvinistic reasons, of course, since the Beaujolais is to them their own vineyard.

# BURGUNDY

## CHABLIS

*Principal wines:*

*Chablis Grand Cru (1)*
*Chablis Premier Cru (1)*
*Irancy (3)*
*Petit Chablis (1)*
*Sauvignon de Saint-Bris VDQS (2)*

## CÔTE DE NUITS (4)

*The great or best known red burgundies:*

*Bonnes Mares (Grand Cru)*
*Chambertin and Chambertin-Clos de Bèze (Grand Cru)*
*Chambolle-Musigny (Grand Cru)*
*Chappelle-, Charmes-, Griottes-, Latricières-, Mazis-, and Ruchottes-Chambertin (Grand Cru)*
*Clos de la Roche (Grand Cru)*
*Clos de Vougeot (Grand Cru)*
*Côte de Nuits (and Villages)*
*Echézaux and Grands Echézaux (Grand Cru)*
*Gevrey-Chambertin*
*Morey-Saint-Denis*
*Musigny (Grand Cru)*
*Nuits-Saint-Georges*
*Richebourg (Grand Cru)*
*Romanée-Conti (Grand Cru)*
*Romanée-Saint-Vivant (Grand Cru)*
*Vosne-Romanée (Grand Cru)*

## CÔTE DE BEAUNE (5)

*The great or best known red burgundies (all 100 per cent Pinot Noir):*

*Aloxe-Corton*
*Beaune*
*Côte de Beaune (and Villages)*
*Pommard*
*Santenay*
*Savigny-Lès-Beaune*
*Volnay*

*The greatest of the great white burgundies (all 100 per cent Chardonnay):*

*Bâtard-Montrachet (Grand Cru)*
*Chassagne Montrachet*
*Chevalier-Montrachet (Grand Cru)*
*Corton-Charlemagne (Grand Cru)*
*Meursault*
*Montrachet (Grand Cru)*
*Puligny-Montrachet*

## CÔTE CHALONNAISE (6)

*The great or best known burgundies:*

*Mercurey (red)*
*Rully (white)*

## MÂCONNAIS (7)

*Mâcon (white)*
*Pouilly-Fuissé (white)*

## BEAUJOLAIS (8)

*Beaujolais Villages*
*The ten Crus Beaujolais:*

*Brouilly*
*Chénas*
*Chiroubles*
*Côte de Brouilly*
*Fleurie*
*Juliénas*
*Morgon*
*Moulin-à-Vent*
*Régnié*
*Saint-Amour*

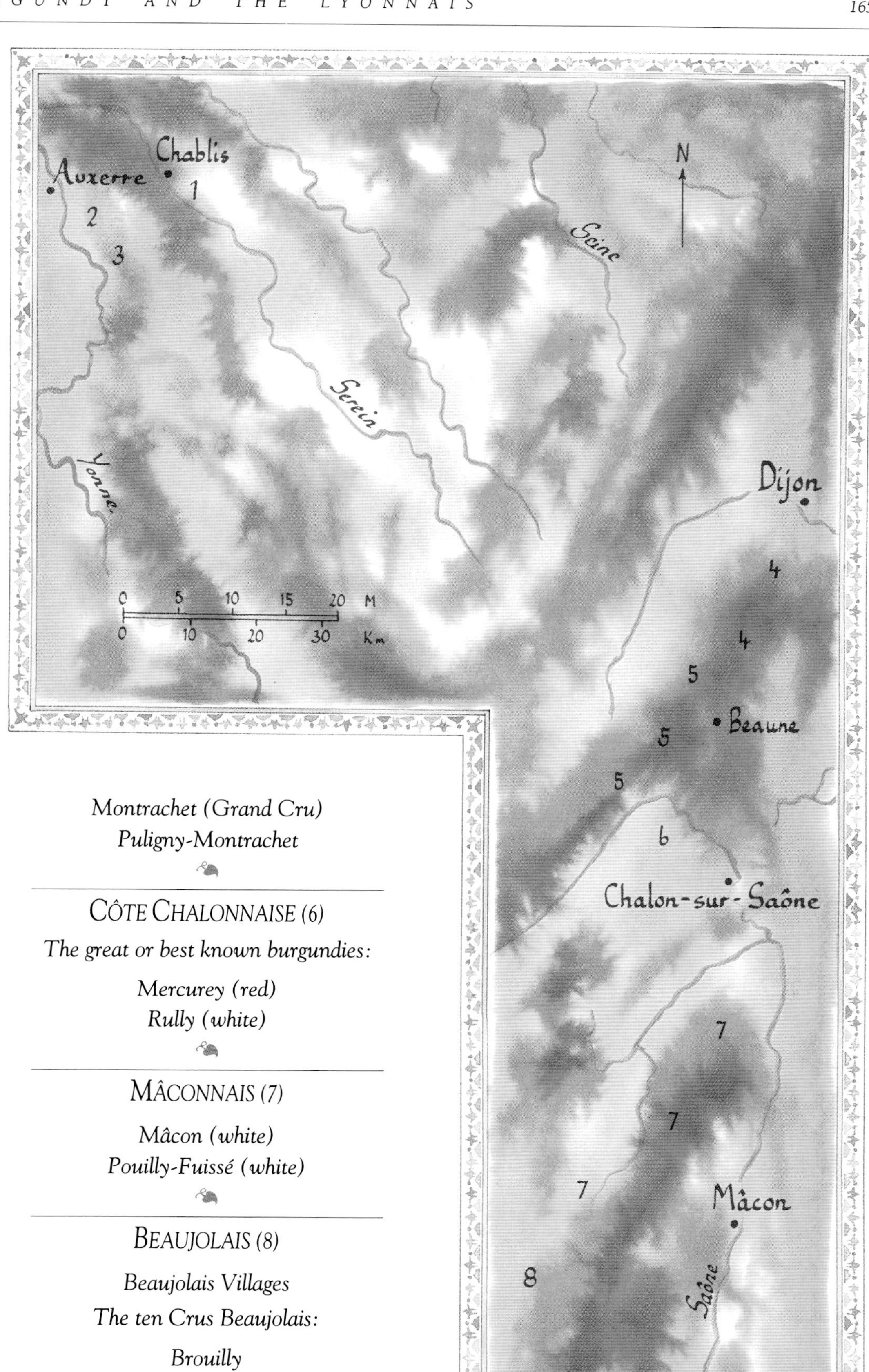

# Recipes of Burgundy and the Lyonnais

Maria Donovan

PETER JOHNSON

## Pâté de Foies de Volaille

*Chicken Liver Pâté*

One of the classic ways to begin a meal in Burgundy is with a terrine or a pâté.

*10 tablespoons (5 oz/155 g) butter*
*1 garlic clove, finely chopped*
*2 lb (1 kg) chicken livers, coarsely chopped*
*milk (optional)*
*salt and freshly ground black pepper*
*2 tablespoons brandy*
*2 slices white bread, crust removed, diced*
*1 cup (8 fl oz/250 ml) canned consommé, or stock made with a bouillon cube*
*juice of 1/2 lemon*

In a heavy, preferably cast-iron, skillet melt half the butter. Add the garlic and chicken livers which have been soaked overnight in milk and carefully dried. (The process of soaking the livers can be omitted. It serves to "whiten" them, so that they resemble *foie gras*, goose liver.)

Stir-fry livers for about 6 to 8 minutes, until they have changed color completely. Add salt and pepper, and gently stir in the brandy. Off the heat, blend in the rest of the butter while the livers are still hot. Add the bread and the stock, then blend the whole mixture in a food processor until smooth, adding lemon juice to taste.

Serve the pâté with toasted white bread, French bread, or *brioche*.

SERVES: 6 to 8

## Jambon Persillé

*Ham in Aspic with Parsley*

This dish is still made in many homes in Burgundy in the traditional way. Stock is made with veal knuckles, calf's feet, and a bouquet garni, simmered for at least 3 hours. Raw ham is then poached in the stock, which is clarified once more to make the aspic.

This recipe is for those who do not have the time or cannot find the ingredients to make a veal stock at home.

*1 1/2 envelopes or 1 1/2 tablespoons (3/4 oz/20 g) powdered gelatin*
*4 cups (1 qt/1 l) water*
*2 tablespoons sherry*
*2 teaspoons white wine vinegar*
*1/4 cup (2 fl oz/60 ml) rosé wine*
*1 1/2 lb (750 g)cooked unsmoked ham, thickly sliced then diced (fatty rind removed)*
*1 1/2 cups finely chopped flat-leafed parsley*

Prepare the aspic by dissolving the gelatin in 1/2 cup hot water and then adding it to the remaining water. Then add the sherry, vinegar, and rosé.

Use a round glass bowl large enough to accommodate the meat and aspic. Pour a layer of aspic over the bottom of the bowl and let this set in the refrigerator. Place a layer of ham, generously sprinkled with parsley, over the hard aspic and cover with liquid aspic. Refrigerate once again.

This procedure should be repeated until all the ingredients have been used up. If necessary, increase the amount of parsley. Refrigerate. Serve unmolded, sliced in wedges like a cake.

SERVES: 6

*Ham in Aspic with Parsley, Chicken Liver Paté*

## Carpe à l'Ancienne

*Carp in the Classic Fashion*

This is the traditional way of cooking carp, a fish that is easy to find in Burgundy, but not so common at city fishmongers. The recipe can be used for any whole fish, fresh-water or salt, even frozen.

*1 carp or other whole fish (pike, bass, trout, bream), about 3 to 4 lb (1.5 to 2 kg)*
*10 tablespoons (5 oz/155 g) butter*
*3 shallots, finely chopped or minced*
*2 tablespoons chopped parsley*
*salt and freshly ground black pepper*
*2 cups (16 fl oz/500 ml) dry white wine*
*1/2 cup (1 oz/30 g) breadcrumbs (preferably freshly made from toasted bread)*
*3/4 cup (6 fl oz/180 ml) heavy (double) cream*

Scale, wash, and gut the fish but leave on the head and tail. Butter an oval baking dish. Preheat the oven to 450°F (230°C).

By hand, work the butter, shallots, and parsley into a thick paste. Salt and pepper the inside of the fish and dry it well on the outside. Coat the fish all over with the butter mixture. Lay the fish in the baking dish. Cover it with the breadcrumbs, pressing them down firmly with your fingers. Pour in the wine.

Lower oven temperature to 300°F (150°C). Place fish in the oven and bake for 45 minutes. Remove from the oven. Pour the cream over the fish, letting it melt and blend with the breadcrumbs and juices, then serve immediately.

SERVES: 4

*Carp in the Classic Fashion*

PETER JOHNSON

## Soupe aux Carottes Nivernaises

*Nivernais Carrot Soup*

This soup is a specialty of Nivernais, which ennobles the carrot in its coat-of-arms. A recipe dating from the time the Gonzaga of Italy ruled Nevers specifies twice as much sugar as carrots. In modern recipes the sugar is greatly reduced.

*1/2 cup (4 oz/125 g) butter*
*1 lb (500 g) carrots, sliced*
*1/4 cup (2 oz/60 g) sugar*
*salt*
*1/2 cup (2 oz/60 g) all purpose (plain) flour*
*6 cups (1 1/2 qt/1.5 l) veal or chicken stock*
*2 teaspoons cream*
*2 teaspoons chopped chives or parsley (optional)*

Heat three-quarters of the butter in a heavy saucepan. Add carrots and sugar, and salt to taste. Sauté uncovered for 10 minutes, stirring frequently. Put carrots in blender and blend until a smooth purée.

Return the puréed carrots to the saucepan, and with a wooden spoon blend in the flour. Dilute with cold stock, stirring carefully. Bring to a boil, reduce heat, take off the lid and simmer for 10 minutes.

Remove from heat. Add the remaining butter and the cream, sprinkle with chopped chives, if desired, and serve.

SERVES: 4

## Potée Bourguignonne

*Burgundy Three-in-one Soup*

Rustic and robust, the *potée* is not so much a soup as a dish of meat garnished generously with vegetables. It makes an ideal one-course meal.

*2 lb (1 kg) salt pork (shoulder, riblet, or neck), soaked overnight*
*1 lb (500 g) unsmoked bacon, soaked overnight*
*1 small ham knuckle, soaked overnight (a smoked knuckle would give added flavor)*
*2 lb (1 kg) green cabbage, coarsely chopped*
*8 carrots, whole*
*5 turnips, whole*
*3 or 4 leeks, white parts only, whole*
*salt, preferably coarse*
*12 black peppercorns*
*6 potatoes, cut in large pieces*
*1 lb (500 g) green beans, whole*

Drain the meat well. Place in a large saucepan, cover with water and bring quickly to a boil. Drain. Cover with fresh cold water, bring to a boil, covered, and let simmer for 1 hour. Add cabbage, carrots, turnips, and leeks. Season with salt, and add peppercorns. Bring to a boil again and simmer for 45 minutes. Add the potatoes and the beans and simmer for a further 30 minutes.

The *potée* in Burgundy is served as follows: the soup strained into a soup tureen, with the meat and vegetables served either on two separate plates, or together on a large serving dish.

SERVES: 8

## Oeufs à la Dijonnaise

*Baked Eggs Dijon Style*

Recipes which say *"à la dijonnaise"* always contain mustard. The mustard, of course, must be of the Dijon variety, and not English mustard, which is far too hot.

*6 hard-boiled eggs*
*salt and freshly ground black pepper*
*2 teaspoons Dijon mustard*
*1 shallot or small white onion, finely chopped*
*2 teaspoons chopped mixed fresh herbs: tarragon, chervil, parsley*
*2 tablespoons heavy (double) cream*
*4 tablespoons (2 oz/60 g) butter*
*sprinkle of vinegar*
*2 teaspoons chopped chives (optional)*

Halve the eggs. Remove the yolks and place them in a bowl with salt, pepper, mustard, shallot, and the mixed fresh herbs. (Do not use dried herbs. If the other fresh herbs are unavailable, simply use fresh parsley.) Add the cream and mix until smooth with a fork, or blend in a food processor.

Preheat oven to 425°F (220°C). Fill the egg whites with this mixture. Lay them in a well-buttered ovenproof dish. Melt the rest of the butter, add a drop or two of vinegar and pour over the eggs. Bake for 10 minutes. Serve hot, sprinkled with the chives, if desired.

SERVES: 4

*Burgundy Three-in-one Soup, Nivernais Carrot Soup, Fish Soup with White Wine, Baked Eggs Dijon Style*

PETER JOHNSON

## La Pauchouse

*Fish Soup with White Wine*

This recipe demonstrates that a fine soup can be made entirely with fresh-water fish.

*5 lb (2.5 kg) mixed fresh-water fish, such as pike, carp, perch, trout, and eel*
*salt*
*8 to 10 black peppercorns*
*bouquet garni: 1 bay leaf, 1 thyme sprig, 5 parsley sprigs*
*1 red onion, sliced*
*5 garlic cloves, peeled*
*4 cups (1 qt/1 l) dry white wine*
*4 tablespoons (2 oz/60 g) butter*
*3 tablespoons all purpose (plain) flour*
*$^3/_4$ cup (6 fl oz/180 ml) cream*
*fried croûtons, rubbed with garlic*

Wash, scale, and gut the fish, removing the heads, tails, and fins. Cut the fish into 2-in (5-cm) chunks. Place the heads, tails, and fins in a saucepan and cover them with cold water. Add a pinch of salt, the peppercorns, and the bouquet garni. Cover and bring to a boil. Remove the lid and simmer for 20 minutes. Strain the stock, and set aside. Discard the heads, tails and fins.

Place the fish pieces in a large soup pot. Add the onion, garlic, fish stock, and the wine. Bring to a boil, reduce heat and simmer for 15 minutes.

Meanwhile melt the butter in a skillet, add the flour, and stir-fry for a few minutes until golden. Stirring continuously, blend in enough cold water to make the mixture the consistency of thick cream. Add to the soup and simmer for a further 5 minutes.

Just before serving, add the cream. The soup should be served immediately, very hot. You may serve the fish separately on a warmed platter or in the soup, in deep bowls, accompanied by the croûtons.

SERVES: 8

*Veal Scallops Dijon Style*

PETER JOHNSON

## Escalopes de Veau Dijonnaises

*Veal Scallops Dijon Style*

This straightforward dish from Dijon takes little time to prepare. It can also be made with veal chops, pork chops, or chicken or turkey breast.

*2 tablespoons vegetable oil*
*6 veal scallops (escalopes), about 4 oz (125 g) each*
*salt and freshly ground black pepper*
*2 tablespoons Madeira or sweet sherry*
*1 tablespoon Dijon mustard*
*1 cup (8 fl oz/250 ml) heavy (double) cream*

Ideally, use a heavy skillet that is large enough to accommodate at least three scallops at a time. Otherwise the scallops can be fried one at a time, but all of them will later need to be placed in a large pan to complete the cooking process with the cream sauce.

Heat the oil and when very hot, fry meat on both sides until golden brown. Add salt and pepper, and pour over the Madeira, stirring to scrape up any brown bits clinging to the pan.

Mix the mustard thoroughly with the cream and blend in with the meat, off the heat. Return to the heat, bring sauce to a boil and serve immediately.

SERVES: 6

## Mouton à la Bourguignonne

*Burgundy Mutton Stew*

The method of simmering meat or poultry for several hours in wine, and seasoned with herbs, is used widely throughout France, but nowhere more than in Burgundy, home of so many of the country's finest wines.

The dish can be cooked in the oven instead of on top of the stove.

*$2^1/_2$ lb (1.25 kg) shoulder of mutton or lamb, cut into bite-sized pieces*
*all purpose (plain) flour for coating*
*8 oz (250 g) lean smoked bacon, chopped*
*salt and freshly ground black pepper*
*bouquet garni: 1 bay leaf, 1 thyme sprig, 5 parsley sprigs*
*4 tablespoons (2 oz/60 g) butter*
*1 lb (500 g) champignons (button mushrooms)*
*1 lb (500 g) small pickling onions, peeled*
*1 bottle (3 cups/24 fl oz/150 ml) Burgundy-style red wine*

PETER JOHNSON

*Burgundy Mutton Stew*

Roll the meat in flour. Fry the bacon in a heavy saucepan. Add the meat and fry, stirring frequently, until golden all over. Season with salt and plenty of freshly ground black pepper, and add the bouquet garni. Whilst stirring, slowly pour in enough wine to cover the meat. Bring to a boil, reduce heat and simmer, covered, for 1 hour.

In a skillet, melt the butter and stir-fry the champignons and onions over moderate to high heat for 5 minutes. Add these to the meat, replace the lid and cook for another hour. Serve with boiled potatoes or long-grain rice.

SERVES: 6

## Coq au Vin

*Rooster Stewed in Red Wine*

There are as many recipes for *coq au vin* as there are cooks. However, there are two ingredients about which there is total agreement: it must be made with a rooster, and a *good* red wine. If you cannot get a rooster, settle for a boiling fowl, but *never* a battery-raised chicken!

*1 rooster or boiling fowl, about 5 lb (2.5 kg), cut into 10 pieces*
*all purpose (plain) flour for dusting*
*salt and freshly ground black pepper*
*2 tablespoons lard or oil*
*3 oz (90 g) bacon, cut into small pieces*
*2 large red onions, finely sliced*
*2 garlic cloves, finely chopped*
*2 tablespoons brandy*
*4 cups (1 qt/1 l) red Burgundy or Beaujolais wine*
*bouquet garni: 1 bay leaf, 1 thyme sprig, 5 parsley sprigs*
*pinch of nutmeg (optional)*
*fried croûtons*

Roll each piece of fowl in flour seasoned with salt and pepper. In a large heavy stewing pot, heat the lard and stir-fry the bacon for a few minutes. Remove bacon and fry the fowl pieces until golden all over (adding more fat to the pot if necessary). Remove. Toss the onions and garlic in the fat for a few minutes.

Return the fowl and bacon to the pot, pour on the brandy, ignite, and stir thoroughly. Add the wine, the bouquet garni, a little more salt and pepper, and nutmeg if desired.

Bring to a boil, cover tightly with the lid, reduce heat and simmer for 2½ to 3 hours, or until the meat is tender but does not fall off the bones.

Place fowl pieces on a preheated serving dish, check sauce and, if necessary, reduce over high heat until thick and creamy. Pour sauce over the meat and serve with croûtons.

SERVES: 6

## Boeuf Bourguignon

*Burgundy Beef*

The secret of this famous dish lies in the quality of the wine that is used. You do not have to buy a vintage château Burgundy, but neither should you make do with the cheapest red from the supermarket. This simple recipe was obtained from a butcher's wife in Mâcon.

*2 white onions, finely chopped*
*2 carrots, finely chopped*
*2 sticks of celery heart, finely chopped*
*3 tablespoons oil*
*3 lb (1.5 kg) beef suitable for braising, such as round, topside or chuck steak, cut into 2-in (5-cm) cubes*
*salt and freshly ground black pepper*
*bouquet garni: 1 bay leaf, 1 thyme sprig, 5 parsley sprigs*
*1 bottle (3 cups/24 fl oz/750 ml) good quality Burgundy or Burgundy-style red wine*
*3 tablespoons all purpose (plain) flour*
*3 tablespoons softened butter*
*2 teaspoons chopped parsley*

Mix together the onions, carrots, and celery. Heat the oil in a large, heavy stewing pot and fry the meat with the chopped vegetables over high heat for 6 minutes, stirring frequently.

Season with salt and pepper, add the bouquet garni and pour in the red wine. Bring to a boil, reduce heat, cover with lid and simmer very gently on top of the stove for 3 hours.

Work the flour in with the butter and thicken the gravy with this mixture, stirring until well blended. Cook, uncovered, for a further 10 minutes. Sprinkle with parsley and serve with boiled potatoes.

SERVES: 8

## Porc en Civet

*Pork Stewed in Red Wine*

"*En civet*" usually means braising in red wine, a method used mostly for game, such as hare and wild boar. The difference here is that pork does not require marinating first.

*2 lb (1 kg) boned shoulder or leg of pork*
*3 tablespoons bacon fat or vegetable oil*
*3 tablespoons all purpose (plain) flour*
*salt*
*8 peppercorns*
*bouquet garni: 1 bay leaf, 1 thyme sprig, 5 parsley sprigs*
*1 unpeeled red onion*
*2 garlic cloves*
*1 bottle (3 cups/24 fl oz/750 ml) Burgundy-style red wine*

If using shoulder, chop it into small cubes. Leg should be left whole and sliced after cooking, then served with the gravy.

In a stewpot, heat the fat and fry the meat until golden. Blend in the flour, then add salt, peppercorns, the bouquet garni, onion and garlic. Add the red wine and stir with a wooden spoon until the mixture comes to a boil. Reduce heat, cover, and cook slowly for $1\frac{1}{2}$ hours.

Once meat is done, check the gravy. If it is too liquid, remove the meat with a slotted spoon, set aside and keep warm. Boil off surplus liquid over a high heat until the sauce is thick. Replace the meat and serve very hot, with boiled potatoes.

SERVES: 6

## Pommes de Terre au Beaujolais

*Potatoes in Red Wine*

This is a popular dish when the grapes are being harvested, eaten either on its own or with sausages cooked on an open fire.

*3 lb (1.5 kg) potatoes, unpeeled*
*3 tablespoons butter*
*4 tablespoons chopped flat-leafed parsley*
*3 tablespoons chopped chives*
*salt and freshly ground black pepper*
*1 tablespoon all purpose (plain) flour*
*$\frac{1}{2}$ cup (4 fl oz/125 ml) canned consommé or stock made with a bouillon cube*
*1 cup (8 fl oz/250 ml) Beaujolais or other light red wine*

*Pork Stewed in Red Wine, Rooster Stewed in Red Wine, Burgundy Beef*

PETER JOHNSON

*Mushroom and Leek Stew, Burgundy Meat Pie, Potatoes in Red Wine*

Cook the potatoes in boiling, salted water. Peel and slice them in rings. Keep warm.

In a casserole, heat the butter with the parsley, chives, salt and pepper. Blend in the flour, stir for 2 minutes and then slowly dilute the mixture with the consommé and the wine. Bring to a boil, reduce heat and simmer, uncovered, for 10 minutes or until it is of the consistency of thick cream.

Add the sliced potatoes to the sauce, mix well and serve hot, either as a side dish or on its own, followed by a green salad.

SERVES: 4 to 6 as a main course, 6 to 8 as a side dish

## Ragoût de Champignons aux Poireaux

*Mushroom and Leek Stew*

Cultivated mushrooms, champignons, are available widely, although a dedicated French gourmet would pay anything for wild mushrooms, such as *cèpes* and *chanterelles*.

Great chefs do, however, admit that rather than use dried mushrooms, they are willing to make do with champignons for most sauces and dishes — provided they are very fresh and firm.

*2 oz (60 g) fatty bacon, diced*
*2 red onions, chopped*
*1 rounded tablespoon all purpose (plain) flour*
*1 bottle (3 cups/24 fl oz/750 ml) Burgundy-style red wine*
*salt and freshly ground black pepper*
*1 thyme sprig*
*1 lb (500 g) leeks, both white and green parts, cut into 2-in (5-cm) pieces*
*2 lb (1 kg) champignons (button mushrooms), or wild mushrooms, washed and sliced thickly*
*1 or 2 tablespoons cream (optional)*

Cook bacon and onion in a heavy saucepan over low heat until onions are golden. Stir in the flour and wine. Add the salt and pepper, thyme and leeks. Bring to a boil, remove lid and cook slowly for 20 minutes. Add the champignons and cook for a further 5 minutes.

Remove champignons and leeks and reduce sauce by boiling it without a lid over moderate heat until it is the consistency of thick cream. Add a tablespoon or two of cream, if desired. Place the leeks on a warmed serving dish, cover them with the champignons, and pour the sauce over the top. Reheat and serve.

SERVES: 6

## Tourte Bourguignonne

*Burgundy Meat Pie*

This is a classic dish of the region, served after feast days in large households.

*Rough Puff Pastry:*
*3 cups (12 oz/375 g) all purpose (plain) flour*
*$^1/_2$ teaspoon salt*
*$1^1/_4$ cups (310 g/10 oz) butter*
*6 tablespoons cold water*
*Filling:*
*$2^1/_2$ cups sliced roast meat or chicken, cut into pieces $1^1/_2$ in x $^1/_2$ in (4 cm x 1 cm)*
*salt and freshly ground black pepper*
*3 eggs*
*1 cup (8 fl oz/250 ml) heavy (double) cream*
*butter for greasing pie pan*
*yolk of 1 egg for glazing the pie*

For the pastry: Sift the flour and salt into a mixing bowl. Cut the butter into pieces and add to the flour. Using two knives, cut the butter into the flour until it forms small lumps, about the size of your little fingernail. Stir in the cold water and gather dough into a ball. Chill for about 10 minutes.

Place on a floured surface and roll out into a rectangle about 6 x 13 in (15 x 33 cm). Fold the dough in three, bringing one end over, then folding the other end over it, and give a half turn, so the sides face you rather than the folded edge. Roll out again, rolling the strip a little longer, fold in three again and give a half turn. Chill for 10 minutes.

Repeat this process, giving the pastry six turns in all and chilling after every second turn. Chill before using.

To assemble: Preheat oven to 425°F (220°C). Roll out a little more than half the pastry and line a 9-in (23-cm) buttered pie pan with it. Fill three-quarters full with meat. In a bowl, beat eggs and cream with a fork and season with salt and pepper. Pour over the meat.

Roll out the smaller piece of pastry so that it is about 1 in (2.5 cm) larger than the pie pan. Cover the top with it, pressing together the top and bottom edges to seal. Beat the egg yolk with a spoonful of water and brush the mixture over the top of the pie. Cut a hole in the center and insert a funnel made with aluminum foil. This will let steam escape.

Bake in the oven for 45 minutes. Serve warm, with a green salad.

SERVES: 6

PETER JOHNSON

*Duck Stewed in Red Wine*

## Civet de Canard

*Duck Stewed in Red Wine*

The Bresse, famous for its *poularde*, chicken, is also known for its duck.

*goose fat or oil for frying*
*1 medium-sized duck or a small goose, cut into 8 or 10 pieces (cut breast lengthwise)*
*5 to 10 small pickling onions, or 1 large onion, finely sliced*
*3 tablespoons Marc de Bourgogne or other brandy*
*3 tablespoons all purpose (plain) flour*
*salt*
*9 peppercorns*
*1 bouquet garni: 1 bay leaf, 1 thyme sprig, 5 parsley sprigs*
*1 bottle (3 cups/24 fl oz/750 ml) good quality Burgundy-style red wine*
*2 to 3 tablespoons chopped parsley (optional)*

In a large heavy saucepan melt the fat and fry the duck pieces slowly, making sure the skin becomes crisp. Remove the meat and quickly fry the onions until they color a little. Remove onions and pour off all excess fat, then add the Marc de Bourgogne and ignite, stirring to scrape up any brown bits clinging to the pot.

Return the duck and the onions to the saucepan and blend in the flour. Season with salt, then add the peppercorns, bouquet garni, and wine. Bring to a boil, reduce heat and cover with lid. Cook very slowly for 45 minutes to 1 hour, until duck is tender. The gravy should be rich and creamy. If necessary reduce it for a few minutes over high heat.

Serve the duck pieces in the gravy, sprinkled with freshly chopped parsley, if desired.

SERVES: 4 to 6

## *Cassis de Dijon*

*Blackcurrant Syrup*

This is an old recipe from Burgundy, still much in use. Blackcurrants are a Dijon specialty, but various other fruit such as redcurrants, strawberries, raspberries, or blackberries are equally suitable for turning into syrup.

Fruit syrups are an essential ingredient in French cooking, being used in desserts and sorbets and in long cooling drinks with soda water, or in aperitifs with white vermouth or vodka.

*2 lb (1 kg) blackcurrants*
*2 lb (1 kg) sugar*
*1 liqueur glass Marc de Bourgogne, other brandy, or any* eau-de-vie *for each quart (liter) of syrup*

In a large enamel or glass bowl, make a layer of blackcurrants, cover it with a layer of sugar and continue alternating blackcurrants and sugar until both ingredients are used up.

Leave in a cool place (but not in the refrigerator) for 24 hours, then extract the juice using a fine wire sieve. Add the Marc de Bourgogne, then pour the mixture immediately into sterilized bottles.

## *Crêpes au Cassis*

*Blackcurrant Pancakes*

This elegant dessert is served with much fanfare in expensive restaurants, but it is not difficult to make. *Crêpes* can be made in advance and frozen, if desired.

*1 cup (4 oz/125 g) all purpose (plain) flour*
*$1^1/_2$ cups (12 fl oz/475 ml) milk*
*1 egg*
*1 teaspoon Marc de Bourgogne or other brandy*
*1 teaspoon light olive oil*
*pinch of salt*
*$^3/_4$ cup (8 oz/250 g) blackcurrant jam*
*butter for frying*
*powdered (icing) sugar for dusting*

Place the flour in a bowl, break the egg in the middle, and add a pinch of salt. Using a wire whisk, slowly mix in the milk, Marc de Bourgogne and finally the olive oil. (A food processor can be used for this.) Leave the batter to rest for a few hours, covered, in a cool place.

In an 8-in (20-cm) skillet, melt a walnut-sized piece of butter, spreading it evenly over the bottom of the skillet. When hot, pour in the batter, which should be the consistency of running cream. Allow half a small ladleful of batter for each pancake, tilting the skillet so that the mixture spreads evenly to cover the bottom. When the pancake has turned golden on the bottom, in about 40 seconds, turn it with a spatula and cook for a further 30 seconds. Turn out, fold in quarters, and keep warm.

If pancakes have been made in advance, they can be placed on a plate and reheated over gently boiling water.

In a small saucepan, dilute the blackcurrant jam with a spoonful of cold water. Bring it to a boil, then remove from the heat. Pour jam over the pancakes and, if desired, sprinkle with powdered sugar.

As a variation, instead of folding the pancakes, roll them up after putting a tablespoonful of *fromage blanc*, cream cheese, in the middle. Place the pancakes on a serving platter and over the top pour a thick, smooth purée of blackcurrants.

SERVES: 4

*Blackcurrant Pancakes, Blackcurrant Syrup*

PETER JOHNSON

## Meringues au Fromage Blanc et Fraises

*Meringues with Cream Cheese and Strawberries*

*Fromage blanc*, cream cheese, is one of the delights of Burgundy. Much smoother than cottage cheese, *fromage blanc* is made with unpasteurised sour milk, placed in a muslin bag to drain off most of the liquid.

This is a most elegant dessert, but one that is extremely straightforward to prepare.

*4 egg whites*
*1/2 cup (4 oz/125 g) superfine (caster) sugar*
*1/2 cup (3 oz/90 g) powdered (icing) sugar*
*8 oz (150 g) strawberries*
*1 tablespoon superfine (caster) sugar for the strawberries*
*10 oz (315 g)* fromage blanc

Butter and flour a baking sheet. Preheat oven to 200°F (100°C). Beat the egg whites in a bowl until soft peaks form, then slowly add the superfine sugar and then the powdered sugar, beating continuously until the mixture is stiff and shiny.

Using a piping bag, pipe the meringues onto the baking sheet in swirls. This quantity will make about 24 small meringues or 12 large ones. Bake for about 1 hour, taking care that the meringues do not brown. They should be a pale ivory color. If necessary, open the oven door slightly during the last 15 minutes of cooking.

Using a metal spatula, remove the meringues from the baking sheet and set them on a metal rack to cool.

Halve the strawberries and put them in a bowl with the tablespoon of superfine sugar. When ready to assemble the meringues, drain any liquid from the strawberries and gently mix half of them with the *fromage blanc*. Sandwich the meringues in pairs, using generous amounts of the *fromage blanc* mixture. Stud the outsides of the mixture with the remaining strawberry halves, for decoration. Serve at once.

SERVES: 6

## Charlotte au Chocolat

*Chocolate Charlotte*

Chocolate mousse is a classic French dessert, and in the following recipe it becomes the filling of a layer cake made with ladyfingers (sponge biscuits).

On its own, served in ceramic pots or small glass compote dishes, the mousse will serve 8 people.

*Cake:*
*24 ladyfingers (sponge fingers)*
*1 cup (8 fl oz/250 ml) milk*
*2 teaspoons rum*
*Mousse:*
*8 oz (250 g) unsweetened (bitter cooking) chocolate, broken into small pieces, or grated*
*3 tablespoons strong Italian mocha coffee*
*2 teaspoons rum*
*1 teaspoon olive oil*
*5 eggs*
*sweetened whipped cream (optional)*

For the mousse: Prepare at least 8 hours before serving. In a saucepan or a double boiler melt the chocolate in the coffee, rum, and oil. Stir until smooth. Remove and let cool.

Separate the eggs and one by one add the yolks to the cold melted chocolate, beating with a wire whisk. In a separate bowl stiffly beat the whites. Fold the beaten whites in with the chocolate mixture. Leave in a cool place to set.

To assemble the cake: Pour the milk and the rum into a bowl. One by one lightly dip the ladyfingers into the milk and line the bottom and the sides of an 8-cup (2 qt/2 l) springform cake pan. Fill with half the chocolate mousse. Cover with a layer of ladyfingers, then with the remaining mousse. Finish with another layer of ladyfingers.

Keep the charlotte overnight in the refrigerator. After unmolding, decorate, if desired, with swirls of sweetened whipped cream.

SERVES: 10

*Chocolate Charlotte, Meringues with Cream Cheese and Strawberries*

PETER JOHNSON

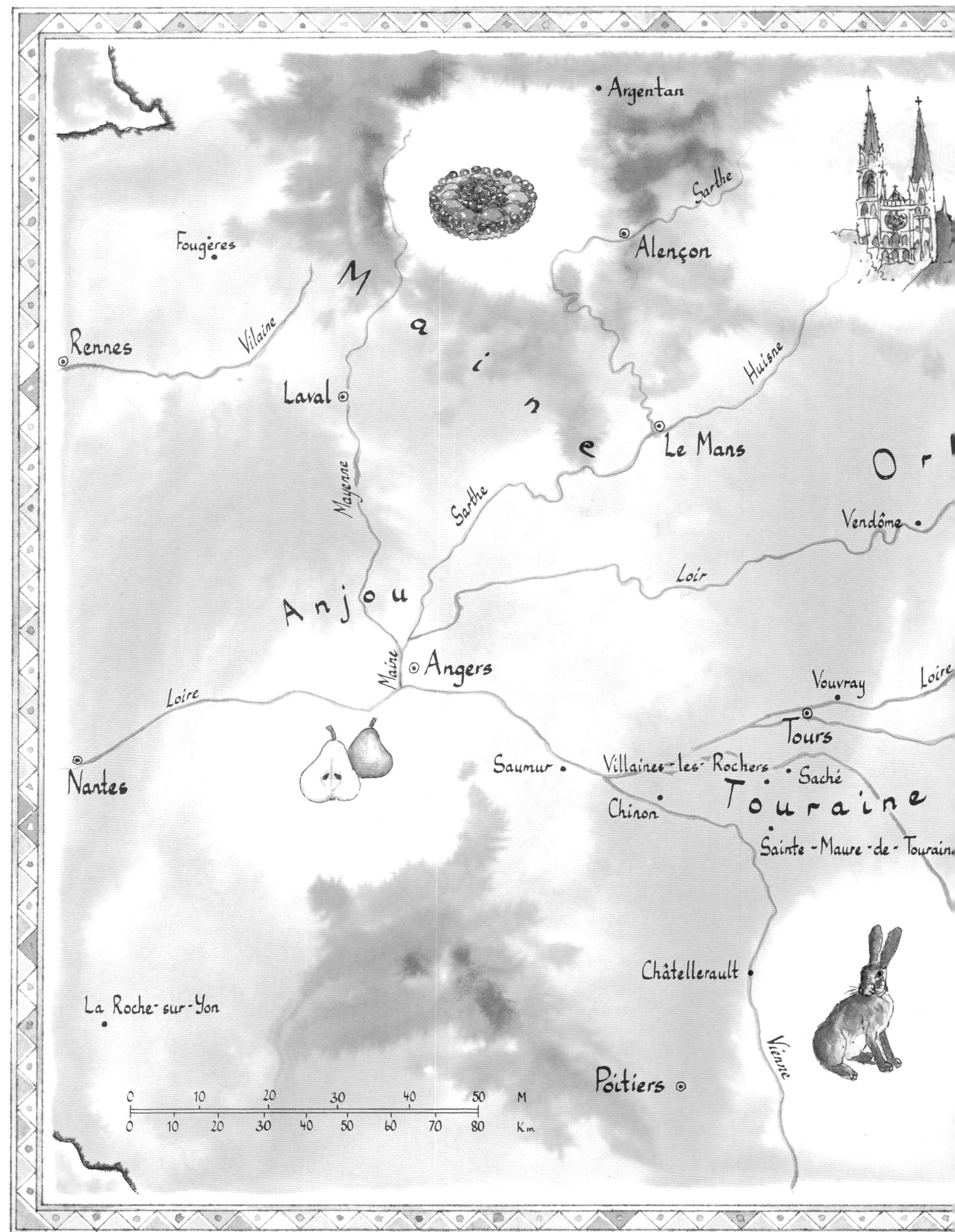

Argentan
Sarthe
Alençon
Fougères
Maine
Rennes
Vilaine
Laval
Huisne
Le Mans
Or
Mayenne
Sarthe
Vendôme
Loir
Anjou
Angers
Maine
Loire
Vouvray
Loire
Tours
Nantes
Saumur
Villaines-les-Rochers
Saché
Touraine
Chinon
Sainte-Maure-de-Tourain
Châtellerault
La Roche-sur-Yon
Vienne
Poitiers
0 10 20 30 40 50 M
0 10 20 30 40 50 60 70 80 Km

# THE LOIRE

*Gregory Usher and Isabelle Bachelard*

The fertile Loire valley is rich both in produce and in history, and is home to some of the country's finest white wines. Fruit trees, vines, and vegetables thrive, and everywhere there are châteaux, from forbidding Medieval fortresses to glorious Renaissance stately homes. The trip from Paris initially takes the visitor across the seemingly endless flat grain fields of the Beauce, but then the scenery becomes delightfully varied as you travel past orchards, market gardens, vineyards, woodlands, and graceful, winding rivers lined with poplars and willows. Little wonder that this region is known as the garden of France.

QUENTIN BACON

*A hardworking nurseryman takes a short break. The Loire valley is known for its glorious gardens.*

## France's Longest River

Outside the main cities of Orléans, Tours, and Angers, the Loire valley remains largely rural. Estates are relatively small, and even wine is often produced by farms growing a variety of produce. It is the Loire, France's longest river, that gives this region its unity. Rising in the rugged Massif Central, it follows a 600-mile (960-kilometer) course northwest through Burgundy and Berry to Orléans, where it turns and heads west across Touraine, Anjou, and the Pays Nantais to the Atlantic Ocean. The ocean's gentle influence gives the region a generally mild climate, with warm, damp air being carried to the inland valleys by the Loire's tributaries — the Cher, the Indre, the Vienne, and the Maine. This moderation seems to extend to the character of the people, too, who are relaxed and gracious. The French they speak is unaccented, and many scholars consider the Loire to be the cradle of the language in its purest form.

Until the advent of the railways in the mid-nineteenth century, the Loire provided an important transportation route for both people and goods, and was busy with barges and sailing boats. The river linked the Atlantic Ocean and southwest France with Paris and the north. But it is an unruly waterway, and never offered ideal passage. Its flow is irregular, its bed is often wide and shallow, and dead ends, islands, and strong currents hamper navigation. Floods have repeatedly broken the river's levees since they were first built in the twelfth century, but those of today, made of sturdy material and with sluiceways that allow controlled runoff, provide the surrounding countryside with reliable protection. In some places these levees are the height of nearby rooftops, and sometimes roads run along the top.

Fish are plentiful in the Loire's capricious waters, and anglers are a common sight. Their catches include sandre, pike, lamprey, eel, shad, and salmon. Traditional menus still feature *fricassée d'anguille*, eel stewed in local wine, and *civelles*, baby eels cooked in oil and butter. Some chefs combine local ingredients in fresh, new ways, creating dishes like *andouillette de sandre*, a rich fish-mousse sausage, and *mille-feuille de brochet*, pike cooked in puff pastry. Even the tiniest fish are never thrown back; they are deep-fried for *petite friture*. Salmon was once plentiful, but pollution and engineering works to control the river's flow have adversely affected spawning, and stock is dwindling.

In ancient times the roving river and its tributaries deposited alluvium throughout the valley, creating rich fields, ideal for growing early vegetables and melons. Over the years levees and irrigation systems have extended the area under cultivation, and now the region also contributes significantly to the national production of apples, pears, raspberries, and strawberries. Flowers too, are grown commercially, such as roses and orchids.

Along the banks of the Loire huge caves have been created through the quarrying of limestone to build the region's great cathedrals and châteaux, and the traditional one-storey, slate-roofed cottages of Anjou. Houses were even carved out of the chalk cliffs, and sometimes their chimneys would poke out among the vines planted on the slopes above. Today the darkness, the steady cool temperature and the high humidity of these vast quarries provide perfect conditions for maturing wine and growing mushrooms.

Neat, brown goats can be seen everywhere, grazing in the fields, and goat's milk cheese is made throughout the region. These cheeses are made in a variety of shapes and are bought at different stages of aging, according to taste. A fresh *chèvre* is soft, with a fresh, lactic taste, while the most mature ones are hard and dry, with a powerful odor. Almost every town seems to produce its own *chèvre,* made in a characteristic way: Vendôme's is a small disk; Sainte-Maure-de-Touraine's is a cylindrical shape with a straw running through the center. Only Orléanais offers cow's milk cheeses — Pithiviers au Foin (in hay), and Olivet Bleu or Cendré (in ashes) — both soft, mild cheeses.

*Following pages: The beautiful Château de Saumur, reflected in the waters of the Loire.*

## Orléanais and Sologne

Orléanais is the Loire's easternmost province, and its capital, Orléans, was once second only to Paris in importance. In 1429 Joan of Arc, at the head of the French forces, drove the British from the city, and in May each year Orléans holds a great celebration to commemorate her exploits. In the cathedral there is a Joan of Arc chapel, with stained-glass windows illustrating scenes from her life.

Although there are few vineyards around Orléans today, a large industry derived from wine has long prospered here. Before rapid transport, much of the wine consigned to the city had soured by the time it reached its destination. Enterprising businessmen turned the spoiled wine to profit by making it into vinegar. Orléans is still the vinegar capital of France.

*Dahlias in the grounds of the sixteenth-century Château de Chenonceaux, which was once the home of Diane de Poitiers.*

LEO MEIER/WELDON TRANNIES

LEO MEIER

# CHAMPIGNONS DE PARIS

Successful attempts were made to grow *Agaricus bisporus*, now known as the cultivated mushroom, in the seventeenth century, but it was not until the nineteenth century that the champignon de Paris, the button mushroom, the least mature form of the cultivated mushroom, was systematically produced. Mushroom farming first flourished around Paris, then spread to the Loire valley, which is now the mushroom center of France.

The Loire's vast limestone quarries, which furnished stone for the region's famous châteaux, provide the dark, cool, moist environment ideal for raising mushrooms. They are grown by impregnating sterilized manure and peat moss with mushroom spores. Air circulation, temperature, and humidity are strictly controlled, sometimes electronically.

Five or six weeks after planting, the first crop is ready for harvesting. Each mound produces five crops, about one a week, and then the compost is discarded or used for potting soil. Working in the dark, wearing a headband with a light, pickers pull out the mushrooms, or cut them with a knife.

Cooked within hours of picking, these mushrooms have a better flavor than even the fanciest day-old wild variety.

LEO MEIER

There is a good deal in Orléanais to please anyone with a sweet tooth. Shops display jars of local honey, *pain d'épice,* spiced honey bread, and *cotignac*, a traditional quince-jelly candy. *Tart Tatin* can be seen everywhere, but fans of this caramelized apple tart are likely to want to visit the Hôtel Tatin in the small town of Lamotte-Beuvron, where this fabled dish was created. According to legend, the Tatin sisters invented the upside-down tart to repair a baking error.

It was the forests of the Loire valley, once teeming with wildlife, that attracted French kings and the nobility to the region. Nothing gave them greater pleasure than hunting. Just south of Orléans, in Sologne, woods and misty marshland still harbor duck, hare, pheasant, and deer, but the animals are now raised by gamekeepers. Hunting continues to be important to the local economy, and wealthy businesspeople from Paris come here to shoot during the winter months. A dozen varieties of wild mushrooms grow in the woods, and they are often cooked in traditional game dishes. Carp and perch netted in the lakes are prized, and beehives dot the region, heather on the moorland providing food for the bees. Sologne is also known for fine vegetables, particularly its slender leeks and its white asparagus.

The game terrines and pâtés of northern Orléanais are particularly highly regarded. Chartres, known for its magnificent, soaring Gothic cathedral, is also home to a celebrated partridge pâté, the *pâté de Chartres*. Pithiviers has long been known for its *pâté d'alouettes*, lark pâté, which consists of a whole, unboned lark, stuffed with forcemeat and wrapped in pastry. Even today the bakers of Pithiviers still make this dish, although how they come by the little birds is a mystery, as they are now protected by law. Pithiviers' other great specialty is its puff pastry tart filled with almond paste, named after the town.

## ROYAL CUISINE AND CHARCUTERIE

To the west of Orléanais lies Touraine. The great sixteenth-century writer Rabelais was born here, at La Devinière. Balzac and the poet Ronsard also lived in Touraine for a time, and wrote about the region. The stifled provincial atmosphere of Saumur was captured brilliantly in Balzac's novel *Eugénie Grandet*.

Tours' fame began in the fourth century with its bishop, later to become Saint Martin. It was he who improved upon nature by inventing pruning: he noticed that vines gnawed by errant donkeys produced better grapes than those that had been left unscathed. But the region's full flowering came during the Renaissance, when the French kings came to live in the splendid castles they had built here. The *haute cuisine* dish, *carpe à la Chambord*, an elaborate preparation of stuffed carp with a garnish of fish *quenelles*, truffles, fluted mushrooms, and fried caviar, takes its name from the largest of the Renaissance châteaux, which has a moat stocked with carp.

Food talk in the Loire valley revolves around *rillons* and *rillettes,* and there are many different versions of these local specialties. *Rillons* are chunks of pork belly or breast which have been macerated with aromatic vegetables in white wine, and then cooked slowly in lard. They are eaten, either hot or cold, as a first course, in the same way as a terrine. Today some chefs lighten this hearty specialty by tossing the pork chunks with greens for *salade aux rillons*. *Rillettes* are a sort of pâté made from pork or sometimes rabbit trimmings which have been gently cooked for hours. The *rillettes* from Vouvray and Tours are of a finer texture than those from nearby Le Mans.

*Preceding page: A group of cottages and farm outbuildings in the Loire valley, surrounded by neatly cultivated fields.*

LEO MEIER/WELDON TRANNIES

Traditional Touraine recipes are generally simple and light, such as *fricassée de volaille au Vouvray*, based on good quality poultry, the area's plentiful vegetables, fresh herbs, and local wine. *Lièvre au Chinon*, roast hare with a red wine and cream sauce, is another dish which takes advantage of the local wine, as does *poires belle angevine*, pears poached in red wine.

Chinon is a delightful Medieval town on the river Vienne, built into the side of a hill, and it boasts a magnificent ruined château. Beneath a hilltop vineyard here you can visit wine cellars carved out of the limestone cliff. It is worth visiting one of the clifftop vineyards and then one of those planted on the ancient riverbed, to compare the red wines. The chalky soil produces robust, long-lasting wines, while the gravelly river soil produces pleasant wines with a raspberry aroma that are ready to drink while still young.

*These neat little homes, with their shutters and lace curtains, are built into the cliffs not far from Les Roches.*

LEO MEIER

No one who has ever toiled in a garden should miss the glorious formal sixteenth-century fruit, vegetable, and flower gardens recreated at the Château de Villandry, west of Tours. These are at their best in late summer. In his letters, Balzac wrote admiringly of the weavers of the nearby village of Villaines-les-Rochers, and today visitors can still watch them at work. Willow reeds are made into everything from cheese trays to baskets for hot-air ballooning. A few miles from Villaines, at Saché, Balzac was a frequent visitor, and this house is now a museum with several handsome period rooms and all sorts of Balzac mementos.

At the border of Touraine and Anjou, the abbey of Fontevrault, which once comprised five separate convents, is one of the most impressive religious complexes in France. In addition to its ornate church, housing the tombs of the Plantagenets, the abbey has the most remarkable Romanesque kitchen. This huge octagonal building, surmounted by a tower and flanked by apses and twenty open fireplaces, gives an indication of the scale of cooking that once took place here.

QUENTIN BACON

*Freshly-picked tulips for sale at the markets, a welcome sign that spring has arrived.*

## Anjou

The French statesman Georges Clémenceau said, "In Anjou France is more French than anywhere else." Certainly the region offers all the attractions for which the Loire is best known: vineyards, châteaux, ancient cathedrals and churches, and wonderful restaurants.

Named after its main city, Angers, Anjou spreads from the white chalk country around Saumur to a darker landscape of schist and granite to the west. Anjou's proximity to the sea and clients in England and northern Europe spurred the growth of its vineyards. Vintners developed sparkling wines here because Anjou wines, like those of Champagne, can easily be made to effervesce, and the local stone quarries provide natural cellars in which to age the wine. In fact, until French law dictated that Champagne wine could be made only with grapes from Champagne, many Loire grapes wound up in Champagne bottles.

Anjou is the land of *la fillette*, a half-bottle measure of wine, and *boule de fort*, a game of bowls similar to Mediterranean *pétanque*. *La fillette* generally accompanies a game of *boule de fort*, and clubs offer their members numbered cubby holes in which to keep their glasses while playing. When in Mazé, home of the *boule de fort* club l'Avenir, one of 350 such clubs in the region, it is worth visiting the Château de Montgeoffroy. The château has the most elaborate kitchens, filled with eighteenth-century copper and pewter utensils.

Angers' gigantic thirteenth-century fortress, once home to the dukes of Anjou, is now the largest tapestry museum in the world. A few Medieval houses remain in the city and there are several late-Gothic churches in the Angevin style. There is also a small wine museum, and you can visit the Cointreau distillery to see this fine orange-flavored liqueur being made.

Doyenné de Comice and Belle Angevine pears were developed in Anjou, and the region has a reputation for raising new fruit varieties, but in recent years many local varieties of fruit and vegetables have been dying out. L' Association pour l'Inventaire et la Conservation des Plantes Cultivées has been set up to track down old plant varieties and restore the worthwhile ones to the culinary repertoire. As a result of their efforts, Guignolet, a cherry liqueur popular early in this century, can still be made with the traditional Guigne cherry. The association is currently redeveloping sea kale, a wild plant which was widely cultivated in the Loire in the nineteenth century.

*Large amounts of fruit and vegetables grow in the rich alluvial soil of the Loire valley. Here a bed of pumpkins is ready for harvesting.*

LEO MEIER

*A woman making* chèvre, *goat's milk cheese. All sorts of* chèvres *are made throughout the region, in shapes ranging from disks, to little pyramids, to cylinders.*

ANTHONY BLAKE/HORIZON

Both Angers and Nantes claim to have invented *beurre blanc*, a white butter sauce made by whisking butter into a reduction of shallots and wine (or vinegar, or both, depending on the chef). It is best to try this delicate sauce in one of the country inns along the Loire, which have served *beurre blanc* with river salmon and pike for generations.

While Anjou shops sell their share of *rillons* (here called *rillauds*) and *rillettes*, they also sell all sorts of fresh sausages. Look for *boudin blanc*, a white sausage made with pork, chicken, veal, and sometimes sweetbreads, and *gogue*, a blood sausage flavored with Swiss chard and herbs. Another regional dish is the almost mythical *cul de veau à l'angevine*, veal sirloin simmered in white wine with onions and carrots, herbs and pork rind. Anjou farmers still grow the old-fashioned *mogettes*, white beans, and green cabbage. Local cooks simmer cabbage with potatoes to make *soupe aux piochons*, or stew it in butter for *chouée*. Fruit desserts are the region's pride, particularly tarts and pies, and there are the classic *crémets d'Anjou*, small molded delicacies made with fresh sweetened cheese that are generally served with strawberries or raspberries.

## Wines of the Loire

The vineyards of the Loire spread from the Pays Nantais on the Atlantic, which is in Brittany, far inland to the communes of Sancerre and Pouilly-sur-Loire in Burgundy. The wines vary from village to village, but they all share the same charm and freshness that makes them a perfect match for the region's unpretentious food. All can be drunk young, although many gain from aging.

The Loire's mild climate favors white grapes, and the versatile Chenin Blanc grape is grown extensively. It is used to produce a wide range of wines, from everyday drinking wines to wines of exceptional quality that age well. Whether still, sparkling, dry, semi-sweet, or sweet, Chenin Blanc wines acquire their full complexity after eight to twelve years.

Montlouis and Vouvray are among the more notable Touraine white wines. From Anjou come Saumur, Anjou Coteaux de la Loire, Coteaux de Saumur, and the outstanding Coulée de Serrant from Savennières, one of the country's great wines, which can be aged for years. There are some fine sweet wines, including Bonnezeaux, Coteaux de l'Aubance and Coteaux du Layon. The sparkling Crémant de Loire, made in Touraine, Anjou and Saumur, makes a delightful aperitif.

The best red wines in the region are made with Cabernet Franc grapes. Of the Touraine reds, perhaps the most interesting are Bourgueil, Saint-Nicolas-de-Bourgueil, and Chinon. Anjou's red wines include Saumur, Anjou-Villages, and Saumur-Champigny.

Still and sparkling pink wines are produced all along the Loire and provide refreshing summer drinking. Cabernet d'Anjou is a medium-dry to medium-sweet rosé, and Rosé d'Anjou is extremely popular, produced in large quantities throughout the region. Saumur Mousseux are sparkling wines made in a variety of styles, including some high quality rosé.

## PAYS NANTAIS

*Muscadet (1)*
*Muscadet de Sèvre-et-Maine (3)*
*Muscadet des Coteaux de la Loire (2)*

## ANJOU-SAUMUR

*White wines:*
*Anjou (dry and sweet) (4)*
*Anjou Coteaux de la Loire (dry and sweet) (5)*
*Bonnezeaux (sweet) (7)*
*Coteaux de l'Aubance (semi-sweet) (6)*
*Coteaux de Saumur (semi-sweet) (8)*
*Coteaux du Layon (sweet) (9)*
*Savennières (dry and semi-sweet) (10)*

*Red wines:*
*Anjou-Villages (4)*
*Saumur (8)*
*Saumur-Champigny (8)*

*Rosés:*
*Cabernet d'Anjou (4)*
*Rosé d'Anjou (4)*
*Saumur Mousseux (sparkling) (8)*

## TOURAINE

*Bourgueil (red) (11)*
*Chinon (red) (12)*
*Crémant de Loire (dry and semi-sweet white, and sparkling) (4, 8, 13)*
*Montlouis (dry and semi-sweet Chenin blanc) (14)*
*Saint-Nicolas-de-Bourgueil (red) (11)*
*Touraine (white, red, and sparkling) (13)*
*Vouvray (dry and sweet white, Chenin blanc, sparkling) (15)*

## UPPER LOIRE

*Though in Burgundy, the following are classified as Loire wines:*

*Coteaux du Giennois VDQS (very light white, and red) (20)*
*Menetou-Salon (white, red, and rosé) (17)*
*Pouilly Fumé (dry white) (19)*
*Quincy (dry white) (16)*
*Reuilly (white, red, and rosé) (16)*
*Sancerre (dry white, red, and rosé) (18)*

### Other Loire Wines

*Châteaumeillant VDQS (21)*
*Saint-Pourçain VDQS (22)*

# RECIPES OF THE LOIRE

*Gregory Usher*

PETER JOHNSON

## Rillons

*Confit of Pork Breast*

Before the advent of refrigeration, the traditional method of preserving meat so that it could be used throughout the winter was this process known as *confit*. This recipe for pork *confit* is from chef Pascal Niatel at Le Relais d'Antan, Lavardin.

*1 fresh pork breast, about 5 lb (2.5 kg), sliced*
*$^3/_4$ cup (6 oz/185 g) salt*
*1 bottle (3 cups/24 fl oz/750 ml) dry white Loire wine*
*1 carrot, sliced*
*1 onion, sliced*
*1 thyme sprig*
*1 bay leaf*
*1 clove*
*1 teaspoon whole peppercorns*
*1 parsley sprig, chopped*
*3 lb (1.5 kg) rendered fresh pork fat*

Arrange the pieces of pork in layers in a large plastic or glass container, sprinkling the salt generously and evenly between each layer. Leave to stand in a cool place overnight.

Remove the pork from the salt. Brush off excess salt and place the pork in a large, shallow container with the wine, carrot, onion, thyme, bay leaf, clove, peppercorns, and parsley. The pork pieces should be completely covered by the wine. Leave in the marinade for at least 12 hours.

Remove the pork from the marinade and drain. Melt the rendered pork fat in a large, heavy-bottomed saucepan or a stock pot. Add the pork and simmer over very low heat for about $2^1/_2$ hours. The pork should be completely covered with fat and the mixture should not boil.

Using a slotted spoon, remove the pork from the fat and drain on a baking sheet lined with paper towels. Serve at room temperature.

(Note: The pork breast can be cut into smaller pieces to serve with an aperitif rather than as a first course, in which case total cooking time should be reduced by about $1^1/_2$ hours.)

SERVES: 10 to 12

*Rabbit Terrine in Aspic,*
*Confit of Pork Breast,*
*Salad with Warm Confit of Pork Breast*

## Salade aux Rillons Chauds

*Salad with Warm Confit of Pork Breast*

*Rillons* are often served alone as a first course, but are delicious in a salad such as this one from chef François Salle at the Auberge de la Brenne, at Neuille le Lierrt.

*Vinaigrette:*
*2 tablespoons red wine vinegar*
*salt*
*$^1/_3$ cup (3 fl oz/80 ml) walnut oil*
*freshly ground black pepper*
*Salad:*
*about 6 cups mixed salad greens, such as butterhead (cabbage) lettuce,* radicchio *and lamb's lettuce*
*6 large cultivated mushrooms, coarsely chopped*
*2 tomatoes, coarsely chopped*
*6 large* rillons
*2 small onions, chopped*
*$^1/_2$ cup ($1^1/_2$ oz/45 g) walnut halves*
*2 tablespoons chopped parsley*

For the vinaigrette, place the vinegar in a small bowl, season with salt, and whisk until the salt has dissolved. Whisk in the oil drop by drop until thoroughly blended. Season with the pepper.

Divide the greens equally among six serving plates. Sprinkle with mushrooms and tomatoes. Drizzle a tablespoon of the vinaigrette over each salad.

Slice the *rillons* thinly. Place in a large skillet with the onions and sauté over medium-high heat until the *rillons* are lightly browned and the onions are cooked.

Divide the hot *rillons* and onions evenly between the six salads. Sprinkle with walnuts and parsley and serve.

SERVES: 6

*A well-fed Loire valley pig.*

VARIN VISAGE/JACANA/AUSCAPE INTERNATIONAL

## Gelée de Garenne

*Rabbit Terrine in Aspic*

Marc de Vouvray, an *eau-de-vie* distilled from the grape residue from Vouvray winemaking, flavors this rabbit terrine from chef Alain Couturier at La Roche le Roy in Tours.

*1 rabbit, ideally a wild one, about 4 lb (2 kg), cut into serving pieces*
*1 onion, thinly sliced*
*1 carrot, cut into thin rounds*
*1 teaspoon whole peppercorns*
*$^1/_2$ cup (4 fl oz/125 ml) Marc de Vouvray*
*1 calf's foot, blanched and halved lengthwise*
*1 bouquet garni: 1 bay leaf, 1 thyme sprig, 6 parsley sprigs*
*salt*
*1 bottle (3 cups/24 fl oz/750 ml) dry Vouvray or other dry white wine*
*1 large bunch mixed fresh herbs, including parsley, chervil, tarragon, dill, and chives*

Place the rabbit pieces in a terrine with the onion, carrot, and peppercorns. Sprinkle the Marc de Vouvray evenly over the rabbit and vegetables and let marinate, refrigerated, for 12 hours, turning the rabbit occasionally.

Transfer the contents of the terrine to an ovenproof casserole. Add the calf's foot, and bouquet garni. Season with salt. Pour the Vouvray over the rabbit. Add enough water to cover the contents of the casserole. Place over medium-low heat and let simmer, covered, for $1^1/_2$ hours.

Meanwhile, thoroughly rinse and dry the herbs, then chop them finely. When the rabbit has cooked, remove from the heat and let cool. Bone the rabbit pieces and set aside. Bone the calf's foot and dice finely. Pour the cooking liquid through a fine strainer and reserve.

In the bottom of a greased pâté terrine or bread pan, arrange the boned rabbit in layers, sprinkling the diced calf's foot and the chopped fresh herbs generously over each layer. Add enough of the strained cooking liquid to come up to the rim of the terrine. Cover and refrigerate for 24 hours.

To serve, dip the bottom of the terrine in hot water for several seconds to loosen, and then invert onto a serving platter. Slice and serve.

SERVES: 6

## Mille-feuille de Brochet à l'Emincée de Poireaux et Duxelles du Champignons Beurre Blanc

*Puff Pastry Filled with Pike Mousse, Leeks, and Mushrooms in White Butter Sauce*

Some fine Loire valley products — pike, cultivated mushrooms, and the rich white butter sauce called *beurre blanc* — are combined in this elegant dish from chef M. Oudry at Les Chandelles in Saumur.

*1 sheet puff pastry, 12 x 6 in (30 x 15 cm)*
*$1^1/_4$ lb (625 g) fillet of pike*
*salt and freshly ground white pepper*
*1 egg white*
*$1^1/_4$ cups (10 fl oz/310 ml)* crème fraîche *or heavy (double) cream*
*4 tablespoons (2 oz/60 g) unsalted butter*
*2 shallots, finely chopped*
*3 oz (90 g) cultivated mushrooms, finely chopped*
*3 oz (90 g) leeks, white parts only, finely chopped*
Beurre Blanc *(White Butter Sauce):*
*4 shallots, very finely chopped*
*$1^1/_2$ tablespoons white vinegar*
*$1^1/_2$ tablespoons dry white wine*
*$1^1/_4$ cups (10 oz/310 g) unsalted butter, softened*
*salt and freshly ground white pepper*

Preheat the oven to 450°F (230°C). Cut the pastry into six rectangles, each measuring 6 x 2 in (15 x 5 cm). Place the rectangles on a baking sheet and bake until dry and flaky, but not browned. Remove from the oven and set aside.

Place the pike in a food processor and process as finely as possible. Force the pike through a sieve to remove all bones and nerves. Return it to the processor and season with the salt and pepper. Add the egg white and process for 1 minute. Add the *crème fraîche* and process on high until the mixture attains the consistency of very firm whipped cream. Refrigerate until ready to use.

Melt half the butter in a skillet, add the shallots and cook over medium heat for 1 minute. Add the mushrooms, season with salt and pepper, and cook over medium-high heat until all the liquid they give off in cooking has evaporated. Set aside.

Wipe the skillet clean. Melt the remaining butter. Add the leeks and cook over medium-low heat until just tender. Season with salt and pepper and set aside.

When ready to assemble, preheat the oven to 400°F (200°C). Cut the pastry rectangles into three 2-in (5-cm) squares. Spread the chilled pike mousse evenly over six of the pastry squares. Spread a layer of the mushroom mixture on top of the mousse, followed by a layer of the sautéed leeks. (You should have used up about half of each of the three mixtures.) Top each square with another square of pastry and spread with successive layers of the mousse, mushroom mixture, and leeks as before. Top with the remaining squares of pastry. Place the six squares on a baking sheet and bake for 15 to 20 minutes.

While the pastries cook, prepare the sauce. Place the shallots, vinegar, and wine in a small saucepan and reduce over medium-high heat until the liquid has nearly evaporated. Remove the saucepan from the heat and add the softened butter, a little at a time, whisking briskly after each addition and returning to the heat from time to time to warm. (Be careful not to overheat, or the butter will melt rather than thicken into a full-bodied sauce.) Season with salt and pepper.

To serve, spoon the *beurre blanc* over the bottoms of six warmed serving plates. Place the warm filled pastry squares in the center of each plate and serve immediately.

SERVES: 6

## Cassolette d'Escargots aux Champignons

*Snails and Wild Mushrooms*

Cool Loire valley forests provide the perfect conditions for wild mushrooms, and cultivated mushrooms are grown in great quantities in limestone caves. In this recipe from chef François Salle of the Auberge de la Brenne, the woodsy flavor of two types of wild mushrooms is paired with snails and garlic.

*12 oz (375 g) oyster mushrooms or other wild mushrooms*
*10 oz (300 g)* chanterelles *or other wild mushrooms*
*7 tablespoons ($3^1/_2$ oz/105 g) unsalted butter*
*1 tablespoon chopped fresh parsley*
*$^3/_4$ cup (3 oz/90 g) ground blanched almonds*
*6 garlic cloves, crushed*
*$^1/_2$ cup (4 fl oz/125 ml) water*
*6 dozen canned snails*
*salt and freshly ground pepper*

Trim and wash the mushrooms. Cut into large cubes and place in a heavy-bottomed saucepan. Add half the butter, the parsley, ground almonds, half the garlic, and water. Place over low heat and simmer for 15 minutes.

In a skillet, melt the remaining butter, add the remaining garlic and cook over low heat for 1 or 2 minutes. Add the snails, season with salt and pepper, and sauté over medium heat until the snails are lightly browned.

Divide the mushroom mixture evenly among six warmed serving plates. Arrange the snails on top and serve immediately.

SERVES: 6

## Andouillette de Sandre à la Moutarde à l'Ancienne

*Perch-Pike Sausage with Mustard Sauce*

*Sandre*, a particularly delicious large perch, is found in many Loire valley rivers.

*1 perch-pike, cod, or any firm white fish, about 4 to 5 lb (2 to 2.5 kg)*
*3 tablespoons unsalted butter*
*2 leeks, white parts only, finely diced*
*1 celery stalk, finely diced*
*1 carrot, finely diced*
*3 cups (24 fl oz/750 ml)* crème fraîche *or heavy (double) cream*
*1 egg white*
*$1^1/_2$ tablespoons green peppercorns*
*2 teaspoons finely chopped chives*
*6 sheets nonstick paper*
*1 cup (8 fl oz/250 ml) peanut oil*
*about 2 cups (16 fl oz/500 ml) fish stock*
*1 tablespoon old-style, grainy mustard*
*salt and freshly ground black pepper*

Fillet the fish, and slice off six large diagonal slices. Flatten these scallops gently and refrigerate. After filleting and slicing the fish, place the flesh that remains, (about 2 lb/1 kg) in a food processor, and process to a purée.

Melt the butter in a large skillet. Add the leeks, celery, and carrot, and cook gently until they are crisp-tender. Set aside to cool. In a mixing bowl, combine the puréed fish flesh with the cooled vegetable mixture, 1 cup (8 fl oz/250 ml) of the *crème fraîche*, the egg white, green peppercorns, and chives.

Spread the sheets of nonstick paper out on a work surface. Brush each sheet generously with the peanut oil. Place one

*Puff Pastry Filled with Pike Mousse, Leeks, and Mushrooms in White Butter Sauce; Snails and Wild Mushrooms*

fillet of fish on each sheet. Spoon a generous tablespoon of the puréed fish and vegetable mixture in the center of each fish fillet. Starting on the long edge of the paper, roll up the fish jelly-roll fashion, twisting the two ends tightly. Place the parcels in a shallow baking pan, then add enough fish stock to come about halfway up the sides of the parcels. Simmer gently over medium-low heat, turning the parcels to poach evenly for 10 to 12 minutes. Remove the fish and keep warm while preparing the sauce.

Place the poaching stock in a saucepan with the remaining *crème fraîche* and reduce until slightly thickened. Pour through a fine strainer. Stir in the mustard and season to taste with salt and pepper.

To serve, remove the fish sausages from their papers and slice. Arrange on the sauce on six warmed serving plates. Serve immediately.

SERVES: 6

## Petits Flans aux Courgettes et Carrottes

*Carrot and Zucchini Molds*

These vegetable molds are a specialty from chef Pascal Niatel of Le Relais d' Antan. They go well with fish or chicken.

*5 oz (155 g) carrots*
*3 oz (90 g) zucchini (courgettes), unpeeled, cut into 2 to 3-in (5 to 7-cm) lengths*
*2 cups (16 fl oz/500 ml) milk*
*7 oz (220 g) Bleu d'Auvergne or other blue-veined cheese*
*5 eggs*
*3/4 cup* crème fraîche *or heavy (double) cream*
*salt and freshly ground pepper*

Preheat the oven to 300°F (150°C). Steam the carrots and zucchini over salted boiling water until fork tender. Place the milk in a small saucepan. Crumble the cheese into the milk and warm over low heat, stirring occasionally, until the milk bubbles and the cheese is melted.

Place the eggs in a mixing bowl and beat thoroughly. Add the *crème fraîche* and mix together. Season with salt and pepper. Gradually pour the warm milk in a thin stream into the egg mixture, whisking constantly.

Chop the steamed carrots and zucchini as finely as possible or shred them with a large grater. Stir the vegetables into the milk and egg mixture. Divide the mixture evenly among six individual generously oiled small cylindrical molds, or ramekins.

Place the molds in a bain-marie with the water coming about halfway up the sides of the molds. Place in the oven and cook for about 30 minutes, or until the mixture is set. Turn out of the molds and serve warm, at room temperature, or chilled with mayonnaise.

SERVES: 6

## *Lièvre à la Crème*

*Hare in Cream Sauce*

France's inimitable *crème fraîche* tames the gamey taste of hare in chef Alain Couturier's recipe, served at La Roche le Roy in Tours.

*3 tablespoons unsalted butter*
*3 tablespoons vegetable oil*
*10 shallots, halved lengthwise*
*2 slices (10 oz/315 g) smoked bacon, diced*
*3 saddles of hare, about 1 lb (500 g) each, or about 4 lb (2 kg) rabbit pieces*
*salt and freshly ground black pepper*
*1½ tablespoons white wine vinegar*
*1½ cups (12 fl oz/375 ml) dry Vouvray wine or other dry white wine*
*1½ cups (12 fl oz/375 ml)* crème fraîche *or heavy (double) cream*
*6 parsley sprigs, finely chopped*

Melt the butter in the oil in a large saucepan. Add the shallots and the bacon and cook for about 10 minutes. Add the hare and cook until lightly browned on all sides. Season with salt and pepper.

Sprinkle the vinegar over the hare and let evaporate for a few minutes. Pour in the wine. Cover the saucepan and simmer over low heat for about 50 minutes, turning the hare occasionally. (If using rabbit, cook for about 30 minutes.)

Stir in the *crème fraîche*. Correct the seasoning. Cover the pan and simmer over low heat for about 10 minutes longer. Arrange the hare on a warm, shallow serving dish. Spoon the sauce over the hare, sprinkle with the chopped parsley and serve. This dish is even more tasty when served with braised chestnuts and celery, and a cranberry compote.

SERVES: 6

## *Fricassée d'Anguilles au Vin Blanc*

*Fricassee of Eel in White Wine*

Eels are cooked in white wine in this recipe of Chef Pascal Niatel at Le Relais d'Antan. Small sole fillets make a suitable substitute if eels are unavailable.

*4 oz (125 g) smoked bacon, coarsely diced*
*9 tablespoons (4½ oz/140 g) unsalted butter*
*2 tablespoons vegetable oil*
*4 oz (125 g) champignons (button mushrooms)*

PETER JOHNSON

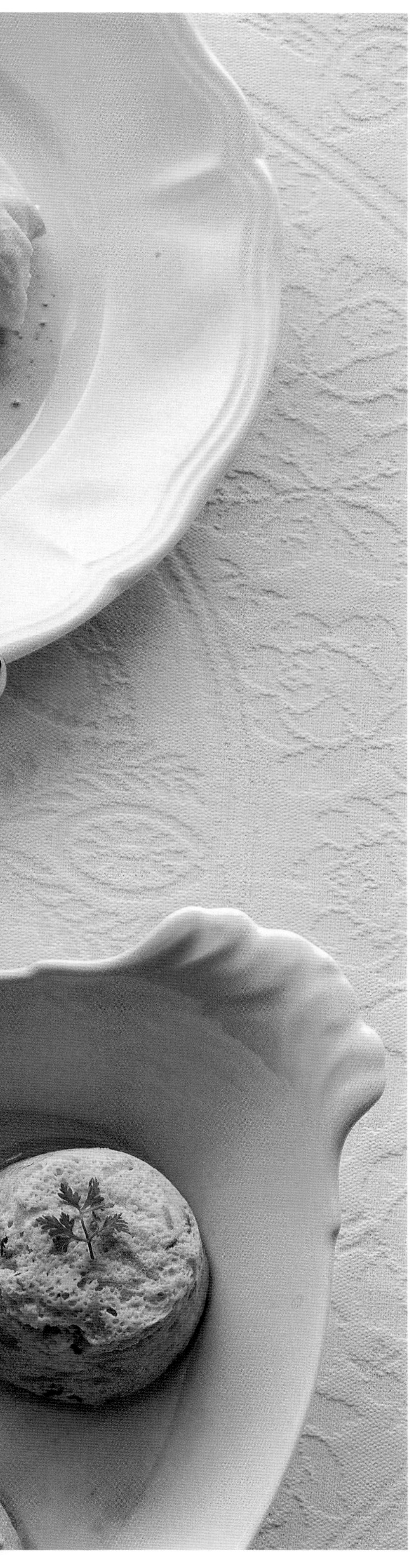

*4 oz (125 g) baby (pearl) onions*
*or small pickling onions*
*salt*
*2 teaspoons sugar*
*2 tablespoons water*
*2 lb (1 kg) small eels, skinned*
*2 tablespoons all purpose (plain) flour*
*1 bottle (3 cups/24 fl oz/750 ml)*
*dry white wine*
*4 cups (1 qt/1 l) fish stock*
*2$^1/_2$ cups (20 fl oz/625 ml)* crème fraîche
*or heavy (double) cream*
*pinch cayenne pepper*

Blanch the bacon in a pan of boiling water for 2 minutes. Drain and pat dry. Place the bacon in a skillet and cook over medium heat until lightly browned. Set aside.

Wipe out the skillet. Add 1 tablespoon each of the butter and oil and heat until the butter melts. Add the champignons and sauté over medium-high heat until the water they give off in cooking has evaporated and they are lightly browned.

In a separate skillet, melt 1 tablespoon of the butter with the remaining oil. Add the onions, season lightly with salt, sprinkle with the sugar and moisten with the water. Cook over medium-low heat, shaking the pan to turn the onions, until the water has evaporated. (If the onions begin to burn, reduce the heat and add a few drops more water.)

Cut open and clean the eels. Slice them into 2-in (5-cm) lengths. Heat the remaining butter in a large casserole. Add the eels and sauté over medium-high heat until well browned on all sides.

Pour off the excess fat and sprinkle the eels with the flour. Add the white wine and the fish stock, and cook over medium-low heat for about 15 minutes. Remove the eels and set aside. Let the liquid in which they cooked reduce over medium heat for 10 to 15 minutes. Pour the reduction through a fine strainer. Return the strained liquid to the casserole and stir in the *crème fraîche*. Add the sautéed bacon, mushrooms, and onions. Return the eels to the casserole and warm over medium-low heat until heated through. Season to taste with salt and cayenne pepper and serve at once.

Boiled potatoes and crisply fried croûtons make excellent accompaniments.

SERVES: 6

*Hare in Cream Sauce,*
*Perch-Pike Sausage with Mustard Sauce,*
*Carrot and Zucchini Molds*

## *Saumon à la Chouée*

*Salmon with Cabbage*

Salmon is paired with the humble cabbage in this recipe from chef Bignon of the Toussaint Restaurant in Angers.

*1 head Savoy or roundhead cabbage*
*2 lb (1 kg) fillet of salmon*
*12 shallots, finely chopped*
*$^1/_2$ cup (4 fl oz/125 ml) white wine vinegar*
*1$^1/_4$ cups (10 fl oz/310 ml) dry white wine*
*1$^1/_4$ cups (10 oz/310 g) unsalted butter*
*salt and freshly ground white pepper*
*1 tablespoon chopped fresh herbs,*
*such as chervil or dill*

Peel off and discard the dark outer leaves of the cabbage, saving only the white inner leaves. Cut a deep triangle at the base of each leaf to remove the core. Rinse and pat dry. Place in a steamer over lightly salted simmering water for 2 minutes. Remove and rinse immediately under cold water to preserve the fresh color. Drain on paper towels and pat dry.

Cut the salmon into six thin, diagonal slices. Place in a steamer and steam over simmering water for 2 to 3 minutes. Set aside.

To prepare the sauce, place the shallots, vinegar, and wine in a small saucepan and reduce over medium-high heat until the liquid has nearly evaporated.

Fill a shallow roasting pan with about 1 in (2.5 cm) of water. Place a cake rack covered with aluminum foil over the water and bring water to a simmer. Arrange six pairs of cabbage leaves on the rack. Cover with another sheet of foil and steam for 2 minutes. Remove the foil and place a piece of salmon between each pair of leaves. Replace the foil and steam over simmering water for another 2 to 3 minutes.

Meanwhile, finish the sauce. Remove the wine mixture from the heat and add the softened butter a little at a time, whisking briskly after each addition and returning the saucepan to the heat from time to time to warm. (Be careful not to overheat, or the butter will melt rather than thicken into a full-bodied sauce.) Add a few drops of water if necessary. Season with salt and pepper.

Place each cabbage parcel on a warmed individual serving plate. Spoon the *beurre blanc* over each portion, sprinkle with herbs and serve immediately.

SERVES: 6

## Sandre au Beurre de Palourdes et au Fenouil

*Perch-Pike with Baby Clams and Fennel*

Clams from nearby Brittany feature in this recipe from chef Michel Lecomte at La Licorne in Fontevraud-l'Abbaye.

*4 large fennel bulbs*
*$2\frac{1}{4}$ cups (1 lb 2 oz/560 g) unsalted butter, softened*
*3 shallots, chopped*
*$1\frac{1}{2}$ lb (750 g) small clams*
*$\frac{2}{3}$ cup (5 fl oz/150 ml) dry white wine*
*6 perch-pike fillets, or any firm white fish fillets, about 5 oz (155 g) each*

Trim the fennel, peel off the leaves and cut them into julienne strips. Melt 5 tablespoons ($2\frac{1}{2}$ oz/75 g) of the butter in a large skillet. Add the fennel and sweat, covered, over low heat for about 30 minutes.

In a separate skillet, melt another 5 tablespoons ($2\frac{1}{2}$ oz/75 g) of the butter, add the shallots and sweat briefly over low heat. Add the clams and the white wine and cook for 5 minutes. Remove the clams from their shells and set aside, reserving the liquid in which they cooked.

Preheat the oven to 350°F (180°C). Place the fish fillets in a buttered baking pan. Add the liquid in which the clams cooked and bake for about 10 minutes.

Remove the fish fillets from the pan with a slotted spatula, being careful not to break them. Pour the cooking liquid through a fine strainer into a small saucepan. Warm over low heat, whisking in the remaining butter a little at a time, being careful not to overheat the sauce.

Divide the fennel strips among six individual serving plates. Arrange the fish and the clams on top. Spoon the sauce over each serving.

SERVES: 6

*Perch-Pike with Baby Clams and Fennel, Salmon with Cabbage, Fricassee of Eel in White Wine*

PETER JOHNSON

## Fricassée de Volaille au Vouvray

*Fricassee of Chicken with Vouvray Wine*

Full flavored, free-range chickens and a rich, white Vouvray wine distinguish this classic fricassee from chef François Salle served at the Auberge de la Brenne, just a few miles from the heart of the Vouvray wine-growing region.

*1 large free-range chicken, about 4 lb (2 kg)*
*2 bouquets garnis: totaling 2 bay leaves, 2 thyme sprigs, 12 parsley sprigs*
*2 carrots, halved*
*1 onion, quartered*
*3 tablespoons unsalted butter*
*2 tablespoons all purpose (plain) flour*
*$1\frac{1}{2}$ cups (12 fl oz/375 ml) dry Vouvray wine or other dry white wine*
*salt and freshly ground black pepper*
*3 oz (90 g) cultivated white mushrooms, chopped*
*pinch of chervil*
*pinch of chopped tarragon*
*1 egg yolk*
*2 tablespoons* crème fraîche *or heavy (double) cream*

Cut the chicken into serving pieces, reserving the carcass, neck, gizzard, and heart to make a stock. Place the carcass, neck, gizzard, and heart in a large saucepan with 1 bouquet garni, the carrots, and onion. Add enough cold water to cover the bones and vegetables by about 1 in (2.5 cm). Bring to a boil and simmer for 30 minutes.

While the stock cooks, melt the butter in a large cast-iron casserole. Add the chicken pieces and sauté over medium-high heat until lightly browned on all sides. Sprinkle the flour evenly over the

PETER JOHNSON

*Fricassee of Chicken with Vouvray Wine*

chicken pieces. Add the Vouvray and the remaining bouquet garni.

When the stock has simmered for 30 minutes, pour it through a fine strainer and add enough of it to the chicken to cover by about 1 in (2.5 cm). Season with salt and pepper and simmer, covered, over low heat for 35 minutes.

Remove 4 cups (1 qt/1 l) of the cooking liquid from the chicken. Place it in a saucepan with the mushrooms, chervil, and tarragon, and simmer briskly. Combine the egg yolk and *crème fraîche*, and whisk it into the mushroom mixture without allowing the sauce to boil.

Arrange the chicken pieces on a warmed serving platter. Spoon the sauce evenly over the chicken and sprinkle with chopped parsley, if desired. Serve with steamed potatoes.

SERVES: 6

## *Pêches de Vigne au Vin Rouge*

*Vine Peaches Poached in Red Wine*

Pêches de Vigne, a particularly succulent variety of French peach, are said to take their ruby-red color from the grape vines next to which they ripen. In this recipe from chef Pascal Niatel of Le Relais d'Antan they are poached in red wine and sweetened with a peach-flavored liqueur. They can be served with vanilla or praline ice-cream, if desired.

*12 small ripe vine peaches, or other peaches*
*1 bottle (3 cups/24 fl oz/750 ml) red wine, preferably Chinon, Bourgueil or a Cabernet Sauvignon*
*3/4 to 1 cup (6 to 8 oz/185 to 250 g) sugar*
*pinch of ground cinnamon*
*1 teaspoon* crème de pêche *or other peach-flavored liqueur*

Peel the peaches. Place them in a saucepan large enough to hold them in one layer. Add the wine, sugar, and cinnamon. There should be enough liquid to completely cover the peaches. Bring to a boil, then reduce the heat and let simmer for 15 minutes. Using a slotted spoon, remove the peaches and set aside.

Continue to cook the liquid over medium-high heat until reduced by about one-third. Remove from the heat and let cool to room temperature. Stir in the *crème de pêche*. Arrange the peaches in a compote and spoon the syrup over them. Serve at room temperature, or chilled.

SERVES: 6

## *Tarte Tatin*

*Upside-Down Apple Tart*

This is chef Pascal Niatel's version of the famous caramelized apple tart created by the Tatin sisters at their hotel at Lamotte-Beuvron early this century.

*10 Golden Delicious apples, peeled, cored, and quartered*
*1 cup (8 oz/250 g) sugar*
*3 tablespoons water*
*3/4 cup (6 oz/185 g) unsalted butter, cut into small pieces*
*8 oz (250 g) sweet short (shortcrust) pastry*

Preheat the oven to 400°F (200°C). Place the apples in a well-buttered nonstick cake pan or deep-sided tart pan, arranging them as snugly as possible. Sprinkle the sugar evenly over the apples. Drizzle the water over the sugar. Distribute the butter evenly over the top. Cook on top of the stove over low heat until the sugar and butter mixture boils and begins to caramelize. This will take about 15 minutes.

Place in the preheated oven and cook for about 10 minutes until the caramel bubbles and lightens.

Meanwhile, roll out the pastry into a disk large enough to cover the top of the cake pan. Place over the apples and return to the oven to cook for a further 20 minutes, or until the pastry is cooked.

Remove the tart from the oven and let cool a few minutes before inverting it onto a serving platter. Serve warm or at room temperature.

SERVES: 6

PETER JOHNSON

*Upside-Down Apple Tart, Warm Pears Glazed with Almond Cream, Vine Peaches Poached in Red Wine*

## Gratin de Poire

*Warm Pears Glazed with Almond Cream*

Plump, ripe pears are the fruit *par excellence* of the Anjou-Touraine region. In this recipe from pastry chef Jean Michel Bezille of La Licorne, they are sautéed, topped with almond cream, and passed under a hot broiler just before serving.

*Almond Cream:*
*¾ cup (6 oz/185 g) unsalted butter, softened*
*¾ cup (6 oz/185 g) sugar*
*1⅔ cups (6 oz/185 g) ground blanched almonds*
*4 large eggs*
*Pears:*
*10 to 12 firm William or Bartlett pears*
*6 tablespoons (3 oz/90 g) unsalted butter*

For the almond cream: Place the butter in a large mixing bowl. Add the sugar and beat with a wire whisk until creamy. This will take about 5 minutes. Add the ground almonds and the eggs and beat until thoroughly blended.

Peel and core the pears. Cut into ¼-in (5-mm) rounds. Melt 3 tablespoons of the butter in a large skillet over medium heat. When the white foam subsides, add enough of the pear slices to line the bottom of the skillet without overlapping, and sauté briefly, turning once. Transfer pear slices to paper towels to drain, and continue in this manner, adding more butter as needed, until all the pear slices have been sautéed.

Divide the pear slices evenly among individual heatproof serving plates, arranging them in overlapping rings. Spoon some of the almond cream evenly over each serving. Just before serving, place the plates under a preheated broiler (grill) for 1 to 3 minutes, or until lightly browned on top. Serve immediately.

SERVES: 6

## Crémets d'Anjou

*Anjou Cream Desserts*

Chef Bignon of the Toussaint Restaurant in Angers uses a 60 per cent fat-free *fromage blanc* to cut down on the calories in this classic dessert. Small porcelain molds, often heart-shaped, with draining holes in the bottom, can be found in kitchen supply stores. As an alternative a larger heart-shape mold, with holes punched for drainage, can be used, or a 6-in (15-cm) diameter rattan basket lined with cheesecloth.

*1¼ cups (10 fl oz/310 ml)* crème fraîche *or heavy (double) cream*
*2½ cups (20 fl oz/625 ml)* fromage blanc, *preferably 60 per cent fat free*
*4 egg whites*
*pinch of salt*
*10 oz (315 g) strawberries*
*10 oz (315 g) raspberries*
*¾ cup (6 oz/185 g) sugar*
*juice of 1½ lemons*

Line six individual ceramic *crémet* molds (see introduction) with double squares of cheesecloth large enough to generously fold over the top once the mold is filled.

Place the *crème fraîche* in a large mixing bowl. Add the *fromage blanc* and whisk or mix at low speed with an electric mixer until thoroughly blended.

Place the egg whites in a separate very clean, dry bowl. Add the salt and whisk or beat with an electric mixer until firm peaks form. Using a rubber spatula, gently fold the firm egg whites into the *fromage blanc* mixture, being careful not to deflate the whites.

Spoon the mixture into the cheesecloth-lined molds. Fold the cheesecloth over the tops of the mixture and place, pierced side down, over a shallow dish in the refrigerator to chill and drain for at least 3 hours. (The excess liquid will drain out of the holes in the bottom of the molds.)

Meanwhile, prepare the fruit. Rinse the strawberries and remove the stems. Sort the raspberries. One of the two berries will be used to decorate the *crémets*, the other will be puréed into a fresh fruit sauce. Place the fruit that you wish to purée in a food processor and process, or force it through a fine sieve. Stir the sugar and lemon juice into the purée and chill until ready to serve.

To serve, spoon a pool of the purée over the bottom of six individual serving plates. Unfold the cheesecloth from the top of each mold and invert the *crémets* onto the serving plates in the center of the purée. Remove the molds and the cheesecloth. Decorate with the remaining whole fruit.

SERVES: 6

*Anjou Cream Desserts*

# BRITTANY

*Martha Rose Shulman*

Brittany is a region of windswept, rugged shorelines, known for its fishermen since ancient times, and nowhere in France can you find a more tempting array of seafood. In the center the farmlands are rich. This is a province where the best food is simple and unadulterated. Here you can eat briny oysters and glistening fresh fish sauced with nothing more complicated than a *beurre blanc* made with slightly salted Breton butter, or grilled lobsters, washed down with crisp, dry Muscadet.

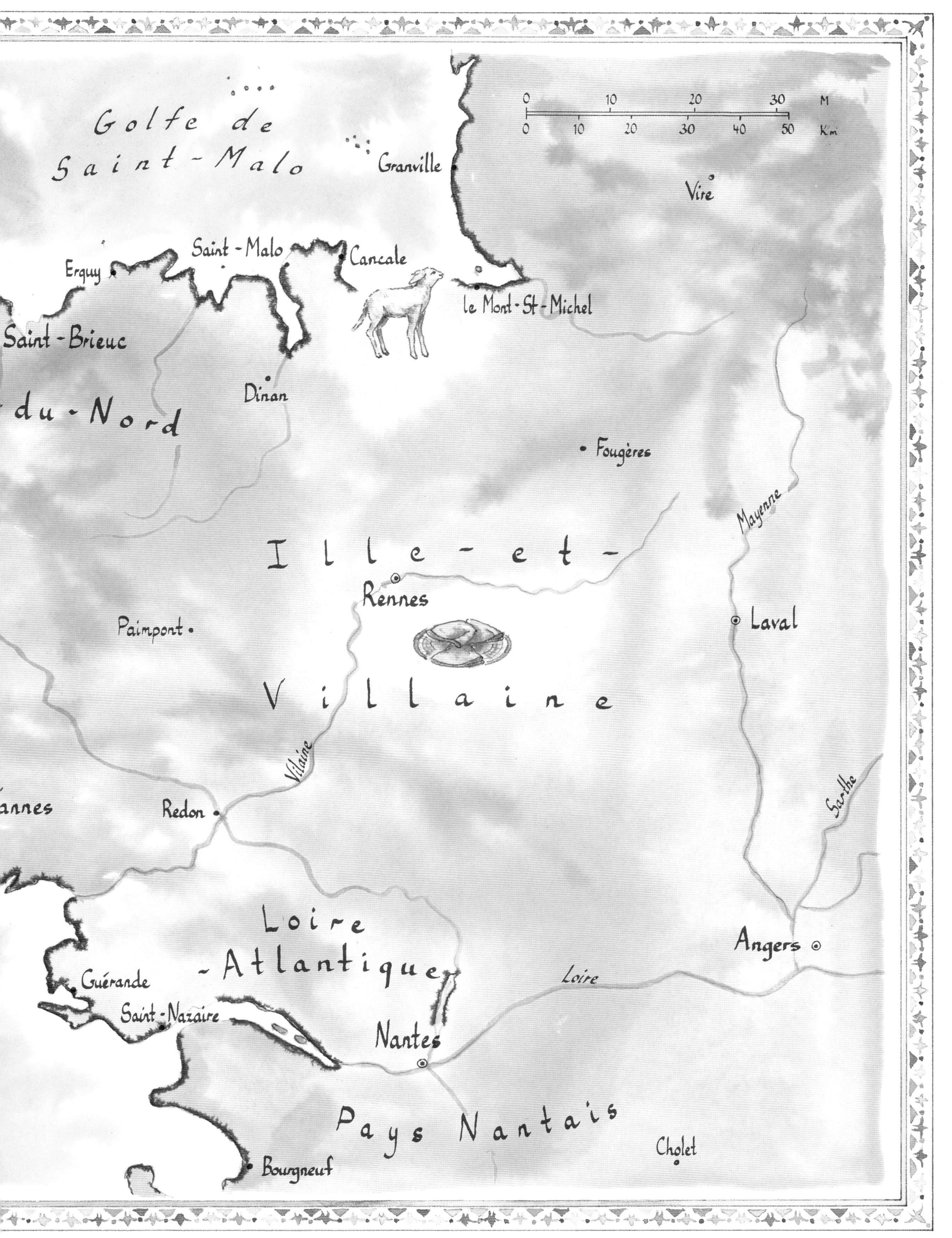

0
10
20
30
M
0
10
20
30
40
50
Km
Golfe de
Saint-Malo
Granville
Vire
Saint-Malo
Cancale
Erquy
le Mont-St-Michel
Saint-Brieuc
Dinan
du-Nord
Fougères
Mayenne
Ille-et-
Rennes
Laval
Paimpont
Villaine
Vilaine
Sarthe
annes
Redon
Loire
-Atlantique
Angers
Loire
Guérande
Saint-Nazaire
Nantes
Pays Nantais
Cholet
Bourgneuf

## LAND OF THE BRETONS

Here you will find earthy buckwheat *crêpes*, sparkling Breton cider, and delicious cakes. Along country roads you will see signs reading "*crêpes* (or *galettes*) *maison*," and the *crêpes* will be made from wonderful fresh milk, butter, and eggs from the farm. The farmers will probably have cider for sale as well.

Brittany is as far west as you can go in France. The region juts out into the Atlantic, with the English Channel to the north and the Bay of Biscay to the south. Finistère, the westernmost department, means "the end of the earth." Breakers pound the cliffs, but the coast has many natural harbors, and the French navy's main base is in the Brest estuary. Ferries from England dock at Roscoff and Saint-Malo on the north coast, and in the summer holidaymakers in their thousands flock to the beaches.

Brittany was a Celtic duchy for over one thousand years before being annexed by France in 1532. The Celts, called Bretons because they had come from nearby Britain following the Anglo-Saxon invasions, were preceded by the Romans, who had themselves followed the Gauls. The Gauls gave the region the name of Armor, meaning "the country by the sea," and Brittany continues to be referred to as the Armorican peninsula.

It is a region of ancient ritual and legend. In parts of Brittany, particularly around Carnac, megaliths, massive stones, stand in lines and circles similar to Stonehenge, erected by the tribes who lived here before the Gauls. And it is said that King Arthur and his knights did not, in fact, live in England, but in the forest of Paimpont in central Brittany. To this day the Breton language, a Celtic language similar to Welsh, is very much alive. So too are the Breton people's Christian

*The port of Cancale, one of the country's prime oyster-growing areas. Louis XIV is said to have had Cancale oysters sent to him at Versailles twice a week.*

LEO MEIER/WELDON TRANNIES

customs and traditional dress, marked by the women's elaborate lace headdresses, called *coiffes*, which differ from region to region. Brittany is a very devout part of France. Shrines and crosses dot the countryside, and it seems that every week some village is celebrating its patron saint with a ceremonial procession called a *pardon*. This is especially true in the west, often referred to as Bas Bretagne, or Bretagne Bretonnante. Haute Bretagne, which comprises northern and eastern Brittany, is more Gallic in nature.

Brittany has long been known for high quality produce. In 1514 an English traveler reported that the country was rich in wheat, rye, oats, rice, saffron, peas, broad beans, garlic, onions, and other vegetables and fruits. The wines were good and the meat plentiful. The quality of its butter was remarked upon as far back as 1650. Its cities were important ports until Napoleonic times, and there was much trading with Mediterranean, Indian, and New World merchants. Salt, salted butter, fish, meat, and woven fabrics were traded for oranges, dried fruits, wines, and spices. Apothecaries made curries from the Indian spices, and the seasoning became part of the traditional cuisine. Today you will see *homard au cari* (or *au kari*) on many a menu, and there is a version in virtually every Breton cookbook.

PASKALL/CEDRI

*A woman from southern Finistère wearing a traditional Breton headdress. These tall ones from around Pont-l'Abbé are called* bigoudens.

## Shellfish and Fish

Brittany's many bays and inlets provide a perfect environment for oysters, scallops, and mussels. Lobsters, both the big *homards* and the smaller, spiny, clawless *langoustes*, thrive further out in the shoals. They are served either grilled, boiled, or roasted, or cut up and stewed in a tomato and shallot-based sauce. This latter is the much disputed *homard à l'amoricaine*, or *à l'américaine*. Most non-Breton food authorities insist that the correct name is *à l'américaine*, and that the dish was actually invented by a Parisian chef (from the Languedoc) who had spent some time in America. Breton gastronomes fiercely disagree, insisting that the dish is thoroughly Breton. The tomatoes and olive oil required for the dish are not indigenous, but perhaps, because they have been available in Brittany for so long, the sauce did develop in the region.

Some of the best scallops in France — *coquilles Saint-Jacques* — come from the bay of Saint-Brieuc on the north coast. The little port of Erquy is a good place to sample them, along with clams called *praires*, and the larger *palourdes*, tiny bay scallops called *olivettes*, periwinkles, and mussels. As for crustaceans, as well as the *homards* and the *langoustes*, there are *langoustines*, crayfish-like but more delicate, and with much less flesh. There are also delicious crabs: *tourteaux* are the large ones with round bodies and relatively short legs, and *araignées de mer* are spider crabs, with great long legs.

If you order a plateau de fruits de mer, you will be served an assortment of seafood laid out on a huge seaweed-strewn platter. The selection varies from place to place. Restaurants in the major oyster-producing areas, like Cancale, Morlaix, and the Morbihan coast, will always offer oysters, as well as raw clams, cooked periwinkles, small shrimp, cooked crab broken in pieces, and sometimes cooked langoustines. Occasionally there will be sea-urchins, split in half, and you are given a little spoon for scooping out their roe, a great delicacy. The accompanying sauce will either be a mixture of red wine vinegar and shallots, a vinaigrette, or a mayonnaise, and the platter will also be served with lemon wedges, slices of rye bread, and Breton butter.

*Following pages: A tiny hotel stands alone among the gorse bushes at Pointe du Raz in southern Finistère.*

EBERHARD GRAMES/BILDERBERG

HOTEL DE L'IROISE

At coastal restaurants oysters come to the table so fresh that they have not even needed chilling on ice. At room temperature they are at their sweet, briny best — the purest taste the sea has to offer. The highly regarded Belon oysters are becoming quite rare and expensive because a parasite has been killing them in recent years, but Brittany also produces the smaller, less expensive crinkly shelled *creuse* oysters. Among the best of these are the *spéciales* and the *papillons*. Mussels, available widely, are also sometimes served raw, and are cooked *à la marinière*, gratinéed, and in *soupe aux moules*.

For centuries Bretons have fished for cod as far away as Greenland and the Newfoundland Banks, and fishing fleets continue to operate out of numerous ports, both large and small, all along the coast. At Guilvinec, in southwestern Finistère, you can watch the fishermen come and go in their small colorful vessels, bringing in fish from nearby waters. They return every day at around 5 p.m. with their catch — including lots of *langoustines* in wicker traps — and the wholesale market begins as they unload.

In general, Breton cooks do not complicate their fish with sauces. Fish are poached in a *court-bouillon*, grilled, fried, or baked, and served with *beurre blanc,* a sauce made with a little vinegar, shallots, and a good deal of butter. It is the usual accompaniment for river fish like pike and shad, and for salmon. More elaborate sauces contain oysters, shrimp, and *crème fraîche* (*à la cancalaise*), or shallots, white wine, and mustard (*sauce Saint-Malo*). Monkfish, is often prepared *à l'amoricaine*, for its flesh is similar to lobster, and it goes well with the heady sauce.

The most traditional Breton fish dish is the *cotriade*, a soup made with onions, potatoes, and the day's catch. There are many different versions, some containing a variety of fish, others just one or two, and some include sorrel. The soup can be made with salt pork and butter, or just butter alone. In a *cotriade* containing several fish you will usually find mackerel, conger eel, and whiting or cod. It is simpler than a Mediterranean *bouillabaisse*, although one version resembles it, called a *bouillabaisse des Kermokos*, Kermokos being the children of Breton sailors and Provençal women. This soup contains tomatoes, garlic, olive oil, and saffron. As Mediterranean as this sounds, most of its ingredients are cultivated in Brittany. Garlic and saffron have been grown here since the fifteenth century.

LEO MEIER/WELDON TRANNIES

## The Guérande Salt Beds

During the Middle Ages, Brittany provided most of Europe's salt, a commodity that was vital for preserving food as well as seasoning it. It was gathered from the salt marshes in the bays of Bourgneuf, Guérande, and Rhuys. The Bretons had salt at their disposal for salted fish, salt pork, and butter, which they also traded with their European neighbors. When Brittany was annexed to France a tax was imposed on salt, which led to a decline in trade.

Today there are about 1000 men working in Brittany in salt beds along the Guérande Peninsula. The salt is gathered during the evenings from late June through early September. Sea water is trapped in shallow beds called *oeillets*, and allowed to evaporate. The coarse, grey, crystalline salt left behind is raked into huge mounds, then gathered up and sold. In good years the yield is 25 000 to 30 000 tons.

*Sel de mer de Bretagne*, highly valued for its flavor, can be bought at roadside stands in this part of Brittany, and in health food stores throughout France. *Fleur du sel*, the greyish-white salt from the top of the evaporating beds, is particularly prized by bakers and chefs.

LEO MEIER/WELDON TRANNIES

*Massive blocks of stone have been used to build this thatched farmhouse at La Larronniere. Opposite: Friends having a chat at the fair at the little town of Landévant, near Lorient.*

## FROM THE FARM

Brittany's most important crops are cabbage, cauliflower, artichokes, potatoes, carrots, and onions, and various seasonal green vegetables also grow well. The beautiful globe artichoke called *gros camus de Léon*, with its meaty leaves that curl at the top, is the province's pride. At the height of the season these artichokes are sold from farmers' trucks for next to nothing. Artichoke hearts are often served sautéed with lamb, or used as a stuffing for fish.

Brittany's *pré-salé* lamb, tender and delicately flavored with salt from the marshes where the sheep graze, is much prized. *Gigot à la bretonne,* roast leg of lamb served with white beans and tomatoes, is a favorite traditional dish, and lamb is also often eaten with potatoes. Pork is widely produced, and exported to the rest of France, as is poultry.

Cider is the drink of the region, a perfect accompaniment for *crêpes*, many fish dishes, and pastries. Cider apples and a number of dessert varieties — used in delicious tarts, baked, and made into apple *crêpes* and purées — are grown mainly in the Saint-Malo region. Brittany is also known for its strawberries, and over twenty different kinds are grown in the Plougastel region, near Brest. There are as many strawberry tart recipes in this area as there are villages.

There is no Breton word for cheese, and the only cheeses made in the region are varieties that resemble cream cheese which comes from the Rennes area. But Gruyère is imported, and you will find it sprinkled on *crêpes* and gratins. Traditionally, warm *crêpes* are dipped into *lait ribot*, buttermilk.

*A wide selection of fruit and vegetables on display at the Quimper market, much of it grown locally in Finistère.*

LEO MEIER/WELDON TRANNIES

## FARS BRETON

The only *far* that tourists usually see is the *far breton,* a rich prune flan, baked all over Brittany. But the traditional peasant *fars* are simple savory dishes. Flour, eggs, and water are made into a thick batter, which is poured into a linen bag. This is tied and placed in a *pot-au-feu*, and cooked for several hours, until it resembles crumbly dumpling. It is then usually served with the *pot-au-feu*.

The most elaborate is *kig ha fars*. The *pot-au-feu* for this dish is made with beef, lamb, and salt pork, a cabbage (cooked separately), carrots, turnips, onions, cloves, leeks, coriander, salt and pepper, celery, thyme, and bay leaves. The *fars* contains buckwheat flour, butter, milk, cream, an egg, sugar, prunes or raisins. This is cooked for 1½ hours, after the meat has boiled for about 2 hours. The meat and vegetables are then piled on a platter, the *fars* crumbled around them, and everything moistened with the gravy.

Every village seems to have its own *fars*. Morbihan versions called *kouign-pod, kouign-forn,* and *farz-dorn* are made with wheat flour, eggs, cream, butter, and sugar. The Groix *fars*, called *le kaloup*, is made with barley flour. Some contain raisins, others pears, others rum.

LEO MEIER

*Above: Cakes and chocolates on display at a* pâtisserie *in Dinan in northeastern Brittany. Opposite: A typical Breton bar, clouds of cigarette smoke surrounding the patrons.*

## PORRIDGE, PASTRIES, AND CRÊPES

Like their northern Celtic neighbors, the country people in Brittany eat various kinds of porridge. The most common one, *bouillie d'avoine*, or *youd kerc'h*, is made from oatmeal. A little like polenta, *bouillies* are cooked in and eaten from copper cauldrons. What is not consumed hot is cut into blocks and reheated. Oatmeal and buckwheat *bouillies* are packaged and sold in *crémeries* and *crêperies*, to be reheated at home and eaten with *lait ribot*.

You can spend many enjoyable hours in Brittany tasting traditional pastries. There are numerous versions of the *gâteau breton*, which in its simplest form is a pound cake, or what the French call *quatre-quarts*, made with equal parts flour, butter, sugar, and eggs. Sometimes it is flavored with a little orangeflower water and orange peel. *Kouign-amann* is made with yeasted dough which is spread with butter and sugar, sometimes ground almonds and angelica, and folded over itself. Then there are the famous butter cookies, *sablés bretons,* and, of course, *crêpes*.

*Crêpe* is Breton, and *galette* is French, but they are actually one and the same, although some would say that the *crêpe* is thinner, and crispier on the edges, that a *galette* is always made with buckwheat flour, and a *crêpe* with wheat flour. The difference is really linguistic: the pancakes served at home in Haute Bretagne are called *galettes*, and those served in Basse Bretagne are called *crêpes*. Both are served in *crêperies*, the *galettes* usually being the savory buckwheat ones, and the *crêpes* those with sweet fillings. Traditional savory *galettes* are filled with egg, cheese, or ham (a *complète* contains all three), and sometimes seafood. A sweet *crêpe* generally contains jam, honey, apple purée, or chocolate.

Finally, Brittany has its wine — Muscadet, made at the mouth of the Loire. A flinty, dry white wine, made from grapes bathed in the salt air, it has the same no-nonsense quality that characterizes all Breton food. (Wines of the Pays Nantais are shown in the wine list and on the map on page 189.)

TONY STONE WORLDWIDE/THE PHOTO LIBRARY

PETER JOHNSON

## *Coquilles Saint-Jacques à la Bretonne*

*Baked Scallops with Butter and Breadcrumbs*

Scallops are rarely absent at a fancy Breton meal, and this is probably the most frequently served scallop dish, not only in Brittany, but throughout France.

*12 large scallops, or 18 to 24 smaller scallops*
*6 tablespoons (3 oz/90 g) butter*
*3 large or 6 small shallots, finely chopped*
*2 or 3 garlic cloves, finely chopped or put through a press*
*handful of finely chopped parsley, or a combination of parsley and chervil*
*pinch of cayenne*
*the water from the scallop shells*
*salt and freshly ground pepper*
*$^3/_4$ cup ($1^1/_2$ oz/45 g) fine breadcrumbs*

Open the scallops and retain the liquid. Remove the layer of skin and the muscle covering the white flesh and discard. Remove the flesh and the coral, rinse thoroughly and dice finely. Retain six shells, discard any remaining flesh inside them and rinse well. Set aside.

Heat a large, heavy-bottomed skillet over low heat and add half the butter. When it has melted, add the shallots and garlic, and sauté, stirring, until they become transparent. Add the herbs and the chopped scallops and coral, and stir. Strain the liquid from the shells through a fine-meshed sieve and add to the skillet. Stir everything together, add a little cayenne, salt and pepper, and cook over medium heat, stirring often, for 8 to 10 minutes, or until the the water has evaporated. If the water has not completely evaporated after 10 minutes, pour off what remains and remove from the heat.

Preheat the oven to 450°F (230°C) or preheat the broiler (grill).

Rub the insides of the six shells with half the remaining butter. Fill the shells with the scallop mixture and sprinkle with the breadcrumbs. Dot with the remaining butter. Heat in the oven or under the broiler until the breadcrumbs brown. This will take 5 to 10 minutes. Serve at once.

SERVES: 6

*Baked Scallops with Butter and Breadcrumbs, Stuffed Clams, Buckwheat Galettes Filled with Cheese and Egg*

## Paloudes Farcies

*Stuffed Clams*

Found throughout Brittany, this dish is said to have been devised by a poor fisherwoman in order to please her children, who had a daily diet of shellfish. She became rich, apparently, when she decided to market her invention.

*3 lb (1.5 kg) clams*
*1 cup (8 fl oz/250 ml) dry white wine, such as Muscadet*
*1 shallot, finely chopped*
*6 large garlic cloves, finely chopped or put through a press, or 2 shallots, finely chopped*
*8 tablespoons finely chopped parsley, or a mixture of parsley and other herbs such as chervil, tarragon, and basil*
*1 tablespoon finely chopped chives*
*6 to 8 tablespoons (3 to 4 oz/90 to 125 g) butter, softened*
*1/4 teaspoon paprika*
*salt and freshly ground pepper*
*3/4 cup (1 1/2 oz/45 g) breadcrumbs*

Rinse the clams well, scrub them with a little brush (such as a toothbrush) and put them in a large bowl of water, to which either a tablespoon of salt or a tablespoon of vinegar has been added. Let them soak for 15 to 20 minutes. Drain and rinse thoroughly. Soak again in salted or vinegared water for 15 minutes, and drain and rinse thoroughly once more.

Combine the wine and shallot in a large, wide, lidded saucepan and bring to a boil. Add the clams, cover and cook, stirring occasionally, for 5 minutes, or until they have all opened. Remove from the heat and allow to cool.

Preheat the oven to 450°F (230°C), or preheat the broiler (grill). When the clams are cool enough to handle, remove one shell from each. Leave each clam resting in the other shell, and place them on a large baking sheet or in a wide flameproof ceramic dish.

Mix together the garlic, herbs, chives, butter, and paprika. Taste for seasoning. Place a spoonful of this butter on each clam. Sprinkle with the breadcrumbs.

Place under the broiler for 2 or 3 minutes, or bake in the hot oven for 4 or 5 minutes, until the breadcrumbs brown and the clams are bubbling. Do not over cook or the clams will become rubbery. Serve at once.

SERVES: 6

## Galettes de Sarrasin au Fromage et à l'Oeuf

*Buckwheat Galettes Filled with Cheese and Egg*

*Galettes* freeze well and are handy to have on hand to wrap around fillings of all sorts.

Galettes:
*1 cup (8 fl oz/250 ml) milk*
*1/3 cup (3 fl oz/90 ml) water*
*3 eggs*
*1/2 teaspoon salt*
*2/3 cup (3 oz/90 g) buckwheat flour*
*1/4 cup (1 oz/30 g) unbleached all purpose (plain) flour*
*2 tablespoons melted butter*
*butter for the pan*
*Filling per* galette:
*1 egg*
*salt and freshly ground pepper*
*1/2 tablespoon butter*
*2 or 3 tablespoons freshly grated Gruyère cheese*

For the *galettes*: Place the milk, water, salt, and eggs in a blender jar and turn on. Add the flours, then the melted butter and blend at high speed for 1 minute. Refrigerate for 1 to 2 hours.

Use a *crêpe* pan (or a larger one for a more authentic *galette*), or a nonstick skillet. Place the pan over moderate heat and brush the bottom with butter. When the butter just begins to smoke, remove from the heat and pour in about 3 tablespoons of batter.

Immediately tilt the pan to distribute the batter evenly, and return to the heat. Cook the *galette* for about 1 minute and gently loosen the edges by running a thin spatula around the edge. If the *galette* comes up from the pan easily and is nicely browned, turn it and cook for 30 seconds on the other side. If it sticks, wait another 30 seconds, then turn. Turn each *galette* out once it is cooked. Continue cooking them in this way until all the batter is used up. If freezing, stack the *galettes* between sheets of wax paper and seal in a plastic bag.

For the filling: Put a cooked *galette* in the pan over low heat and break an egg over it. Spread the egg over the *galette* with a spatula. Season with salt and pepper, add butter and sprinkle with Gruyère. Heat for a few seconds, then fold it in half and in half again. Serve hot.

SERVES: 6 (approximately 12 *galettes*)

*Cream of Artichoke Soup*

PETER JOHNSON

## Crème d'Artichauts

*Cream of Artichoke Soup*

In Brittany the artichoke is often boiled or steamed and eaten with a vinaigrette or hollandaise sauce, or with mayonnaise. Here, the hearts are used for a marvelous thick soup. The leaves can be served as an appetizer.

*10 large globe artichokes*
*8 to 12 cups (2 to 3 qt/2 to 3 l) water, or more, to cover the artichokes*
*2 to 3 teaspoons salt*
*2 tablespoons butter*
*1 onion, chopped*
*2 large garlic cloves, finely chopped or put through a press*
*1 potato, diced*
*salt and freshly ground pepper*
*$^1/_2$ cup (4 fl oz/125 ml) heavy (double) cream*
*4 to 6 tablespoons chopped parsley or chervil*
*thin slices of lemon*

Break off the stems of the artichokes, and with a pair of kitchen scissors cut away the tops of the leaves. Place in a large pot, cover with the water, add salt and bring to a boil. Reduce heat, cover and cook for 30 minutes, or until tender on the bottom and the leaves pull away easily. Drain, retaining the water, and allow to cool.

When the artichokes are cool enough to handle, remove all the edible leaves, and set on a platter to serve as an appetizer. Discard any tough leaves and the choke, and dice the hearts finely.

Heat the butter in a large, heavy-bottomed saucepan or soup pot and add the onion and garlic. Cover and cook over very low heat for 5 minutes, stirring often. Add the diced artichoke hearts and continue to cook over low heat, covered, for 10 minutes. Stir often and do not let the mixture brown. Add 6 cups ($1^1/_2$ qt/1.5 l) of the cooking liquid from the artichokes, and the diced potato, and bring to a boil. Cover and simmer for 30 minutes. Remove from the heat and purée in a blender or put through a food mill fitted with the finest attachment. Return to the pot and taste for seasoning. Stir in the cream and serve. Garnish each bowl with parsley or chervil, and a thin slice of lemon.

SERVES: 6

PETER JOHNSON

Breton Lobster Stew

## Homard à l'Americaine

*Breton Lobster Stew*

Some authorities claim that this dish was invented by a chef from the Midi, who had spent many years in America, hence the name. But patriotic Bretons insist that 'américaine' is simply a corruption of 'Amoricaine', l'Amorique being the ancient name for Brittany.

*3 lobsters, about 1 lb (500 g) each, cut into 4 or 6 chunks each, corals and creamy interiors from the heads removed and set aside*
*2 tablespoons olive oil*
*2 tablespoons butter*
*$^1/_2$ cup (4 fl oz/125 ml) Cognac*
*3 shallots or 2 onions, finely chopped*
*3 large garlic cloves, finely chopped or put through a press*
*3 large tomatoes, peeled, seeded, and chopped*
*$1^1/_2$ cups (12 fl oz/375 ml) dry white wine, such as Muscadet*
*3 cups (24 fl oz/750 ml) fish, meat, or chicken stock*
*bouquet garni: 1 bay leaf, 1 thyme sprig, 1 parsley sprig*
*salt and freshly ground pepper*
*pinch of cayenne*
*handful of parsley*

Heat the olive oil in a large, heavy-bottomed casserole and sauté the lobster over high heat until it turns red. Flame it with the Cognac, and when the flames die down, remove the lobster from the pot and set aside on a plate.

Heat the butter in the same casserole and add the shallots. Cook over medium-low heat, stirring often, until they begin to soften. Add half the garlic and the tomatoes, and cook together for 5 to 10 minutes, until almost dry. Add the white wine, the stock, the remaining garlic, the bouquet garni, salt and pepper, and a pinch of cayenne. Bring to a boil, cover partially and simmer for about 20 minutes, until the mixture has thickened a little. Add the lobster and simmer, covered, for another 15 to 20 minutes.

Remove the lobster from the sauce and place on a serving platter. Remove the shells if you wish.

Add the reserved corals and creamy interiors from the heads to the sauce, stir well and reduce over medium heat for a minute or two. Taste for seasoning. Put the sauce through a food mill fitted with the finest attachment. Pour the sauce over the lobster, sprinkle with parsley, and serve.

SERVES: 6

## Morue Brestoise

*Gratin of Salt Cod and Potatoes*

Since the Middle Ages, salt cod has been a staple in Brittany.

*$1^1/_2$ lb (750 g) salt cod fillets*
*8 cups (2 qt/2 l) water*
*2 bay leaves*
*4 garlic cloves, peeled, left whole*
*5 tablespoons ($2^1/_2$ oz/75 g) butter*
*3 onions, chopped*
*4 leeks, white parts only, chopped*
*2 tablespoons all purpose (plain) flour*
*$1^1/_2$ lb (750 g) potatoes, scrubbed*
*salt and freshly ground pepper*
*$^1/_4$ cup ($^1/_2$ oz/15 g) breadcrumbs*

One or two days before you wish to make the dish, place the salt cod in a colander and set the colander in a large bowl. Fill the bowl with water and soak the fish for 24 hours or longer, changing the water at least eight times. Drain.

Combine the salt cod, water, garlic cloves, and bay leaves in a large saucepan and bring slowly to a simmer over medium-low heat. As soon as the surface of the water begins to tremble, turn off the heat, cover and leave for 10 minutes. Do not allow the water to boil. Remove the fish and strain the liquid, reserving 2 cups (16 fl oz/500 ml). Place the fish on a board and remove all the bones and skin. Break the fish into small flakes and discard any pieces which seem hard or dry. Set aside.

Heat 3 tablespoons of the butter in a large, heavy-bottomed saucepan and add the onions and leeks. Cook, stirring, over medium heat, until they begin to color. Add the flour and mix well, and continue to cook over medium heat for another few minutes. Slowly stir in the reserved cooking water from the fish, stirring all the while with a wooden spoon. Simmer over low heat for 15 minutes, stirring often, or until thick. Taste for seasoning.

Meanwhile, cook the potatoes in a large pot of water. When they are done, drain, and remove the skins, if desired. Slice into thin rounds.

Preheat the oven to 450°F (230°C). Butter a 2-qt (2-l) gratin dish and spoon in a small amount of sauce. Make alternating layers of the potatoes and salt cod. Pour on the remaining sauce, top with the breadcrumbs, and dot with remaining butter. Bake in the oven for 10 minutes, until browned and bubbling. Serve at once.

SERVES: 6

## Lapin au Cidre et aux Pruneaux

*Rabbit Cooked in Cider with Prunes*

This is actually a combination of two Breton recipes. Breton cider makes an ideal cooking medium for the rabbit, and the prunes complement the mixture perfectly.

*3 cups (24 fl oz/750 ml) Breton cider*
*$1^1/_4$ cups (8 oz/250 g) dried prunes*
*1 large rabbit, cut into 12 pieces*
*3 tablespoons unsalted butter*
*1 tablespoon vegetable oil*
*$^3/_4$ cup (6 fl oz/180 ml) Cognac*
*8 oz (250 g) shallots, finely chopped*
*3 garlic cloves, finely chopped or put through a press*
*3 oz (90 g) streaky bacon, trimmed of rind and diced*
*$1^1/_2$ tablespoons all purpose (plain) flour*
*$1^1/_2$ cups (2 fl oz/375 ml) chicken stock*
*bouquet garni: 1 bay leaf, 1 thyme sprig, 1 parsley sprig*
*salt and freshly ground pepper*
*handful of raisins*

Two hours before cooking, place the prunes in a bowl and pour in the cider. Leave for 2 hours. Drain and reserve the cider.

Rinse the rabbit pieces and pat dry. Heat two-thirds of the butter with the vegetable oil in a large, heavy-bottomed casserole and brown the rabbit pieces on all sides. Add the Cognac and flame. When the flames have died down, remove the rabbit pieces from the casserole and drain on paper towels. Pour off the liquid and fat that remain in the casserole.

Heat the remaining butter and add the shallots, garlic, and bacon. Cook, stirring, over medium-low heat, and when the shallots begin to brown add the flour and continue to sauté together for a few minutes, stirring all the while. Return the rabbit pieces to the casserole and add the cider, the chicken stock and the bouquet garni. Add salt and pepper to taste, bring to a boil, boil for 10 minutes, then reduce heat to low. Cover and simmer for about 45 minutes, stirring every once in a while, or until the rabbit falls away easily from the bones.

Add the prunes and raisins and simmer for a further 5 minutes. Taste for seasoning and serve with rice, potatoes, or pasta.

SERVES: 6

*Rabbit Cooked in Cider with Prunes, Gratin of Salt Cod and Potatoes*

PETER JOHNSON

PETER JOHNSON

*Roast Leg of Lamb with White Beans*

## Gigot à la Bretonne

*Roast Leg of Lamb with White Beans*

Brittany is known for its delicious *pré-salé* lamb, raised along the coast. "*A la bretonne*" often refers to a garnish of white beans.

*Beans:*
*1 lb (500 g) dried white beans*
*1 tablespoon olive oil*
*3 onions, chopped*
*6 garlic cloves, finely chopped*
*2 bay leaves*
*1 tablespoon salt*
*2 tablespoons butter*
*1 1/2 lb (750 g) tomatoes, peeled, seeded, and chopped*
*1/2 teaspoon thyme*
*salt and freshly ground pepper*
*Lamb:*
*1 leg of lamb, about 4 lb (2 kg)*
*1 tablespoon unsalted butter or olive oil*
*4 garlic cloves, peeled and cut into slivers*
*salt and freshly ground pepper*
*1/2 cup (4 fl oz/125 ml) dry white wine*

For the beans: Soak the beans overnight, or for at least 6 hours, then drain. Cover with water in a large soup pot and bring to a boil. Skim off all of the scum that rises to the top, remove from the heat, and drain.

In the same large pot, heat the olive oil and add 1 chopped onion and 1 chopped garlic clove. Cook over low heat, stirring, until the onion begins to soften. Add the beans and water to cover by 2 in (5 cm), and bring to a boil. Add the bay leaves, cover, reduce heat and simmer for 45 minutes. Add the salt and another chopped garlic clove, cover and continue to cook for another 30 to 45 minutes, or until the beans are tender but not mushy. Taste and adjust salt, remove the bay leaves, and set aside.

While the beans are cooking, heat the butter in a wide, heavy-bottomed skillet and add the remaining onions and garlic. Sauté over low heat for 5 to 10 minutes, stirring, until the onions are golden. Stir in the tomatoes, some salt and pepper, and the thyme. Cook over medium heat, stirring from time to time, for 15 minutes. Add this mixture to the beans.

For the lamb: Preheat the oven to 400°F (200°C), or to 450°F (230°C) if you wish to sear the meat in the oven (see below). Trim off the thicker portions of fat from the leg. Make small incisions here and there in the meat and slip in the slivers of garlic. Rub with butter. Sear the lamb on all sides in a roasting pan over high heat, or in the oven, for 10 minutes. Then either place the lamb in the oven, or turn the oven down to 400°F (200°C), depending on the searing method used. Roast for about 1 hour, or until a meat thermometer inserted in the thickest part of the leg registers 112°F (45°C). After the first 15 minutes, add 3/4 cup (6 fl oz/180 ml) boiling water to the pan. From time to time during the cooking, baste the lamb with this liquid.

Remove the lamb from the roasting pan and place on a cutting board. Lightly season with salt and pepper, cover loosely with aluminum foil and let stand for 20 minutes.

Meanwhile, bring the bean and tomato mixture to a boil. Simmer until slightly thickened and aromatic, adding more garlic, salt, pepper, and thyme if you wish.

Degrease the roasting pan, deglaze with the white wine and reduce the liquid by half. Stir these pan juices into the beans. Transfer to a large warmed serving platter. Slice the lamb and lay the slices over the beans. Serve at once.

SERVES: 8

## Pommes Bonne Femme

*Baked Apples*

In Brittany, the apples used for this recipe are usually Reine de Reinettes.

*6 large, tart baking apples*
*6 tablespoons (3 oz/90 g) slightly salted butter, softened*
*1/2 cup (4 oz/125 g) sugar*
*ground cinnamon*

Preheat the oven to 375°F (190°C). Core the apples. Work the butter and sugar together, and fill the cored apples with the mixture. Sprinkle with cinnamon.

Bake for 40 minutes, or until the apples split and are soft when pierced with a knife. Serve hot.

SERVES: 6

## Gâteau Breton

*Breton Pound Cake*

There are hundreds of recipes for the popular *gâteau breton*, a rich butter cake which, in its simplest form, is identical to a pound cake. The slightly salted butter from Brittany contributes to the cake's flavor.

*1/3 cup (2 oz/60 g) raisins*
*1/4 cup (2 fl oz/60 ml) rum*
*1 tablespoon butter for the cake pan*
*6 large egg yolks*
*2 1/4 cups (9 oz/280 g) all purpose (plain) flour*
*1 cup (8 oz/250 g) slightly salted butter, at room temperature*
*1 cup (8 oz/250 g) sugar*
*2 tablespoons finely chopped orange peel*

Combine the raisins and rum in a small bowl and let soak for about 15 minutes. Preheat the oven to 350°F (180°C). Butter a 9-in (23-cm) diameter cake pan or a 4 x 8-in (10 x 20-cm) loaf pan.

Beat the egg yolks in a bowl and reserve a couple of teaspoons for the glaze.

Place the flour in a large bowl, or in the bowl of an electric mixer with a paddle attachment. Make a well in the center and put the sugar and butter in the middle. Using your fingers or the mixer, work the sugar and butter into the flour. Add the egg yolks, raisins, rum and the orange peel, and work gently to a smooth dough.

Transfer the dough to the cake pan and gently press it out to the edges of the pan. Brush the top with the reserved egg yolk and, with a fork, make a lattice design across the top.

Bake for 50 minutes to 1 hour, until a knife comes out clean when inserted. Remove from the oven and allow to cool completely, then unmold.

SERVES: 8 to 10

*Baked Apples, Breton Pound Cake*

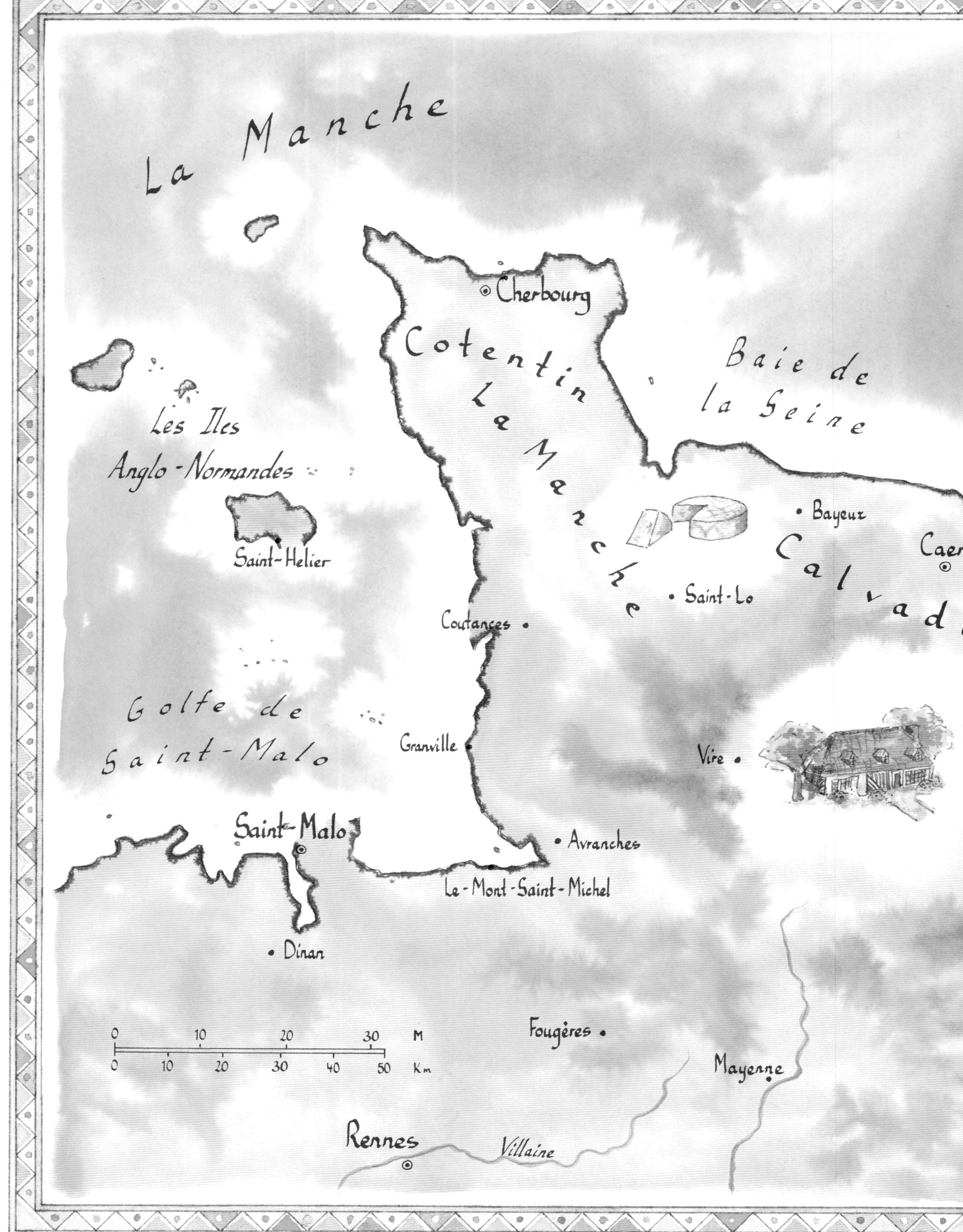

La Manche
Cherbourg
Cotentin
La Manche
Baie de la Seine
Les Iles Anglo-Normandes
Saint-Helier
Bayeux
Caen
Calvad
Saint-Lo
Coutances
Golfe de Saint-Malo
Granville
Vire
Saint-Malo
Avranches
Le-Mont-Saint-Michel
Dinan
Fougères
Mayenne
Rennes
Villaine
0 10 20 30 M
0 10 20 30 40 50 Km

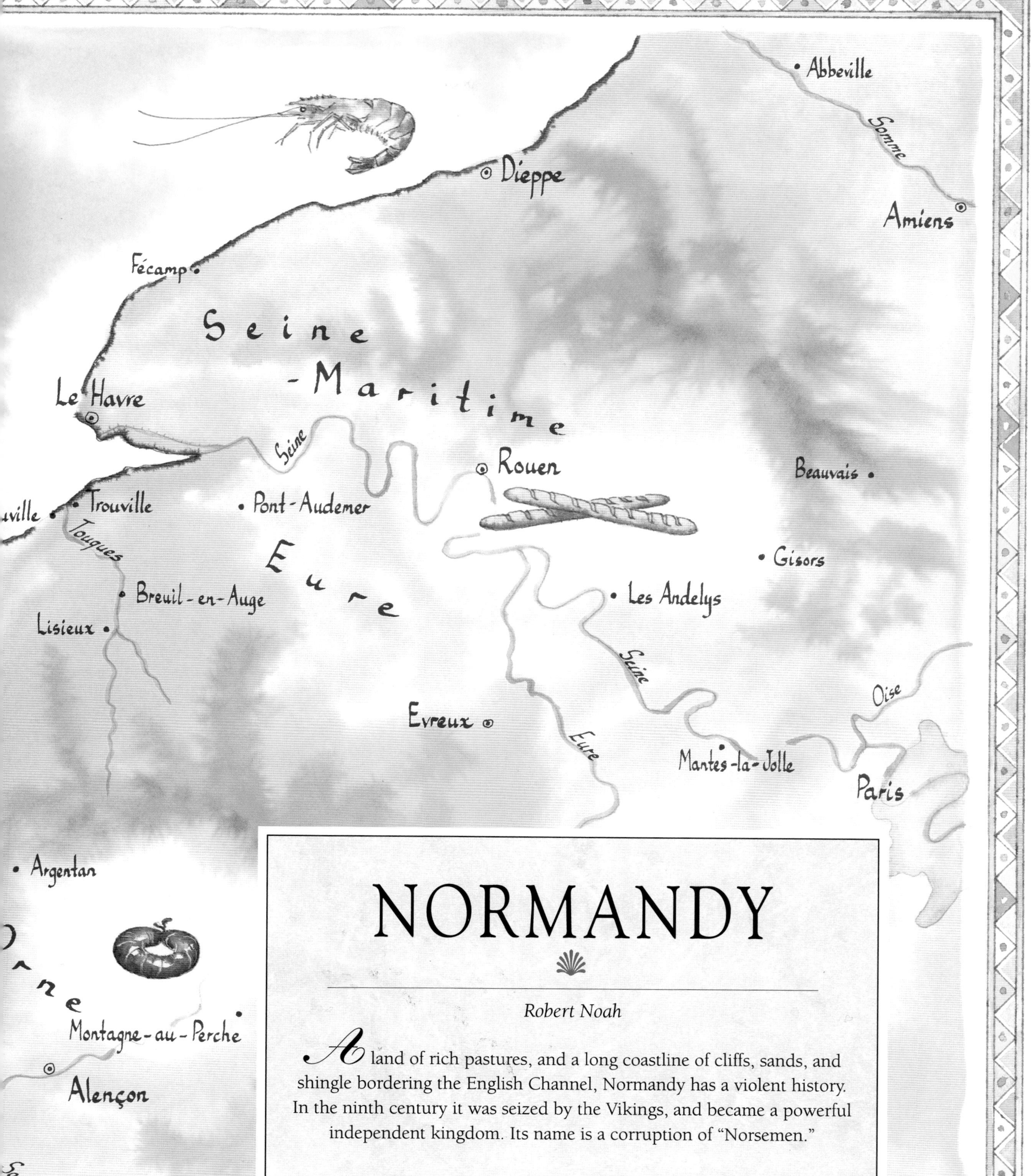


# NORMANDY

*Robert Noah*

A land of rich pastures, and a long coastline of cliffs, sands, and shingle bordering the English Channel, Normandy has a violent history. In the ninth century it was seized by the Vikings, and became a powerful independent kingdom. Its name is a corruption of "Norsemen."

LEO MEIER

*Fishing fleets operate out of ports all along the Normandy coast, notably Dieppe and Fécamp, and supply a vast catch to the markets of France.*
*Opposite: Milk churns await collection outside a Norman farmhouse. This style of building, using a timber frame in-filled with clay, is typical of the region.*

M. CAMBAZARD/EXPLORER

In 1066 William, Duke of Normandy, invaded England and defeated King Harold, becoming king himself, and he was well on the way to conquering the kingdom of France at the time of his death. During the Hundred Years' War the English captured Rouen, where they tried Joan of Arc for heresy and burnt her at the stake. Subsequently expelled, the English eventually returned, with the Allies, in the D-Day landings of 1944, a time when many of the region's towns were severely damaged by bombing.

From earliest times the Normans have been industrious farmers and daring sailors, and the people are of solid stock. While delicate dishes based on cream and butter abound, the Norman culinary tradition is also rich in hearty, sometimes coarse fare. *Graisse normande*, rendered pork and beef fat simmered with vegetables and herbs, gives certain traditional dishes a distinctive flavor. The Normans love pork products, and the regional *charcuterie* is excellent and varied. Specialties include *andouillettes* and *andouilles,* sausages made with the stomach and intestines of the pig, *boudin noir*, blood pudding, and *rillettes*, potted pork. Pâtés and terrines abound. *Boudin blanc,* a delicately flavored fresh sausage made with chicken, veal, or fish, is another regional delicacy.

## Cream, Butter, and Apples

Normandy's more refined culinary creations are based on cream and butter, with apples, cider, and Calvados, apple brandy, featuring prominently. The term *"à la normande"* refers to a dish that includes one or more of these local products. Rich, sweet Norman butter is used in a multitude of wonderful tarts, *sablés*, *galettes*, candies, and other specialties.

As the land has been kind to the province, so has the sea. The channel ports supply a vast catch of fish and shellfish, not only for Normandy, but for Rungis, the central market of Paris, which in turn supplies much of France and even certain demanding restaurateurs in Brussels, London, and New York. Sole is king, but other noble fish include brill, monkfish, and turbot, and humbler varieties such as flounder, gurnard, hake, and mackerel are becoming increasingly popular.

*Le Mont-Saint-Michel, built by Benedictine monks between the eleventh and sixteenth centuries. On the salt marshes nearby, which belong as much to Brittany as to Normandy, graze the region's famous* pré-salé *lamb.*

LEO MEIER

TRIPELON-JARRY/CEDRI

*Nothing could be more Norman than the sight of lazy, well-fed cows in an apple orchard. Not surprisingly, butter, cream, apples, and cider form the basis of much of the local cuisine.*

Since ancient times the region's oyster beds, which are mainly in the Cotentin peninsula, have been famous, but by the middle of the nineteenth century they were largely exhausted. Intense restocking efforts have been made recently, with considerable success. A wide range of other shellfish is also available and the scallops are among the world's best, though they are only available for a limited time in the fall and winter, to protect them from overfishing.

Elements of these products and cuisines can be found throughout Normandy, yet there are differences and specialties unique to each of the province's five departments. Like the rest of France, Normandy has in recent years become somewhat homogenized, traditional dishes being ignored and allowed to disappear, but the locals are now showing an increasing concern for their heritage. With a little research, and if you address yourself to young, local chefs, you can ferret out what is good and truly Norman.

## The Cotentin Peninsula and Le Mont-Saint-Michel

In the north of Normandy lies the department of the Manche, "the sleeve." This refers to the English Channel, which surrounds it on three sides. Cherbourg, at the tip of the rugged Cotentin peninsula, is its major city, and a busy port, with ferry connections to Ireland and England. The delicately flavored *pré-salé* lamb of the salt marshes — most notably around Le Mont-Saint-Michel — is justly famous. *Charcuteries* are abundant. The *andouille* of Vire is probably the best known version of this traditional smoked sausage and the town of Avranches specializes in *boudin blanc* made with fish.

While the Manche uses butter in its cooking, it is also the region fondest of *graisse normande*. So popular is this cooking fat that it is sometimes referred to as *graisse de Cherbourg*. Its use makes one of the staples of the local cuisine, *soupe normande*, a dish composed of rather ordinary ingredients (white beans, potatoes, leeks, and cabbage cooked in water), into something special, with tiny telltale "eyes" of fat forming on the surface. Another specialty unique to the Manche is the famous *omelette de la Mère Poulard* from Le Mont-Saint-Michel. Mère Poulard opened her inn here in 1888 and became eternally famous for her frothy omelettes. People are welcome to watch as dozens of these omelettes are made in the restaurant's stone fireplace every day.

Fish and shellfish are eaten widely in the Manche. Shrimp and lobster are particularly reputed, with the best coming from around Cherbourg. *Les demoiselles de Cherbourg* are really baby lobsters served with their cooking bouillon, flavored with Calvados. This prettily named dish has become a classic of the French repertoire. Cod was once a valuable catch, and the local fishermen would salt it and sell it not only at home, but along the coast of Portugal and Spain and as far away as southern France. *Morue à la cherbourgeoise*, salt cod with potatoes and onions, serves as a reminder of this trade. Salmon has disappeared from the rivers, but trout are still fished, and oyster farming is booming.

Traditional breadmaking has to some extent survived in the Manche. *Pain brié*, a dense, white rectangular loaf, is an old-style bread from here which can be found all over Normandy. *Pain de Cherbourg* is unique to the region. Originally Cherbourg's bakers were the only ones in France allowed to make their dough with sea-water, which contained just the right amount of salt. Today, for health reasons, that custom is illegal, and these loaves, which resemble *pains pliés* (with a folded top), are made with ordinary water. *La gâche* is another bread from the Cotentin peninsula, variations of which can be found elsewhere in Normandy. It is a hard kind of *galette*, with a shiny crosshatched top.

## The Riches of Calvados

Eastwards lies the department of the Calvados, and its picture-perfect vallée d'Auge. This is the Normandy found on postcards and travel posters — tiny villages of timbered houses, and fields cut into patchwork by thick beech hedges. Cows rule here, and the black and white Norman breed, prized for its meat, can produce as much as 6½ gallons (30 liters) of milk a day. It is this milk, so rich in cream, that gives the local butter its wonderful flavor. Isigny butter is among the best in the country, and the finest is sold in distinctive wooden containers. It is always sweet, unlike some other Norman butters, and Brittany's famous *demi-sel*. Its low whey content makes it ideal for preparing puff pastry, and it is used in fine kitchens throughout the country.

Cheese is another important product of the happy cows of the Calvados. Until recently, only cow's milk cheeses were produced, though today a small amount of goat's milk cheese is made. Calvados is the home of Camembert, France's best known and most widely imitated cheese, and it represents 90 per cent of all cheese production in the region. But the area is equally and rightfully proud of Pont l'Evêque and Livarot, both of them, like Camembert, protected by *appellation d'origine contrôlée* labels. At their best these soft, creamy cheeses are rich and strongly flavored, and are excellent served with dry cider.

## Camembert

Camembert cheese is a great Norman symbol. Though today it is produced throughout France, true Camembert must be made from the milk of Norman cows from certain delimited areas. In fact, over 2000 brands of so-called Camembert using milk brought in from all over France can carry "Camembert made in Normandy" labels, but they will not bear the *Appellation "Camembert" Contrôlée* stamp guaranteeing their origin.

The story goes that Marie Harel and her daughter, farm women living near the village of Camembert, created the cheese in the nineteenth century. Originally made with a blue mold, it had been sold in local markets since the seventeenth century, but it was the Harels who standardized production, and were involved in the introduction of a new penicillium which produced the crusts that we know today. Another important development was the creation of the wooden box in the 1890s which permitted the cheese to be sent far afield. It thus became an international delicacy.

True Camemberts, ideally from the Calvados, are now rare. Various producers claim to be the last suppliers of the genuine article, but the consumer should look for the ACC label. An authentic ripe Camembert will have a white crust with reddish marks and will be soft from the outside to the center.

## Cider and Calvados

Normandy is one of the few regions in France that does not produce wine. The popular local drink instead is cider — fermented apple juice. The best French cider comes from Normandy, with that of the highest quality coming from the vallée d'Auge in the Calvados. The highly regarded *cidre bouché* is bottle fermented. The effervescence of cheap, sparkling ciders is added artificially. When cooking with cider, always use a *cidre sec*, dry cider.

Calvados is brandy made from cider. The Arabs introduced distilled alcohols into France in the Middle Ages, and this *eau ardente*, fire water, was initially used mainly as a medicine. Apple brandy is first mentioned in 1533, and those produced in the west of France were first referred to as Calvados in the nineteenth century.

Calvados is not only served at the end of a meal. The day can begin with a *café Calva*, a most effective wake-up call, and mealtimes are sometimes punctuated with a mid-menu shot of Calvados, the *trou normand*, to stimulate the appetite. The chilled aperitif *pommeau*, appropriate at any time of the day, is a mixture of apple juice and Calvados. And of course Calvados gives character to dozens of Norman dishes.

LEO MEIER

Apple trees — over one hundred varieties of them — grow everywhere in the Calvados, both in tended rows and wild. The famous cider is made from the juice of *pommes à cidre*, apples that are unfit for ordinary consumption. Through fermentation this unpalatable juice becomes highly drinkable and it blends well with a variety of ingredients when cooked. Caen, William the Conqueror's ducal seat, is the principal town of the department. This thriving university town, which has some of the finest Romanesque architecture in the country, is known gastronomically for its *tripes à la mode de Caen*, tripe cooked with cider. Calvados also appears in many dishes. What could be more Norman than *poulet vallée d'Auge*, that uses cream and Calvados?

Eggs cooked in many ways are common throughout Normandy, and the Calvados area prepares its *omelette normande* with, not surprisingly, apples and Calvados. Apple tarts abound — with pastry cream, apple sauce, caramelized or plain. *Bourdelots* are cored apples filled with fruit jelly or butter and sugar, which are then wrapped in pastry and baked. A pear given the same treatment is called a *douillon*. Local *crêpes,* thicker than those of Brittany, are delicious stuffed with Calvados-soaked apples and then flamed.

Like the Manche, the Calvados enjoys a long coastline. At the resorts of Deauville and Trouville the world of fashion took to the beach in the nineteenth century, and the towns still attract the wealthy during the summer months. Trouville has a delightful market along the docks on the Touques river, where the fishermen unload their catches. All along the seaboard you will find the freshest seafood. A fine meal anywhere on the northern coast commonly begins with a shellfish platter, a mixture which could include oysters, cockles, mussels, sea snails, periwinkles, shrimp, *langoustines*, halved sea-urchins, and perhaps a tourteau crab. Southern Calvados still boasts trout streams, and the fat fish can be well accommodated *"à la normande"* or *"à la vallée d'Auge."*

## Rouen and the Seine-Maritime

The next department along the coast is the Seine-Maritime, with Rouen as its capital. Despite the destruction of the Second World War, many of the city's glorious Gothic buildings still remain, with their spires, gables, and gargoyles, and there has been extensive reconstruction. Rouen boasts several famous gastronomic specialties. The classic garniture, *sauce normande*, though created in Paris in 1837 by chef Langlais at the restaurant Le Rocher de Cancale, was based on a Rouen recipe for *matelote normande*, a fish stew. It can be used, with variations, for saucing fish, meat, and vegetables. And the city has given its name to *canard à la rouennaise,* a dish made famous in the last century by Frédéric Delair, one of the owners of the Tour d'Argent in Paris. The duck is killed by suffocation so that the blood is retained, giving the meat a particularly rich flavor. Rouen also excels in desserts, and its *mirlitons,* almond puff pastry tartlets, are a Norman classic. At Christmas time, *sucre de pommes* appears — a sugar confection flavored with apple and sometimes tinted with cherry.

Dieppe is another city in the Seine-Maritime whose name is connected with a famous garniture. Any recipe using the term *"à la dieppoise"* should properly include shrimp, mussels, mushrooms, and cider or white wine. *Sole dieppoise* is the best known version, though any variety of fish can be used. *Marmite dieppoise* is a rich fish stew made with cider and cream, and consists of scallops and an assortment of noble fish such as sole and turbot. The third classic garniture to come from Normandy, *"à la trouvillaise,"* named after the town of Trouville, is a *dieppoise* with a shrimp butter.

Apple production is important in the Seine-Maritime and cider and Calvados are plentiful, including the famous cider of the Caux plain, north of Rouen. Another local drink is the liqueur, Bénédictine, first made by the Benedictine monks of Fécamp in the sixteenth century. This is also cream and butter country, and milk is a major source of income. Local cheeses include Neufchâtel, produced in the Bray region, and Carré de Bray.

QUENTIN BACON

*Over a hundred different varieties of apples can be used to make cider, and producers commonly mix sweet, sweet-sour, bitter, and tart apples together.*

## Fresh-water Fish and Wild Rabbits

Normandy's fourth department is the Eure, named after one of the three rivers that flow through its forests and fields. With only a small portion of coastline, fresh-water fish is of greater importance here than fish from the sea, and the local *matelote* is made with trout. The region has fine wild rabbits, and the town of Gisors is known for its rabbit *rillettes*. Les Andelys is the place to go for honey, and the local butter is also well-considered. The town of Pont Audemer is known for its *mirliton* pastries, which is not surprising, for Gaston LeNôtre, France's current king of pastry, was born here.

Further still from the sea lies the Orne department, also named after a river. Geographically an extension of the Calvados, it too has rich pastures, and produces high quality dairy products and cider. The Orne excels in fine *charcuterie*, and the *boudin noir* of Mortagne-au-Perche is exceptional. Each year the town's contest for the best *boudin* draws charcutiers from miles around, and even overseas. *Sanguette*, black pudding made with rabbit's blood, takes advantage of the region's prolific rabbits. And the tripe are second only to those of Caen. River fishing is a popular pastime but, unfortunately for the visitor, little of the catch finds its way to restaurant tables. Hunting is also popular, and dishes such as daube of goose (almost always domestic these days) *"à la normande"* continue the Norman tradition of garnishing with cream and apples.

LEO MEIER

*A gardener busy tidying up one of his potted plants in a garden near Le Mont-Saint-Michel.*

# RECIPES OF NORMANDY

Robert Noah

PETER JOHNSON

## *Terrine de Canard au Calvados*

*Duck Terrine with Calvados*

This terrine of Michel Bruneau's uses the local Rouennais-style ducks that have been suffocated, leaving the meat a dark color and heightening its flavor. However, any duck can be used for this recipe.

*1 duck, about 5 lb (2.5 kg), boned, with liver*
*2 strips pork fatback, about 1/4 in (5 mm) thick*
*1/2 cup (4 fl oz/125 ml) Calvados*
*2 truffles, coarsely chopped (optional)*
*1 fresh thyme sprig*
*1 bay leaf*
*a mixture of lean and fatty pork that equals weight of boned duck*
*1 tablespoon fresh coriander, finely chopped*
*1 tablespoon fresh chervil or parsley, finely chopped*
*salt and freshly ground pepper*

Slice the duck breasts thinly and marinate with the strips of pork fat, half the Calvados, the truffles, thyme, and bay leaf for 2 hours. Meanwhile, finely chop the remaining duck meat with the duck liver and the pork, then add the remaining Calvados, the herbs and salt and pepper. Preheat the oven to 400°F (200°C). Line an 8-cup (2-qt/2-l) terrine with slices of pork fatback and add half the duck and pork mixture, topped by half the truffles, if they are being used. Pack the mixture down into the terrine. Over the top arrange half the strips of duck breast and some fatback and then pack in the remaining meat mixture, sprinkling over the remaining truffles. Top with the remaining duck breast and slices of fatback, prick with a fork, then cover with aluminum foil. Cook in a bain-marie. First bring it to a boil on the stove then continue cooking in the oven for 1 1/2 hours, or until a knife inserted into the center of the terrine is hot after 20 seconds. Remove from bain-marie and cool. Refrigerate for at least four days before serving.

To facilitate serving, cut a few slices of the terrine and place them beside it, overlapping, on the serving platter.

SERVES: 6

*Duck Terrine with Calvados,*
*Foie Gras Soup with Lentils,*
*Oysters in Pommeau,*
*Omelette de la Mère Poulard*

## *Soupe de Foie Gras aux Lentilles*

*Foie Gras Soup with Lentils*

In this dish Michel Bruneau combines duck *foie gras*, which is now being produced in Normandy, with lentils — a mix of the noble and the humble. While called a soup, it contains relatively little liquid and can be served on plates rather than in bowls, as an appetising first course, or as a satisfying light meal on its own.

*3 oz (90 g) light-colored lentils*
*2 cups (16 fl oz/500 ml) chicken stock*
*2/3 cup (5 fl oz/150 ml) vegetable broth (the cooking liquid of a mixture of vegetables)*
*2 onions, chopped*
*2 large carrots*
*bouquet garni: 1 bay leaf, 1 thyme sprig, 6 parsley sprigs*
*6 slices bacon, each about 1/4 in (5 mm) thick*
*2 tablespoons cream*
*salt and freshly ground pepper*
*3 tablespoons butter*
*10 oz (300 g) fresh duck* foie gras, *cut into slices weighing 1 1/2 to 2 oz (40 to 60 g) each*
*fresh chervil, coarsely chopped (optional)*

Cook the lentils in the chicken stock and vegetable broth, with the onions, carrots, bouquet garni, and bacon. Remove the bacon after 15 minutes. After a further 15 minutes remove the carrots and one-third of the lentils, which should be firm. Combine these lentils with the cream and keep warm. Continue cooking the remaining lentils until very tender, almost a purée, then force them through a fine mesh strainer. Correct the seasoning and whisk in the butter. Slice the carrots thinly and put aside.

Season the slices of *foie gras* on both sides with salt and pepper and cook in a dry, nonstick skillet for 30 seconds per side. Drain on paper towels.

To serve, divide the lentil purée between six warmed serving plates, placing a spoonful of the lentils in cream in the center of each serving. Scatter the carrot slices around the creamed lentils (they will reheat in the warm soup) and place a slice of *foie gras* on top of each serving, with a slice of bacon to the side. Decorate, if desired, with the chervil.

SERVES: 6

## *Huîtres au Pommeau*

*Oysters in Pommeau*

This recipe of Michel Bruneau's is unmistakably from Normandy, with its combination of oysters, apples, *pommeau*, and cream.

*24 large oysters in their shells*
*3 shallots, finely chopped*
*2 apples, peeled, cored, and coarsely chopped*
*$^{1}/_{3}$ cup (3 fl oz/90 ml)* pommeau *($^{1}/_{2}$ dry cider, $^{1}/_{2}$ apple brandy or Calvados)*
*2 tablespoons Calvados*
*$^{1}/_{2}$ cup (4 fl oz/125 ml) cream*
*freshly ground white pepper*

Open the oysters, keeping as much of their juice in the shell as possible. Combine in a pan the shallots, apples, *pommeau*, and Calvados. Over high heat reduce by three-quarters, then add the cream. Reduce the heat to low and continue cooking the sauce. Detach the oysters from their shells and strain their liquid into a bowl. Add the oyster liquid to the sauce and strain through a fine mesh strainer. The sauce should heavily coat the back of a spoon.

Put the oysters back in their shells and cover with the sauce. Add a little pepper to each oyster and place under a hot broiler (grill) until lightly colored.

SERVES: 6

## *Omelette de la Mère Poulard*

Mère Poulard, who established her inn on Le Mont-Saint-Michel in 1888, earned her fame with one recipe — her soufflé omelette. Today the same hotel-restaurant is many times bigger than in her day, but it continues to serve her egg specialty.

*12 eggs, separated*
*for savory omelettes: salt and freshly ground pepper*
*$^{1}/_{3}$ cup (3 fl oz/90 ml) cream, whipped stiff*
*4 tablespoons (2 oz/60 g) butter*
*for dessert omelettes: powdered (icing) sugar, and rum*

Season the separated eggs with salt and pepper (if you are making a savory omelette). Beat the yolks until they are light-colored, and beat the whites until they form stiff peaks. Gently fold the yolks into the whites, alternating with the whipped cream.

Meanwhile, heat the butter in a heavy 10-in (25-cm) skillet until it foams up and is very hot. Pour in the egg mixture, stirring only occasionally. The omelette is cooked when it has formed a light brown crust on the bottom but remains slightly runny in the center. Fold it in half in the skillet and then place it on a warmed serving platter.

If the omelette is to be served as a dessert, sprinkle the top generously with powdered sugar and flame with heated rum.

SERVES: 6

## *Graisse Normande*

*Norman Cooking Fat*

Though butter is characteristic of Norman cuisine, this flavored fat is also widely used as a substitute for oil or butter when roasting meat, or sautéing vegetables.

*1 lb (500 g) pork fat, chopped*
*1 lb (500 g) beef fat (ideally, from around the kidneys), chopped*
*an assortment of fresh vegetables such as:*
*2 carrots, coarsely sliced*
*1 large onion, quartered*
*1 leek, white and green parts, coarsely chopped*
*1 turnip, quartered*
*bouquet garni: 1 bay leaf, 1 thyme sprig, 6 parsley sprigs*
*salt and freshly ground pepper*

Melt the porkfat and beef fat in a heavy pan over low heat, covered, for about 35 minutes, or until most of the fat has melted, then add the vegetables, bouquet garni, and a pinch of salt and pepper. Continue to cook slowly, covered, until virtually all the fat has dissolved. Correct the seasoning and strain the fat through a fine mesh strainer or cheesecloth into a heavy crock or other container. When cool, cover and store in the refrigerator.

## *Sauce Normande*

*Norman Sauce*

This ubiquitous sauce, based on an old Norman dish, is said to have been created in the Parisian restaurant Le Rocher de Cancale in 1837. It is frequently used today in Norman meat and vegetable dishes. To transform it into a version suitable for fish, use only 1 cup (8 fl oz/250 ml) of cider and reduce with 1 cup of well-flavored fish stock.

*Norman Cooking Fat*

PETER JOHNSON

PETER JOHNSON

Norman Sauce, Norman Soup

*$\frac{1}{2}$ cup (4 oz/125 g) butter*
*1 onion, finely chopped*
*2 tablespoons all purpose (plain) flour*
*$1\frac{1}{2}$ cups (12 fl oz/375 ml) dry cider*
*$1\frac{1}{2}$ cups (12 fl oz/375 ml) cream*
*pinch of grated nutmeg*
*salt and freshly ground pepper*
*several drops of lemon juice*

In a medium saucepan melt 2 tablespoons of the butter and then add the chopped onion. Cook until the onion is tender, then sprinkle on the flour and continue cooking for a further minute or so. Pour in the cider and whisk vigorously for several minutes, or until the mixture thickens slightly and is smooth. Simmer for 10 minutes. Add the cream and nutmeg and taste for seasoning. Let the sauce reduce and thicken until it coats the back of a spoon. Whisk in the remaining butter and the lemon juice.

SERVES: 6

## Soupe Normande

*Norman Soup*

This soup contains no meat, its flavor deriving from an assortment of vegetables which can be varied with the seasons, and the *graisse normande*.

*$\frac{2}{3}$ cup (4 oz/125 g) dried white beans*
*1 lb (500 g) potatoes, quartered*
*3 leeks, white parts only, cut into $\frac{3}{4}$-in (2-cm) pieces*
*1 celery stalk, cut into $\frac{1}{4}$-in (5-mm) slices*
*3 tablespoons Norman cooking fat (see recipe page 228)*
*bouquet garni: 1 bay leaf, 1 thyme sprig, 6 parsley sprigs*
*6 cups ($1\frac{1}{2}$ qt/1.5 l) water*
*1 small cabbage, parboiled and cut into 6 or 8 pieces*
*3 oz (90 g) green beans, cut into $\frac{1}{2}$-in (1-cm) lengths*
*3 to 4 tablespoons butter*
*2 to 4 tablespoons coarsely chopped parsley or chervil*

Soak the white beans overnight in cold water and drain. Put in a saucepan with sufficient water to cover and boil for 20 to 30 minutes, until barely softened. Put the potatoes, leeks, celery, white beans, cooking fat and bouquet garni in a pot and pour on the water. Simmer uncovered for 25 minutes. Add the cabbage and the green beans and continue cooking at a simmer, covered, until all the vegetables are tender. Correct seasoning, adding more cooking fat if desired. Whisk the butter and herbs into the soup immediately before serving.

SERVES: 6

## Sole Trouvillaise, Fondue de Pommes

*Sole Trouvillaise with Apples*

Régis Lecomte of l'Auberge du Dauphin in Breuil-en-Auge, a typical Norman village between Lisieux and Deauville, devised this recipe. A less costly fish can be substituted for the sole, but it should remain firm after cooking for attractive presentation.

*3 sole, about 14 oz (440 g) each, trimmed and filleted*
*$1\frac{1}{2}$ cups (12 fl oz/375 ml) dry cider*
*$1\frac{1}{4}$ cups (10 oz/310 g) butter, softened*
*6 apples, firm and slightly tart, peeled*
*2 tablespoons peanut oil, or a vegetable oil with little flavor*
*salt and freshly ground pepper*
*2 tablespoons chopped chives*

Cut the sole fillets on the diagonal into $\frac{3}{4}$-in (2-cm) strips. In a small saucepan over high heat reduce the cider by half, then whisk in $\frac{3}{4}$ cup (6 oz/180 g) butter. Keep warm. Cut the apples into sticks approximately $\frac{1}{4}$ in (5 mm) thick and sauté in 2 tablespoons (1 oz/30 g) of the butter. Keep warm.

Heat the oil and the remaining butter in a skillet large enough to comfortably accommodate the sole fillets without excessive crowding. When hot, cook the fish until it firms, then cover and continue cooking over low heat for a further 5 minutes. Taste for seasoning.

To serve, arrange the apple sticks in the middle of six warmed serving plates and place the sole strips on top, pouring the sauce around the apples and fish. Sprinkle with the chives.

SERVES: 6

## *Barbue Braisée au Cidre*

*Brill Braised with Cider*

Brill is a firm-fleshed, flat white fish similar to turbot. Any similar fish can be used in the recipe. The sauce is an updated version of *sauce normande*, using the cooking liquid instead of fish stock. The meat glaze is optional, but does add dimension to the dish.

*2 brill, about $2\frac{1}{2}$ lb to 3 lb (1.25 to 1.5 kg) each, skinned and filleted*
*2 shallots, chopped*
*3 to 4 cups (24 fl oz/750 ml to 1 qt/1 l) dry cider*
*1 tablespoon meat glaze (optional)*
*$\frac{1}{2}$ cup (4 fl oz/125 ml) Calvados*
*$1\frac{1}{2}$ cups (12 fl oz/375 ml) cream*
*6 tablespoons (3 oz/90 g) butter*
*salt and freshly ground pepper*
*2 leeks, white parts only, cut into thin strips*
*2 apples, scooped into small balls*
*1 tablespoon lemon juice*

Preheat the oven to 350°F (180°C). Cut the fish into six portions and put in a skillet large enough to hold them comfortably with 1 tablespoon ($\frac{1}{2}$ oz/15 g) of butter, the shallots, cider to cover, and the meat glaze, if it is being used. Cover, bring to a simmer on top of the stove and then cook in the oven for 3 to 4 minutes, or until the fillets resist when pressed, or a knife inserted into the thickest part of a fillet comes out warm after 20 seconds. Remove the fish, put it aside, and keep warm.

Reduce the cooking liquid to a glaze, add the Calvados, then the cream, and cook slowly until the sauce barely coats the back of a spoon. Strain and whisk in 4 tablespoons (2 oz/60 g) of butter. Taste for seasoning. Cook the leeks in the remaining butter until soft. Cook the apple balls in the lemon juice and water to cover until they are tender, but still hold their shape.

To serve, arrange the leeks in the center of six warmed serving plates and place a piece of fish on top. Pour over the sauce and decorate with the apple balls.

Serves: 6

*Sole Trouvillaise with Apples, Brill Braised with Cider*

## *Navarin d'Agneau*

*Lamb Stew*

Lamb is one of the staple meats of Normandy. The following recipe is a good way to use less expensive cuts.

*2 tablespoons butter*
*2 tablespoons peanut oil*
*3 lb (1.5 kg) lamb neck or shoulder, trimmed and cut into pieces weighing approximately 2 oz (60 g) each*
*1 onion, finely chopped*
*2 tablespoons all purpose (plain) flour*
*2 garlic cloves, crushed in their skins*
*bouquet garni: 1 bay leaf, 1 thyme sprig, 6 parsley sprigs*
*salt and freshly ground pepper*
*2 cups (16 fl oz/500 ml) veal, beef, or chicken stock*
*18 pearl onions, or small pickling onions*
*12 baby carrots, or fewer larger carrots, cut into pieces*
*12 baby turnips, or fewer larger turnips, cut into pieces*
*12 small potatoes, or fewer larger potatoes, cut into pieces*
*2 to 4 tablespoons coarsely chopped parsley or chervil (optional)*

Heat the butter and oil in a heavy casserole, until very hot. Add the meat and color it lightly on all sides. Add the chopped onion, and continue cooking until onion is soft. Sprinkle on the flour and cook for another minute, then add the garlic, bouquet garni, salt and pepper, and the stock. The liquid should barely cover the meat.

Cover the pan and simmer for approximately 1 hour. Add the onions, carrots, and turnips and continue cooking, covered, until the vegetables are barely tender. Add the potatoes and finish cooking. Total cooking time should be about $1\frac{1}{2}$ hours.

Remove the meat and vegetables to a warmed serving platter and reduce the sauce for 1 or 2 minutes, skimming to remove any fat that might boil to the surface. Stir in the parsley, if desired, and pour over the meat.

Serves: 6

*Norman Potato Salad, Lamb Stew, Green Beans in Cream*

PETER JOHNSON

## Salade Cauchoise

*Norman Potato Salad*

The truffles in this salad, though not regional, combine particularly well with the potatoes – a vegetable eaten with most main courses in this part of the country.

*1½ lb (750 g) new potatoes, unpeeled*
*¾ lb (375 g) celery, (white center part only), cut into thin strips*
*3 tablespoons cider vinegar*
*5 oz (150 g) ham, thinly sliced*
*salt and freshly ground pepper*
*1 or 2 truffles, thinly sliced (optional)*
*1 cup (8 fl oz/250 ml) crème fraîche or heavy (double) cream*

Boil the potatoes until just tender. Remove from water and peel while they are still warm. Cut the warm potatoes into strips (there should be approximately twice as many strips of potatoes as there are of celery), add the celery and pour on the cider vinegar. Add ham, salt and pepper, and the truffles, if desired.

Refrigerate the salad until shortly before serving, when the cream is carefully folded in. Taste for seasoning and add more cider vinegar if necessary. Spoon onto individual plates or into one large salad bowl.

SERVES: 6

## Haricots Verts à la Crème

*Green Beans in Cream*

Success with this recipe depends on the freshness of the beans and the quality of the cream. Sterilized cream, with its particular flavor, is best avoided.

*2 lb (1 kg) green beans, trimmed and strings removed*
*1½ cups (12 fl oz/375 ml)* crème fraîche *or heavy (double) cream*
*butter*

Plunge the beans into a large saucepan of salted, boiling water. Cook until they are still firm (cooking time will depend on their size and freshness). Drain and refresh in cold water.

Preheat the oven to 350°F (180°C). Butter an ovenproof gratin dish just large enough to hold the beans in two or three layers, and cover with the cream. Add pepper (and salt if the beans were insufficiently salted during cooking). Cook in the oven for about 20 minutes, until the cream has reduced slightly and begun to thicken. Serve the beans at the table in the gratin dish.

SERVE: 6

*Norman Crêpes Flamed with Calvados*

PETER JOHNSON

## Crêpes Normandes Flambées au Calvados

*Norman Crêpes Flamed with Calvados*

More commonly found in Brittany, *crêpes* are also popular in Normandy. This recipe fills the *crêpes* with apple purée. The finished, stuffed *crêpes* can be made ahead of time, refrigerated, and then reheated.

*2 eggs*
*1 egg yolk*
*¾ cup (3 oz/90 g) all purpose (plain) flour*
*2 cups (16 fl oz/500 ml) milk*
*2 tablespoons (1 oz/30 g) melted butter*
*2 lb (1 kg) apples, peeled, cored, and quartered*
*1 cup (8 oz/250 g) sugar (more or less, depending on the sweetness of the apples)*
*¾ cup (6 fl oz/180 ml) Calvados*

Prepare the *crêpe* batter by mixing in a bowl the eggs, flour, milk, and melted butter. Meanwhile cook the apples in a heavy pan, covered, over low heat, with three-quarters of the sugar. The apples are done when they can be easily mashed with a fork. Mash most of the apples, but leave some of them whole. Mix in 3 tablespoons of Calvados.

Place a 6-in (15-cm) *crêpe* pan over moderate heat and brush the bottom with butter. Heat until a drop of batter in the pan sizzles, then pour in 2 to 3 table-

PETER JOHNSON

*Caramel Rice Pudding, Apple Fondant with Pommeau and Caramel Sauce*

spoons of batter, tipping the pan to coat the base evenly. Cook for about 1 minute, until light brown, then toss or turn with a spatula. Cook for 30 seconds, then turn out onto a plate. Cook all the *crêpes* in this way until the batter is used up. Preheat the oven to 350°F (180°C).

Spoon 4 tablespoons of the apple mixture into the center of each *crêpe*. Fold the sides of the *crêpe* over the apples. Place the *crêpes* folded-side down in a single layer in a buttered ovenproof dish.

When ready to serve, sprinkle the *crêpes* with the remaining sugar and put them in the oven to warm, and to partially caramelize the sugar. While they are heating, warm the remaining Calvados in a pan and transfer it to a bowl or small pitcher for serving. Present the *crêpes*, pour on the hot Calvados and flame at the table.

SERVES: 6 (12 *crêpes*)

## Fondant de Pommes, Sauce Caramel au Pommeau

*Apple Fondant with Pommeau and Caramel Sauce*

Régis Lecomte created this delightful dessert and serves it in his restaurant.

*Fondants:*
*1/2 cup (4 oz/125 g) sugar*
*3 tablespoons butter*
*2 lb (1 kg) apples, firm and slightly tart, peeled, cored, and quartered*
*powdered gelatin*
*1/3 cup (3 fl oz/90 ml)* pommeau *(1/2 dry cider, 1/2 apple brandy or Calvados)*
*Sauce:*
*1 cup (8 oz/250 g) sugar*
*1/3 cup (3 fl oz/90 ml) water*
*3/4 cup (6 fl oz/180 ml) cream*
*3/4 cup (6 fl oz/180 ml)* pommeau *(1/2 dry cider, 1/2 apple brandy or Calvados)*

Line four individual soufflé molds with plastic wrap. Preheat the oven to 325°F (160°C). Put the sugar and butter in a heavy skillet and place the apple quarters on top. Over moderate heat, caramelize the apples. When they are golden all over, arrange some of them to make a single layer in each mold, then sprinkle on a little gelatin. Add another layer of apples, then some more gelatin, repeating the process until the molds are filled. Deglaze the skillet with the *pommeau* and pour the liquid evenly over the molds. Cover and bake in a bain-marie in the oven for 20 minutes.

Let the molds cool then weigh each one down and place them in the refrigerator. (Cardboard rounds can be cut slightly smaller than the diameter of the molds, covered in plastic wrap, placed over the apple mixture and weighed down.)

For the sauce: In a medium saucepan over moderate heat make a caramel with the sugar and water. When it is light gold in color, add the cream and cook until the caramel has completely dissolved. Add the *pommeau* off the heat. Cool. To serve, turn out the molds onto individual serving plates and pour the sauce around each fondant.

SERVES: 4

## Terrinée

*Rice Pudding*

This is a dessert found all over Normandy that is made at home rather than in restaurants. Many variations exist, and the dish is known by a number of names, including *tordgoule*, *teurgoule*, and *bourgoule*.

*6 cups (1 1/2 qt/1.5 l) milk*
*3/4 cup (5 oz/150 g) short-grain rice*
*1/3 cup (3 oz/90 g) sugar*
*1 teaspoon ground cinnamon*
*salt*

Preheat the oven to 275°F (140°C). Bring the milk to a boil and let it cool off completely. Meanwhile, wash the rice and mix with the sugar, cinnamon, and a pinch of salt. Pour on the cool milk and stir. Pour into a well-buttered baking dish and bake in the oven for 2 1/2 hours. The pudding will form a light-colored crust and be firm. Serve warm or hot.

SERVES: 6

Bourges
Nevers
Berry
Châteauroux
Cher
Moulins
Loire
Bourbonnais
Montluçon
Saint-Pourçain-sur-Sioule
Nouhant
Vichy
Gannat
Allier
Vienne
Limoges
Riom
Clermont-Ferrand
Billom
Limousin
Massif
Auvergne
Brioude
Perigueux
Brive-la-Gaillarde
Salers
Mts de la Margaride
Le Puy
Cantal
Central
Sarlat
Dordogne
Vic-sur-Cère
Aurillac
Mts d'Aubrac
Laguiole
Lot
Cahors
Rodez
Tarn
0 10 20 30 40 50 M
0 20 40 60 80 Km.

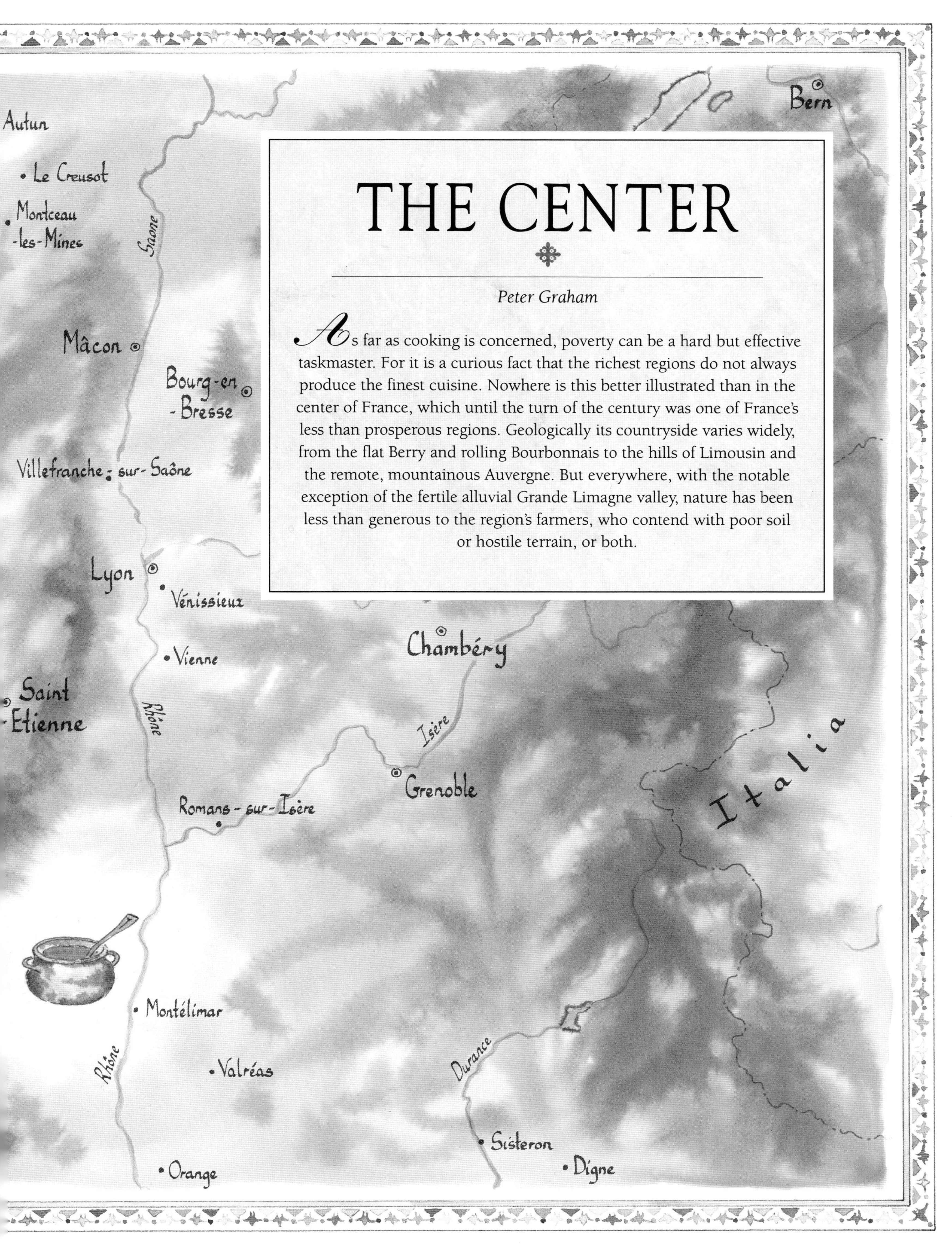


# THE CENTER

*Peter Graham*

As far as cooking is concerned, poverty can be a hard but effective taskmaster. For it is a curious fact that the richest regions do not always produce the finest cuisine. Nowhere is this better illustrated than in the center of France, which until the turn of the century was one of France's less than prosperous regions. Geologically its countryside varies widely, from the flat Berry and rolling Bourbonnais to the hills of Limousin and the remote, mountainous Auvergne. But everywhere, with the notable exception of the fertile alluvial Grande Limagne valley, nature has been less than generous to the region's farmers, who contend with poor soil or hostile terrain, or both.

CATHERINE KARNOW

*A farmer from the Auvergne poses with his scythe. The bracken around him is dead and soon the winter snows will arrive.*

## Berry's Wild Larder

In the Berry, where bleak limestone plains alternate with woods and marshland, people have always relied on wild produce, such as fish, frogs, game, and mushrooms, to supplement their diet. Even in bourgeois households such as those described by George Sand in several of her novels (she was a native of Nohant, in the heart of Berry), the fare was usually down-to-earth and relied on local produce. The soil of the Berry is mainly poor. While some areas produce excellent white and light red wines such as Reuilly, Quincy, Menetou-Salon, and Châteaumeillant, much of the region is used for grazing sheep and goats. Lamb raised in this part of the country, particularly the Berrichon breed, is highly prized, as are the local goat's milk cheeses, Valençay and Crottin de Chavignol. The latter goes particularly well with the wines from neighboring Sancerre.

## The Grande Limagne Valley

*Brilliant orange pumpkin being sliced and weighed at the markets. Pumpkins are often used to thicken soups and stews.*

LEO MEIER/WELDON TRANNIES

To the south the Berry merges imperceptibly into the Bourbonnais. The dark soil of the Grande Limagne valley is rich with volcanic ash and its beef and poultry are renowned. Every year, just before Christmas, a large and cacophonous poultry fair is held in the small fortified town of Gannat, home of the classic Bourbonnais dish, *poulet au fromage*. In the attractive market town of Riom, on 11 June every year, local farmers dressed up as Brayauds (devotees of the fifth-century Saint Amable) march through the streets. The Brayauds give their name to several dishes, such as *omelette brayaude,* with potatoes, ham, and cheese, and *gigot brayaude*, which resembles the Berrichon *gigot de sept heures*.

Around Saint-Pourçain-sur-Sioule lie some of the oldest vineyards in France. Saint-Pourçain wine and its lesser known neighbors to the south, Corent and the now almost defunct Chanturgues, are robust, homely wines. It is with Chanturgues that the Auvergnat version of *coq au vin* should properly be made.

The Bourbonnais is better known for its waters than its wines: a third of the bottled water consumed in France comes from here and the Auvergne. Vichy is the region's pre-eminent and largest spa, but the city is also known for its confectionery — barley sugar, pastilles and *pâtes de fruits*. (Vichyssoise soup is not, by the way, a local dish, but was developed in the United States.) Vichy water is known to be beneficial to the digestion, and the various spa waters in the region will, it is claimed, cure anything from rheumatism to skin complaints.

The Limagne valley runs southwards into the Auvergne, bordered by two attractive Medieval towns — Billom, long a major center of garlic growing and processing, and Brioude, which has a bustling food market. The river Allier used to teem with salmon at this point: nineteenth-century monks at the monastery of Lavoûte-Chilhac near Brioude became so sick of eating salmon that they begged their abbot not to serve it more than once a day, or three times a week.

## Le Puy and its Lentils

To the southeast lies the town of Le Puy, with three remarkable spurs of volcanic rock towering over it. One is topped by an eleventh-century chapel, another by a statue of the Virgin Mary, and the third is favored by hang gliders. Le Puy's food market is most definitely worth a visit. In the Velay, around the town, farmers grow a delicious variety of green-grey lentil, *lentilles vertes*, marked with dark speckles. When cooked the lentils turn a rich brown. They are integral to the classic Auvergnat salt pork dish, *petit salé aux lentilles,* and are also served with sausages and ham, and used to thicken soups.

*The Château d'Anjony, with its four huge towers, looks out over the surrounding countryside. It was built in 1439 and has remained in the same family ever since.*

CATHERINE KARNOW

LEO MEIER

*Chestnuts from the Châtaigneraie, the "sweet chestnut grove," west of the Aubrac plateau, are used in all sorts of dishes, from soups to stuffings and desserts.*

## The Aubrac Plateau, the Chataigneraie, and the Monts du Cantal

To the west of Le Puy the Auvergne becomes considerably more rugged, with the Margeride mountains and the windswept Aubrac plateau, which rises to 3300 feet (1000 meters). Not so long ago the docile local cows were used as draft animals as well as dairy cattle, with only calves being used for meat. From around Laguiole, in the plateau's center, comes an excellent cheese of the same name, and the town is also famous for its elegantly curved folding knives. Most farmers in the Auvergne carry such knives, using them in the fields to cut up sausage and cheese for snacks, and at table in place of a meat or bread knife.

To the west of the Aubrac plateau lies a more clement area known as the Châtaigneraie, literally "the sweet chestnut grove." Its rounded hills and steep valleys are carpeted with chestnut trees, and local meat and poultry dishes often contain chestnuts. The Châtaigneraie and a small area to its southwest are the only part of France, apart from the Côte d'Azur, where stockfish, wind-dried, unsalted cod, is traditionally eaten. Nice and Marseille were introduced to stockfish centuries ago by Norwegian sailors, but no one knows how it found its way into the southern Auvergne. This most outlandish ingredient — it is pungent-smelling and hard as a plank before soaking — is cooked with eggs, cream, potatoes, and garlic to make *estofinado*, a great local favorite.

North of the Châtaigneraie and the town of Aurillac lies a group of extinct volcanoes, the Monts du Cantal. Their grassy slopes provide excellent grazing land, and the region is famed for Cantal, a cheese similar to Laguiole, which is made in cylinders weighing up to 110 pounds (50 kilograms) and sold at several stages of maturity. Whereas the cows of the Aubrac can, come spring, amble straight from their cozy sheds onto the pastures, in the Monts du Cantal the cowherds take their animals up the mountains to graze at altitudes sometimes in excess of 5000 feet (1500 meters). In the old days they would spend summer there, milking the cows and making butter and cheese in *burons*, stone huts. No longer houses for the cowherds, the *burons* are still used for maturing the cheese.

The best Cantal, called Salers, is made mainly from the milk of Salers cows, hardy, nimble cattle with a rust-red coat and elegantly curved, pointed horns. Both the cheese, the cow, and a local aperitif flavored with gentian root take their name from the austerely beautiful mountain village of Salers. Beef and veal from Salers cattle, which are often crossed with Charolais, are of exceptional quality.

Anyone interested in learning about Salers cheese can visit a *buron* by applying to the Syndicat d'Initiative of either Salers or Vic-sur-Cère during the summer months. Those unwilling to tramp up a mountain should at least visit the wholesale cheese market at Besse-en-Chandesse, in the heart of another group of extinct volcanoes, the Monts Dore, to the north. Every Monday farmers from all around come to the market to sell their Saint-Nectaire cheeses. At its best Saint-Nectaire is perhaps the finest of all Auvergne cheeses. Made from unpasteurized milk, and therefore carrying the *fermier* appellation, it has a greyish rind tinged with red and yellow. Several blue cheeses are also made in the Auvergne, including Bleu d'Auvergne and the distinctive Fourme d'Ambert, which some consider superior to Roquefort.

To the west of the Auvergne lies Limousin, which is mainly given over to stock breeding. This region shares many culinary specialties with the Auvergne, though

JEAN-PAUL FERRERO/AUSCAPE INTERNATIONAL

they often have other names. The Limousin *clafoutis*, baked cherry custard, for example, is called *milliard* or *millard* in the Auvergne, while the latter's *soupe au chou* goes by the name of *bréjaude* in the Limousin, where it sometimes contains a kind of dumpling called a *farcidure*. But one dish peculiar to Limousin is *boudin aux châtaignes*, a delicious, slightly sweet black pudding with fragments of chestnut taking the place of the usual cubes of fat.

*Limousin is known for the quality of its cattle. Here a pair of cows are being used for ploughing.*

Three breeds of farm animal are named after the province of Limousin: a black and pink pig that is particularly fond of chestnuts, a hardy sheep, and a small reddish cow, all of which produce excellent meat. Its capital, Limoges, famous for its porcelain, has also long been known for its butchers. One of the city's oldest and most attractive streets is the rue des Bouchers.

## Home of Parisian Catering

The Paris café has its origins in the Massif Central. In the nineteenth century, poverty drove peasants in their thousands from the Auvergne and Limousin to seek work in the capital. Tough, hard-working people, they cornered the market in firewood and coal, which frequently had to be carted up numerous flights of stairs in the new seven-storey apartment blocks. Often such a fuel business would double as a wine shop, with a small zinc counter, and these soon grew into cafés and restaurants. The solidarity that was such a feature of mountain life was maintained in the capital, and today well over three-quarters of the catering trade is owned by people from this part of the country or their descendants. They even have their own weekly paper, *L'Auvergnat de Paris*.

*Page 241: An elderly farm laborer sits in the sunshine outside a house in the Auvergne.*

## CHARCUTERIE

In a joke about the Auvergnats, an Auvergnat child is asked which parent they love most, and replies "bacon." The Auvergne, indeed the center of France as a whole, is celebrated for its *charcuterie*, pork products. Most farmers keep a pig or two, and they are generally fed on kitchen scraps, stale bread, and skimmed milk, sometimes being allowed to forage for acorns and chestnuts in the woods.

Each year the slaughterer is called in, and the pig, after what must be a happy life compared with the lot suffered by many of its kind, is turned into all manner of products by the farmer and his wife, assisted by relatives and neighbors.

The blood goes into *boudin*, black pudding, and the better cuts, the liver, and the kidneys are generally frozen. Fattier cuts are used to make *saucisses fraîches*, fresh sausages, and several types of salami-like *saucisson sec*, the best being *rosette*. The shoulders, back, and spare ribs are wet-salted (*petit salé*), while the hind legs are salted then dried in a corner of the hearth, to make raw ham.

The trotters, tail, snout, lights, heart, spleen, and ears go into coarse, tasty pâtés, such as *fricandeau*, *pâté de tête*, or *fritons*, all of which can be found in country *charcuteries*. Also found in *charcuteries* in the southern Auvergne, though not pork-derived, are *tripous* — delicious little bundles of sheep's tripe flavored with garlic and cloves.

LEO MEIER

These people were successful partly through their willingness to provide value for money. (An Auvergnat proverb says "You can't catch flies with vinegar.") This is certainly true of restaurants in the Massif Central today, for they offer the most generous set menus. Critics of the cooking dismiss it as heavy and greasy, which is not the case, but it probably was in harder times, when fat provided a cheap and readily available source of calories. Strenuous manual labor gives people hearty appetites, and in the days when harvesting was done by hand, each farmer helping their neighbor, farm workers would eat as many as five meals a day. Before the era of the combine harvester, priority had to be given to feeding *"les hommes."* In parts of the Auvergne, until recently, it was customary for the women to stand serving the men, only sitting down to eat when the men had finished.

Even today, men have little to do with preparing or serving meals. Occasionally they may lend a hand to prepare *aligot*, a blend of mashed potatoes, garlic and cheese, which requires considerable muscle power when made in large quantities, as it sometimes is for weddings or for village fêtes, when it is billed as an *aligot géant*. Otherwise men deign only to use their Laguiole knives to cut slices from the huge round half-rye loaves that are kept in ample kitchen-table drawers. Most farmhouses have their own external bread oven, a small igloo-shaped construction usually set against the wall of the house or barn.

## LE JARDIN POTAGER

In most homes, each meal begins with a vegetable soup, often containing bread, cabbage, or cheese. It is traditional to pour a dash of red wine into the soup when only a few spoonfuls are left, a practice that is thought beneficial to the health. Cabbage, an easily grown vegetable that is resistant to cold, looms large in the diet: it goes into the frequently eaten *soupe au chou* and *chou farci*, as well as into *potée*, where it is cooked with various pork meats.

Until the arrival of the railway, many Massif Central communities were cut off from the rest of France and virtually self-sufficient. Even today most country people keep hens and rabbits, and grow their own vegetables. The word *jardin* is generally used to refer to a *jardin potager*, a kitchen garden. The green tops of Swiss chard are used in such dishes as *falette,* stuffed breast of veal, and *pounti*, a curious savory pudding containing meat and prunes. Until recently the only cooking and salad oil used came from their own walnut trees. The most commonly used fat is lard.

Potatoes are important, and are often eaten with cheese, as in the already mentioned *aligot*. *Truffade,* potatoes fried with bacon and cheese, is so called because when the potato was introduced in the eighteenth century the Auvernats nicknamed it *trufa*, the Occitan word for truffle, no doubt because of its shape and earthy origin. Potato pies, made with puff pastry, are also very popular.

Because of their memories of less affluent times, the peasants of the Massif Central, like those of the Berry, rely heavily on the wild larder. They enthusiastically hunt, fish and gather anything edible, whether animal or vegetable: boar, venison, game birds, trout, crayfish (now rare), snails, dandelions, mushrooms, chestnuts, crab apples, wild asparagus, medlars, and blueberries. Even in our age of relative culinary affluence, there is perhaps a useful lesson to be learnt from such thrift combined with a love of variety. (Berry and Bourbonnais wines are listed under Loire Wines on page 189.)

SPECTRUM COLOUR LIBRARY/SCOOPIX

PETER JOHNSON

# *R*ECIPES OF THE CENTER

Peter Graham

## *Pâté de Cèpes*

*Cèpe Pie*

Although associated with southwest France, *cèpe* mushrooms are highly prized and keenly hunted all over the country. Their subtle flavor is brought out particularly well in this old recipe.

*Short pastry:*
*2 cups (8 oz/250 g) all purpose (plain) flour*
*1 teaspoon salt*
*$^1/_4$ teaspoon powdered (icing) sugar*
*$^1/_2$ cup (4 oz/125 g) unsalted butter, diced and chilled*
*$^1/_3$ cup (3 fl oz/90 ml) iced water*
*Filling:*
*2 lb (1 kg) firm* cèpes *(porcini mushrooms), or 3 oz (90 g) dried* cèpes
*4 tablespoons (2 oz/60 g) butter*
*1 onion, finely chopped*
*1 garlic clove, finely chopped*
*7 oz (220 g) ham, sliced*

For the pastry: Mix the flour, salt, and sugar in a mixing bowl. Add the butter. Holding a knife in each hand, cut the butter into the flour. Continue until the mixture has the consistency of fresh breadcrumbs. Gradually sprinkle the iced water over the mixture, stirring all the time with a fork until the dough forms a compact, unsticky mass. (You may need slightly less or more water than the amount indicated.) Shape the dough into a ball, and wrap in aluminum foil. Refrigerate for at least 30 minutes, or overnight if possible, before use.

Preheat oven to 400°F (200°C). Butter an 8-in (20-cm) deep-sided ovenproof china pie plate. Divide the pastry into two pieces, one weighing about twice as much as the other. Roll out the larger piece into an 11-in (27-cm) circle and line the pie plate with it.

For the filling: If using fresh *cèpes*, carefully wipe off all grit with moistened paper towels. Avoid washing them if possible. Cut into small pieces. Cook in a nonstick 10-in (25-cm) skillet with the butter over medium heat until they have given up nearly all their moisture. If using dried *cèpes*, break into small pieces and soak in a little water for at least 30 minutes, then transfer, along with any water not absorbed, to the skillet and cook for a minute or two in the butter. Chop half the ham coarsely. Add the onion, garlic, and chopped ham to the *cèpes* and cook gently for about 10 minutes.

Place a layer of the mixture in the pastry shell and cover with a slice of ham. Add more alternating layers until the ingredients are used up.

Using a pastry brush, moisten the edge of the pastry shell with water. Roll out the remaining piece of pastry into an 8-in (20-cm) circle, lay over the top of the filling and crimp the edges of the pastry to seal. Make a central hole in the pastry and brush the surface with milk.

Bake for about 45 minutes. The crust should be golden and feel cooked when lightly prodded with the finger. If it browns too soon, cover with aluminum foil for the remaining cooking time. Allow to rest for 5 minutes after removing from the oven. Serve in its dish.

SERVES: 6

## *Soupe au Fromage*

*Cheese Soup*

This used to be one of the staple dishes of Cantal cowherds in the days when they spent summer in the mountains, milking their cows and making cheese, but it is much more of a winter dish in character — warming, filling, and nourishing.

*3 oz (90 g) salt pork fatback or unsmoked bacon fat, finely chopped*
*1 large onion, sliced*
*6 cups ($1^1/_2$ qt/1.5 l) vegetable stock*
*freshly ground pepper*
*12 oz (375 g) rye bread, sliced*
*11 oz (350 g) young Cantal cheese or mild Cheddar, very thinly sliced*
*2 tablespoons heavy (double) cream*

Preheat oven to 350°F (180°C). Render the fat in a nonstick 10-in (25-cm) skillet over medium heat and fry the onion until golden (do not allow to burn). Bring the stock to a boil, add the onion, its cooking fat, any remaining scraps of unrendered fat and a little pepper. Simmer for 20 minutes.

Put alternate layers of bread and cheese into a 3-qt (3-l) ovenproof soup tureen, ending with a layer of cheese. Dribble the cream over the top and pour in the boiling-hot stock. Put in the oven for about 15 minutes, then serve in warmed soup plates or bowls.

SERVES: 6

*Left: Savoury Pudding, Cheese Soup, Cèpe Pie*

## Pounti

*Savory Pudding*

*Pounti* is an oddity unique to the Auvergne. In people's homes, it is essentially a vehicle for leftover meat and, depending on the amount available, the proportions of the ingredients can vary considerably. At its best, as in the following recipe, which uses yeast, it is a light dish that offers a refreshing combination of flavors. In some versions the prunes are omitted, which robs the dish of its originality.

*8 prunes*
*1 cup (4 oz/125 g) buckwheat flour or all purpose (plain) flour*
*2 cups (16 fl oz/500 ml) milk*
*5 eggs*
*1/6 oz (5 g) fresh (compressed) yeast or 1/12 oz (2 g) dry yeast*
*1 lb (500 g) sausagemeat or cooked pork leftovers (for example,* petit salé *or roast pork, including a little fat)*
*7 oz (220 g) Swiss chard tops, spinach or lettuce*
*1 onion, quartered*
*1 garlic clove*
*2 tablespoons parsley*
*1 tablespoon chervil*
*salt and freshly ground pepper*
*1 tablespoon walnut oil*

Soak the prunes in water or tea for at least 6 hours and then pit. Preheat oven to 400°F (200°C). Put the flour in a large mixing bowl and add all but 2 tablespoons of the milk, stirring until smooth. Beat in the eggs one by one, then the yeast diluted in the remaining milk, which should be warmed slightly.

Put the meat, Swiss chard tops, onion, garlic, parsley, and chervil in a blender or processor, and blend to a fairly fine consistency. Add plenty of pepper and a little salt. (The amount of salt will depend on how salty the sausagemeat or pork is.) Add the contents of the blender or processor to the ingredients in the mixing bowl. Mix thoroughly.

Turn the mixture into a 2-qt (2-l) deep pie plate, oiled with walnut oil. Arrange the prunes evenly over the surface, then press them down until they are submerged in the mixture. Bake for about 40 minutes or until the *pounti* has puffed up a little and browned on top. It is cooked when a sharp knife inserted in it comes out clean.

Serve immediately, cutting into sections like a cake. *Pounti* is sometimes unmolded before serving, but this is unnecessary, particularly as it should be eaten piping hot, straight from the oven.

SERVES: 6

## Truites au Lard

*Trout with Crisp-fried Ham Fat*

This dish from the Auvergne brings together two flavors which combine surprisingly well. True Auvergnats believe that slightly stale fat produces a better result.

*5 oz (150 g) raw ham fat, salt pork fat or unsmoked bacon fat, trimmed of rind*
*6 trout, about 8 oz (250 g) each*
*2 tablespoons all purpose (plain) flour*
*salt and freshly ground pepper*
*1 garlic clove, finely chopped*
*2 tablespoons flat-leafed parsley, finely chopped*
*1 tablespoon best wine vinegar*

Cut the ham fat into 1/4-in (5-mm) squares and fry gently until crisp in a nonstick skillet large enough to accommodate the trout in a single layer. (If you do not possess a sufficiently large skillet, cook the trout in two batches, keeping the first batch very hot while cooking the second.) Clean the trout, flour lightly and season with pepper and a little salt. (The amount of salt needed will depend on the saltiness of the ham fat.) Remove the ham fat and set aside, leaving the rendered fat in the pan. Turn up the heat. When the fat is just below smoking point, put in the trout and fry over medium heat for about 6 minutes per side, or until the skin is crisp.

Transfer the trout to a very hot serving dish. Discard most of the fat from the pan. Reheat the ham fat pieces briefly in the pan and arrange them over and around the trout. Put the garlic, parsley, and vinegar into the pan, deglaze briskly and pour over the trout. Serve immediately. The trout may be served on their own as a first course, or with boiled potatoes as a main course.

SERVES: 6

*Trout with Crisp-fried Ham Fat*

PETER JOHNSON

## Mourtayrol

*Saffron-flavored Meat Stew*

Saffron was commonly used in Medieval French cuisine. Now it lingers on only in a few Provençal dishes like *bouillabaisse* and this lavish Auvergnat mixed-meat stew, which is traditionally eaten at Easter. Like *pot-au-feu*, it makes up the first two courses of a meal, and usually leaves little room for anything else substantial.

*1 boiling chicken, about 5 lb (2.2 kg), trussed*
*1 lb (500 g) lean beef such as chuck or rump steak*
*8 oz (250 g) raw ham or 1 raw ham bone with a little meat left on it*
*1 celery stalk*
*2 onions*
*4 cloves*
*1 bay leaf*
*salt*
*6 carrots, sliced*
*4 young turnips, quartered*
*3 leeks, sliced*
*4 peppercorns, coarsely crushed*
*5 threads (0.3 g) saffron*

Begin cooking the dish the day before it is to be eaten. Trim the chicken of all excess fat, both external and from the stomach cavity, and place in a 10-qt (10-l) pot with the beef, raw ham, celery, onions, each studded with 2 cloves, and bay leaf. Add enough water to cover. Cover and bring slowly to a boil, skimming from time to time. Simmer for 2 hours, skimming again if necessary. Leave to cool completely, then refrigerate. Next day, remove as much fat as possible from the surface of the liquid. Check the saltiness of the broth. Depending on the saltiness of the ham, it may or may not need additional salt. Bring to a boil again. Add the carrots, turnips, leeks, and peppercorns. Stir in the saffron, making sure it dilutes well. Simmer for about 30 minutes or until the vegetables are cooked. Check seasoning.

Serve the broth as a first course. Away from the table, ladle it directly from the pot onto oven-dried crusts of bread in heated soup bowls and serve. For the main course, transfer the meats (except the ham bone if used) onto a large warmed serving dish and arrange the vegetables around them. Serve immediately.

SERVES: 6

PETER JOHNSON

Saffron-flavored Meat Stew

## *Chou Farci Limousin*

*Limousin Stuffed Cabbage*

All cabbage cultures, from Poland to the Massif Central, have their own ways of stuffing the vegetable. Within the Limousin and Auvergne, there are several different versions of *chou farci*. Often, what goes into the dish will depend on what meat leftovers are available. This Limousin recipe is a light version of a dish calling for fresh meat and chestnuts.

*1 lb (500 g) fresh chestnuts*
*1 large Savoy or roundhead cabbage, or 2 small ones, weighing a total of about 3 lb (1.5k g)*
*2 tablespoons lard*
*5 oz (150 g) raw ham, thinly sliced, trimmed of rind and cut into strips*
*12 oz (375 g) sausagemeat*
*2 onions, finely chopped*
*2 garlic cloves, finely chopped*
*1 tablespoon sweet marjoram or 1 teaspoon thyme, finely chopped*
*2 eggs*
*salt and freshly ground pepper*
*2 cups (16 fl oz/500 ml) veal or other meat stock*

Make a slash on the flat side of each chestnut. Bring a large saucepan of water to a boil. Drop in the chestnuts and boil for 30 minutes.

Meanwhile, cut the cabbage(s) in half and remove a triangular wedge of stem from each half as well as any tough ribs. Break off the leaves one by one. Blanch the leaves in plenty of boiling salted water for 10 minutes. Refresh under cold water and drain.

Remove chestnuts from heat. Take them out of the water in batches of 5 or 6 (they are easier to peel while still hot), and remove the outer shell and all inner skin, breaking open the chestnut to do so if necessary.

Grease a heavy 4-qt (4-l) casserole with the lard. Preheat oven to 375°F (190°C). Make the stuffing by mixing together the chestnuts, meat, onions, garlic, herbs, and eggs very thoroughly. Add salt and pepper to taste. (The amount of salt needed will depend on the saltiness of the ham and the sausagemeat.)

Cover the sides and bottom of the casserole with the largest cabbage leaves. Spread a thin layer of the stuffing on the cabbage. Cover with more leaves, pressing them down firmly so there are no air pockets. Repeat the operation until the stuffing has been used up, finishing with a layer of cabbage. Pour in the stock, which should almost submerge the stuffed cabbage if it has been tightly packed.

Cover the casserole and put in the oven for about $2^1/_2$ hours. The cabbage will give off a varying amount of liquid depending on its freshness. After $1^1/_2$ hours check the liquid level inside the casserole. If it does not seem to have reduced, finish cooking with the casserole lid off.

The *chou farci* is cooked when it can be pierced easily with a pointed knife. Drain off any excess liquid, setting it aside for soup or stock. Turn the cabbage out onto a warmed serving dish. The dish should be slightly bowl-shaped and larger than the *chou farci*, as a certain amount of liquid will ooze out. Serve the *chou farci* on its own, cutting it like a cake.

SERVES: 6

## Aligot

*Mashed Potatoes with Cheese*

Like *soupe au fromage*, this is a dish that cowherds used to eat for weeks on end during their summer spell up the mountains. Its unique consistency — when raised with a spoon, it trails a mass of rubbery threads — is produced by Tomme fraîche de Cantal, an unsalted, unmatured version of Cantal cheese. Despite the amount of garlic it requires, *aligot* does not have a great deal of character when eaten on its own. It goes well with a salty or piquant main dish such as *saucisses fraîches* (very meaty Auvergnat sausages), fried liver deglazed with a dash of vinegar, or crisp-fried bacon.

*2 lb (1 kg) mature (floury) potatoes*
*about 3/4 cups (6 fl oz/180 ml) milk, heated*
*3 tablespoons butter*
*4 large garlic cloves, very finely chopped*
*freshly ground pepper*
*1 1/4 lb (625 g) Tomme fraîche de Cantal or Mozzarella, very thinly sliced*
*salt*

Wash and boil the potatoes. Peel while still hot and mash in a heavy 4-qt (4-l) saucepan with the heated milk, butter, garlic, and pepper until a smooth consistency is obtained.

Place over very low heat and stir in the cheese. Beat vigorously with a wooden spoon until the mixture becomes elastic. Add plenty of salt to taste (the cheese is unsalted) and continue beating. As the mixture heats up it will become slightly softer. If it remains too stiff, add a little more hot milk. As soon as it makes long bubblegum-like strands when lifted with the spoon, serve. Guests and any accompanying dish must be ready: there is nothing more sullen than an *aligot* that has cooled off.

*Aligot* can more conveniently be made in advance, then at the last moment put into a microwave, which reheats dishes with this kind of consistency to perfection.

SERVES: 6

*Limousin Stuffed Cabbage, Mashed Potatoes with Cheese*
PETER JOHNSON

PETER JOHNSON

*Salt Pork with Green Lentils*

## Petit Salé aux Lentilles

*Salt Pork with Green Lentils*

This classic dish is not worth making unless you can obtain genuine green lentils from Le Puy.

It is important to include both a lean and a fat cut of pork as they contribute the contrasting flavors that give the dish its unique character.

*3 lb (1.5 kg) uncooked* petit salé, *salt pork, including, if possible, 1 piece* palette, *blade bone, and/or spare ribs, and 1 piece lean belly*
*2 onions*
*4 cloves*
*3 garlic cloves*
*bouquet garni: 1 bay leaf, 1 thyme sprig, 6 parsley sprigs*
*freshly ground pepper*
*1 lb (500 g) green Le Puy lentils*

Soak the salt pork overnight in plenty of cold water. Place in a 4-qt (4-l) pot with enough fresh water to cover and bring to a boil over medium heat, skimming when necessary. After 10 minutes' boiling, reduce to a simmer and taste the water. If there is no taste of salt, or very little, move straight on to the next step; if it is salty, drain off the water, rinse the pork and cover with fresh water.

Add the onions, each studded with 2 cloves, the garlic, the bouquet garni, and plenty of pepper. Bring to a boil and simmer for 1 1/2 to 2 hours, or until the meat can be pierced easily with a pointed knife.

Rinse the lentils in cold water and add to the pork. Bring back to a simmer. After 20 minutes or so, the lentils will swell and may even begin to emerge from the water. Make sure all the lentils remain immersed, adding a little water from time to time, if necessary.

When the lentils are cooked (this will take between 30 minutes and 1 hour, depending on their freshness; they should not turn to a mush, nor should they remain *al dente*), check seasoning and add salt if necessary. Strain off nearly all the liquid and set aside for a soup. Remove the bouquet garni. Lift out the onions carefully, so they do not disintegrate, and the pork. Arrange on a large, warmed serving dish and pour the lentils around them. Serve with Dijon mustard.

A delicious salad can be made with leftover lentils. Simply add a green onion (scallion or spring onion) and some flat-leafed parsley, both finely chopped, some lemon juice, a little Dijon mustard and vegetable oil, and mix well. The salad is even better eaten the next day.

SERVES: 6

PETER JOHNSON

*Apple Pie, Chestnut Mold*

## *Cadet-Mathieu*

*Apple Pie*

This is a substantial Auvergnat version of apple pie, which is given a distinctive touch by the presence of orangeflower water. The best results are obtained with slightly tart but flavorful apples, such as russets, which resemble the varieties found in the Auvergne (Saint-Germain, Queue de Lièvre).

*13 oz (400 g) short pastry (see cèpe pie recipe, page 243)*
*3/4 cup (3 oz/90 g) all purpose (plain) flour*
*2 cups (16 fl oz/500 ml) milk*
*1/3 cup (3 oz/90 g) superfine (caster) sugar*
*4 egg yolks*
*1 tablespoon orangeflower water*
*2 lb (1 kg) tart apples, peeled, cored, and finely sliced*

Preheat oven to 400°F (200°C). Butter an 8-in (20-cm) deep-sided ovenproof china pie plate. Divide the pastry into two pieces, one weighing about twice as much as the other. Roll out the larger piece into an 11-in (27-cm) circle and line the pie plate with it.

Mix the flour with 1/2 cup (4 fl oz/125 ml) of the milk. Put the rest of the milk in a heavy 1-qt (1-l) saucepan and bring to just below boiling point. Lower heat and stir in the flour-and-milk mixture until smooth. Add half the sugar and cook gently, stirring, for about 10 minutes or until fairly thick. Remove from heat and quickly beat in the egg yolks, one by one, and the orangeflower water.

Pour the mixture into the pastry shell. Cover with layers of apples and sprinkle with the rest of the sugar.

Using a pastry brush, moisten the edge of the pastry shell with water. Roll out the remaining piece of pastry into an 8-in (20-cm) circle, lay over the top of the filling and crimp the edges of the pastry to seal. Make a central hole in the pastry and brush the surface with milk.

Bake for 45 to 60 minutes. The crust should be golden and feel cooked when lightly prodded with the finger. If it browns too soon, cover with aluminum foil for the remaining cooking time. Allow to rest for 5 minutes after removing from the oven. Serve in its dish.

SERVES: 6

## *Gâteau de Châtaignes*

*Chestnut Mold*

A typically rich dessert with a velvety texture, this comes from the Limousin — the heart of chestnut-eating country.

*3 lb (1.5 kg) fresh sweet chestnuts*
*14 tablespoons (7 oz/210 g) butter*
*2/3 cup (5 oz/150 g) sugar*
*5 eggs*
*3 drops vanilla extract (essence)*

Make a slash on the flat side of each chestnut. Bring a large saucepan of water to a boil. Drop in the chestnuts and boil for 30 minutes. Remove from heat. Take the chestnuts from the water in batches of 5 or 6 (they are easier to peel while still hot), and remove the outer shell and all inner skin, breaking open the chestnut to do so if necessary. Preheat oven to 375°F (190°C).

Lightly butter a 1 1/2-qt (1.5-l) charlotte mold, soufflé dish, or cake pan. Purée the chestnuts and other ingredients in a blender or processor. Turn the mixture into the charlotte mold, pressing it down firmly so there are no air pockets. Place in a bain-marie of very hot water in the oven: the water should come three-quarters of the way up the outside of the mold. Bake for 45 to 60 minutes, taking care that the water in the bain-marie never quite bubbles. The dish is cooked when a pointed knife inserted into the filling comes out clean.

Remove from oven and the bain-marie and leave to cool for 5 minutes. Run a knife round the edge of the mold and unmold with a sharp tap onto a serving plate. Serve with whipped cream or chocolate sauce.

SERVES: 6

## *Clafoutis*

*Baked Cherry Custard*

Every village in the Limousin is proud of its own recipe for *clafoutis*, but the basic proportions do not vary much. A similar dish, called *milliard* or *millard*, is made in the Auvergne. Ideally, the tiny, tart yet sweet fruits of the wild cherry tree should be used; failing that, use small black cherries. They should not be pitted — it is a good idea to warn your guests about this — because the pits add a touch of astringency.

*1 lb (5 oz/650 g) wild cherries or small black cherries*
*5 tablespoons (2½ oz/75 g) butter*
*1 cup (4 oz/125 g) all purpose (plain) flour*
*4 eggs*
*⅓ cup (3 oz/90 g) sugar*
*1 cup (8 fl oz/250 ml) milk*
*powdered (icing) sugar (optional)*

Preheat oven to 375°F (190°C). Wash, stem, and dry the cherries, but do not pit them. Use 2 tablespoons butter to grease a shallow baking dish large enough to hold the cherries in a single layer. Sprinkle with 2 tablespoons of flour and shake vigorously to spread evenly over the surface. Turn the dish over and tap out excess flour. Melt the rest of the butter in a small saucepan and leave to cool. Put the rest of the flour, the eggs, and the sugar into a mixing bowl, add the melted butter and beat well. Warm the milk and add gradually, stirring all the time until a smooth batter is obtained.

Place the cherries in the baking dish and gently pour the batter over them. Bake for about 45 minutes, or until well browned. Dust, if desired, with powdered sugar. *Clafoutis* is best served lukewarm, from the baking dish, though it can also be eaten cold.

SERVES: 6

PETER JOHNSON

*Baked Cherry Custard*

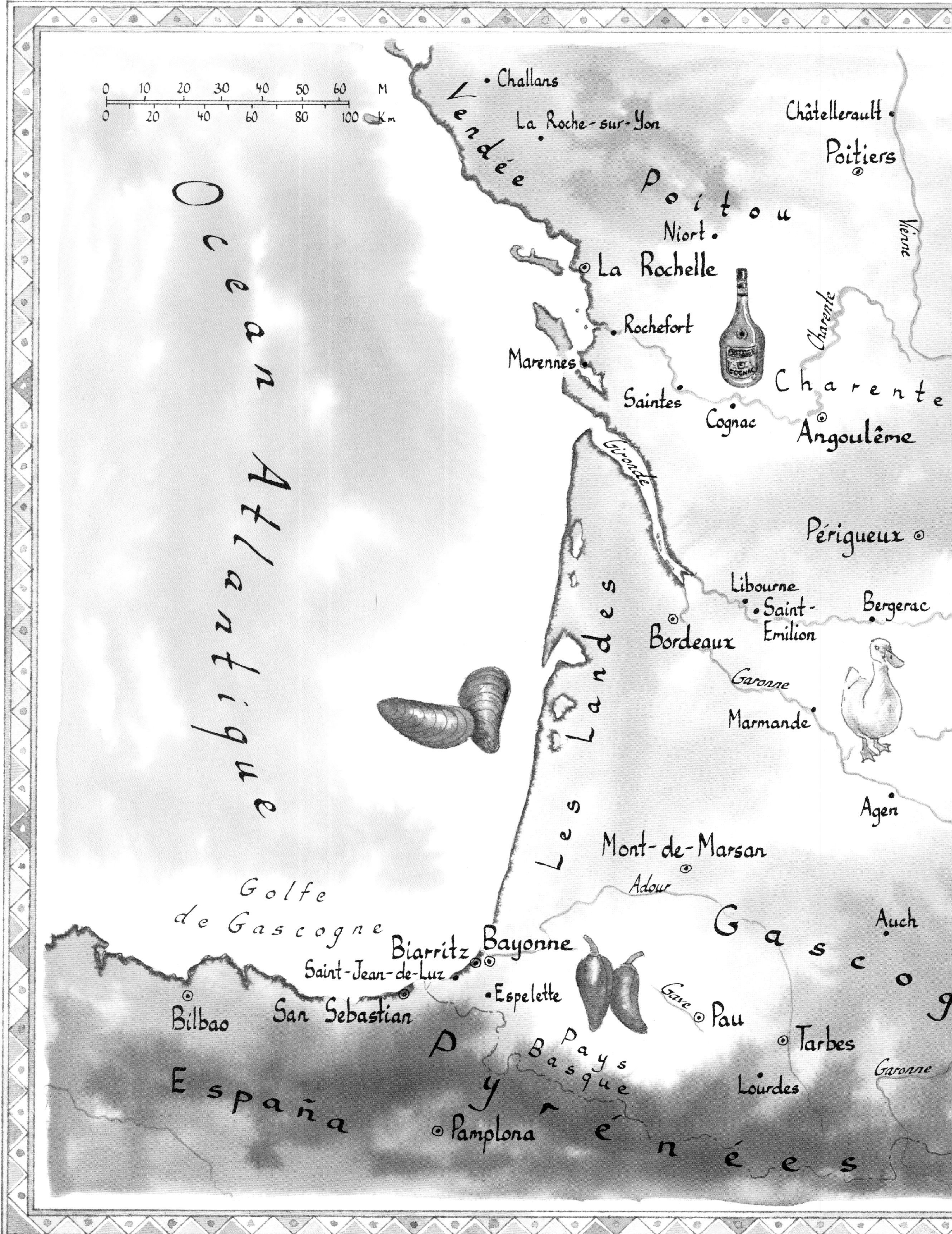

0 10 20 30 40 50 60 M
0 20 40 60 80 100 Km
Challans
Vendée
La Roche-sur-Yon
Châtellerault
Poitiers
Poitou
Niort
Vienne
La Rochelle
Rochefort
Charente
Marennes
Saintes
Cognac
Charente
Angoulême
Ocean Atlantique
Gironde
Périgueux
Libourne
Saint-Emilion
Bergerac
Bordeaux
Garonne
Marmande
Les Landes
Agen
Mont-de-Marsan
Adour
Golfe de Gascogne
Auch
Biarritz
Bayonne
Saint-Jean-de-Luz
Espelette
Bilbao
San Sebastian
Gave
Pau
Tarbes
Pays Basque
Garonne
Lourdes
España
Pamplona
Pyrénées

# THE ATLANTIC COAST, THE BASQUE COUNTRY, AND THE PYRENEES

*Diane Holuigue*

Nowhere in France could the traveler find such a diversity of cultures in so small an area than by journeying down the Atlantic coast from the Loire to the Spanish border. The people of the Vendée, the bourgeois, conservative Bordelais, and the fiery, proud Basques have only the ocean to their west in common.

Dominated by the cities of Bordeaux and Bayonne, the coast is studded with fishing villages and small trading ports and everywhere there is evidence of the sea's bounty. Along the marshy, flat coastlands of the Vendée jetties push out into the water, from which square fishing nets are suspended. Hoisted at dusk, these *carrelets* bob and sway from their slender poles, silhouetted eerily against the darkening sky. Further south, in the great bay of Arcachon, spread acre upon acre of oyster and mussel beds. The regions also attract holidaymakers in huge numbers. In the north there are the great sandy beaches of Charentes; southwards, in the Basque country, lie the resort of Biarritz and the enchanting coastline near the Spanish border.

Inland, the area divides into distinctive rural zones, the most northerly of which is the Vendée, whose populace looks towards the Loire. This region produces some of the country's best beef and dairy cattle, goat, lamb, and poultry, and high quality vegetables. To the east, the Vendée melts imperceptibly into the Poitou, where the rich river valleys yield similar produce. These two areas thrive on a dairy-based cuisine, rich in creamy sauces and great *pâtisserie*.

*Fishing boats in the port of Saint-Jean-de-Luz. Despite the vast numbers of tourists that come in the summer, the town is still very much Basque in character.*

GERARD SIOEN/CEDRI

## Charentes, Bordeaux, and the Landes

Further south lies the province of Charentes where some of France's best butter is produced, but the region's wealth comes primarily from the vineyards that provide the wine distilled for Cognac. The quiet town of Cognac stands on the banks of the Charente river, and many of the great houses, such as Martell and Hennessy, offer visitors tours and tastings. The municipal Musée de Cognac, which traces the history of this remarkable *eau-de-vie,* is well worth a visit.

The city of Bordeaux lies on the river Garonne, near where it converges with the Dordogne in the Gironde estuary. Fabulous wines from the vineyards lying to the south, resulting in immense export earnings, have made Bordeaux one of France's principal cities, and a great gastronomic center. The Romans planted the vines on which are based the great wines of the Bordelais, and it was the English, during the many years they ruled here, who encouraged their growth and subsequently introduced them to the world.

On her marriage to Henry II of England in 1152, Eleanor of Aquitaine brought as her dowry the powerful Duchy of Aquitaine, along with most of the southwest corner of France. This made the English crown more powerful than the King of France, and so began a struggle for supremacy between the two countries that lasted for three centuries. It was from Bordeaux that Eleanor ruled, and since those days the city has had the air of a capital city. Over the years a magnificent cathedral, imposing public buildings, wide avenues, exhibition halls, theaters, and art galleries were built, although the city has declined since the turn of the century, and many now consider its lifestyle slow and conservative.

South again lie the great, marshy lowlands of the Landes. Here local shepherds traditionally worked balanced on stilts, both to keep their feet dry and to keep an eye on their sheep. Afforestation, to prevent the giant coastal sand dunes from moving eastward, has created a vast and rather tedious landscape of pine trees. Wild birds flourish in the shelter of the pines, which has broadened the diet of the locals and made the area popular with hunters. To the east, where the Landes melds into the Gers and Gascony, the land is more fertile, and peasant smallholdings produce duck and geese for fattening for the *foie gras* market.

## The Basque Country

In the southwestern corner of France, on the Spanish border, lies the Basque country. The fiercely independent Basques have their own language, and an ancient culture that has more in common with the Basques of Spain than with the neighboring French. The Basque's color is red, and the men wear large, floppy red berets to show solidarity with their Spanish brothers. On feast days they wear these berets, white tee-shirts and pants, and red cummerbunds to run the bulls or to attend bullfights. This is the only region in France where bullfighting is permitted; a tribute to Basque culture, or perhaps a sop to calm separatist sentiments that are never far from the surface.

Inland, on the foothills of the Pyrenees in the winter, and up into the heights as the weather clears, graze huge flocks of sheep. From here comes some of the country's highest quality lamb, but the Basques tend to eat fish and seafood, reserving the lamb for valuable export income.

Traditionally shepherds and fishermen, the Basques were once the world's greatest whalers. (They were also pirates and smugglers too, given half a chance.) The Bay of Biscay yields a bountiful harvest, and large quantities of anchovies, sardines, cod, and tuna are caught and exported.

Tourism here is big business. Biarritz is the grand resort, its casinos and beaches packed with people during the summer months, but the small ports and picturesque mountain villages also attract numerous visitors. Saint-Jean-de-Luz, at the mouth of the Nivelle river, is an enchanting small town with a fleet of tuna boats. Little whitewashed houses with brightly painted doors and shutters and angular red-tiled roofs line the narrow cobblestoned streets. Pots of geraniums hang from iron balconies, and everywhere strings of chili peppers hang from the shutters, drying for the off-season.

Bayonne, the capital of the Pays Basque, has been a major port and military base since the twelfth century. The region's political and cultural center, it is a lively city with winding streets, bustling markets, and some fine buildings. For anyone interested in investigating the Basque way of life, the Musée Basque is fascinating, and has an extensive library.

Along the coast, from the Loire to Spain, fish and seafood dominate the diet, although the dishes of the Vendée differ greatly from those on Basque tables. In the north butter and cream dress the rich sauces served over fresh-water fish from the rivers that criss-cross the region, and over produce from the ocean — shrimp, sardines, and mussels. Sardines appear in pâté, fish is made into a stew known as *la chaudrée,* and shrimp are dressed in creamy sauces akin to those of Normandy. Mussels are served in many guises, one of the best known being the *éclade*, a picnic dish of mussels grilled and then flambéed on a bed of pine needles.

*Bunches of peppers hang drying outside a house in Espelette, in the Basque country.*

S.MARMOUNIER/CEDRI

## OYSTERS

Along the Atlantic coast, from Brittany to Spain, there are numerous natural oyster beds. In the area south of Bordeaux, around the flat, sandy estuaries of the Landes, oysters have done much for the fortunes of a region not blessed with great agricultural potential.

Until the nineteenth century oyster stocks were thought to be inexhaustible. Although their collection was forbidden from April to October, few attempts were made to encourage development, and by the 1850s many beds were not being replenished through spontaneous regeneration. From this time on, oysters have been farmed in the region, particularly around the Arcachon basin.

There are two main types of oysters farmed: the "flat" oyster, of which the Belon and Claire are considered the finest, and the "hollow" oyster, most notable of which is the Portugaise. Some of the most prized oysters are grown around Marennes, where there is an algae that tinges them green and gives them an especially prized flavor.

It is said that the French eat their oysters with a few drops of lemon juice and nothing else, but in fact they are often eaten with chopped shallots and vinegar, and are quite frequently cooked, mainly in soups and creamy sauces.

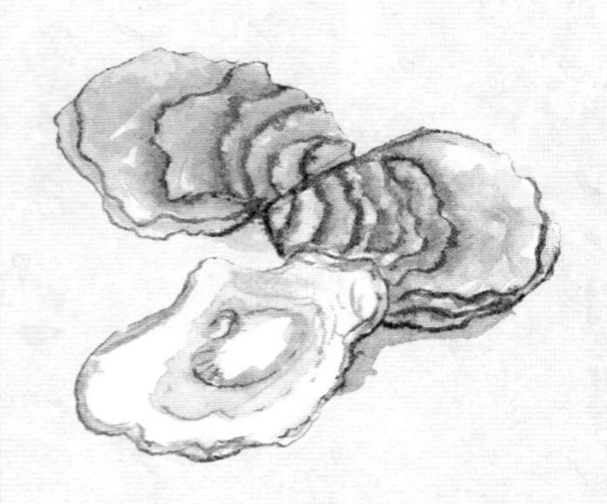

The famous *mouclade* is a creamy, curry-flavored mussel stew. In Poitou *bouilleture d'anguilles* is eels stewed in white wine, a dish similar to the *matelote d'anguilles* of the Loire valley. Special eels to look out for are the skinny spaghetti-like ones known as *piballes*, most often cooked in oil with garlic.

From the town of Challans comes the prized *canard de Challans*, the great restaurant duck of France, and the chickens in this part of the country are second in quality only to those of Bresse. Rabbit is popular, and wild rabbit is used to make *pâté vendéen*. Goats graze on the plains, and some excellent goat's milk cheese is made in Poitou. The small Chabichou, shaped like a truncated cone, is soft and mild when fresh, becoming sharper and harder with age. La-Mothe-Saint-Héray is a delightful *chèvre* with a Camembert-like texture. Fresh goat's milk cheese is used to make the area's famous *tourteau fromagé*, and there are all sorts of other delicious tarts, flans, and creamy desserts. Among the wonderful fruits of the region, the tiny pumpkin-skinned Charentais melon has a pungency and texture that has won it a world market.

The cuisine of Bordeaux is undoubtedly the most sophisticated of the region. The term *"à la bordelaise"* most often refers to a red wine sauce. *Sauce bordelaise* is a reduction of gently simmered red wine and shallots, and *daube bordelaise* is beef braised in red wine, often served cold with the wine set in aspic surrounding the meat. *Entrecôte bordelaise* is porterhouse steak served with *sauce bordelaise*, but in its most rustic form it was simply a steak rubbed with oil and grilled over a fire made from old wine barrels, served with a garnish of chopped raw shallots. More generally, *"à la bordelaise"* means cooked in the Bordeaux manner. Such is the name given to *cèpe* mushrooms or eggplant when cooked in oil and flavored with garlic and shallots, to eels when fried in oil, and to mussels when stewed in red wine and tomatoes. The *tourin bordelais* is an onion soup thickened with egg yolks. Oysters, when served *"à la bordelaise"* are served with spicy little sausages, a rather curious treatment, unlike any other in France.

Southward to the Landes and on into the foothills of the Pyrenees, the cooking is more rustic and more likely to include lamb, though the famous *agneau de Pauillac*, served either with *cèpes* or the first vegetables of the season, is a specialty of Bordeaux. In this poorer country potatoes predominate, generally sautéed in goose fat. Potatoes or pumpkin slices cooked *"à la landaise"* are gratinéed. Particular to the area are the small birds that scratch their way through the pine forests, such as woodcock, pigeon, ortolan and guinea-fowl. They tend to be braised in red wine and served as *salmis*, but tiny birds such as the ortolan are often just spit roasted.

## A PROFUSION OF BELL PEPPERS

In the Basque area bell peppers are served with practically everything. Grown around the town of Espelette, Basque peppers are smaller than most, and somewhat sweeter, though a spicy one, the *poivron d'Espelette*, features in many dishes. *Pipérade* is a stew of tomatoes and bell peppers into which beaten eggs are gently stirred. Bell peppers also appear in *poulet basquaise*, a braised chicken dish. *Morue à la biscaiana* is cod tossed in olive oil and simmered with white wine, tomatoes, bell peppers, and pimiento. *Morue à la bayonnaise* is scarcely different, but once the fish is cooked it is layered with mashed potatoes, topped with breadcrumbs and gratinéed. *Chiperons*, cuttlefish, are braised with tomatoes and bell peppers, *axoa d'Espelette* is a veal casserole made with the same vegetables, and even rabbit takes its turn to bask in the red and green garnish. Sometimes, for a change, the peppers are stuffed, either with fish, meat, or rice. Local goat's milk and ewe's milk cheeses, known as *olorons*, are served as a first course alongside roasted, peeled bell peppers drizzled with olive oil.

Abandoning the bell pepper, there is also *ttoro*, a peppery fish soup, and the famous *gâteau basque*, a covered tart with a pastry cream filling, sometimes made with cherries, apricots or prunes. Most famous internationally is the *jambon de Bayonne*, the region's ham. Its wonderful flavor comes from first being rubbed with salt for three days, then being cured in brine containing red wine and herbs, rubbed with red Espelette pepper and milled black peppercorns, and finally being hung raw to dry for up to two years.

There are rustic, not to say rasping, red wines made in the Basque area, and Pittara is the local cider. Better known is the liqueur Izarra, which is made from herbs and flowers. There are two versions, the strong one being a bright green color, and the milder one yellow.

*The ruins of the Cathar castle at Peyrepertuse, in the Central Pyrenees, one of a string of seven fortresses built by the French in the twelfth century to keep out the Spanish.*

GERARD SIOEN/CEDRI

# THE WINES OF BORDEAUX

The area surrounding Bordeaux nurtures some of the greatest, most celebrated wines in the world, vineyards thriving along the rich although somewhat gravelly banks of the Gironde estuary, along the lower reaches of the Dordogne and the Garonne rivers, and on the land that lies between them. For centuries the great ports of Bordeaux, and Langon further up the Garonne, have shipped these wines to the world.

Originally known as *clairet* (hence the English term "claret"), light wine, to distinguish them from the heavier, darker wines of Gascony with which they were at one time associated, these wines were not at first much favored by the French. For centuries, dating from the marriage of Eleanor of Aquitaine to the Plantagenet King Henry II of England, it was the English who, producing no wines of their own, encouraged the growth and development of the wines of Bordeaux.

By the sixteenth century, Bordeaux was the greatest wine port of Europe, and the Bordelais were exporting their wine not only to the home counties of their liege English lords, but were also provisioning the whole of northern Europe.

It was under the Plantagenets that the first legislation to safeguard the appellation of origin came into being, and since 1911 Bordeaux has been legally defined as being the wine grown within 425 communes of the department of the Gironde. Within these boundaries, there are sixty wines classified as *Grands Crus*, the mark of highest distinction. Their greatness depends not only upon the particularities of the soil and microclimate, but upon rigorous quality control regarding grape varieties and methods of cultivation. The principal grape varieties for red wines are Cabernet Sauvignon, Cabernet Franc, Merlot and Malbec. The fine whites are blended mostly from Sémillon, Sauvignon, and Muscadelle grapes.

LEO MEIER

*One of the retailers in Saint-Emilion that sells produce direct from local winemakers. Shops such as these are happy to provide wine tastings for prospective customers.*

The names of the viticultural regions conjure up the romance of the great wine growths: Médoc, Graves, Sauternes, and Saint-Emilion. Divided further, areas such as the Haut-Médoc, Pauillac, Margaux, and Pomerol are synonymous with the world's greatest red wines — among them Château Lafite-Rothschild, Château Margaux, Cos d'Estournel and Château Latour (from the Médoc), Château Cheval Blanc (from Saint-Emilion) and Château Pétrus (from Pomerol).

LEO MEIER/WELDON TRANNIES

*A Bordeaux cooper at work. Making barrels is an extremely skillful business, and the tools and methods used have changed little for centuries.*

The name Graves is associated with fine ıite wines, although the most famous aves of all, Château Haut-Brion, :helieu's favorite wine, is a red, ısidered by many to rate with the atest reds of the Médoc.

The world sets its sweet white wine ındards by the legendary Chateau d'Yquem, in Sauternes, with its never-cloying, flinty, sweet flavor. The great sweet wines of Sauternes in their finest years are made with grapes affected by a fungus, *Botrytis cinerea*. This brings about *pourriture noble*, noble rot, that concentrates the sugars in the grapes, giving the wines the most intense bouquets and flavor.

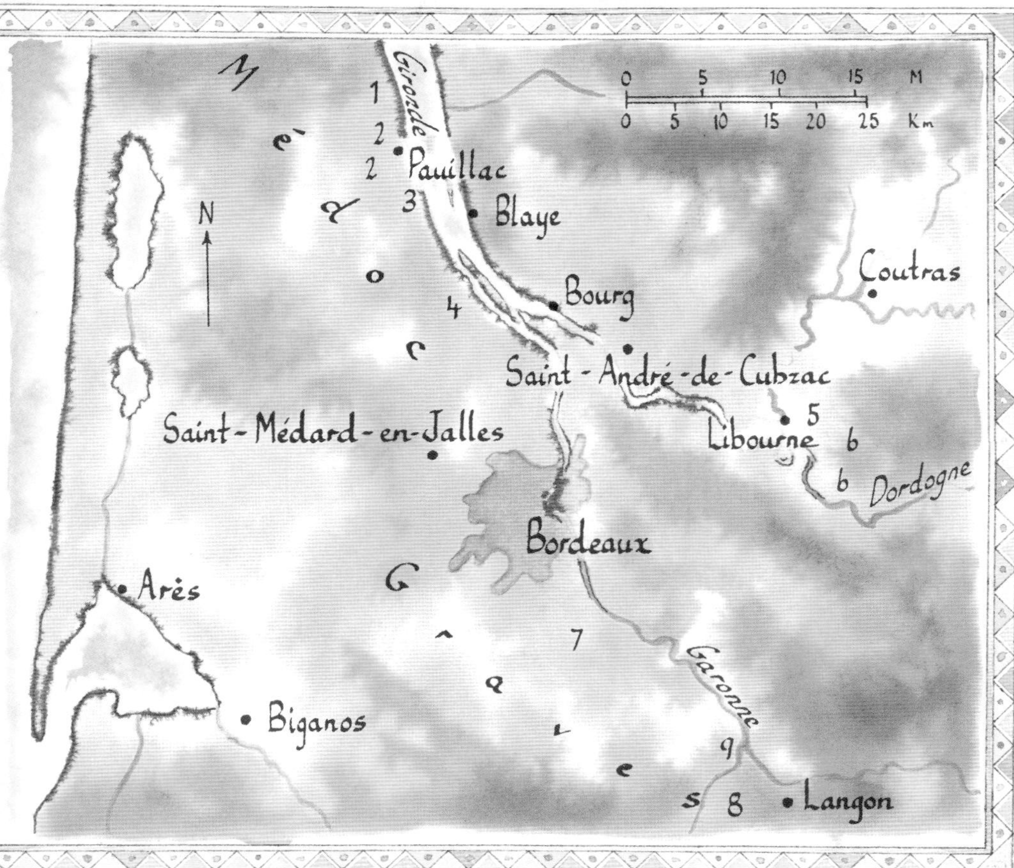


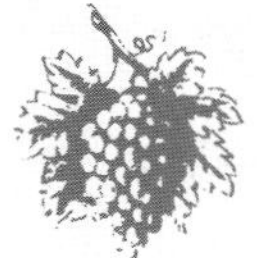

## BORDEAUX

*Each of the châteaux listed here is merely an outstanding representative of the wine-producing district to which it belongs. Such a selection will produce disagreements, and inevitably leaves out wines of equal stature.*

*Red wines:*

*Château Ausone (6)*
*Château Cheval Blanc (6)*
*Château Cos d'Estournel (1)*
*Château Ducru-Beaucaillou (3)*
*Château Gruaud-Larose (3)*
*Château Haut-Brion (7)*
*Château La Mission-Haut-Brion (7)*
*Château Lafite-Rothschild (2)*
*Château Lafleur (5)*
*Château Latour (2)*
*Château Léoville-Las Cases (3)*
*Château Lynch Bages (2)*
*Château Magdeleine (6)*
*Château Margaux (4)*
*Château Montrose (1)*
*Château Mouton-Rothschild (2)*
*Château Palmer (4)*
*Château Pétrus (5)*
*Château Pichon-Lalande (2)*
*Château Trotanoy (5)*

*Sweet white wines:*

*Château Coutet (9)*
*Château Climens (9)*
*Château Guiraud (8)*
*Château Rieussec (8)*
*Château Suduiraut (8)*
*Château d'Yquem (8)*

PETER JOHNSON

# RECIPES OF THE ATLANTIC COAST, THE BASQUE COUNTRY, AND THE PYRENEES

*Diane Holuigue*

## Pipérade

*Bell Pepper and Tomato Ragoût with Eggs*

The *pipérade* is a form of vegetable stew, with beaten eggs gently stirred through it. It is a wetter dish than most people expect, and is often eaten with a spoon or with lots of bread to take up the sauce. It is traditionally served with slices of Bayonne ham.

*1/4 cup (2 fl oz/60 ml) olive oil*
*2 large onions, sliced or chopped*
*2 small hot red chili peppers, sliced*
*6 large, very red tomatoes, peeled, seeded, and chopped*
*3 garlic cloves*
*2 thyme sprigs, leaves stripped*
*2 bay leaves*
*salt and freshly ground pepper*
*pinch of sugar*
*4 large red bell peppers (capsicums), cored and seeded, cut into uneven chunks and slices*
*3 large green bell peppers (capsicums), cored and seeded, cut into uneven chunks and slices*
*5 eggs*

Heat the oil in a deep skillet, and toss the onion until softened but not colored. Add the chili peppers, tomatoes, garlic, thyme, and bay leaves. Cover and simmer for 4 or 5 minutes, mashing occasionally.

Add salt and pepper to taste, plus the sugar, then stir in the bell peppers. Cover and simmer for a further 15 to 20 minutes, until the bell peppers are softened.

Break the eggs into a bowl, beat them with a fork and stir into the mixture. Cook for a further 5 minutes, gently stirring the eggs through the mixture with a fork or wooden spoon. The mixture should thicken but remain moist. Transfer to a warmed serving dish and serve immediately.

SERVES: 6

*Garlic Soup,*
*Bell Pepper and Tomato Ragoût with Eggs,*
*Mussel Stew*

PETER JOHNSON

*Chicken with Bell Peppers Basque Style, Chicken Stew Henry IV, Ragoût of Tuna Basque Style*

## Mouclade

*Mussel Stew*

The salt marshes and sandy coast of the Vendée are rich in mussels, scallops, cockles, baby clams, sea snails and shrimp. *Moucle* is the word for mussel in the local dialect.

*4 lb (2 kg) mussels, cleaned, scrubbed, and debearded*
*$\frac{1}{4}$ cup (2 fl oz/60 ml) dry white wine*
*4 tablespoons (2 oz/60 g) butter*
*1 tablespoon curry powder*
*1 scant tablespoon all purpose (plain) flour*
*pepper*
*several drops of lemon juice*
*pinch of saffron stamens*
*3 tablespoons cream*
*1 egg (optional)*

Place the cleaned mussels in a pan with the white wine. Cover tightly and place over high heat until the mussels open. (This will take 2 to 4 minutes, depending on their size.) Remove mussels when cool enough, and discard one shell from each, leaving only the half shell on which the mussel sits. Set aside. Retain the poaching liquid.

In a saucepan, heat the butter and fry the curry powder for 30 seconds, stirring with a whisk, then add the flour and stir for a further 30 seconds or so. Add $2\frac{1}{2}$ to 3 cups of strained poaching liquid and bring to a boil, stirring. Season with pepper and a little lemon juice to taste.

To finish the sauce, infuse the saffron stamens in the sauce for 2 minutes, then add the cream. If adding an egg, whisk it in quickly, and do not allow the sauce to return to the boil.

Arrange the mussels on a large, flat dish, spooning the sauce into the half shells over the mussels. Serve immediately.

SERVES: 6

## Soupe à l'Ail

*Garlic Soup*

A soup from the shepherds of the Pyrenees that is said to ward off colds, so rich is it in vitamin C. It is quite commonly served as a whole meal in the evenings with a lightly poached egg slipped into each bowl. Don't worry about all the garlic. If you don't tell anyone what it is made of, you may get compliments for your fish soup!

*3 garlic bulbs (about 50 cloves)*
*6 slices country-style bread*
*6 cups ($1\frac{1}{2}$ qt/1.5 l) water*
*salt and freshly ground pepper*
*2 tablespoons chopped parsley*
*cream for garnish (optional)*

Peel the garlic. Place all the cloves in a large soup or stock pot with the bread slices and water and boil for 20 minutes. Purée the soup. Season to taste, sprinkle with parsley, and serve.

To serve for guests, you may dress the soup up by drizzling cream over the surface, and scattering a little more parsley over the cream.

SERVES: 6

## Marmitako

*Ragoût of Tuna Basque Style*

Of all the fish at the disposal of seafaring Basques, probably cod and tuna are the most loved. Most at home with fish cookery are those in fishing communities along the coasts of France, and they cook their fish the easiest way: stewed slowly in a large pot with the produce of the region. In Saint-Jean-de-Luz, close to the Spanish border, they make *marmitako* — the most flavorsome fish stew of all.

*$\frac{1}{4}$ cup (2 fl oz/60 ml) olive oil*
*2 large onions, chopped*
*4 red bell peppers (capsicums), seeded, and cut into wide slices*
*3 green bell peppers (capsicums), seeded, and cut into wide slices*
*4 to 6 very red tomatoes, peeled, seeded, and chopped*
*2 large garlic cloves, finely chopped*
*2 bay leaves*
*6 small potatoes, halved*
*$\frac{2}{3}$ cup (5 fl oz/150 ml) dry white wine*
*2 lb (1 kg) fresh red tuna, skinned, boned, and cut into large cubes*
*salt and freshly ground pepper*
*1 or 2 hot red chili peppers, shredded*

Heat the oil in a wide saucepan or deep skillet and sauté the onions and bell peppers. When the heat has brought out the colors, add the tomatoes, garlic, bay leaves, and potatoes, along with the white wine. Simmer until the potatoes are just softened (about 8 to 10 minutes).

Add the tuna and cook a further 10 minutes, then season to taste with the salt, pepper, and chili. Cover and transfer to the oven and cook very gently for 30 minutes. Serve at once.

SERVES: 6

## Poulet Basquaise

*Chicken with Bell Peppers Basque Style*

Variations to this colourful ragoût include the addition of mushrooms, hot chili peppers, Bayonne ham, or even a few slices of the local garlic sausage.

*1/3 cup (3 fl oz/80 ml) olive oil*
*1 large onion, chopped*
*2 garlic cloves, finely chopped*
*2 green bell peppers (capsicums), seeded and sliced*
*2 red bell peppers (capsicums), seeded and sliced*
*6 very red tomatoes, peeled, seeded, and chopped*
*2 bay leaves*
*1 thyme sprig*
*salt and freshly ground pepper*
*1 chicken, about 3 lb (1.5 kg), cut into 8 pieces*

In a deep skillet, heat a little less than half the oil and sauté the onion and garlic until they soften but do not color. Toss the bell peppers in the mixture for 30 seconds, then add the tomatoes and herbs, and a little salt and pepper. Reduce heat, cover and simmer for 20 minutes.

In the meantime, in a second deep skillet, heat the remaining oil and brown the chicken pieces. This will take 15 to 20 minutes. Pour the cooked peppers and their sauce over the chicken. Cover and simmer for a further 20 minutes. Remove the chicken pieces to a warmed serving dish. Check the sauce for seasoning, and remove the herbs. Spoon the sauce over the chicken. Serve hot with boiled rice or boiled potatoes.

SERVES: 6

## Poule au Pot Henri IV

*Chicken Stew Henri IV*

"Every Frenchman," vowed Henri IV, the hero-son of Navarre who became king of France, "shall have a chicken for his pot on Sunday." Hence the name of this one-pot family meal.

*4 oz (125 g) stale bread, crusts removed*
*6 oz (185 g) Bayonne ham or* prosciutto, *chopped*
*1 chicken, about 4 lb (2 kg) with liver, gizzard, and heart*
*2 shallots, finely chopped*
*1 garlic clove, finely chopped*
*2 tablespoons chopped parsley*
*1 tablespoon chopped tarragon*
*3 eggs, beaten*
*salt and freshly ground pepper*
*3 carrots, cut into thirds*
*3 to 4 turnips, halved*
*4 onions or 2 thin leeks*
*3 large potatoes, quartered*

In a bowl, make the stuffing for the fowl by crumbling the bread and adding the chopped ham, chopped liver and gizzard from the bird, shallots, garlic, and herbs. Bind with the eggs and season with salt and pepper. Stuff the chicken with this mixture and truss to pull the legs into the carcass and hold the stuffing in place.

Place the chicken in a large stockpot with enough water to cover, and bring to a boil. Reduce heat and simmer very slowly, covered, for 1 hour (45 minutes for a younger chicken). Skim from time to time. Add all the vegetables except the potatoes and continue to cook slowly for a further 1 to 1¼ hours. Cook the potatoes in salted water, and add to the stockpot just before serving. Check seasoning.

Classically, the broth is served as a soup course, spooned over a thick slice of stale country-style bread. Then the meat and vegetables are served directly into the emptied soup plates, with a bowl of rock salt passed from person to person to season as desired.

SERVES: 6

*Porterhouse Steak Bordeaux Style*

PETER JOHNSON

## *Entrecôte à la Bordelaise*

*Porterhouse Steak Bordeaux Style*

One of the great classics of French cookery, the entrecôte of the Bordeaux area, derives its fame from the sauce made from the breathtaking regional wines, and the wonderful combination of marrow and shallot in the garnish. It is the *haute cuisine* version of the old recipe of the Bordelais vignerons, who grilled their steaks over fires made from broken up, old wine barrels.

*six 2-in (5-cm) pieces of marrow bone, sawn from the central part by the butcher*
*3 porterhouse steaks cut 2 in (5 cm) thick (or 6 steaks for those with large appetites)*
*butter and/or oil for cooking the steaks*
*salt and freshly ground pepper*
Sauce Bordelaise:
*7 tablespoons (3½ oz/105 g) butter*
*3 tablespoons finely chopped shallots*
*1¼ cups (10 fl oz/310 ml) red Bordeaux wine*
*2 thyme sprigs*
*3 black peppercorns, crushed*
*1¼ cups (10 fl oz/310 ml) high quality veal or beef stock, preferably with a good, natural gel*
*salt and freshly ground pepper*

Remove the marrow from the bones, using a small knife. Place the pieces of marrow in a bowl of cold water and soak out the blood for a minimum of 2 hours, preferably 4. Change the water at least once.

Ideally the steaks should be cooked on an oiled cast-iron ridged griddle, in which case rub them with oil and set aside. If they are to be pan-fried omit this step.

For the sauce: Heat 4 tablespoons of the butter in a medium saucepan, and cook the chopped shallots until softened. Add the wine, thyme, and peppercorns, bring to a boil and reduce by half. Add the stock and simmer slowly for about 30 minutes. Remove the thyme sprigs, season with salt and, if necessary, pepper. Set aside.

To cook and assemble the dish: Heat the griddle well, then quickly oil it and sear the steaks. Cook for 4 minutes, after 2 minutes changing the angle of the steaks by 45° to imprint the characteristic grill marks. Turn the steaks over, season with salt and pepper and cook for about 3 minutes longer. (The meat will be rare. Adjust the cooking time as desired.) Alternatively, the steaks can be cooked on a barbecue, under a broiler (grill) or fried in a skillet in a mixture of butter and oil.

When cooked, leave the steaks to stand, covered, on a board for 3 or 4 minutes so that the juices don't flow when carving, and finish the sauce.

Return the sauce to the stove to reheat, then quickly add the remaining butter off the heat, whisking well to bind the sauce.

Place the marrow in a small saucepan with fresh water and cook it by bringing the temperature to just under the boil. Remove immediately and slice into discs. Add to the sauce.

Carve the steaks into thin slices, cut slightly on the diagonal. Fan the slices of half a steak per person onto each plate, then spoon over the sauce. (If serving one steak per person they can be left whole.) Serve with green beans or a potato dish. In season, a dish of sautéed *cèpes* is a traditional accompaniment.

SERVES: 6

## *Gratin des Landes*

*Pumpkin and Ham Gratin*

Accompanied by a tossed green salad, this creamy dish of layered pumpkin — also often made with potatoes — can be served as a simple but satisfying light meal.

*2 tablespoons butter*
*1½ lb (750 g) pumpkin, finely sliced*
*5 slices Bayonne ham or* prosciutto, *roughly chopped*
*6 oz (185 g) grated Gruyère cheese*
*salt and freshly ground pepper*
*2 cups (16 fl oz/500 ml) milk, warmed*
*½ cup (4 fl oz/125 ml) cream*

Preheat the oven to 325°F (160°C). Butter an oval ovenproof baking dish and alternate the slices of pumpkin, ham, and cheese. Season each layer with salt (lightly, because the ham is salty) and pepper. Dot with small nobs of butter. Finish with a pumpkin layer sprinkled with grated cheese, then pour over the milk and cream. Bake in the oven for 50 minutes, or until tender. Serve hot.

Note: Some cooks beat an egg with the hot milk so that the mixture sets a little while cooking. In this case, the oven should be set at 300°F (150°C), and the dish cooked for 1 hour, so that the egg will not curdle.

SERVES: 6

## *Haricots Secs à la Charentaise*

*Dried Haricot Beans Charentes Style*

This method of cooking dried beans is at once easy and flavorsome, and the dish is an ideal partner to meats on winter days.

*1 lb (500 g) dried white beans (haricot or cannellini)*
*3 tablespoons butter*
*1 onion, chopped*
*1 tablespoon all purpose (plain) flour*
*water or chicken stock to cover*

PETER JOHNSON

*Dried Haricot Beans Charentes Style, Pumpkin and Ham Gratin*

*1 bay leaf*
*1 thyme sprig*
*salt and freshly ground pepper*
*walnut oil for serving*

Soak the beans overnight, or for a minimum of 4 hours, in cold water, changing the water once. Drain, and dry the beans well with a cloth or paper towels.

In a deep skillet with a lid, heat the butter and fry the onion until softened. Add the beans and turn until greased.

Sprinkle in the flour, stir, then cover the beans with water or chicken stock. Add the bay leaf, thyme, salt and pepper, bring to a boil, reduce heat and simmer until the beans are tender. This will take from 45 minutes to 1 hour, depending on the quality of the beans and the length of time they were soaked. Remove the herbs and discard.

Serve hot, with each person drizzling a light coating of walnut oil over the beans.

Serves: 6

## Tourteau Fromagé

*Cream Cheesecake*

This cheesecake of the Vendée and Poitou is made from fresh white goat's milk cheese, enriched with egg. Although a form of deep-dish tart, it is relatively light and fluffy, and resembles a cake as it rises into a rich brown dome while baking.

*Pastry:*
*1 1/2 cups (6 oz/185 g) all purpose (plain) flour*
*5 tablespoons (2 1/2 oz/75 g) butter, softened*
*1 egg*
*pinch of salt*
*2 or 3 tablespoons water*
*Filling:*
*9 oz (280 g) fresh goat's milk cheese or cottage cheese*
*1/4 cup (2 fl oz/60 ml) milk*
*3/4 cup (6 oz/185 g) sugar*
*6 eggs, separated*
*2/3 cup (2 1/2 oz/75 g) all purpose (plain) flour*
*several drops of vanilla extract (essence)*

For the pastry: Place the flour on a work surface, make a well in the center and add the butter, egg, salt and the water. Mix the ingredients in the well, then gradually work in the flour until the mixture forms a pliable ball. Add slightly more water if the mixture is a little dry.

Roll out the dough and line a 9-in (23-cm) circular straight-sided pie pan. Make a slight lip on the edge to attach the pastry to the dish so that it will not shrink down the sides. Refrigerate for 20 minutes to rest the elasticity of the pastry.

For the filling: Place the cheese in a bowl and mash well with a wooden spoon until it is smooth, then work in the milk and sugar. Add the egg yolks one by one, creaming to a smooth, white, fluffy paste, then add the flour in a stream and fold in well. Flavor with vanilla extract.

Preheat the oven to 350°F (180°C). Beat the egg whites until they are firm, then fold gently into the cheese mixture. Spoon into the pastry-lined pan and bake for 45 minutes, or until a skewer inserted into the center comes out clean. The top should turn a rich caramelized brown. If the top has not colored well, lightly dust it with powdered sugar and return it to the oven for a minute or two.

Remove from oven and cool before unmolding. Serve at room temperature.

Serves: 6 to 8

## Merveilles

*Cognac Fritters*

In Lyon these sweet, deep-fried fritters are called *bugnes*, and in Nice they are known as *ganses*. In Gascony they are fried in goose fat rather than oil.

Throughout the Charentes and along the Garonne they are known both as *merveilles*, marvels, and *oreillettes*, little pillows. The addition of Cognac gives them the distinctive stamp of the region.

*4 cups (1 lb/500 g) all purpose (plain) flour*
*1 teaspoon baking powder*
*1/3 cup (3 oz/90 g) sugar*
*8 eggs*
*7 tablespoons (3 1/2 oz/105 g) butter, softened*
*1 teaspoon orangeflower water*
*1 tablespoon Cognac*
*oil for deep-frying*
*superfine (caster) sugar for sprinkling*
*powdered (icing) sugar for dusting*

Place the flour in a bowl, make a well in the center and add the baking powder, sugar, eggs, butter, orangeflower water and Cognac. Stir with a wooden spoon, briskly, until all the ingredients in the center are blended, then break down the wall of flour and gradually incorporate this into the dough. Form into a ball, wrap in plastic wrap and rest in the refrigerator for 2 hours.

Heat the oil in a deep fryer to 325°F (160°C). On a floured board, roll out the dough about 1/6 in (4 mm) thick and cut into strips about 1 in (2.5 cm) wide and 3 in (7.5 cm) long. The strips may be fried singly, but it is typical also to cut a few longer ones and tie them in bows, or to take some of the strips and tie them together in a loose knot. Cutting the dough with a crinkly edged pastry wheel will give the fritters a lacey appearance.

Drop the fritters into the deep fryer three or four at a time, depending on the size of the basket, and cook until golden brown. (This usually takes only about 20 to 30 seconds.) Ensure that the oil does not become too hot, or it will discolor the fritters.

Remove the fritters with a slotted spoon and turn onto paper towels sprinkled with superfine sugar. Dust with powdered sugar and serve either immediately or at room temperature.

MAKES: 25 to 30 strips

## Gâteau Basque

*Basque Cake*

This popular Basque cake is really a double-crust deep-dish tart. Generally it has a pastry cream filling, but occasionally it is filled with prunes or cherries.

*Pastry:*
*2 3/4 cups (11 oz/345 g) all purpose (plain) flour*
*2 eggs, beaten*
*13 tablespoons (6 1/2 oz/200 g) butter, softened*
*3/4 cup (6 oz/185 g) sugar*
*1 tablespoon rum*
*Filling:*
*2 cups (16 fl oz/500 ml) milk*
*1 egg*
*3/4 cup (6 oz/185 g) sugar*
*2 tablespoons all purpose (plain) flour*
*several drops of vanilla extract (essence)*
*4 or 5 tablespoons apricot jam*
*1 egg, beaten, for the glaze*

For the pastry: Place the flour on a work surface, make a well in the center and add the eggs, butter, sugar, and rum. With the fingers, blend together the ingredients in the well, then gradually work in the flour until the mixture forms a pliable ball. If it is sticky, add a little more flour. Cover in plastic wrap and rest in the refrigerator for 1 hour.

For the cream: In a saucepan, bring the milk almost to a boil. Set aside. In a bowl, whisk the egg and sugar, then add the flour. Blend with a little of the hot milk, then add this mixture to the remaining milk in the saucepan, and return to a boil, whisking, until the mixture thickens. Flavor with vanilla, then allow to cool.

Preheat the oven to 400°F (200°C). Roll out two-thirds of the pastry and line an 9-in (23-cm) tart mold, brush with apricot jam, then spread with the cream filling.

Roll out the remaining pastry and place it over the top, trimming it to the correct size. Press the edges of the two layers of pastry together with the fingers. With the prongs of a fork, score a lattice pattern across the top of the tart, then brush with beaten egg. Bake for around 30 minutes, or until brown and crisp. Serve cooled.

SERVES: 6

*Cream Cheesecake, Cognac Fritters, Basque Cake*

PETER JOHNSON

OBREMSKI/THE IMAGE BANK

*A quiet corner in a Paris park.*


## ACKNOWLEDGMENTS

A number of people and organizations were of assistance to the publishers in the preparation of this book. Many thanks to the following for photographic props: Appley Hoare Antiques, Woollahra; Country Trader, Paddington; Accoutrement, Mosman; Sandy de Beyer, Mosman; Corso di Fiori, Chatswood; The Bay Tree, Woollahra; Parterre Garden, Woollahra (pages 148, 172, 175, 242, 258, 265); Country Floors, Woollahra; Sentimental Journey at Mosman Antiques, Mosman; Ventura and Co. for Alessi; Hale Imports and Villeroy and Boch, Brookvale; Incorporated Agencies, Rosebery; Royal Copenhagen, Artarmon; Studio Haus, Double Bay; Fragrant Garden, Erina; In Residence, Woollahra; John Normyle, Paddington; and Porter's Original Limewash, Surry Hills. Susan Whitter, Ronda Hertz, Inger Marchant, Maureen Simpson, David Furley and Peter Johnson kindly lent privately-owned items for photographic propping. Many thanks to Elizabeth McLeod and Beth Geale for food preparation and styling, and to Joanne Chiswell for photographic assistance.

# Glossary

ANCHOVIES: Preserved anchovies are used for flavoring a variety of southern dishes. Initially they are preserved in salt in large steel barrels and aged from three months to a year. Then they are either left whole and packed again in fresh salt, or filleted and packed in oil. Salted anchovies are sold by weight. Anchovy fillets are sold in small cans or jars.

*APPELLATION D'ORIGINE CONTRÔLÉE (AOC):* Any product that carries such an appellation, such as a particular wine, cheese, butter, fruit, or type of poultry, is recognized by law as having been produced in a given region, and having specific attributes, such as being made in a certain way, or being of a particular breed or plant type.

ARMAGNAC: A pungent brandy produced in Gascony, to the south of Bordeaux. Because it is distilled only once, unlike Cognac, which is distilled twice, it has a more earthy taste. It is often drunk at the end of a meal, and is used to intensify the flavor of a variety of main dishes and desserts. Some producers market fruit bottled in Armagnac. (See box on page 138.)

*BAGUETTE*: The traditional long, thin, crusty French loaf, most commonly made with bleached white flour.

BAIN-MARIE: A pan filled with hot water that is kept near boiling point, in which vessels containing certain delicate dishes are cooked, which might break up or become "oily" if they are cooked over direct heat. Custards, various puddings, terrines, mousses, and so on are cooked in this way.

BARDING FAT: Thin slices of fat bacon or pork fat for wrapping around poultry, game, and terrines before they are cooked.

BAYONNE HAM: This is the best-known raw, salt-cured ham from France, but most regions have their own version, broadly known as *jambon de pays*. Such hams are eaten as a first course, and are used to flavor many cooked dishes.

*BEURRE BLANC*: A classic reduced sauce made with vinegar and/or white wine, shallots, and butter.

*BEURRE MANIÉ*: Flour and butter blended together and used as a thickening agent in sauces.

BLANCH: To place food in boiling salted water for varying lengths of time, either to soften, or to partially or fully cook it. Food is also sometimes blanched to remove an over-strong taste, as in the case of onions or green cabbages, or meat that is salty or has a strong smoked flavor. Certain vegetables and fruit, such as tomatoes and peaches, are blanched so that they are easier to peel.

BOUQUET GARNI: A combination of bay leaf, thyme, and parsley that is used to flavor stocks, soups, stews, and sauces. If the herbs are fresh they are tied together with string; if they are dried they are placed in a cheesecloth bag. Either way, they can then be removed easily from the dish once it has been cooked.

According to the region and the type of dish, the *bouquet garni* might be varied to include such aromatics as basil, chervil, tarragon, rosemary, savory, fennel, celery stalks, leek leaves, or orange peel.

*BRIOCHE*: A buttery, egg-enriched yeast bread, usually made in the shape of a ball, topped by a smaller ball, and cooked in a fluted mold. This type of *brioche* is known as *brioche à la tête*, and is made either in a large mold or in small individual ones. *Brioche* dough is also used to make cases for a variety of sweet and savory dishes, and to make cakes.

BUTTER: Most of the butter used in France is unsalted, and it is particularly delicious when farm-produced, rather than made commercially, as it is then made from unpasteurized milk. *Demi-sel* is lightly salted butter, a specialty from Brittany. The finest butter in the country comes from Isigny in Normandy and from the Poitou-Charentes region.

CALVADOS: The name of a department in Normandy, which is also used for the famous fiery local brandy which is distilled from cider. Calvados is used widely in Norman cooking, and can be used to flavor cakes and pastries. (See box on page 224.)

*CÈPES*: *Porcini* or boletus mushrooms. Big and fleshy, these are among the most widely used of the wild mushrooms.

CHAMPIGNONS: *Champignons de bois*, and *champignons sauvages* are wild mushrooms, but the word is generally used to refer to *champignons de Paris*, which are the least mature form of the cultivated mushroom. They are also known as button mushrooms. (See box on page 184.)

*CHANTERELLES*: Prized apricot-colored, trumpet-shaped wild mushrooms, also known as *girolles*.

CHEESES: There are so many cheeses available in France (one expert claims there are at least 750) that it is impossible to begin to list them in this glossary, but most of the best-known ones are referred to in the text of the book. They are made from cow's milk, ewe's milk, or goat's milk (see following entry), and the finest ones are protected by *appellations d'origine contrôlées*.

*CHÈVRE (FROMAGE DE)*: The word literally means "goat," but it is used to refer to cheese made from goat's milk. A wide variety of *chèvres* are produced throughout France in all sorts of shapes and packing, and they can be eaten at varying stages of maturity. Fresh *chèvre* is soft and relatively mild in flavor, whereas mature cheeses can be hard and pungent.

*CHOUCROUTE*: Sauerkraut — finely sliced cabbage fermented in brine and flavored with juniper berries. The word is also used for the dish consisting of *choucroute*, various sausages, bacon and pork, served with potatoes.

COGNAC: A brandy distilled from wine, made in the region around the town of Cognac, in Charentes. Its characteristic flavor comes from the grapes of the region and aging in oak barrels. Most Cognac is aged for only two or three years, but the best may be left to mature for up to fifty years. Well-aged brandy is usually mixed with younger vintages in order to produce standard blends of varying quality.

Cognac is frequently served after a meal, and is used as a preservative in terrines and pâtés, and to intensify the flavor of a range of sauces.

*CONFIT*: Preserved duck or goose, and sometimes pork, cooked and preserved in its own fat.

CORNICHONS: The young fruit of certain kinds of cucumber, picked while they are still green and preserved in vinegar. *Cornichons* are served as a condiment with such dishes as pâtés and terrines and are a traditional accompaniment to *pot-au-feu*.

COURT-BOUILLION: An aromatic poaching liquid for meat, fish and vegetables.

CRÈME FRAÎCHE: A mature, heavy cream with a nutty, slightly sour flavor. It can be made by mixing 2 tablespoons of cultured buttermilk with 2 cups of heavy cream. The mixture should be let stand overnight, at room temperature, then stirred and put in the refrigerator for at least 4 hours, to thicken further.

*Crème fraîche* can be stored for several days in the refrigerator, and its flavor will develop as it matures.

CROÛTONS: Small cubes of bread fried in oil or butter, or simply toasted, generally served as an accompaniment to soup. Sometimes *croûtons* are cut into decorative shapes, such as hearts, and are used to garnish various dishes that are served in sauce.

DIJON MUSTARD: A pungent, creamy mustard from Dijon, in Burgundy, made from mustard seeds steeped in *verjus*, the acidic fermented juice of unripened grapes.

EAU-DE-VIE: Literally "water of life," a brandy distilled from fruit. *Eaux-de-vie* are mostly aged in crockery casks, rather than wood, so they are usually colorless. Any number of *eaux-de-vies* are made throughout France, from every type of fruit. Kirsch, made from cherries, is probably the best known. (See also the entry for Marc, below.)

ENDIVE: Known as Belgian endive in the US, chicory in Britain, and *witloof* in Flanders. A vegetable the length of a hand with tightly overlapping white leaves that are edged with yellow. It is generally used in salads, but it is also popular braised. It is crisp, with a slight bite, but it should not be bitter.

ESCAROLE: A curly-headed salad green of the chicory family, which is known as chicory in the US and curly endive in Britain. It is quite strongly flavored, with a pleasing bite.

GALANTINE: A classical dish of boned meat or poultry that is stuffed or rolled and pressed into a symmetrical shape. Galantines are cooked in a gelatin stock and served cold.

HERBES DE PROVENCE: A mixture of thyme, rosemary, savory, and bay leaf, often dried.

MARC: The word literally means "dregs," but it is usually used to refer to *eau-de-vie de marc* which is a spirit distilled from the skin, seeds and stalks that are left after the grapes have been pressed. Marcs vary from region to region, two of the best known being Marc de Champagne and Marc de Bourgogne.

MATELOTE: A fresh-water fish stew made with red or white wine. *La pauchouse* from Burgundy is a form of *matelote*.

MORELS: Dark brown, conical wild mushrooms, which are highly sought after. They have a very short season in the spring.

OLIVE OIL: In the south of France olive oil is the main cooking medium, and throughout the country many choose it for making salad dressings. Olive trees grow throughout the Mediterranean and most of the ripe olive crop is crushed for oil. The first cold pressing of the olives yields extra virgin oil, the highest quality oil. Additional pressings, which are heated, give progressively lower grades of oil. Olive oil should be a clear amber color. Bright light will make it fade, so it is often stored in green bottles. (See box on page 88.)

OLIVES: Olives are used widely in the south of France as a condiment, an hors-d'oeuvre, and in cooking. Picked unripe, they are green: picked ripe, they are black. Methods of processing and preservation vary, but all olives have to be cured or they are too bitter to eat. They are stored in brine or olive oil, to which flavorings are sometimes added, such as lemon, chili, and garlic. Niçoise olives are small and black.

PERSILLADE: Chopped parsley, often mixed with chopped garlic, added to certain dishes at the end of cooking.

PETIT SALÉ: Salt-cured inexpensive cuts of pork, such as spare ribs, bladebone, and belly, usually served with lentils.

POT-AU-FEU: A traditional dish of beef simmered with vegetables for several hours. The stock is served as a soup, and is followed by the meat and vegetables as the main course.

POTÉE: A traditional soup made with pork and vegetables — mainly cabbage and potatoes. As with a *pot-au-feu*, the stock is usually served as a soup, followed by a main course consisting of the meat and vegetables.

QUATRE-ÉPICES: A traditional spice blend used in France for centuries to flavor terrines, pâtés, and *charcuterie* products. It consists of equal quantities of ground ginger, nutmeg, white pepper, and cloves. Sometimes cinnamon, mace, or chili are also added.

RILLONS: Chunks of pork belly or breast macerated with aromatic vegetables in white wine and then cooked slowly in lard. *Rillons* can be served cold or hot. When cold, they are served like *rillettes*. When hot, they are drained of fat and often crispened in a skillet before serving. Warm, and chopped finely, they are excellent in a salad.

RILLETTES: A kind of pâté made with minced pork trimmings, which can also be made with goose, duck, rabbit, or fish. *Rillettes* are served at room temperature with bread or toast, accompanied by olives and *cornichons*.

SAUCE BÉARNAISE: A sauce made with egg yolks, butter, shallots, white wine, and vinegar, flavored with tarragon. It is usually served with steak, broiled chicken, fish, and egg dishes.

SAUCE BÉCHAMEL: Also known as *sauce velouté*, this is a straightforward white sauce made with butter and stock or milk, thickened with flour. It can be enriched with cream, egg yolks, or additional butter. Many other sauces are derived from *sauce béchamel*, such as *sauce mornay*, cheese sauce, *sauce soubise*, onion sauce, and *sauce à la moutarde*, mustard sauce.

SAUCISSE: A small sausage, generally made from chopped pork meat, which requires cooking. Some *saucisses* are smoked.

SAUCISSON: This term generally refers to a large air-dried sausage which does not require cooking, such as a salami, which is served sliced. The *saucissons* of Lyon, Arles, Lorraine, Brittany, and Strasbourg are among the best known.

SHALLOTS: Small members of the onion family that have a delicate flavor with a slight hint of garlic. There are two varieties — pink and grey. The pink ones are the most common, and have a milder flavor. If shallots are unavailable, the minced white part of green onions (scallions or spring onions) can be used as a substitute.

TERRINE: An earthenware container that is used for cooking meat, fish, or vegetable dishes. The name is also used to refer to a pâté cooked and served in such a dish.

TRUFFLE: A subterranean fungus, of which there are a number of varieties. The most highly regarded are the black ones from Périgord and Quercy, which are about the size of a walnut. They are both scarce and expensive, but only very small amounts are needed to provide a dish with the most delicate and distinctive flavor and aroma. Canned and bottled truffles are widely available. (See box on page 135.)

VINAIGRETTE: A dressing made with oil and vinegar or lemon juice, generally seasoned with salt and pepper. Traditionally used on green salads, vinaigrettes are also served with *crudités*, and a wide range of cold meat, fish, and vegetable dishes. A variety of other ingredients can be added, such as chopped fresh herbs, crushed garlic, mustards, chopped anchovy fillets, and chopped hard-boiled egg. Oils and vinegars of all sorts can be used to vary the flavoring.

VINEGAR: An acid-tasting condiment, which has been used since Biblical times, produced by acetic fermentation in alcoholic liquid, such as wine, cider or beer. The vinegar used most widely in France is made from white or red wine.

Good quality vinegar is clear and transparent. If it is made from white wine it is colorless, while that made from red wine has a pinkish tinge. Vinegar can be flavored with a variety of aromatics such as basil, tarragon, shallots, garlic, and raspberries.

LEO MEIER

*Figs from Provence.*

# INDEX

Page numbers in *italics* refer to illustrations